John Cargill Thompson was educated at Glasgow High School
Dramaic A in the
as an actor, stage manager and director,
the Royal Shakespeare Company in 1964.
Amershar ff of the Drama Department of the
Stanley Hse of North Wales before becoming Senior
Amershag and Coordinator of Academic Affairs at
Telepho eatre, Manchester Polytechnic. He has
This book ty student productions, including many of
d in this volume. His play *No Kind of Hero*
laboration with David Mackail) was produced
.300 elevision in 1966. He is the author of *The Boys'*
dy of some aspects of the work of G. A. Henty,
sent engaged on a reconsideration of the work of

ra
I2
n

Pan Literature Guides
General editor: Andrew Mylett

An Introduction to Shake _____ *raries*
Marguerite Alexa...

An Introduction to Fifty British Novels 1600–1900
Gilbert Phelps

An Introduction to Fifty American Novels
Ian Ousby

An Introduction to Fifty Modern British Poets
Michael Schmidt

An Introduction to Fifty British Plays 1660–1900
John Cargill Thompson

An Introduction to Fifty European Novels
Martin Seymour-Smith

An Introduction to Fifty American Poets
Peter Jones

An Introduction to Fifty British Poets 1300–1900
Michael Schmidt

In preparation
An Introduction to Fifty Modern British Plays
Benedict Nightingale

An Introduction to Fifty Modern British Novels
Andrew Mylett

Pan Literature

An Introduction to
Fifty British Plays
1660–1900

John Cargill Thompson

Pan Books London and Sydney

First published 1979 by Pan Books Ltd,
Cavaye Place, London SW10 9PG
© John Cargill Thompson 1979
ISBN 0 330 25867 2
Printed and bound in Great Britain by
Richard Clay (The Chaucer Press) Ltd, Bungay, Suffolk

to
J. D. Carruthers

Contents

Preface 9

Audience and Taste 18

The Tempest, or The Enchanted Island
Sir William D'Avenant, John Dryden 31

Henry V Roger Boyle, 1st Earl of Orrery 43

An Evening's Love, or The Mock Astrologer
John Dryden 53

The Rehearsal
George Villiers, 2nd Duke of Buckingham 61

Aureng–Zebe John Dryden 68

The Country Wife William Wycherley 75

The Man of Mode, or Sir Fopling Flutter
Sir George Etherege 83

All for Love, or The World Well Lost John Dryden 90

King Lear Nahum Tate 96

Venice Preserved, or A Plot Discovered
Thomas Otway 102

Love for Love William Congreve 111

The Relapse, or Virtue in Danger
Sir John Vanbrugh 119

The Mourning Bride William Congreve 127

The Way of the World William Congreve 132

The Funeral, or Grief à la Mode Sir Richard Steele 139

The Recruiting Officer George Farquhar 148

Cato Joseph Addison 158

Jane Shore Nicholas Rowe 165

The Beggar's Opera John Gay 174

Polly John Gay 180

The Tragedy of Tragedies, or The Life and Death of Tom Thumb the Great Henry Fielding 189

The London Merchant, or George Barnwell George Lillo 195

The Gamester Edward Moore 202

Douglas John Home 208

The Way to Keep Him Arthur Murphy 214

The Country Girl David Garrick 220

The Clandestine Marriage George Colman 229

The West Indian Richard Cumberland 239

She Stoops to Conquer Oliver Goldsmith 248

The Rivals R. B. Sheridan 258

The Duenna R. B. Sheridan 270

A Trip to Scarborough R. B. Sheridan 277

The Castle Spectre M. G. Lewis 283

Pizarro R. B. Sheridan 292

Rob Roy Macgregor Sir Walter Scott, Isaac Pocock 301

The Doom of Devorgoil Sir Walter Scott 307

The Cenci P. B. Shelley 316

Prometheus Unbound P. B. Shelley 323

Swellfoot the Tyrant P. B. Shelley 328

Virginius James Sheridan Knowles 340

The Lady of Lyons Edward Bulwer 348

London Assurance Dion Boucicault 356

The Colleen Bawn Dion Boucicault 363

Caste T. W. Robertson 373
London by Night Dion Boucicault and others 381
Charley's Aunt Brandon Thomas 388
An Ideal Husband Oscar Wilde 396
The Importance of Being Earnest Oscar Wilde 403
The Liars Henry Arthur Jones 414
Trelawny of the 'Wells' Arthur Wing Pinero 423

Bibliography 433
Index 440

Preface

The theatre is the Devil's pulpit. If this is so then England must be a veritable fortress of evil, for she has inherited one of the strongest theatre traditions in the world. The high market value which the 'angels' of other countries place on English writers, actors and critics is the direct result of a sense of style inculcated by this heritage, which was consolidated during the period considered by this work. Proper respect for the word genius allows only Shakespeare and this is reflected in the tendency to study the Elizabethan and Jacobean activity of which he is the apex without proper regard for the evolving tradition which is our strongest asset. Drama is an essentially tribal activity and its health rests not on isolated genius but on cooperation. It is easy to understand that the success of a play is shared by all its present contributors: writers, actors, designers *et al*, but this success should never be seen out of the context of the theatre tradition. It is this which has conditioned the expectations and response of critics and audience.

Although we shall discover an occasional Scots and a dominant Anglo-Irish contribution to this development, British drama centres on London and the satellite theatres royal during the period covered by this book and it is the evolving mores of the English way of life which have shaped and fashioned it to its present form. Theatre is shaped by the world which it mirrors and the proud, aggressive opulence of eighteenth- and nineteenth-century England is reflected in the drama of this period.

The strong continuity from development to development is entirely the result of a performing tradition. English theatrical scholarship from its early days in the eighteenth century has concentrated on the pre-Restoration drama to the detriment of all that follows. The result has been an old fashioned view that English drama, with the exception of the plays of Sheridan and Goldsmith, takes a downward path from Congreve till the end of the nineteenth century, when it is implied that the mini-renaissance spearheaded by Jones, Pinero and Shaw is but the pale reflex of the continental activity of Ibsen, Strindberg and Chekov. During the early part of the twentieth century changes in theatre practice transferred the custodianship of this tradition from the performers to the scholars. The same Victorians who had laid the foundation for profitable argument and debate on the Elizabethan and Jacobean period must be blamed for initiating the absurd practice of grouping Restoration and eighteenth-century comedy. As we shall see, the last years of the seventeenth century are years of transition and uncertainty and Restoration drama marks the end of the era dominated by Shakespeare and Jonson rather than the beginning of a new one. Goldsmith and Sheridan for all their protestations of revolt against sentimentalism have much more in common with Steele and Colman than they have with Etherege, Wycherley and Congreve. Another grave disservice to future critical consideration was the tendency of early critics to judge the drama of the Restoration from their own moral standpoint. The result of this was that the unconventional 1920s took up Wycherley and Congreve as a gesture against their elders, so that in 1923, Allardyce Nicoll felt it necessary to begin his standard *History of Restoration Drama* with a warning:

... he who would now bring the works of Ravenscroft and of Tate to light lies in the danger of being accused by modern moralists of a perverted judgement and of an uncultured taste.

Nicoll was ahead of his time and Bonamy Dobrée's *Restoration Comedy*, (1924) is aggressively defensive in its assurance that the late seventeenth-century playwrights are men of judgement and intellect, mainly concerned with distilling a new moral balance from the chaos of Restoration morality. Nicoll and Dobrée were supported by the activity of professional experimenters, particularly at the Lyric Theatre, Hammersmith, where a young Edith Evans first gave us her unique recreations of Millamant and Mrs Sullen. It was the success of these productions which led the BBC to take up Dryden, Congreve, Farquhar and others, establishing the drama of this period as a normal part of our theatrical heritage. However, the BBC, by making Restoration drama respectable, removed the need for its enthusiastic defence and the scholars of the 1920s who had gleefully turned to it as a means of scoring over their elders were succeeded by generations who preferred to rummage in the dustbins and attics of the Elizabethan and Jacobean period. There was a secondary flurry of activity in the 1940s and 1950s led by L. C. Knights (*Explorations: Essays in Criticism Mainly on the Literature of the Seventeenth Century*, pp 131–49 'Restoration Comedy: The Reality and the Myth', 1946) and ably supported by Norman Holland (*The First Modern Comedies*, 1959), John Loftis, Clifford Leech and others but this activity has tended to be specialized and selective, homing in on particular authors and plays and neglecting their relationship to the overall picture. The reason for this is historical; the study of English drama is an offshoot of the study of English literature and this has led to judgements being passed on play texts as finished works rather

than as the potential starting points for theatrical creation.

We are now at a stage of transition in our approach to
studying plays. Nineteenth-century drama has only won
the approval of the selectors of course material in the
last twenty years or so and critical writing on this period,
as exemplified by the work of George Powell (*The Victorian Theatre*, 1956); Allardyce Nicoll (*A History of Late
Eighteenth-Century Drama 1750–1800*, revised edition,
1952; *A History of Early Nineteenth-Century Drama
1800–50*, revised edition 1955; *A History of Late Nineteenth-Century Drama 1850–1900*, 1946) and Michael R.
Booth, Richard Southern, Frederick and Lise-Lorne
Marker and Robertson Davies (*The Revels History of
Drama in English*, volume VI, 1750–1880, 1975), reflects a
very different approach to the study of theatre from that
commonly employed for the period 1660 to 1800. Writers
on what we loosely label Victorian theatre are fully aware
of the interrelationship of scripts and the shared process
of creation between writers, designers and actors, with the
result that considerable strides have been taken to select
material for study that demonstrates the positive evolution of British theatre. This work is embodied in the two
standard collections: M. R. Booth's *English Plays of the
Nineteenth Century*, five volumes, 1969 and George
Rowell's *Nineteenth-Century Plays* (The World's
Classics), 1953.

What is not fully appreciated by the general student is
the vast output represented by these distillations. The
period 1750 to 1900 saw an unprecedented increase in the
number of plays written, performed and published. It has
been suggested that the Elizabethan period is that of the
greatest English theatrical activity. Such a suggestion is
arrant nonsense but that it can be seriously advanced is
indicative of our unbalanced approach to the study of
English theatre and emphasizes the need for a more ob-
jective appraisal of the vast amount of work produced

after the Restoration. It is work that is often so varied
that all distillations, be these anthologies or surveys, must
by the process of selection fall short of perfect. This can
only be corrected by the student exploring for himself
the many collections of eighteenth- and nineteenth-
century plays. Even the better known of these represent
only the upper storeys of a monumental edifice of activity. There is Bell's *British Plays*, 1777 (95 plays); *The
British Drama*, in two volumes, 1824–6; Inchbald's
British Theatre, 1808 (100 plays in twenty-five volumes);
T. J. Dibdin's one hundred plays *London Theatre* 1815–
18; *Oxberry's Edition*, 1820–22; the four volume *London
Stage*, 1824–7 (172 plays); and the two series launched in
the 1880s by Dicks, *The British Drama* and *Dicks Standard Plays* which include over 300 separate items. At the
beginning of this avalanche of dramatic publication the
plays were confined to those presented at the theatres
royal of Drury Lane and Covent Garden:

> O superb theatres, too small for parks, too enormous for
> houses, which exclude comedy and comfort, and have a
> monopoly for performing nonsense gigantically!
>
> Bulwer-Lytton, *Paul Clifford*

With the break-up of their monopoly and the rise of the
minor theatres in the nineteenth century there was a
further increase. The seminal collection of plays is *Lacy's
Acting Edition* 1851–60. This firm absorbed *Cumberland's British Theatre* (exclusively Covent Garden and
Drury Lane texts) and *Cumberland's Minor Theatre*,
which had previously absorbed the earlier *Dolby's British
Theatre*, 1823–5. Lacy in its turn was taken over by
Samuel French in 1872. Tragically the great mass of the
repertory of the Surrey Side and East End theatres of
London were never printed.

Having made the student aware of the almost limitless
dimensions of the subject under consideration it is the

aim of this work to shrink these dimensions in order to provide a basic framework of study within the context of known drama courses. The study of drama is fast coming of age and the process of reconsideration of a critical tradition which studied plays out of their theatrical context is already well advanced. Even so it is as well to underline for the reader that music, design, acting, the shape of the auditorium and the values and taste of the audience for whom a play was written must be borne in mind if a text is to be fully appreciated. The reading of a play is a recreative adventure where the reader is invited to enlarge on the matter given him in the printed script.

There is also a need to understand conventional short cuts in communication. Throughout the plays under consideration writers employ certain stock characters over which their actors have full control. The author can therefore concentrate the script on the intricacies of plot and leave the element of characterization to the performer. This respect for the actor's contribution survives today for the writer of a television series. A series creator lays down the guide-lines for the characters and as a series progresses new authors accept these characters which they have inherited. In the total picture of English drama there is considerable inheritance from the dramatic past. What often appears in isolated first sight to be weak characterization becomes rich and fully developed when understood in the context of our dramatic tradition.

Scenic means of communication are often more telling than verbal. Most people's imaginations and memories are pictorial. When relating what has taken place off stage a good playwright works to produce a series of mental pictures. He does this with the sound and meaning of words and with sheer narrative. The bigger the acting area and auditorium the more difficulty there is for words alone to clearly communicate. In the vast theatres of the early nineteenth century, as in the outdoor arenas of the Middle Ages, spectacle became the pre-eminent means of communication. Medieval drama wished to create an image of Hell in the minds of the audience, so it showed a glimpse of Hell through frightening gates from which could be seen smoke, fire and shadowy devils. It threatened with rumbling thunder and a terrifying use of scenic sound. The nineteenth-century managers faced the problem of an acoustically poor auditorium by employing scenic spectacle, procession and visual action as major narrative elements. The best professional playwrights of this era accepted the limitations of their medium and co-operated with the designers and carpenters to produce masterpieces of total entertainment of which the script was but a single part.

A play distils the world outside the theatre to something that can be managed in a playhouse. In a play everything must happen within a couple of hours. The audience makes allowances for certain conventions. Thus the theatre accepts love at first sight or recognition between a long parted brother and sister because the actors on the stage tell them they are true. Often moments such as these prove most difficult in rehearsal because the actors must create the reality of an emotion in an unnaturally encapsulated space of time. It is the actor's problem, his art must solve it and if he is successful the audience is not even aware of its existence. The reader, without the assistance of the performing artist between him and the text, may misinterpret an author's trust to the art of the actor as slight or sentimental writing. Other short cuts are easier for us to recognize so long as we are looking for them. Often they are the use by an author of contemporary attitudes to a class of people or type of situation. Thus in the eighteenth century the character of a lawyer does not have to be explained, for the audience share a common distrust of tautology. In the nineteenth century a city audience possessed distrust for the interests of land, thus the squire becomes the villain. It is essential not to lose sight of this background and continu-

ous tradition if individual plays are to be fully appreciated.

It is with great regret that introductory material on the
actors and theatres of this age is omitted. The space dictated by the size of a work of this kind allowed only a
superficial study of these elements which would have confused rather than clarified; for details in these areas the
reader is referred to Allardyce Nicoll's *History of English
Drama 1660–1900*.

This work concentrates on fifty selected texts intended
to give a representative picture of the period. As the
ability to follow a plot is essential to an understanding of
a play, this work aims to familiarize the reader with plays
he expects to read and thus clarify the complexities of un-
familiar language and structure. At the other end of this
process is the aim of providing a handy reminder, with
cast list and a built in anthology of scenes and speeches,
for the student who has read a play but wishes to refresh
himself on the main outline. It would be dishonest to
suggest that a student will not on occasion use this book
as a substitute for reading the actual text. This is not as
reprehensible a practice as is often made out. One builds
up one's own reading over a period which extends well
beyond any academic apprenticeship. Yet one is often
expected to have a broad knowledge supporting that
already acquired in depth. It is no shame to read selec-
tively and this study should in places support a detailed
knowledge of only a fraction of the contents.

It is to be hoped that this book will have some relevance
to practitioners as well as to the conventional student. All
the plays selected could still arouse interest on the modern
stage and some might well replace the more timeworn
established favourites.

The criterion of selection has been dramatic excellence
at the time the play was written. Thus a play which may
well not speak directly to us but which answered a contemporary need is preferred over a text which accident

has given a reconsidered value. As far as possible selection for the period 1800 to 1900 has borne in mind availability of texts, except in those cases, such as *The Castle Spectre*, when it was felt that an obscure play significantly clarified the development of the tradition.

Plots have been outlined act by act and scene by scene, although in a few cases where scenic divisions have no narrative significance these have been ignored. Continuity and coherence have been the main concern so that occasionally scenes between minor characters are glossed over. In the cast lists characters are mentioned only to be ignored in the outline. The full cast list is of immense significance to the practitioner; he needs to know how many roles there are. If a part is then not referred to in the outline its size is clearly indicated.

I would like to acknowledge the assistance of Mr David Harris, Head of the Manchester Polytechnic School of Theatre, A. L. J. Connolly, Head of the Department of Communication Arts and Design, and finally Mrs Joan Taylor and Miss Pat Madden who typed the manuscript in its various stages.

John Cargill Thompson, 1979

Audience and Taste

Although L. C. Knights, in *Drama and Society in the Age of Jonson* (1936) clearly demonstrated that it was the rise of the capitalist system in the early years of the seventeenth century which radically altered the native tradition inherited from the individual and social morality of the Middle Ages, and by so doing pointed the way to a more positive view of the starting and finishing points of cycles of dramatic development, we are caught up in a course structure which generally divides English drama into four major sections: Medieval, Shakespeare and his contemporaries, the Restoration to 1900, and Modern. This book serves such a structure but it would fail in its duty if it did not at the outset point out that any such division can be dangerously misleading.

Two natural breaks occur in the history of English drama. The first comes at the beginning of the seventeenth century as rising capitalism and speculation swept away the old Tudor world order. The second great change of direction takes place two hundred years later around 1800, when the increase in urban population creates a vast new working-class audience. These change the conventional view of dramatic development in the following way: Shakespeare and Marlowe are no longer an explosive starting point from which all that follows is a decline, but a glorious climax to the medieval dramatic tradition. From the early 1600s to the middle of the eighteenth century the theatre searches for a new identity. No sooner is this achieved in the second half of the eighteenth century and before it can explore the stability gained by the achievements of Garrick, than there is a violent change in the composition of the audience and from the end of the eighteenth century to the second half of the nineteenth century a new audience has to be wooed and civilized. The achievement of the English theatre in leading the audience from sensational melodrama and spectacle to the subleties of social comedy is very great. The period 1800 to 1900 far from being one of theatrical decline is one of consistently positive improvement.

From the beginning to the end of the period which we cover contemporary 'critics' inveigh against the poor taste of the time, the corrupt state of the drama and the general excellence of the age before. Foreign models are held up for our admiration. It would almost appear from this general air of gloom that the theatre as an art form is in continuous danger. Yet people still kept going to the theatre and the bulk of the complaints come from those who didn't. One of the problems arises from the fact that since the Elizabethan age it has been impossible to serve all classes satisfactorily. Differences in education and class aims and values widen to such an extent that, by pleasing one section of the community, a theatre must necessarily alienate another. The general movements in taste reflect the opinions of the bulk of the audience for which the plays were written. At our starting point the most popular plays are city comedy with speculation and usury as its targets, idealized romantic comedy, serving a classic platonic ideal, and tragedy or tragi-comedy, which upholds such absolutes as honour, obedience and love. Such drama reflects the attitudes of a largely upper-class audience and rejects the citizen and apprentice element in the city of London which is now coming more and more under the influence of Puritanism. The next age sees a shift to a comedy of witty sexual intrigue and exaggerated heroic tragedy which excites our pity and admiration. The young men of the court of Charles II lived very much in the present. In spite of the King's protestations to the contrary, there was a considerable fear that they might have to resume their travels in yet another social upheaval. The old values of their fathers and grandfathers had failed them. Their comedy reflects a fear that too strong a reliance on ideals might again prove fatal, while their tragedy mirrors this distrust by placing heroism outside the bounds of day to day existence. After the glorious revolution of William of Orange society stabilizes, the middle classes return to the theatre and this is reflected in the rigid division of types. Comedy becomes serious, sentimental and improving. Tragedy becomes sober and classical. This stability is maintained till the second half of the eighteenth century. The first signs of change are not in individual plays but rather in varied bills of entertainment. The custom was, after the third act of the main piece to allow further customers into the theatre at half-price. The half-price customers were of a different, less literate class and the farces, pantomimes, entr'acte songs and dances, speciality numbers, orchestral music before and between pieces, together with an ingenious variety of prologues and epilogues demonstrate the growing eclecticism of theatrical taste. This eclecticism is at the heart of the anarchic blends of melodrama, song and musical spectacle which make the drama of the first half of the nineteenth century so difficult to classify. Allardyce Nicoll has formulated, or tried to formulate, eighty-five different categories of dramatic writing during this period. This herculean task can be simplified into a statement that early nineteenth-century dramatists, moving away from the formal division of genres of the eighteenth century, presented the whole play bill, entr'actes and all, together in the one play. This delighted a working-class audience whose main demand was for show.

As this audience became more responsible so the nine-teenth century moved from the romantic to the realistic, from illusion to something more solidly physical and from poetry to prose. With this movement away from illusion the paraphernalia of real life had to be reproduced in settings, costumes and properties. Theatres became more solid and respectable, the middle and upper classes renewed their patronage and working-class realism was replaced by society drama.

The two ages that require most preliminary explanation are those of the Stuart–Restoration period and the late eighteenth to early nineteenth century. It has now become generally accepted by specialists that Victorian rejection of the sexual nature of Restoration comedy led to our inheriting a very imperfect and superficial view of that period. The reconsideration of that period together with a much more detailed study of the much neglected Caroline drama now presents the view that the physical break caused by the closing of the theatres in 1642 is of much less significance than was previously thought. The old idea that Restoration drama is, if not an offshoot of French theatre, at least heavily influenced by it, has been rejected in favour of a continuing tradition as expressed by Bonamy Dobrée in *Restoration Comedy* and Allardyce Nicoll in *History of English Drama 1660–1900*.

This native tradition has been protected by the Englishman's inability to understand any foreign culture, so that anything incorporated into the English way of life is immediately adapted and anglicized to the point that whatever its origins it becomes essentially English. Thus the French influence on Restoration drama is minimal.

It is convenient for the student of theatre to accept the theory that an organic Elizabethan–Medieval society was suddenly replaced by an anarchic Jacobean swirl of individual competition. In historical terms this is a gross oversimplification but the nature of drama is to oversimplify and the concern of Restoration drama with speculators and moneylenders presents just such a straightforward conflict between ruthless materialism and the old order. The ideally stable and morally coherent model of the previous era, as exemplified by Hooker's *Ecclesiastical Policy* gives place to the world described by Hobbes in *Leviathan*:

> To this war of every man, against every man, this also is consequent; that nothing can be unjust. The notions of right and wrong; justice and injustice have there no place. Where there is common power, there is no law: where no law, no injustice. Force and fraud are, in war, the two cardinal virtues. Justice and injustice are none of the faculties neither of the body nor the mind ... It is consequent also to the same condition, that there be no propriety, no dominion, no *mine* and *thine* distinct; but only that to be every man's, that he can get: and for so long as he can keep it.

This anarchy is common to Dorimant (*The Man of Mode*) and to Overreach (*A New Way to Pay Old Debts*) and gives us the link between English dramatic writing before and after the Commonwealth. It is easy enough to grasp the relationship of Stuart city comedy in terms of this social revolution which was to lead to a shift of power from crown to Parliament, merchants and industrialists. We must also understand that the host of usurping dukes and shaky thrones represented in Stuart tragedy, reflects a similar fear of pragmatism.

The Cavaliers believed that their hope lay in a series of absolute values such as love, honour and obedience to order. Is it any wonder that after a period of twenty years of exile they should at the best question these values and at the worst cynically reject them?

The most superficial study of the period of the immediate restoration of the monarchy reveals an open licence and libertinage unparalleled in any other period. The King set the example. Pepys reports that Charles, with

Mrs Stewart: '... gets into corners, and will be with her half an hour together, kissing her to the observation of the world'. The brazen, barely concealed erotic intrigues of the court seem so wildly incompatible with the platonic idealism of Charles I that it is easy to misinterpret this as a moral and social revolution. When we look closer, there is a frenetic quality about the merriment of this court which is decidedly unreal. It was almost inconceivable that intelligent men like Rochester and Buckhurst could smash up the astronomical balls in Whitehall simply for amusement. Underneath this picture of debauchery we find an age of curiosity and serious inquiry. In the drama, Dryden and others begin to ask serious questions as to how plays should be written but this is simply a literary aspect of the scientific curiosity which led to the founding of the Royal Society. This curiosity and scientific reason is to a certain extent cross-referenced with the sexual attitudes. Men and women discovered that sexual desire and love were separate and we must credit them with an almost scientific experimentation in this area. The platonic code had collapsed with Cromwell; the code he and his fellows offered was rejected; a new code had been discovered. The strongest feeling that comes out of both the tragedy and comedy of the reign of Charles II and James II is a serious search for identity. It is not that people do not believe in anything but that everything in which their fathers believed has collapsed. Thus, not all the bawdy elements are attempts to amuse but rather the majority represent a striving towards honesty, a serious attempt to discover anything which might be. Pre-Restoration comedy had attempted to expose the hidden recesses of human passion and desire, the comedy of Etherege and Wycherley does not need to expose anything hidden and can simply show the same passions and desires as they appeared in daily life. The pre-Restoration comedy can appeal to a supposedly absolute standard of morality, but the comedy of the Restoration has no such guide-line. It is not so much that Restoration comedy is less profound than that written during the Jacobean period but it is necessarily more uncertain. In the same way the tragedy searches for its heroes in unreality because it is unable to discover any lasting heroism in its own age. The subject matter of English plays prior to 1642 is identical with that of the end of the century. Granted Shakespeare holds out marriage as a happy haven for lovers but we must not let this blind us to the fact that the vast bulk of early seventeenth-century drama as exemplified by the work of Marston, Massinger and Shirley reveals what superficially we might call the Restoration flavour:

> *Beatrice* My love here.
> *Crispinella* Prithee call him not love, 'tis the drab's phrase; nor sweet home, nor my coney, nor dear duckling, 'tis the citizen's terms, but call him –
> *Beatrice* What?
> *Crispinella* Anything.
>
> Marston, *Dutch Courtezan*

And again from Massinger's *The City Madam*, when Anne Frugal answers Sir Maurice Lacy's proposal of marriage:

> *Anne*   I require first,
> And that, since 'tis in fashion with kind husbands,
> In civil manners you must grant, my will
> In all things whatsoever, and that will
> To be obeyed, not argued ...
> *Sir Maurice* This in gross contains all:
> But your special items, lady.
> *Anne*   When I am one.
> And you are honoured to be styled my husband,
> To urge my having my page, my gentleman-usher

My woman sworn to my secrets, my caroch
Drawn by six Flanders mares, my coachman,
   grooms,
Postillion, and footmen.

Sir Maurice   Is there aught else
To be demanded?

Anne   Yes, sir, mine own doctor.
French and Italian cooks, musicians, songsters,
And a chaplain that must preach to please my
   fancy:
A friend at court to place me at a masque;
The private box ta'en up at a new play,
For me and my retinue; a fresh habit,
Of a fashion never seen before, to draw
The gallants' eyes, that sit upon the stage, upon
   me;
Some decayed lady for my parasite,
To flatter me, and rail at other madams;
And there ends my ambitions.

A comparison between the two quotations above and the famous 'proviso' scene in *The Way of the World* reveals how the ingredients of Restoration comedy exist in Jacobean drama and how far the later period continued and developed from the earlier. We can safely reject the naïve and old fashioned view that Restoration drama is in the main an offshoot of French drama transplanted by the exiled Cavaliers on their return. The comedy of Molière is closer to Jonson than it is to Congreve and the attitude to French manners is identical in the drama of Shirley to that in the plays of Etherege. Indeed the French court had more influence on that of Charles I than on the courts of his sons.

During the Commonwealth the theatre-going habit had been lost but by the 1690s the middle classes had returned and the age of William and Mary and the age of Queen Anne place a growing stress on judgement, sound sense, good nature and restraint. This clearer attitude to life is reflected in different ways in the work of Rowe, Congreve, Farquhar, Steele and Addison. The result is that wit is tempered by a clearer morality. We must not interpret this new reserve as coldness so much as a greater concern to avoid malice. The drama becomes fundamentally more affectionate and sober and, while it is natural for us today to prefer gossip to wet handkerchiefs, we must respect the sincerity of these men who felt they had discovered truths hidden from their fathers and looked forward to an enlightened future with a careful, sober hope. It is this responsibility to the future which superannuates all the wits, coquettes and libertines in the drama from Steele onwards. The main impression that we obtain from a study of mid-eighteenth-century theatre is its stability. The most radical change and upheaval covered in this study comes at the end of the nineteenth century. Again this reflects non-theatrical factors.

In 1790 London contained approximately 900,000 persons, by 1850 this figure had risen to over three million. The constant flow of people from the provinces into London during the eighteenth century had been checked by a death rate which exceeded the birth rate. A sharp rise in migration from the rural areas in the agricultural depression of the early nineteenth century combined with improved sanitation was the reason for this explosion. In the eighteenth century the town was the arbiter of theatrical taste. This right of arbitration was protected by the Licensing Laws which effectively placed the national theatre in the hands of the patent theatres, Drury Lane and Covent Garden. The new working-class colonies in the East End and directly south of the Thames gave birth to minor theatres providing theatrical entertainment especially written for this semi-literate audience and very different in flavour from the official national drama as represented by the patent theatres. In broad terms the early nineteenth century saw the educating and civilizing of this new audience whose previous ideas of entertainment stopped at cock fighting, badger baiting and bare-knuckle pugilism. This audience not only patronized its own local minor theatres but also overran the patent theatres. Considered in these terms the so-called decline of drama during the nineteenth century becomes the colossal and positive achievement of taking this audience from spectacle and show to social drama in just over fifty years.

From 1750–90 the audience at the patent theatres was mainly fashionable gentry and middle-class tradesmen. The lower classes were confined to the gallery. The theatre was relatively more expensive in the eighteenth than the nineteenth century. The predominant pattern of taste was that of the educated middle classes, spiced with aristocratic embellishment.

In the period 1792–1812 both Covent Garden and Drury Lane underwent considerable enlargement whilst at the same time the minor theatres began to challenge seriously the monopoly of the patent. Larger theatres and new audiences affected the type of material that was presented. Hearing and seeing became most difficult which obviously brought about an increase in spectacle and a broader more obvious style of acting, but the rash of performing animals and simpler plots must be put down to the influence of the new audience. In the first years of the nineteenth century managers found boxes and pit poorly attended while the galleries were full, particularly after the third act of the main piece when half price was accepted. The auditorium class war reached its climax in 1809 when John Philip Kemble tried to raise the price of the pit and turn more than half the gallery space into additional private boxes. The result was the two month 'old price' riots during which not a word of text was heard for the rattles, jeers and catcalls of the rioters. Such behaviour discouraged the middle classes and the only course open to managements was to reduce prices in an

attempt to woo the gallery audiences into other parts of
the theatre. Thus Kemble's new prices were 7s 6d for a
box, 4s for the pit, and the galleries 2s and 1s. By 1835
these had been reduced to 4s, 2s and 1s and they remained
that low until 1852. Hence the working- and lower-
middle-class effect upon the plays that were written.

In the early nineteenth century the theatre became
openly low class. From Elizabethan times prostitutes had
frequented the theatre but in the eighteenth century these
had confined themselves to the gallery and stage boxes. In
the early nineteenth century they began to make the public foyers their main sphere of operation. Sir Walter Scott
complained in 1819:

> The best part of the house is openly and avowedly set off for
> their reception; and no part of it which is open to the public
> at large is free from their intrusion, or at least from the
> open display of the disgusting improprieties to which their
> neighbourhood gives rise ... No man of sense would wish
> the female part of his family to be exposed to such scenes.

In 1833 the *Edinburgh Review* after complaining about
indecency in theatre foyers goes on to point out the following anomaly:

> ... while we are blessed with a Censor [George Colman]
> who scrupulously changes 'damn it' into 'hang it', and
> cannot allow the public ear to be polluted with 'my angel!'
> we have theatres where open profligacy revels with a
> freedom scarcely known in civilized lands, and which the
> wives and daughters of our citizens can scarcely enter
> without a blush.

Macready was the first person to take action against these
practices when, in 1842, as manager of Drury Lane he
gave orders that prostitutes were to be refused admission.
We may share Scott's civilized objections but we must
accept open prostitution as a fact of the age. They came
with the brutal semi-civilized audience which had taken

over the theatre auditorium. Kemble's new prices had been a last loyal attempt to protect the interests of the middle classes. His successors in management accepted the situation and their achievement in reforming it reveals great patience in adversity. Prostitutes in the foyer were not a symbol of the decline of the stage but just another of the new factors with which the nineteenth-century theatre had to cope. Macready was able to prosecute his order because the situation had stabilized and improved. Similarly at Sadler's Wells between 1844 and 1862 Samuel Phelps was allowed to change an unruly minor theatre into a respectable place of entertainment. The royal patronage which had an accelerating influence on the return of society to the theatre was only possible because of the advances made within the profession itself. In 1848, Queen Victoria placed on Charles Kean the responsibility for bringing companies to perform at Windsor Castle. These command performances continued until the death of the Prince Consort in 1861. *The Times* acknowledged the royal contribution in its article of 16 January 1849:

> When the highest patronage in the land considers that an English dramatic performance is such an entertainment as to merit the construction of a stage in her drawing-room, with all the appurtenances of a regular theatre, the opinion that the native drama is unfashionable receives an authoritative rebuke.

At the Prince of Wales and later the Haymarket theatres, the Bancrofts wooed society with carpets, curtains and white lace antimacassars on the stall seats. In contrast to the 'old price' riots of 1809, apart from a few cries of 'where's the pit?', its replacement by stall seats costing 10s each passed almost unheeded.

This was possible because theatre audiences had again divided. When society returned to the West End the lower and working classes concentrated their patronage on neighbourhood theatres and music halls whose function was eventually to be taken over by cinema and the mass media. Even in the working-class theatres respectability prevailed and the audience demanded good acting of worthwhile material. Family groups predominated. Dickens describes the scene in *The Uncommercial Traveller*:

> Many of us – on the whole the majority – were not at all clean, and not at all choice in our lives or conversation. But we had all come together in a place where our convenience was well consulted, and where we were well looked after, to enjoy an evening's entertainment in common. We were not going to lose any part of what we had paid for through anybody's caprice, and as a community we had character to lose. So we were closely attentive, and kept excellent order.

In spite of the dirt, the smell, the noise and the crush of the rude multitude, just as in its West End counterparts, the standards of the Victorian neighbourhood theatre were dictated by an intense interest in what was going on on the stage.

The Tempest, or
The Enchanted Island
Sir William D'Avenant (1606–68)
John Dryden (1631–1700)

The Puritan government had closed the theatres in 1642. A further edict was passed in 1647 which gave magistrates the right to enter playhouses and imprison the actors. There was a third act in 1647–8. The need for three edicts and various petitions, such as *The Actors Remonstrance, or Complaint ... for the Silencing of their Profession, and banishment of their several Playhouses* (1643) and *The Players Petition to Parliament*, would seem to indicate that there was a fair amount of surreptitious performance.

Whitelock's *Memorials* tell us that troops interrupted an entertainment at the Red Bull on 20 December 1649, imprisoning the actors and destroying their costumes. Many of the actors and playwrights served in the Civil War on the Royalist side, so that we can deduce that the bulk of those that were left were the very old, the very young and the incompetent. At the beginning of the Civil War players still performed in the Royalist towns and cities, or in the private houses of the nobility, but in general drama became a furtive underground occupation attracting little new talent. Because of the theatre's underground nature during this period it was possible to make a large fortune out of the second rate.

The two writers to emerge from the interregnum as major influences are Thomas Killigrew (1612–83) and William D'Avenant (1606–68). Both these men had been members of the 'tribe of Ben', or disciples of Ben Jonson.

D'Avenant was the son of the wife of an Oxford inn-keeper called John Davenant. Gossips seeking to interpret Shakespeare's hidden biography have identified Mistress Davenant with the dark lady of the sonnets and William D'Avenant as Shakespeare's godson or even illegitimate child, but there is nothing to support any of the assertions.

When William D'Avenant altered the spelling of his name by the addition of an aristocratic apostrophe thus claiming descent from an ancient Norman family, a contemporary writer remarked: 'Useless, everybody knows that D'Avenant comes from the Avon; this river is the cradle of his muse.'

Prior to the Civil War D'Avenant held a number of minor posts in noble households, until he became the boon companion of Sir John Suckling. He was always in debt. He also suffered from syphilis and the resulting mercury poisoning from the treatment. He was convicted for the murder of an inn servant. It was while he was awaiting the King's pardon that he wrote a masque for the Queen which brought him into prominence as a writer. In 1640 he became manager of Beeston's Boys Company at the Cockpit. He served with the King's Army and was knighted for his services to the Royalist party in 1643. In 1650 he was appointed Lieutenant Governor of Maryland but on his way to America was captured in the Channel and imprisoned in the Tower. After his return, in 1656, he was the first to revive the theatre with operatic productions which made great use of scenic machinery he had observed on the continent.

Killigrew, too, had served the Royalist cause, both during the Civil War and the exile. In 1660 the theatre was formally legalized when patents were granted to Killigrew and D'Avenant. These patents were an attempt to control and regularize an existing professional theatre which contained 'much matter of prophanation and scurrility' and 'for the most part tend to the debauching of the manners of such as are at present at them'. The patents stated the

intention to establish a theatre that could 'serve as innocent and harmless divertisement for many of our subjects'.
The patent goes on to empower Killigrew and D'Avenant
to recruit two companies of players and build two playhouses. The new playhouses were to be equipped with
new scenery. Provision for the introduction of women on
to the stage was also made. The sole performance rights
to most of the best known plays of the Jacobean and Caroline periods were divided between the two companies.

John Dryden is the towering figure of the Restored
theatre. The family had provided squires and rectors for
generations and his great-grandfather was said to have
been a friend of Erasmus. During the Civil War his family
supported the Puritans. Coming from such a background,
with a family tradition for scholarship, Dryden's education at Westminster and then Trinity College, Cambridge, is what we would expect. He took his degree of
BA in 1654 and probably remained at Cambridge for the
next three years. In 1657 he came to London. Family influence obtained him a minor government office.

It would appear that he turned to the stage for financial
reasons, yet he was one of the great theatrical theorists.
The prefaces to his plays are full of balanced criticism.
Dryden's great critical work was planned, if not written,
during the Great Plague, when he was living in Wiltshire.
This was printed in 1668 and called an *Essay of Drama-
tick Poesy*. It takes the form of a dialogue between
Neander (Dryden), Eugenius (Charles, Lord Buckhurst),
Crites (Sir Robert Howard) and Lisideius (Sir Charles
Sedley). Crites held the classics up as the only model;
Lisideius maintains the rules of French drama; Neander
defends the pre-Restoration English drama, while agree-
ing that there is much to gain from a study of more formal methods of composition.

Dryden's prolific writings for the stage show many
different phases. At the beginning of his theatrical career

he specialized in coarse comedy. As late as 1780, *The Kind Keeper, or Mr Limberham* was banned after three performances as indecent. His comedies are much more correctly Restoration than those of his successors to which we incorrectly apply the term: they serve as the link between Jacobean comedy and the plays of Wycherley, Congreve and others. His comic work lacks the formal artistry of his successors, yet it is not without wit. He is attempting to create a new form of English comedy which would combine the romanticism of Beaumont and Fletcher with the reality of Jonson. He states very clearly in the introduction to *An Evening's Love, or The Mock Astrologer*:

> I will not deny but that I approve most the mixed way of comedy; that which is neither all wit, nor all humour, but the result of both.

His wit is mainly displayed through the use of a pair of lovers, around whose exchanges of repartee the characters revolve. What Dryden was able to do, because of the introduction of actresses on to the stage, was to carry these pairs of lovers several degrees further than Shakespeare.

Dryden's heroic dramas, such as *The Indian Queen* (1664), written in collaboration with Sir Robert Howard, the sequel *The Indian Emperor* (1665), *Tyrannic Love* (1669) and the vast two part *The Conquest of Granada* (1670) take the form to an extreme of bombastic vigour. The Duke of Buckingham's *The Rehearsal* (1671), although it had been conceived with D'Avenant as the original target, ridicules Dryden's work in this field.

Dryden was created poet laureate and historiographer to the King in 1670. At the very end of his career he abandoned rhymed tragedy for blank verse to produce what most acknowledge to be his best play, *All For Love, or The World Well Lost* (1678). The story is the same as Shakespeare's *Antony and Cleopatra* but Dryden, representing the two lovers as entirely under the dominion of

love, concentrates on the culminating point in their relationship.

On the accession of James II in 1685 Dryden became a
Roman Catholic. There is still discussion as to the sincerity of his conversion but he did not abjure his new
faith in the revolution. The result of this was that he lost
his office and pension as laureate and historiographer
royal. His last years were spent in translating the classics,
presumably for a living. He was still venerated as the
greatest living poet, holding court at Will's coffee-house.
Congreve, Vanbrugh and Addison were among his disciples and Pope, as a boy of twelve, was taken to see the
veteran poet. Unmolested by the new government he died
in May 1700 and was buried in Westminster Abbey.

DATE 1667
CAST
Alonzo, Duke of Savoy and usurper of the dukedom of Mantua
Ferdinand, his son
Prospero, right Duke of Milan
Antonio, his brother, usurper of the dukedom
Gonzalo, a nobleman of Savoy
Hippolyto, one that never saw woman, right heir to the
dukedom of Mantua
Stephano, master of the ship
Mustacho, his mate
Trincalo, boatswain
Ventoso, a mariner
Miranda ⎫
Dorinda ⎬ daughters to Prospero that never saw man
Ariel, a spirit attendant on Prospero
Milcha, a second spirit
Caliban   ⎫
Sycorax, his sister ⎬ two monsters of the Isle
SCENE An uninhabited island

Plot

Act I The first scene presents the shipwreck of Alonzo, Ferdinand, Antonio, Gonzalo and the sailors. Dialogue is overshadowed by scenic embellishment, spirits fly down among the sailors, rise and cross in the air. The ship sinks, the theatre is darkened: there is thunder and lightning, and a shower of fire illuminates the stage. The next scene is composed of three walks of cypress trees, each walk leading to a cave. In one of these Prospero keeps his daughters, in another, Hippolyto, and the middle walk leads to an open part of the island. Prospero explains to Miranda how fifteen years previously his brother Antonio, with the help of Alonzo, usurped his dukedom and cast Prospero and his family adrift in a rotten boat. At the end of Prospero's tale Miranda sleeps. Prospero summons Ariel, who relates how he raised the storm. None of those shipwrecked are harmed but Ariel has divided them in separate groups each unaware of the salvation of the others. Ariel reminds Prospero of his promise to release him from service and Prospero assures him that but two days remain of his servitude. Ariel requests that his love Milcha is summoned to help him in his final tasks. Prospero grants this request. The two spirits 'fly up and cross in the air' before making their exit.

Act II A wild part of the island. Stephano, Mustacho and Ventoso enter drunk. Believing themselves the sole survivors of the wreck they set about dividing the island. As Stephano was master at sea he is to be duke on land. After some disagreement it is decided that Mustacho and Ventoso shall be viceroys. Trincalo then appears, with a barrel of sack he has rescued. This possession investing him with authority he refuses to accept these arrangements and declares himself a rival duke. Stephano declares him rebel and exits to confer with his viceroys. Caliban enters and after a drink or two of sack readily hails Trincalo as king. In the second scene Prospero explains that Hippolyto,

the right duke of Mantua, is also concealed on the island.
Because of a prophecy that women will bring him into
great danger he has been kept in ignorance of the existence of Miranda and Dorinda and they of him. Prospero
warns Hippolyto against women. The scene continues
with Dorinda and Miranda peeping at Hippolyto. Miranda, frightened, runs away when Prospero calls, leaving
Dorinda and Hippolyto alone together.

Act III The invisible Ariel and Milcha (to whom is given
the lyric 'Full fathom five thy father lies') lead Ferdinand
by song, while in his cave Prospero is relieved to discover
that Miranda does not love Hippolyto: he promises to
introduce her to one 'of which this youth was but the
opening bud'. He upbraids Dorinda for encouraging Hippolyto. Elsewhere, after a dance of fantastic spirits a table
laden with food is brought in by two spirits, only to be
flown away just as the lords approach it. Discord is sown
between Caliban, Trincalo and his intended wife Sycorax
when an invisible Ariel turns the sack in the bottle to
water. Stephano and his colleagues enter and suggest a
truce, but this dissolves when Trincalo refuses to share his
bottle of sack. The next scenes are set by Prospero's cave.

Ferdinand and Miranda meet and immediately fall in
love, but Prospero harshly pretends to mistake Ferdinand
for an enemy to the peace of his isle. Later Ferdinand is
vastly amused by Hippolyto's naïve questions about
women but Hippolyto begins to suspect that he is being
mocked and concludes that Ferdinand intends to steal
Miranda and Dorinda and that Prospero's warnings
against women were but a cunning ploy by the old man
to preserve the women for himself.

Act IV Prospero releases Ferdinand to Miranda, only requiring that she make the two young men friends. Ferdinand interprets Miranda's request to this effect as love
for Hippolyto. Hippolyto meanwhile, inflamed by Ferdinand's information that there are more women than
Dorinda and Miranda is determined to enjoy them all.

He unsuccessfully tries to enlist Dorinda's assistance. Hippolyto and Ferdinand quarrel, and arrange to fight. Elsewhere Stephano, Mustacho and Ventoso agree to Trincalo's title provided he shares his sack. A table rises and four spirits dance round it with bottles of wine only to disappear again with everything. The sailors become very drunk and Trincalo confesses that he cannot abide Sycorax and only married her to improve his title to the island. Stephano takes this opportunity to undermine the new state by retailing Trincalo's babblings to Sycorax. Ferdinand seems to kill Hippolyto. Prospero commands Ariel to bring the lords to him. He reveals himself, telling them that he had intended to end their quarrel by the marriage of Ferdinand and Miranda. This is no longer possible as Ferdinand must die for murdering Hippolyto. Act V Before Prospero's cave. Miranda pleads for Ferdinand's life with a seemingly intractable Prospero, but Ariel enters to announce that Hippolyto is still alive. His near escape has matured him. Prospero is reconciled with his enemies, and Miranda and Dorinda marry Ferdinand and Hippolyto. Stephano, Trincalo and the other sailors are driven in and as their sack is finished they are content to return to the ship, which Prospero, by his magic, had saved from the storm. Ariel is freed and the play concludes with a masque between Neptune, Amphitryon and a chorus of Tritons and Neriads. Aeolus descends summoning the winds who fly in from the four corners. In the final scene Ariel flies directly out of the rising sun, and sings Shakespeare's song 'Where the bee sucks, there suck I'.

Critical commentary

The temptation to draw superficial conclusions from a comparison between Shakespeare's play and the present text must be fought. Such a comparison would appear to give the lie to the theory that there is no significant break in our dramatic tradition during the hiatus of the Commonwealth. There is a vast critical gap between Jacobean and Restoration drama which any quick comparison between the two plays ignores. No play can ever be studied in isolation either of its background or its place in our evolving dramatic tradition. A play must be examined in the context of the audience taste and expectation.

There is a dangerous tendency to exaggerate the difference between early and late seventeenth-century drama because the critical gap we have already referred to masks significant evolutionary factors. Proper attention to its content reveals that the Restoration treatment of *The Tempest* is exactly what we would expect at this point in the development of English drama. Even the technical differences are not nearly so great as they appear to be when we examine the play via a comparison with Shakespeare's *Tempest* written for an Elizabethan playhouse. Certainly the Elizabethan playhouse continued in existence until the closure of the theatres in 1642 but during the Jacobean period the smaller indoor private theatres catering for a more exclusive courtly audience had much more effect on the type of plays written than their public counterparts. The court masques of Inigo Jones and his successors had introduced movable scenery and there are strong arguments for suggesting that embryo 'Restoration' scenic techniques were employed in the indoor theatres during the Caroline period. The increase in spectacle in this play over plays written just prior to 1640 is no greater than the corresponding increase of the use of spectacle in Caroline drama over Jacobean. Dryden's and D'Avenant's reliance on scenic device as a main dramatic means, typifies the difference between their play and that of Shakespeare. The audience are shown things rather than asked to imagine them. From Sir Walter Scott onwards critics have pointed out that many of the orders given in the opening shipwreck scene are either meaningless or would have resulted in quite the opposite from the author's' intent. Such criticism is irrelevant. In the 1600s the play might have attracted the critical attention of sailors and Thames watermen but a restricted court audience in 1667 would have been highly unlikely to have understood the terms sufficiently for their acceptance of the scene to be undermined. It is a quibbling point, the new first scene communicates confusion and most readers, without the assistance of footnotes, would pass on unaware of the nautical inaccuracies and impressed by the clear use of visual means. At other times this scenic concept of the play is totally detrimental. Internal development of character is always to be preferred over external effect. The essence of Shakespeare's play is badly diluted in D'Avenant and Dryden by the device of bringing the lords to repentance through the scenic pressure of the devil masque. Again we can close the gap between Shakespeare and Dryden if we understand what lies between. The 'external' began to make headway on the stage from early in the seventeenth century. The Jacobean private theatres replaced philosophical debate with lavish production, extravagant plot and refined sentiment. Similarly with depth of characterization. All the characters are coarsened from their originals: particularly Caliban, Stephano and Trincalo. Shakespeare's monster provokes the audience to something akin to sympathy and it is a daring stroke of genius to place the beautiful speech redolent of immortal longings, beginning 'Be not afeared, the isle is full of noises', in the mouth of the deformed slave. The Restoration Caliban is all debased caricature. Jacobean drama began to order and simplify, this process continues through the Caroline period so that by the 1660s a monster who dreamed immortal dreams would have been an untidy violation of order. Likewise the buffoonery of Shakespeare's clown and butler takes on a sinister meaning as these characters, transformed by the adaptors to sailors, quarrel over the state. Harmless fun becomes sharp satire on the late Commonwealth. Sad too are the alterations to Ariel, that lonely asexual being, supplied with a girl-friend, Milcha. Such change, in despite of a new found ability to fly through the air, confines the spirit world to a scenic earth. Nothing is left to our imagination.

The language is similarly shorn of the poetic. A comparison between the treatments of Prospero's first act exchange with Miranda demonstrates this point:

> My brother and thy uncle called Antonio:
> I pray thee mark me, that a brother should
> Be so perfidious: he, whom next thyself
> Of all the world I loved, and to him put
> The manage of my state, as at that time
> Through all the signories it was the first,
> And, Prospero, the prime duke, being so reputed
> In dignity; and for the liberal arts,
> Without a parallel; those being all my study,
> The government I cast upon my brother,
> And to my state grew stranger, being transported
> And wrapt in secret studies, thy false uncle
> (Do'st thou attend me?) ...
>
> Shakespeare

This is altered to:

> My brother, and thy uncle called Antonio, to whom I
> trusted then the manage of my state, while I was wrapped
> with secret studies: that false uncle having attained the
> craft of granting suits, and of denying them; whom to
> advance, or lop, for over-topping, soon was grown the
> ivy, which did hide my princely trunk, and sucked my
> verdure out: thou attend'st not.

The latter speech is written in that disjointed blank verse/ prose typical of the late Stuart period, which Dryden was one of the first to discard in favour of heroic couplets. The overwhelming preponderance of speeches of this kind has led most editors of Dryden to blame D'Avenant

as the main begetter of the play. Such a view is in direct
denial of Dryden's own claim that he was responsible for
all the portions in which Hippolyto appears. Dryden was
obsessed with refining the chaotic drama he and his fellows had inherited from the Caroline period, of which
D'Avenant was a survivor, and while one must agree
with critical editorial comparison between the two plays,
such criticism must be leavened with an understanding of
the point in the tradition at which *The Tempest* was
written and with respect for Dryden's ambition to distil
refined simplicity from luxuriant Caroline fertility. It is
wrong to think of Dryden and the other adaptors of
Shakespeare as a reaction against Shakespeare. They are
more truly a reaction against the absurdities of Webster,
Ford and others.

Henry V
Roger Boyle, 1st Earl of Orrery
(1621–79)

Roger Boyle was the third surviving son of the Earl of
Cork. He was educated at Trinity College, Dublin and
also possibly at Oxford. He travelled in France and Italy.
In 1641, on the outbreak of the rebellion he returned to
Ireland. He fought at the battle of Liscarrol in 1642. He
was eventually persuaded to serve under the parliamentary authorities, only resigning on the execution of the
King. For a time he disappeared from public life, living
quietly in Somerset. He was, however, a leading figure in a
scheme to bring about the restoration of Charles II.
Cromwell discovered this and visited him personally to
warn him that all his plans were known. The result of this
meeting was that Boyle agreed to serve Cromwell in
Ireland against the rebels. On Cromwell's departure for
Scotland he cooperated with Ireton and was one of the
leading commanders at the siege of Limerick. He had
now become a friend and supporter of Cromwell, particularly in Ireland. He was returned to Parliament in 1654
and 1656 as member for Cork and also, in the latter parliament, for Edinburgh. In 1657 he became lord president
of the council in Scotland, by which time he was one of
Cromwell's most trusted advisors. He was a strong advocate of Cromwell assuming the title of King, and also
suggested that Cromwell's daughter, Frances, should
marry Charles II. On the death of the Protector he supported his son, Richard, but subsequently had the fore-

sight to see that a change was coming. He returned to Ireland and anticipated the Restoration by inviting Charles II to land in Cork. He sat for Arundel in the parliament of 1661, having been created Earl of Orrery in 1660. He was appointed a lord justice of Ireland and drew up the Act of Settlement. In 1668 he was impeached for 'raising money by his own authority upon his majesty's subjects' but Charles's dismissal of parliament halted these inquiries and they were never resumed. His plays were all written after the Restoration, although he had written a novel, *Parthenissa*, in 1654.

Boyle's tragedies fall into two groups, his plays with an English historical setting and those framed more exotically. The first includes *Henry V* and *The Black Prince* (both 1667) and the second *Mustapha* (1665), *Tryphon* (1668), *Herod the Great* (printed 1694) and *Altemira* (printed 1704). He also wrote two comedies, *Guzman* (1669) and *Mr Anthony*.

CAST

King Henry V of England
The Duke of Bedford, his brother
The Duke of Exeter, his uncle
The Earl of Warwick
The Archbishop of Canterbury
Owen Tudor
The Dauphin
The Duke of Burgundy
The Earl of Chareloys, his son
The Constable of France
De Chastel, the Dauphin's creature
Bishop of Arras
Count of Blamount
Monsieur Colemore
The Queen of France
Princess Katherine, her daughter
Princess Anne of Burgundy

The Countess of La Marr
SCENE France

Plot

Act 1,*i* Henry V's camp before the battle of Agincourt. This scene establishes the friendship between the King and Tudor. *ii* The palace of the Dauphin. Denied the regency of France, the Dauphin plots with his confidante De Chastel against Burgundy. *iii* The French court. The Queen, Princess Katherine, Princess Anne of Burgundy and the Duke of Burgundy await news of the battle. Although there is no direct or indirect relationship between this play and Shakespeare's play of the same name, in this scene, and this scene alone, Boyle is occasionally reminiscent of his predecessor:

> *Queen*   France justly might the English valour dread,
>   Were it again by that great monarch led;
>   We fear him less who now the crown does wear,
>   His wildness, not his courage brings him here.
> *Burgundy* Whilst his prodigeous father was alive,
>   Some youthful signs of wildness did he give;
>   But when he early on his throne was placed,
>   A Kingly soul his royal title graced;
>   And then whatever misbecoming thing
>   Lived in the Prince, was buried in the King.

News is brought of the French defeat at Agincourt. The Queen and her attendants exeunt to assemble a council, leaving Katherine to confess her love for Owen Tudor to her confidante Anne of Burgundy.

Act II,*i* The English camp. Henry tells Tudor of his love for Katherine and sends him to the French court to request her in marriage. In soliloquy Tudor confesses his own love for the lady but argues that friendship and honour demand he sacrifice his love to the King's. *ii* The French court. The French debate whether or not to continue the war. These deliberations are interrupted by a request from Tudor to speak with the Princess. Katherine receives the King's suit without warmth but promises to follow her mother's wishes in the matter. The scene ends with her restating her love for Tudor in soliloquy.

Act III,*i* The English camp. Henry refuses to be placed under an obligation to Katherine's mother and decides to woo her for himself. *ii* A room in the French court. Burgundy and his son discuss statecraft and morality. Burgundy believes:

> A statesman all but interest may forget,
> And only ought in his own strength to trust:
> 'Tis not a statesman's virtue to be just.

His son argues that this must be tempered by reason and interchange of justice. *iii* Elsewhere in the French court. The Dauphin and De Chastel plan to prevent the marriage between Katherine and Henry. The former conceals himself in his sister's chamber in order to spy on her meeting with the English ambassador. *iv* The French court. The Queen and the Constable discuss the Dauphin, and Henry's love for Katherine. The purpose of this scene is to show that the Constable is gaining favour at the expense of Burgundy. *v* Katherine's apartments. A disguised Henry woos the Princess. When he declares his identity the Dauphin discovers himself and attacks him. Henry quickly disarms the Dauphin but spares his life. Katherine helps Henry to escape. The Princess soliloquizes on reason and love. The audience learn that reason requires she give preference to the King over Tudor. *vi* The Dauphin's apartments. De Chastel urges the Dauphin to allow him to follow Henry and kill him but the Dauphin forbids such an action as dishonourable. *vii* Outside the castle. Warwick waits for the King. *viii* Katherine's apartments. The Princess shares her concern for the King's safety with Anne of Burgundy.

Act IV,*i* The English camp. The French nobles, led by
the Duke of Burgundy, and their English counterparts
are seated in council. The English reject the French
offers of treaty. *ii* The French court. The Queen discovers
a plot between Burgundy and the Dauphin to deprive
her of the regency. She conspires to set the one against the
other. *iii* Katherine's apartments. The King secretly visits
Katherine. The truce ends. A messenger enters with the
news that the Queen and the Dauphin have quarrelled.
The Dauphin has been expelled from court. Burgundy's
son enters with further news that the Dauphin is determined to pursue a quarrel against his father. Although
this is a mainly political scene it is related to the love
theme by the closing couplet: 'Love's queen did rise from
the tempestuous sea;/Which shows that love in storms
must ever be ...' *iv* The English camp. Henry discovers
that Tudor loves Katherine. He demonstrates his honour
by insisting that he will plead his friend's cause for him
and demand that the Princess decide between them.

Act V,*i* The English camp. News arrives of a great English naval victory. This is followed by news to the effect
that Burgundy has been murdered by the Dauphin.
Burgundy's son asks Henry's help to avenge his father.
This deed proves the Dauphin unworthy of a crown. *ii*
The French court. The Queen and Katherine see Henry
as their support, the Dauphin their enemy. News is
brought that Henry will visit them that night. *iii* Elsewhere in the French court. From a conversation between
the Constable and the Bishop of Arras we learn that the
French estates, spiritual and temporal, have condemned
the Dauphin. It has been agreed that Henry marry
Katherine: 'And on their issue would the crown entail.'
iv Katherine's apartments. The Princess is wooed by
Henry and Tudor. The situation is resolved with Henry
and Katherine united, with Tudor retained as an honourable friend to them both. The Queen enters to inform
them of the decision of the French estates. *v* The

Dauphin's apartments. The Dauphin flies on learning of
the approach of the English army. *vi* The French court.
Henry is formally presented with the French crown.

Critical commentary

There is no question but that the rhymed heroic drama
so popular in the 1660s attracts us not at all. But if we are
to appreciate fully the aims and aspirations of the Restoration dramatists we must make ourselves come to terms
with the work done in this field for it is here that they
were most obviously ambitious. In the first stage of the
development of Restoration tragedy, of which Boyle is
fairly representative, heroism is associated with moral
idealism. The dominant theme is self-sacrifice and the
triumph of loyalty and friendship over personal desire.
In the second stage, as demonstrated by Dryden's heroic
plays, the moral emphasis is reduced at the expense of the
power element in heroism. The plays of Boyle are restrained and classical, those of Dryden violently melodramatic.

It is comparatively easy to demonstrate the line of development from early seventeenth-century city comedy to
the Restoration comedy of manners, but Restoration
tragedy still remains partly under the cloud of being dismissed as a largely French importation. Again we are
faced with a woeful ignorance of the drama of the
Caroline period and of the interregnum. The French influence begins to show itself as early as the work of Fletcher
and Massinger who first began to emphasize the heroic
by exploiting the literary vogue of the romance, by intensi-
fying and elevating experience, particularly by the devotion of these characters to honour. The main drama comes
from the dilemma caused by conflict between love and
honour. This predates the drama of Corneille which is
similarly preoccupied.

The court playwrights of the Caroline period, reflecting the taste of the Queen, continued to refine and idealize love after the style of French romance. This is the high point of French influence. In spite of the lip service paid by dramatic theorists to Corneille's immense reputation, by the time of the Restoration a natural suspicion of things foreign was beginning to reassert itself and English drama was essentially rediscovering its native roots.

Even in the one respect where they most imitate the French, in the use of rhymed couplets, the familiar English five foot metre was preferred over the French six. Rhyme is not entirely lacking from Caroline and Jacobean drama and the device should be properly understood in its historical context rather than dismissed as a curious foible of the fifteen or so years of the immediate Restoration. Tudor and early Elizabethan plays had inherited a rhyming dramatic form. This gives dramatic dialogue an antithetical sharpness, discipline and balance. The immediately pre-Shakespearean stage is dominated by a blank verse written as it were in couplets and quatrains. Each thought is rigidly confined to two or four lines and there is a sense of punctuation, or end stopping, at the end of each line. The regularity of blank verse of this type is essentially monotonous but we must allow it great clarity of expression. The rigid form controls the author's thought process and there is usually a sense of weight behind the precepts expressed. The separation into balancing halves which mars dialogue written in rhyme, either couplet or quatrain, is still very much in evidence. Such is the verse of Sackville and Norton in *Gorboduc* but the same pattern is still apparent in the work of Greene, Peele, Marlowe and even early Shakespeare. Shakespeare breaks this pattern, developing the run on line with the thought continued over an irregular number of lines, often beginning and ending in mid line. With him blank verse comes of age but the new freedom sometimes traps him into bathos and we are all aware of glorious speeches which end with some uncharacteristic banality. This is the cause of the more disciplined Jonson's criticism that Shakespeare never blotted or corrected his work. The trap which this luxuriance creates is the reason behind the whole theory of rhyming tragedy, as Dryden clearly states in his 'Epistle Dedicatory' to *The Rival Ladies* (1664):

> That benefit I most consider in it is, that it bounds and
> circumscribes the fancy. For imagination in a poet is a
> faculty so wild and lawless, that like a high-ranging spaniel,
> it must have clogs tied to it, lest it out-run the judgement.
> The great easiness of blank verse renders the poet too
> luxuriant; he is tempted to say many things, which might
> be better omitted, or at least shut up in fewer words: but
> when the difficulty of artful rhyming is interposed, where the
> poet commonly confines his sense to the couplet, and must
> contrive his sense into such words, that the rhyme shall
> naturally follow them, not they the rhyme, the fancy then
> gives leisure to the judgement to come in; which seeing so
> heavy a tax imposed, is ready to cut off all unnecessary
> expenses.

There can be no argument that Shakespeare's run on verse had deteriorated over the Jacobean and Caroline period into little more than crudely cadenced prose. Lines had become so uneven in length and thoughts so arbitrary and uncontrolled that the return to the disciplines of rhyme must be acknowledged as a praiseworthy attempt to reverse the process.

That Dryden and other Restoration dramatists were aware of this heritage is apparent from the dedication of *The Rival Ladies* where Dryden credits Boyle with introducing the rhymed heroic play and reminds us that the form was, 'not so much a new way amongst us, as an old way revised'.

The immediate models for Restoration tragedy were

the Elizabethan and Jacobean plays revived after 1660, but only Fletcher and Shakespeare survived in the repertory. The relationship with Shakespeare is curious and best demonstrated by examining the attempts to regularize and control his genius in adaptation. It is Fletcher who provides the main foundation for Restoration tragedy, *The Maid's Tragedy* particularly, satisfying the craving for patterned behaviour. The conflict in Owen Tudor between love for Katherine and friendship for Henry is essentially Fletcherian – Boyle simply refines the formula. The plot and scene arrangements are considerably more controlled, reminding us almost of the classicism of *Gorboduc* or *The Misfortunes of Arthur*. Any sense of movement comes from the brevity of the scenes and from scenic embellishment rather than from presented action. The only time the plot erupts into violence is in Act III, *v* for the brief fight between Henry and the Dauphin. It could well be that the more restrained and ordered treatment of violence on stage is partly due to a need to control a potentially violent and disorderly audience.

The old politico-morality concerns of the pre-Shakespearean history play are still present in the sub-plot, where both Burgundy and the Dauphin demonstrate, by their lack of honour, unsuitability for government. However, these moral concerns are idealized and unrelated to the contemporary situation; the aim of tragedy is now elevation. There is an inhibiting sense of propriety which avoids any political statement beyond a subtle emphasis of the royal prerogative; this will give place in the tragedy produced after the Glorious Revolution to a stress on the evils arising from despotism. Boyle does not attempt to follow either the unity of time or place but the unity of action is stressed by the tight plot and absence of comic distraction. An Elizabethan would have made the political material the central theme, using this to mirror some issue of the time, and to do this he would have introduced recognizable comic types. The Restoration writers wished to demonstrate how idealized figures were capable of behaving. The introduction of recognizable types would have destroyed the illusion of distance.

An Evening's Love, or The Mock Astrologer
John Dryden

DATE 1668

CAST

Wildblood ⎱
Bellamy ⎰ two young English gentlemen

Maskal, their servant

Don Alonzo de Ribera, an old Spanish gentleman

Don Lopez de Gamboa, a young noble Spaniard

Don Melchor de Guzman, a gentleman of great family, but of a destroyed fortune

Donna Theodosia ⎱
Donna Jacintha ⎰ daughters to Don Alonzo

Donna Aurelia, their cousin

Beatrix, woman and confidant to the two sisters

Camilla, woman to Aurelia

SCENE Madrid in the year 1665 during the last evening of the carnival

Plot

Act I,*i* A street in Madrid. Don Lopez and a servant cross the stage, their carnival costumes give an instant visual impression of intrigue. From their conversation we learn that Don Melchor and Don Lopez are both in love with Aurelia. Don Melchor has commanded his friend to persuade Aurelia that he is in Flanders, thus leaving the way clear for Melchor to court her cousin Theodosia. Lopez has promised to help Melchor and thus lends himself to the deception although it is contrary to his own interest. Don Lopez and the servant are replaced on the stage by two English gentlemen, Bellamy and Wildblood. They are bored with Spain, the carnival and Spanish cooking. Their spirits are revived when Don Alonzo de Ribera, with his two daughters Theodosia and Jacintha pass across the stage. The men and women are kept on separate sides of the stage while Maskal questions Beatrix. He returns with sufficient information to embark his masters upon an adventure. The ladies are on their way to church. *ii* A chapel. Bellamy and Wildblood court the two girls while all are supposedly at their devotions. The women leave and Wildblood sends Maskal to question Beatrix further.

Act II A street before Don Alonzo's house. Maskal reports back. Theodosia's affections are already engaged but Jacintha is not only free but much taken with Wildblood. She enters with Beatrix. Wildblood accosts her. They fence verbally with witty expertise, lines being tossed back and forth between them as though they were participating in a game of tennis. This exchange is interrupted by the arrival of Don Alonzo. Maskal has communicated to Bellamy that Theodosia's lover is the false Don Melchor. He blurts this information out to Theodosia who immediately and correctly blames Beatrix for telling tales. In order to protect the maid Maskal announces that Bellamy has achieved his knowledge of Theodosia's private affairs by astrology. Don Alonzo enters and by a coincidence has studied astrology in his youth. Bellamy parries his questions and by the end of the act his reputation as an astrologer is firmly established. Don Melchor enters accompanied by Don Lopez and a troupe of musicians. He starts to serenade under Theodosia's window. The Englishmen fall upon this party and drive the Spaniards off the stage. Don Lopez re-enters and Maskal

catches him in the net of his master's astrology. Don Lopez
invites Bellamy to his house. It is his intention to
acquaint Aurelia with his skill. She will visit Bellamy and
ask to be shown her lover. She will learn that very far from
being in Flanders as she supposes he is in Madrid. Thus
will Lopez contrive to expose his friend without breaking
his oath to him.

Act III Don Lopez's house. Wildblood has broadcast
Bellamy's fame as a fortune teller. To them comes
Aurelia. Bellamy uses his knowledge of Melchor's dupli-
city to bring about his exposure. He promises to conjure
his spirit into her presence. She writes an ambiguous summons which Bellamy then despatches via Maskal, so that
Melchor on receipt of it will believe Aurelia has discovered his presence in Madrid and meet her as commanded. Don Alonzo enters to question Bellamy further
about astrology. This falls out well for Don Lopez's plans
for it is his intention to persuade Alonzo to bestow his
daughter on Melchor thus leaving Aurelia free to accept
his suit. Lopez and Alonzo speak at the same time at cross
purposes. A quarrel is only avoided by the entrance of
a group of masquers, among them Jacintha disguised as
a moor. Wildblood takes her to one side and courts her
without realizing her identity, Jacintha inveigles him
into a game of dice and wins three hundred pistols he had
promised her earlier. She returns almost immediately in
her own person and presses Wildblood for the promised
loan. He abuses Maskal for losing the money. Jacintha
admits her trick and Wildblood is suitably disconcerted
by her discovery.

Act IV,i The street. Maskal delivers Aurelia's letter to
Melchor. Jacintha, again disguised, this time as a Mulatta, once more tries Wildblood's constancy and once more
he finds himself unable to resist proferred variety. Maskal
hears the Mulatta call out Beatrix as she exits. ii A garden. Don Melchor keeps his appointment with Aurelia.
Believing him a spirit she exits in terror. Theodosia enters

and gives Melchor a diamond as a pledge of her love for him. Alonzo hearing that the ring is lost insists that Bellamy should discover it by means of his supposed powers. This he is able to do as Beatrice has informed him of the gift. Alonzo recovers the ring from Melchor in a scene of confusion and double meaning. When Alonzo uses the word 'jewel' he means the diamond but Melchor misunderstands him to mean Theodosia. When they at last understand each other Alonzo ridicules Melchor's pretensions to his daughter. Maskal maintains to Beatrix and Jacintha that his master was aware of her disguise. Beatrix very reasonably argues that to recognize her and make such shameless advances merely aggravates the crime. Wildblood then pleads his own case, maintaining that the worst Jacintha can say of him is that he has loved her three times over. The act ends with a state of truce between the lovers.

Act V Don Alonzo's house. Aurelia, now she knows Melchor's treachery, welcomes Lopez's attentions. This information is relayed to Theodosia who likewise now welcomes Bellamy's suit. Melchor is carried off by four Englishmen. All this pother brings Alonzo and servants with drawn swords. This is the final test of Bellamy's astrological skill. He tells Alonzo that by his art he has discovered that his niece and daughters were to be carried off this very night. He explains his own presence in the garden as due to his desire to prevent such a happening. In this he has been successful. Alonzo accepts his explanation but insists that he conjure a devil. Bellamy commands that the lights be darkened and there be perfect silence. He orders Maskal to open a door and the lovers are discovered standing motionless. Alonzo immediately forgets his devil and wishes to seize the elopers but Bellamy tells him that what he sees are not his niece and daughters but spirits conjured for his edification. At this point they are interrupted by servants carrying in a bound and gagged Melchor. Again Bellamy conjures Alonzo to stop his ears.

Unfortunately Wildblood starts to sneeze, servants enter with lights and the deception is discovered and the Corigidor sent for before Alonzo fully realizes whom he has caught. The women now blackmail him into accepting their marriages lest by being hauled before the authorities their reputations should be destroyed. Alonzo grudgingly accepts the situation, sending word to the Corigidor that he had mistaken carnival merriment for rape and robbery.

Critical commentary

Allardyce Nicoll in *World Drama* (1949) complains of what he calls the strange eclecticism which prevented Dryden from consolidating his first experimental essays in Comedy of Manners. This is both over generous and a little hard. It seems on the one hand to credit Dryden in *The Wild Gallant* (1663), *An Evening's Love* (1672), and *Marriage-à-la-mode* (1672), with doing something new in comedy, which we shall show to be far from the case, and at the same time to disparage his rare gift for exactly judging the taste of the time.

Nicole credits Dryden with inventing the pair of witty lovers which Congreve was to develop into the ultimate achievement of Millamant and Mirabel. They have their origins in the wit combats of the lovers of Commedia dell 'Arte, are used by Shakespeare to great effect in the scenes between Beatrice and Benedict in *Much Ado About Nothing* and are the main staple of the plays of James Shirley. Dryden is able to carry such scenes one degree further because for the first time an English playwright was able to write parts for women rather than boy players.

It has been suggested that the main difference between early and late seventeenth-century comedy was the post-Restoration restrictive concern with matters exclusively aristocratic. There is no real evidence in the present text of any vast change of attitude since the time of Shirley.

Basically the piece is a comedy of complex intrigue slightly in imitation of the Spanish. True it stresses unconditionally the world of fashionable youth, with the well born Wildblood and Bellamy finding fit aristocratic matches in Jacintha and Theodosia. 'It is also true that, to a certain extent, it transfers the quality of humours from character defects to social manners. Don Melchor is, one feels, not so much condemned on moral grounds but because his behaviour is what a later age would call 'bad form'. Having admitted these trends towards what is critically termed Comedy of Manners, let us at once claim that they are equally apparent in the work of Beaumont and Fletcher (compare *Wit Without Money*, c. 1614, and Fletcher and Middleton *The Nice Valour or The Passionate Madman*, printed 1647).

The present play is very far from what we understand as Restoration drama. There is perhaps a preconception that all the comedy of this period is concerned with incidental wit and sexual relationships. In spite of Pepys's information that he found the play 'very smutty', and his fellow diarist Evelyn's similar comment that it was 'very profane', there is little in the text to merit such a description, beyond such obvious exchanges as:

> [*goes to lay hold of her*]
> *Jacintha* Hold, hold, Sir, I am an ambassadress sent you from a lady, I hope you will not violate the law of nations.
> *Wildblood* I was only searching for your letters of credence.

and again:

> *Lopez* Could you guess what countrymen?
> *Maskal* I imagined them to be Italians.
> *Lopez* Not unlikely; for they played most furiously at our backsides.

The difference between this play and what we think of as typically Restoration is that the plays from Etherege to Congreve all allow a new and experimental freedom to women but here, even allowing for the licence of carnival time, women are presented as the subordinates of their men folk. The idea of Beatrix acting as go-between and at the same time serving as a nominal chaperone adheres to an identical morality to that found in the plays of Shakespeare – a morality which is still basically middle class. As for the wit in the play, it is never incidental or employed for its own sake for Dryden is too fine a dramatist to hold up a fast moving comedy simply for witty chat reflecting the manners of the town. The absence of such dialogue can be in part ascribed to the play's foreign setting and its place is taken by visual incident depicting the colour of the carnival. Some of the scenes, such as Aurelia's panic on seeing what she takes to be the spirit of Melchor and the final act, show that Dryden's superb use of stage picture is as apparent in his comedies as it is in his tragedies and operas. There can be no question that above all dramatists of his time Dryden conceived his plays in terms of the stage picture and of the players who would give them life and that, though this might on occasion trap him into unsuccessful experiments, it was for the most part entirely successful. The humour is remarkably unrefined, as for example when easy laughs are obtained at the expense of Spanish cookery:

> I had a mind to eat of a pheasant, and as soon as I got it into my mouth, I found I was chawing a limb of cinnamon; then I went to cut a piece of kid, and no sooner it had touched my lips, but it turned to red pepper: at last I began to think myself another kind of Midas, that everything I touched should be turned into spice.

Such humour may at first sight appear beneath critical notice, yet it should be noted that it is still successfully employed in the comedy of our own age. It is essentially the same as jokes about curry and chips.

An Evening's Love serves as a reminder of the state of comedy at the start of the Restoration period; such comedy continued to be received with great enjoyment at the same time as the more typical Comedy of Manners plays were achieving their success. Its more obvious appeal was transferred from the main-piece drama to the farces in the early eighteenth century, when sentimentalism began to dominate main-piece comedy.

The Rehearsal

George Villiers, 2nd Duke of Buckingham (1628–87)

A prominent political and literary figure during the years immediately following the Restoration, Buckingham is satirized as Zimri in Dryden's poem *Absalom and Achitophel*. He was educated at Cambridge and then at Christ Church, Oxford. He was made a Knight of the Garter for his attendance on Charles II after the Battle of Worcester.

He wrote three dramatic works: *The Rehearsal*; an alteration of Fletcher's *Chances* and *The Battle of Sedgemore*.

DATE 1671

CAST

Bayes	Sun	
Johnson	Thunder	
Smith	Two Heralds	
Two kings of Brentford	Four Cardinals	
Prince Prettyman	Mayor	mutes
Prince Volscius	Judges	
Gentleman usher	Serjeant-at-arms	
Physician	Amaryllis	
Drawcansir	Chloris	
General	Parthenope	
Lieutenant General	Pallas	
Cordelic	Lightning	
Tom Thimble	Moon	
Fisherman	Earth	

SCENE Drury Lane Theatre and Brentford

Plot

Act I Two gentlemen, Johnson and Smith, are invited by the author, Bayes, to watch a rehearsal of his play. He has great hopes of this, for besides being written to all the best dramatic theories: 'I have printed about a hundred sheets of paper to insinuate the plot into the boxes ...' This is a direct reference to printed sheets given to the audience before the *Indian Emperor,* explaining that that play was a sequel to the *Indian Queen.* Thus the dual identity of Bayes with D'Avenant and Dryden is established. The play begins with a double prologue spoken by Thunder and Lightening which is almost a line by line parody of the second part of the *Conquest of Granada:*

> So boar and sow, when any storm is nigh
> Snuff up, and smell it gathering in the sky;
> Boar beckons sow to trot in chestnut-groves,
> And there consummate their unfinished loves:
> Pensive in mud they wallow all alone,
> And snore and gruntle to each other's moan.

The Rehearsal ridicules this:

> So two kind turtles when a storm is nigh,
> Look up and see it gathering in the sky;
> Each calls his mate to shelter in the groves,
> Leaving, in murmurs, their unfinished loves;
> Perched on some dripping branches, they sit alone,
> And coo and hearken to each other's moan.

The rehearsal can proceed no further as Mr Ivory is not present in the theatre. All adjourn for a pipe of tobacco. Abraham Ivory had been a well known actor of women's parts, but by the time *The Rehearsal* came to be written he had become an alcoholic fit for nothing but running errands. The company still paid his salary out of charity. Act II,*i* Almost the opening line is the physician's. 'Sir, to conclude', he continues with a speech of jumbled metaphor describing a storm 'grasped but by the eye of reason'. This is followed by a scene conducted in a whisper. The joke, 'Sir, to conclude', before anything has been said implying that the conversation has begun off stage, and then followed by an exchange of confidences of which all reason demands both the two characters are already well aware, is not a direct parody of any particular author but simple fun at the expense of all dramatic openings. Sheridan employs almost the same opening for the beginning of *The Spanish Armada* in *The Critic*. The fact that the whispered conversation is carried on by politicians, 'and matters of state ought not to be divulged', is a further joke borrowed by Fielding and Sheridan. *ii* The second scene introduces us to the two kings of Brentford, who enter hand in hand. The humour derives from their introduction in a common place as setting. *iii* They leave the stage to Prince Prettyman who enters to make love to Chloris but falls asleep before he can carry out his intention. *iv* The Gentleman usher and the physician, our whisperers at the opening of the play, usurp the government. *v* [*Enter four men at one door, and four at another, with their swords drawn*]. After exchanging challenges they kill one another. At a given musical note the dead men rise together and dance. They do not do this with any degree of reality so they have to rehearse it several times.

Act III,*i* A scene between Prince Prettyman and Tom Thimble his tailor burlesques the scene between Failer and Bibber his tailor in *The Wild Gallant*. *ii* The two usurpers enter hand in hand, inquiring: 'But what's become of Volscius the Great;/His presence has not graced our court of late.' Cordelic, as a messenger from this same Volscius, enters to tell them that a fair person, it isn't quite clear who, but someone they both do know, is dead. *iii* Confusion mounts as Amaryllis enters and an old fisherman is dragged before her. This person has been hired by Prince Prettyman, or is it by Prince Volscius to

kill Prince Volscius? Prince Prettyman, ridiculing a similar situation in *Marriage-à-la-Mode*, declares the fisherman his father. *iv* Prince Volscius enters, to immediately
fall in love with Parthenope. This causes him a great deal
of trouble with his boots, to whom he soliloquizes before
making his exit hopping on one foot. The act concludes
with a dance, which is spoiled by Bayes teaching the actors
the steps.

Act IV,*i* This opens with the funeral of Lardella.
Smith, as confused as we are, asks who this lady is. Bayes
explains 'Why sir, the sister of Drawcansir; a lady that was
drowned at sea, and had a wave for her winding sheet.'
This is in ridicule of the second part of *The Conquest of
Granada*: 'On seas I bore thee, and on seas I died,/I died,
and for a winding-sheet, a wave/I had; and all the ocean
for my grave.' The two usurpers are about to commit suicide for love of her when Pallas enters and informs them
that Lardella is not dead. This is but a trial of their love.
The coffin is opened to discover a banquet and Pallas
pours wine out of her lance. Drawcansir enters to interrupt these festivities. *ii* This next is a heroic scene where
Prince Volscius and Prince Prettyman quarrel because
they are *not* in love with the same woman.

Act V,*i* The two rightful kings of Brentford descend from
the heavens upon a cloud. The two usurpers steal away.
This is followed by a civil war which takes the form of a
battle between armies of one man on each side. This is
followed by a dance and another battle. Johnson and
Smith leave for dinner as the argument of the fifth act is
read. The players decide rather than rehearse such stuff
to adjourn for dinner. Bayes in pique removes his play
from them. The players change the bills to another play
but conclude by rehearsing the last dance which may, they
feel, prove useful in the future.

Critical commentary

The Rehearsal owes its position in this selection partly as a representative of the continuing burlesque tradition which is present in the Mystery Cycles, is continued in plays such as Peele's *Old Wives' Tale* and Beaumont's *Knight of the Burning Pestle* and reaches perfection in the early nineteenth century, before the censor inhibited its growth in the work of Fielding and Carey: but it also demonstrates that the absurdities which we find in plays like Boyle's *Henry V* and Dryden's *Aureng-Zebe* were just as apparent in the seventeenth century as they are today. *The Rehearsal* provides a useful peg upon which to hang a few final comments on heroic tragedy. In Boyle's play heroism is virtually synonymous with moral idealism. It is dominated by the triumph of friendship and loyalty over private emotion. The solemn logic of Prince Volscius and Prince Prettyman quarrelling because they are *not* in love with the same woman is but a logical extension of this morality which derives to a very great extent from the French romances of Mlle de Scudery and others. For Boyle heroism is entirely a search for moral balance while, in contrast, Dryden is enraptured by the power element. Not for him the self-sacrificing denial of self; his heroes dominate every situation reducing their rivals in an atmosphere of violent melodrama. The behaviour of Drawcansir is in the same vein. Heroic drama was a theoretical experiment and it is arguable if it was ever truly perfected. The student should not be alarmed at his recognition of the ridiculous so long as, unlike Buckingham, he credits the sincerity of the form. Boyle is proposing a moral ideal while Dryden is exploring the dangers of power, which, while it may inspire, can also lead to grotesque exaggeration or distortion. Heroic plays are set in a completely unreal world of fantasy, almost begging the attention of the satirists.

The bulk of English satirical drama in the seventeenth /

eighteenth/nineteenth centuries is literary rather than
political. It is the nature of satire to lash the follies of the
time. Burlesque differs from satire in that it enjoys, even
welcomes, these same follies. It does not wish to correct
them because if corrected there would be less in the world
to laugh at. Satire is justice. Burlesque is the universal
desire to deflate. The harsh immediacy of satire makes it
a rather sterile and destructive form, but the warm irreverence of burlesque retains our sympathy even when the
targets are forgotten, for irreverence and the wish to curb
pomposity is a constant of human nature. *The Rehearsal*
may be intended as satire but it claims our interest today
as a burlesque and as one of the ancestors of a type of
drama which, descending through pantomime and extra-
vaganza, remains, in modern examples such as the plays
of Mr Ernest Wise, *Monty Python's Flying Circus*, and
Beyond the Fringe, one of the most popular of all dramatic forms.

Without an almost encyclopaedic knowledge of Restoration tragedy the bulk of the satirical jokes must pass us by.
Suffice it for us to understand that it attacks the tragedies
of both the Howards, Boyle, D'Avenant and others, with
particular virulence reserved for the work of Dryden. It is
savagely laced with direct parody and demonstrates little
love for its targets. More positively, it establishes certain
burlesque jokes. Its first contribution is in the form of the
rehearsal play, which allows the audience a peep behind
the scenes. The confidential opening, the one man armies,
the badly rehearsed battles and dances that go magnifi-
cently awry, the monotonous elevation of commonplace
thought with its accompanying bathos, and the imperfect
logic together with a solemn defence of the *non sequitur*,
are all stock devices not only in pantomime and burlesque,
but also in farce. This is clearly demonstrated in the final
scene of J. H. Morton's *Box and Cox*, (1847), when the
two men establish that they are long-lost brothers by the
absence of a strawberry mark on Cox's left arm! These

elements remain just as fresh in the modern theatre as they do in the present critical context. The joke against heroic couplets may have long lost its meaning but the form is firmly established in English literature as the only way to express the mock-heroic. The ridicule of scenic machinery and stage business is no longer an immediate concern for the legitimate drama, but modern mockery of ballet, musicals and opera never fails to lampoon this element. It is very significant to English humour to understand the need to prick the bubble reputation: we are a nation of debunkers. This ability to mock what is intended for us to fear or admire, out of its theatrical context, perplexed Napoleon and Hitler and has protected us from the extremes of political frenzy. The dramatic reflection of this national characteristic must be understood if the uniqueness of English theatre is to be appreciated.

Aureng-Zebe
John Dryden

DATE 1675
CAST
The old Emperor
Aureng-Zebe, his son
Morat, his younger son, half-brother to Aureng-Zebe
Arimant, Governor of Agra
Dianet ⎫
Solyman ⎪
Mir Baba ⎬ Indian Lords, or Omrabs,
Abas ⎪ of several factions
Asaph Chan ⎪
Fazel Chan ⎭
Nourmahal, the Empress, mother of Morat
Indamora, a captive-queen
Melesinda, wife to Morat
Zayda, favourite slave to the Empress
SCENE Agra, in the year 1660

Plot

Act I Three of the Emperor's sons are in rebellion. Only
Aureng-Zebe remains loyal. Morat threatens to capture
Agra. He sends an ambassador to his father excusing his
behaviour on the grounds that he believed him dead.
News is brought that Aureng-Zebe has defeated the other
two brothers. Arimant is astonished when the Emperor

forbids Aureng-Zebe entrance to the city. The Emperor loves Indamora, a captive-queen promised to his son. His jealousy blinds his gratitude. Aureng-Zebe's entry cannot be halted and the Emperor sends Arimant to Indamora:

> Bid her conceal my passion from my son.
> Tho' Aureng-Zebe return a conqueror,
> Both he and she are still within my power.
> Say, I'm a father, but a lover too:
> Much to my son, more to myself I owe.

Aureng-Zebe enters. He asks to see Indamora. She greets him coldly. He chides her with inconstancy. She is stung into telling him that the Emperor has made love to her. The act ends with Aureng-Zebe torn between his duty to his father and his love.

Act II Aureng-Zebe is the saviour of Agra, the hero of the hour. The Omrabs aware of his father's treachery offer to support him. Arimant falls under Indamora's spell. She points out not only that she is above him in status, but that she is much younger than he is. The Emperor overhears Arimant's love making. Indamora protests that Arimant was making love on his master's behalf. He half accepts her explanation, being fully convinced when Indamora points out Arimant's fear of Nourmahal's jealous fury. The Emperor urges her to give up Aureng-Zebe. Nourmahal upbraids the Emperor for his treatment of her and is cynically rejected. Aureng-Zebe pleads for his step-mother but the Emperor has her hustled off under guard. He claims Indamora as the reward of his loyalty. When his father refuses this and accuses him of ulterior motives Aureng-Zebe points out that he could take anything he desired. The Emperor's anger flares up. He degrades Aureng-Zebe and raises Morat to be his heir. Aureng-Zebe refuses either to fly or to rebel against his father.

Act III Arimant, now Indamora's slave, agrees to take a message from her to Aureng-Zebe. She and Melesinda, the faithful wife of Morat, meet. They realize that one or other of their loves must fall. The reinstated Morat enters the city. Aureng-Zebe comes to him with offer of service. Again the Emperor offers to restore his elder son if he will resign his interest in Indamora. Aureng-Zebe refuses and is condemned to death. Nourmahal offers to be his executioner. She confesses to Zayda that she loves him. Zayda reminds her that Morat must fall if Aureng-Zebe should rise. Melesinda pleads with her husband for Indamora and Aureng-Zebe. Indamora herself enters and joins in the pleas for Aureng-Zebe's life. Morat too has fallen in love with Indamora. He offers her Aureng-Zebe's life in exchange for her love.

Act IV Aureng-Zebe waits for death. He is amazed at the kindness of Nourmahal. Then he understands her incestuous intentions and rejects her:

> *Nourmahal* I beg my death, if you can love deny.
> [*offering him a dagger*]
> *Aureng-Zebe* I'll grant you nothing; no, not ev'n to die.
> *Nourmahal* Now then, you are not half so kind as I.
> [*stamps with her foot*]
> [*Enter Mutes, some with swords drawn, one with a cup*]

Before his brother can drink Morat enters and stops the execution. He confesses that it is not brotherly love but love of Indamora that is the cause of the reprieve. Morat orders Melesinda to speak on his behalf to Indamora. The Emperor chides Morat for his treatment of Melesinda. Morat replies by demanding his father resign his interest in Indamora. The Emperor sees in this divine justice for his treatment of Aureng-Zebe. Aureng-Zebe chides Indamora for having bought his love by entertaining that of Morat. At the point of reconciliation Arimant enters with news of further treachery. Morat has taken over the citadel. The Emperor enters in despair. His troubles are his just punishment for his treatment of Aureng-Zebe. His

son will have none of this and suggests a way of escape for
them both.

Act V Morat is besieged in the citadel. Contradicting reports come in of Aureng-Zebe's death. Indamora and
Melesinda comfort each other. To them comes Nourmahal curious to see Indamora. Nourmahal gives Indamora a dagger but Morat enters in time to stop her suicide.
The fort has been recaptured by the Emperor and Aureng-
Zebe. Morat is dying. Finding his brother Morat in Indamora's arms Aureng-Zebe again believes she has yielded
to his brother. The Emperor reconciles the lovers. Nourmahal commits suicide.

Critical commentary

Aureng-Zebe is something more than a simple example of
the heroic play. In some ways it is the mirror image of
The Man of Mode for Aureng-Zebe's great quality is
neither bravery, courage nor honour but reason. Apart
from the brief lapses caused by jealousy he is remarkably
free of passion. None of Dryden's previous characters are
temperate men. Montezuma in *The Indian Emperor*
throws away his kingdom for a love he cannot control,
rather after the manner of the old Emperor in *Aureng-
Zebe*. The previous heroic *ethos* of the theatre is undermined right from Morat's first entry:

> To me, the cries of fighting fields are charms:
> Keen by my sabre, and of proof my arms,
> I ask no other blessing on my stars:
> No prize but fame, nor mistress but the wars.

This is the speech of a hero. Dryden very skilfully reveals
such a nature to be primitive and unreasonable and it is
obvious that we are meant to accept Aureng-Zebe's view
of his brother:

When thou wert form'd, Heav'n did a man begin;
But the brute soul by chance was shuffled in.
In woods and wilds the monarchy maintain:
Where valiant beasts, by force and rapine, reign.
In life's next scene, if transmigration be,
Some bear or lion is reserved for thee.

We have already examined the first beginnings of heroic tragedy as exemplified by the work of Roger Boyle. It is important to reiterate that the form is a natural development of the dramatic tradition and not an isolated theatrical aberration. Boyle uses the form to regularize and refine Jacobean and Caroline tragedy, Dryden returns to a basically Renaissance concept of heroic character. The human potential for good or evil is exaggerated in order to create a sense of wonder, or, to use the more common critical term, 'admiration'. This too is a return to the English past rather than imitation of the French. Chapman and Marlowe had created heroes of this ilk. Indeed the main difference between Shakespeare and his predecessors are the checks and balances of human frailty with which he surrounds his characters. The Jacobeans and their successors began to discard these limitations and with Dryden the wheel comes full circle. Even Antony in *All For Love* is presented as irregularly great rather than limited by his inability to control his passions.

Our inability to reconcile the Restoration comic and tragic worlds derives in part from the fact that we tend to identify certain writers, such as Congreve, with comedy and a totally different group, such as Otway, with tragedy. We should note that apart from Nathan Lee who wrote nothing but tragedies and Etherege who wrote nothing but comedies all writers essayed both forms. There is very little difference between the Elizabethan concept of tragedy and comedy. Benedict and Romeo belong to the same world, and speak very much the same language. Elizabethan heroism always seems real and probable and many stage heroes seem almost insignificant against the reality of Drake and Raleigh. Heroism like the old values was something to be distrusted after the Civil War, and such national heroes who like Prince Rupert had survived, were looked upon as embarrassing anachronisms. The Cavalier virtues of love and honour collapsed during the Civil War. Heroism was still admired but it seemed unreal and of another age, and to treat it as a contemporary quality would have seemed almost indecent. There is no doubt that the restored court was more political than honourable. No one wished to go on his travels again. This does not mean that they felt that in their imperfect world ideals had no place. Thus an idealized world had to be created where honour was rewarded. Tragedies came to be set either in classical Greece or Rome, in the East or in the New World from which exotic settings it was easier for exotic characters to appeal for the admiration of the audience. The unreality of chanted verse helps the audience to accept characters and values which would only have inspired sneers in a more realistic or down to earth form.

Aureng-Zebe was written just before the abandonment of rhyme and we note in it the beginnings of the domestication of the super-hero. As Dr Johnson noted in *Lives of the English Poets* 'The personages [in *Aureng-Zebe*] are imperial; but the dialogue is often domestic, and therefore susceptible of sentiments accommodated to familiar incidents.' The old absolutes of love and honour were beginning to give place to filial devotion and reason and pity to replace admiration as the main force in tragedy. In subsequent plays more and more scenes come to work on our tear ducts rather than demonstrate grandeur and evoke wonder. The scenes which show the wronged wife Melesinda are included to this end. Even before the audience see her for the first time she is described as being 'bathed in tears'. Family relationships are more to the fore in this play than in any previous heroic tragedy. One notes that Aureng-Zebe's main claim to virtue is that he is the best of sons, while it is the lack of domestic loyalty in the Emperor which causes his downfall. Morat is a bad son and a bad husband, while Nourmahal is shown to be treacherous both as a wife and as a mother.

The interplay of domesticity and heroism is one of the most fascinating aspects of English drama and the seeds of the social drama of the late nineteenth century are present even in as exotic a form as heroic tragedy.

The Country Wife
William Wycherley (c. 1640–1716)

Of good family, at fifteen Wycherley was sent to France to
be educated. Although in France he came under the influence of the 'precious' circle, it would be wrong to look
for this French refinement in his plays. With Wycherley
in mind Voltaire compared the drama of the two countries: *'Il semble que les Anglais prennent trop de liberté
et que les Françaises n'en prennent pas assez'*. Wycherley
became a fellow-commoner of Queens College Oxford, in
July 1660. He does not seem to have matriculated or to
have taken a degree. He then proceeded to the Inner
Temple, rather to acquire a fashionable polish than to
make a serious study of the law.

Wycherley's first play *Love in a Wood* was produced in
1671. It gained him the patronage of Charles II's mistress,
the Duchess of Cleveland. Voltaire creates the legend, in
Letters on the English Nation, that she used to visit
Wycherley at his chambers in the Temple disguised as a
country wench in a straw bonnet. He followed this the
same year with *The Gentleman Dancing Master*. *The
Country Wife* (1671–2) and *The Plain Dealer* (1674)
established the trends for manipulating dialogue which
were to be continued by Wycherley's successors.

Wycherley's private life may have damaged his career.
In the late 1670s, under the patronage of the Duchess of
Cleveland, it seemed certain that Charles II would choose
Wycherley as the tutor for his bastard son, the Duke of

Richmond. Wycherley saw the Countess of Drogheda in a bookshop at Tunbridge. She was young, pretty and rich. A marriage took place in 1680, but fearing the loss of the royal favour Wycherley kept it a secret. When the King eventually did hear of it Wycherley lost both the appointment and the King's patronage. The Countess died a year later leaving her fortune to her husband. The will was challenged, the costs of litigation were high and, without support, Wycherley ended up in the Fleet prison. There he remained for seven years until he was released by James II who settled a pension of £200 a year on the poet. The year before his death, at the age of seventy-five, he married a young girl. Some biographers have said that this was done to spite his nephew and heir, knowing that the jointure would impoverish his estate.

DATE 1675

CAST

Horner

Harcourt

Dorilant

Pinchwife

Sparkish

Sir Jasper Fidget, a formal fool

Quack, a doctor

Margery Pinchwife, wife to Pinchwife

Alithea Pinchwife, sister to Pinchwife

Lady Fidget, wife to Sir Jasper

Dainty Fidget, Sir Jasper's sister

Mrs Squeamish

Old Lady Squeamish

Lucy, Alithea's maid

SCENE London

Plot

Act I,i Horner's lodgings. Quack has noised it abroad

that Horner is impotent. Horner counts on the strength of this rumour to be trusted with other men's wives. The trick works and Sir Jasper leaves his wife and sister in Horner's care. The ladies refuse to remain but, as Horner assures Quack, having now obtained the confidence of the husbands it will not take him long to win their wives. Pinchwife, because he has been in the country, has not heard Quack's tale and when he calls he is most reluctant to discuss the country wench he has recently married with Horner and his friends. So jealous is Pinchwife that the previous day when he took his wife to the theatre he had her wear a mask and smuggled her into the gallery. Such behaviour is calculated to intrigue a man like Horner and make him more curious.

Act II,*i* Pinchwife's house. Margery questions Alithea about the town. She is naïve enough to praise the actors to her husband, thus feeding his jealousy. In contrast, Sparkish, who is engaged to Alithea, insists on forcing his friend Harcourt upon her and encouraging him in his open advances to that lady. The three representatives of fashionable womanhood: Lady Fidget, her sister-in-law and Mrs Squeamish call on Mr Pinchwife to ask if they can take Margery to the theatre. It is apparent from their dialogue that Wycherley intends to present these ladies as more odious than the Horners and Harcourts of his world:

> *Dainty* I suppose the crime against our honour is the same
> with a man of quality as with another.
> *Lady Fidget* How! no sure, the man of quality is likest
> one's husband, and therefore the fault should be the less.
> *Dainty* But then the pleasure should be the less.

By the end of this scene Horner has told Lady Fidget his secret and Sir Jasper is a fair way to being punished for his jealousy and his stupidity.

Act III,*i* Pinchwife's house. Margery is becoming very disturbed by her husband's jealousy, particularly unsettl-

ing is his unfortunate admission that Horner, after seeing
her masked at the play, loves her. She insists that he take
her to the theatre a second time. *ii* The New Exchange.
Sparkish remains blind to Harcourt's love for Alithea and
insists on thrusting them into each other's company.
Pinchwife is, as he promised, taking his wife to the theatre,
but in a further complicated attempt to keep her to himself has insisted on her dressing as a youth and trying to
pass her off as his wife's brother. This only leaves her open
to more freedoms from Horner:

> He kissed me a hundred times, and told me he fancied
> he kissed my fine sister, meaning me, you know, whom he
> said he loved with all his soul, and bid me be sure to tell
> her so.

The act closes with Sir Jasper carrying Horner off to entertain Lady Fidget.
Act IV,*i* Pinchwife's house the next morning. Alithea
confesses to her maid her preference for Harcourt over
Sparkish. Sparkish enters with Harcourt dressed as a parson. That Sparkish could allow himself to be so deluded
is a final proof of his idiocy. The three exeunt to prepare
for the 'marriage' between Sparkish and Alithea, a ceremony which will be presided over by Harcourt, or as
Sparkish believes by Harcourt's identical twin brother.
ii Margery Pinchwife's bedchamber. Pinchwife forces his
wife to write a letter to Horner telling how greatly she despises his 'nauseous, loathed kisses and embraces'. In being
forced to write what is not true Mrs Pinchwife comes to a
realization of the real state of her feelings towards Horner.
Neither character is treated particularly sympathetically
in this scene. At one point Pinchwife offers to write whore
with a penknife on his wife's face, while she reveals that
her innocence is the result of ignorance and stupidity
rather than inner purity. The idea of writing to Horner
having been suggested by her husband, Margery contrives
that a real love letter is sent in exchange for that which

has been dictated to her. *iii* Horner's lodgings. This is the famous China scene during which Horner contrives to make love to Lady Fidget while her husband guards the door. This scene is elaborated on below. It closes with Pinchwife delivering his wife's love letter to Horner and Sparkish arranging for Mrs Pinchwife, whom he believes his sister-in-law, to dine with Horner. *iv* Pinchwife's house. Pinchwife discovers his wife writing to Horner and threatens her with his sword. Act V,*i* Pinchwife's house. Pinchwife's anger with his wife has cooled. She, learning the ways of the town, contrives to convince him that she was writing to Horner on Alithea's behalf. Pinchwife, believing this, escorts a supposed Alithea, who is in fact his wife, to Horner's lodgings. *ii* Horner's lodgings. Pinchwife leaves his supposed sister with Horner. *iii* The Piazza of Covent Garden. Pinchwife tells Sparkish Alithea is unfaithful to him so that when Alithea enters Sparkish unconditionally renounces her. *iv* Horner's lodgings. Lady Fidget, Dainty Fidget and Mrs Squeamish discover their shared interest in Horner. They decide to be open among themselves in order to preserve their reputation in the world. In contrast Mrs Pinchwife wishes to announce her love for Horner and leave her husband. Pinchwife accuses Horner of dishonouring Alithea. This results in Margery confessing her liaison with Horner. Instead of the customary conclusion with a general exposure of vice and chastisement of erring characters the play ends equivocally with a comforting restatement of the original lie about Horner's impotence, with which Pinchwife is able to satisfy himself. At Horner's instigation Margery's behaviour is explained by Lucy as a contrivance to divide Alithea and Sparkish so as to make the way clear for Harcourt.

Critical commentary

Wycherley, like his contemporaries, was attacked by nineteenth-century scholars, who have had such an influence on future attitudes, for the artificiality of his characters and the loose moral tone of his plays. Yet surely they are an attack on the vices of his age. The husbands who are cuckolded deserve it, being either jealous, tyrannical or foolish. In this play Wycherley is not attacking marriage but the hypocrisy of some contemporary attitudes to marriage. He proposes a natural mean between the extreme jealousy of Pinchwife and the exaggerated carelessness of Sparkish. The lack of jealousy in the latter is not commendable because it is symptomatic of a lack of love and his intended marriage is revealed as one of convenience rather than one of passion. Thus any attack on the relationship between Sparkish and Alithea protects rather than abuses the sanctity of marriage. The beginning of the fourth act sums up, in the short exchange between Lucy, Alithea's maid, and her mistress, the whole moral purpose of the play:

> *Alithea* I was engaged to marry, you see, another man, whom my justice will not suffer me to deceive or injure.
> *Lucy* Can there be a greater cheat or wrong done to a man than to give him your person without your heart? I should make a conscience of it.
> *Alithea* I'll retrieve it for him after I am married a while.
> *Lucy* The woman that marries to love better, will be as much mistaken as the wencher that marries to live better. No, madam, marrying to increase love is like gaming to become rich; alas! you only lose what little stock you had before.

Wycherley uses parallel dramatic devices such as disguising Harcourt and Margery Pinchwife as their own twin brothers to constantly remind us that we are intended to see Pinchwife and Sparkish as each other's reflections.

There is common misunderstanding of the nature of Wycherley's comic world which can be traced back to Charles Lamb's attempt to rationalize his delight in

Restoration comedies by arguing, in his essay 'On the Artificial Comedy of the Last Century', that they are set in a make-believe society where ordinary standards do not apply. It is anything but empty fooling when Pinchwife draws his sword on Margery at the end of Act IV. There is no doubt that since these plays were rediscovered for presentation after the First World War their production has stressed their artificiality at the expense of their reality. This has affected criticism, already predisposed to discover 'a miserably limited set of attitudes' to contrast Restoration comedy with 'such modern literature as deals sincerely and realistically with sexual relationships'. ('Restoration Comedy: the Reality and the Myth', L. C. Knights, 1937).

The implication that all serious social comedy should be written like Henry James is patently absurd, but the gap between early twentieth century social comedy and its Restoration counterpart has been widened by the insistence of actors to present the latter as high camp. The steel of many of the most important scenes has been flawed by frivolity. A good example of a scene where the stage fun fails to communicate the real meaning is the 'China' passage in Act IV:

Lady Fidget And I have been toiling and moiling for the prettiest piece of china, my dear.
Horner Nay, she has been too hard for me, do what I could.
Mrs Squeamish Oh, lord, I'll have some china too. Good Mr Horner don't think to give other people china, and me none, come with me too ...

As Norman Holland pointed out in *The First Modern Comedies* (Harvard University Press, 1959) 'China' is a particularly apt choice as a symbol of sexual relations between Horner and Lady Fidget. Because eating dishes are made from china it stresses that their affair is totally one of appetite. China is worked and decorated clay which has altered its appearance: Lady Fidget and Horner share an embellished artificial relationship without either emotional or biological purpose.

The Country Wife is a sad comment on the morals of the age but it is not an immoral or amoral play. It cannot be an overtly didactic play as the climate of Restoration society precluded anything that smacked of Puritanism, but Wycherley intends reformation. The play reflects the pretence and the pretensions of the society for which it was performed and offers subtle chastisement. An Elizabethan or Jacobean dramatist would have stressed the sadness of Horner's artificial relationships but the state of emotional impotence in which he ends the play is as meaningful if a less obvious punishment than the exposure of Sparkish and Pinchwife.

The Man of Mode, or Sir Fopling Flutter
Sir George Etherege (1634–91)

It is usually thought that Etherege was educated at Cambridge, although if this is so he left without taking a degree. He then spent some time in France. He wrote only three plays: *The Comical Revenge, or Love in a Tub* (1664), a serious verse drama with a blank verse high plot and two prose sub-plots; *She Would if She Could* (1668); and *The Man of Mode*. The two latter are both written entirely in prose.

DATE 1676

CAST

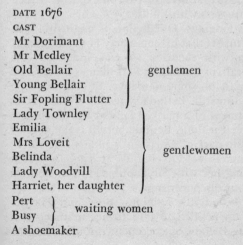

Mr Dorimant
Mr Medley
Old Bellair   } gentlemen
Young Bellair
Sir Fopling Flutter

Lady Townley
Emilia
Mrs Loveit   } gentlewomen
Belinda
Lady Woodvill
Harriet, her daughter

Pert   }
Busy   } waiting women
A shoemaker

An orange-woman
Three slovenly bullies
Two chair men
Mr Smirk, a parson
Handy, a valet de chambre
SCENE London

Plot

Act I,*i* Dorimant's dressing room. Dorimant receives
traders and intimate friends. Foggy-Nan, the orange-
woman, tells him that Harriet is attracted to him but that
her mother has heard of his reputation and is determined
to protect her from him. Harriet is an heiress and both
attractive and witty. He means to break with his mistress
Loveit of whom he has become tired. Medley, Dorimant
and Young Bellair, the last slightly less rakish than his
companions, and in love to the point of marriage with
Emilia, gossip briefly of fashion introducing a description
of Sir Fopling Flutter, a 'person of great acquired follies'.
Bellair receives news that his father is come to town which
will hinder his progress with Emilia.
Act II,*i* Emilia's lodgings. Old Bellair is mightily taken
with Emilia but insists that his son marry Harriet. Medley
comes to gossip with them. *ii* Loveit's lodgings. Mrs
Loveit and Pert talk of Dorimant. Pert blames his absence
these two days past on some new love. Loveit, knowing
him false, loves him still. Belinda visits her and describes
Dorimant's treatment of a masked lady at the playhouse,
thus making Loveit jealous. Belinda herself is the masked
lady and her visit part of Dorimant's plan to be rid of
Loveit. Dorimant enters. Loveit rails at him. Dorimant
retorts by accusing her with Sir Fopling Flutter. Belinda
finds his behaviour disconcerting.
Act III,*i* Lady Woodvill's lodgings. Busy and Harriet
talk, Harriet is disinclined to bow to her mother's will
and marry Young Bellair. She accepts without denial the

teasing suggestion of her maid that she inclines to Dorimant. Harriet and Young Bellair pretend to be in love to dupe Old Bellair and Lady Woodvill. Old Bellair sends them for a drive with Lady Woodvill while he himself hurries back to Emilia. *ii* Lady Townley's house. Dorimant persuades Belinda to make Loveit walk in the Mall. Sir Fopling Flutter makes his elaborate first appearance. Dorimant sends him after Loveit. Lady Townley and Emilia prepare to entertain Old Bellair. *iii* The Mall. Harriet and Young Bellair are walking. Bellair introduces Dorimant to Harriet. Lady Woodvill having heard Dorimant is in the Mall carries Harriet off. Mrs Loveit in order to make Dorimant jealous ignores him in favour of Sir Fopling. Dorimant, under the name of Mr Courtage, is invited to visit Lady Woodvill and Harriet.

Act IV,*i* Lady Woodvill's lodgings. The disguised Dorimant flatters Lady Woodvill and wins her confidence by criticizing the manners of the time. Old Bellair pays court to Emilia. Dorimant excuses himself from the mother to fence verbally with Harriet:

Dorimant [*aside*] I love her and dare not let her know it. I fear sh'as an ascendant o'er me and may revenge the wrongs I have done her sex. [*to her*] Think of making a party, madam; love will engage.
Harriet You make me start! I did not think to have heard of love from you.
Dorimant I never knew what 'twas to have a settled ague yet, but now and then have had irregular fits.
Harriet Take heed, sickness after long health is commonly more violent and dangerous.
Dorimant [*aside*] I have took the infection from her, and feel the disease now spreading in me. [*to her*] Is the name of love so frightful that you dare not stand it?
Harriet 'Twill do little execution out of your mouth on me, I am sure.
Dorimant It has been fatal.

Harriet To some easy women, but we are not all born to
one destiny.

Sir Fopling and others enter. The company try and persuade Sir Fopling to dance. Lady Woodvill, thinking that
Dorimant may be among the new arrivals, hustles Harriet
away. Dorimant is now free to keep a previous engagement with Belinda. The party breaks up with the intention of serenading Dorimant. *ii* Dorimant's lodgings.
Belinda is taking her leave. She entreats him both to be
discreet and not to see Loveit more. Bellair, Medley and
Sir Fopling are heard arriving and Belinda hastily takes
her leave. Dorimant is not to be drawn on the identity of
his visitor. Sir Fopling is questioned on his progress with
Loveit. The scene ends with Dorimant, in spite of his
promise to Belinda, setting out to visit Loveit. *iii* The
Mall. Belinda, in her haste, had given the chair men no
directions. Presuming their fare is Dorimant's usual
female visitor they set her down at Loveit's lodgings.
Act V,*i* Loveit's house. Pert tries to persuade her mistress
to seriously entertain Sir Fopling's suit. A footman enters
with news that Belinda is below. She recognizes the chair
as that which brings her from Dorimant's lodgings and is
suspicious. Belinda allays these suspicions by saying that
she was picked up in the Strand. Dorimant arrives, Belinda, shocked at his so soon breaking his oath, withdraws
in confusion. Dorimant continues to feign jealousy of Sir
Fopling. Belinda reappears and Dorimant is exposed to
both his mistresses, though neither admits the exposure
to the other and Loveit, still unaware that Belinda is her
rival, proposes that they follow Dorimant. *ii* Lady Townley's house. Emilia has just secretly married Young Bellair.
Old Bellair enters and the chaplain is hidden in a closet.
Lady Woodvill and Harriet are on their way. Old Bellair
sends for a chaplain to marry Harriet to his son. Dorimant
arrives. Lady Woodvill still takes him for the sober Mr
Courtage. The chaplain is discovered and Old Bellair in-

sists he marry Young Bellair to Harriet. The chaplain
points out that he has just performed the marriage ceremony for Young Bellair. Old Bellair then states that he
himself will marry Emilia, thus forcing confession of the
secret marriage. Lady Woodvill discovers Dorimant's
identity. Dorimant excuses himself with Loveit by explaining that her rival has been no idle mistress. His suit
to Harriet is honourable. Belinda for the sake of her reputation remains silent. Lady Woodvill who has been
charmed by 'Mr Courtage' agrees to Dorimant paying
court to Harriet.

Critical commentary

It is wrong to consider the comedy of the Restoration a
new form. It deals with exactly the same strata of society
as Jacobean and Caroline city comedy. Jacobean comedy
grows out of satire and complaint. In the hands of Jonson,
Marston and others it sets out to scourge the abuses of the
age. Is Restoration comedy moral in purpose, or is it, as
it professes in prologue after prologue, an empirical form
written purely to divert? If we examine the work of
Wycherley the step between city comedy and the Comedy
of Manners is slight indeed, but Wycherley has a sharply
critical pen and an old fashioned attitude which makes
him untypical of his age. Etherege, Sedley and Dryden
are more truly the norm. All three are educated men
brought up on the classical definition of tragedy as an elevated, idealized form dealing with princes and heroes with
comedy serving as a contrasting mirror of common life. At
the same time all three are of a milieu where a didactic
approach smacks something too much of Puritanism and
the troubles of the last reign. Their drama is classical:
heroic tragedy is elevated and idealized, comedy about
common people. The modern student finds it difficult to
accept that Dorimant, Bellair, Sir Fopling Flutter and the
rest are not of the aristocracy. They are the new society

but their grandfathers were yeomen or city merchants. Their actions are intended as common, elevated action being reserved for tragedy. Assessment of the morality of this type of comedy also has to surmount the hurdle of our association of the word morality with sexuality. This is where Wycherley is atypical, maintaining in *The Country Wife* that sex has become a painted artifact which is replacing the true relationship between man and woman, but on the whole sexual licence is in no way the main target of these plays. The true target is the threat passion and appetite pose to reason. We must not allow the sexuality of Dorimant to obscure the criticism that he is frittering away energy and thought. Given the turmoil which preaching and narrow morality had caused during the Comonwealth it is natural that this type of drama should attempt to reason rather than lash with satire. Society is in the process of finding itself, even of becoming honest. There is a rejection, or at least criticism, of all the values of the last age because the world of these values had collapsed. The individual needed to discover a framework. Patriotism, love, duty and friendship were the values of the age of Charles I, attention to them had resulted in revolution. It seemed to many that they had gone down before the aggression of the commercial speculators which are the targets of city comedy.

Dorimant is Shakespeare's Edmund, Jonson's Volpone and all those anarchic figures governed by appetite in the drama of the previous age. Etherege shows that such individuality is not evil but that it requires the governing quality of reason. Loveit believes in the old fashioned values of honour, faith and constancy, but she is ruled by passion and lacks control. Belinda falls because she allows passion to overcome reason. Harriet has sufficient self control to hold out against the passion, her attraction to Dorimant insists on marriage. It is interesting to note that the two representatives of the former age, Old Bellair and Lady Woodvill, lack the control and manners of the younger generation. Old Bellair's habit of calling on God's name is another example of contempt for old forms. Emilia points out the futility of oaths when Young Bellair begins to swear eternal constancy. Emilia's awareness of reason is essential to the morality of the play. Nature must be restrained by reason. Sir Fopling shows lack of restraint and for this he is mocked. This play is as much a search for the golden mean as anything Ben Jonson penned, perhaps the ending brings this most clearly home to us. Dorimant has not given proof that he is in full control of his appetites, thus instead of being instantly rewarded with Harriet's hand he must, like the King of Navarre and his courtiers in *Love's Labour's Lost*, undergo a trial period which will test the sincerity of his new state.

All for Love, or The World Well Lost

John Dryden

DATE 1677

CAST

Marc Antony
Ventidius, his general
Dollabella, his friend
Alexas, Cleopatra's eunuch
Serapion }
Myris } priests of Isis
Cleopatra, Queen of Egypt
Octavia, Antony's wife
Charmion }
Iras } Cleopatra's maids
SCENE Alexandria

Plot

Act I,i The Temple of Isis. Two priests are discussing the fearful portents in nature. Alexas enters and commands them to keep their fears to themselves. Antony has been defeated at Actium. There is now a pause in the war. Antony has removed himself apart, seeing no one, not even Cleopatra. Ventidius complains to Alexas that Cleopatra is the cause of Antony's ruin. Ventidius tries to rouse Antony to fight. He tells him his soldiers refuse to fight for Cleopatra but if he himself will head them there is hope. He accuses him of throwing away an empire for love.

Antony's anger at this accusation cools and he prepares to fight.

Act II,*i* Cleopatra's apartments. She has learnt from Alexas that Ventidius has persuaded Antony to leave her. Charmion brings news that Antony refuses to see her, as Alexas retorts: 'He shows his weakness who declines the combat . . .' *ii* Antony's camp. Antony is about to give the word to march. Alexas enters with messages and rich gifts from Cleopatra. He is tricked into allowing Cleopatra to fasten her gift herself. She begs him to stay. He upbraids her with her flight at Actium. Cleopatra's defence is her great love for him. Ventidius urges 'but Actium, sir, remember Actium'. Cleopatra replies:

> True, I counselled
> To fight at sea; but I betrayed you not.
> I fled; but not to the enemy. 'twas fear;
> Would I had been a man, not to have feared,
> For none would then have envied me your friendship,
> Who envy me your love.

Her final weapon is a letter from Octavius offering her Egypt and Syria if she will betray Antony. She has rejected this offer. Antony is won over.

Act III The city. The Egyptian soldiers have won a minor victory. Antony is exultant. Ventidius cautiously advises him to make peace and to this end arranges a meeting with Dollabella. Dollabella and Ventidius chide Antony for losing himself in Cleopatra. Antony reminds Dollabella of his first meeting with Cleopatra:

> She came from Egypt,
> Her galley down the silver Cydnos rowed,
> The tacking silk, the streamers waved with gold,
> The gentle winds were lodged in purple sails;
> Her nymphs, like Neriods, round her couch were placed;
> Where she, another sea-born Venus lay.

She lay, and leant her cheek upon her hand,
And cast a look so languishingly sweet,
As if, secure of all beholders hearts,
Neglecting she could take 'em: boys, like cupids,
Stood fanning, with their painted wings, the winds
That played about her face: but if she smiled,
A darting glory seemed to blaze abroad:
That men's desiring were never weary'd;
But hung upon the object: to soft flutes
The silver oars kept time; and while they played,
The hearing gave new pleasure to the sight;
And both to thought: 'twas heaven or somewhat more;
For she so charmed all hearts, that gazing crowds
Stood panting on the shore, and wanted breath
To give their welcome voice.

Dollabella points out that when he then fell in love with
Cleopatra it was a private love, now an empire stands in
the balance. Octavia and Antony's daughters are brought
in in an attempt to shame him into some recognition of
himself. Antony greets her as Caesar's sister and accuses
her of begging his life from Octavius. He still refuses to
make terms. His friends continue to try and persuade him
till almost at the moment of agreement Alexas enters.
There follows the meeting between Cleopatra and Octavia. Octavia accuses Cleopatra of destroying Antony, Cleopatra's defence once again is her great love.
Act IV Antony's camp. Antony is unable face to face to
tell Cleopatra to go. Dollabella urges that he let Ventidius
do it for him. Ventidius, remembering that Dollabella
once loved Cleopatra himself, sees in Dollabella's reluctance to meet her a chance to ruin Cleopatra with Antony.
At the same time, on the other side of the stage, Alexas is
advising Cleopatra to use Dollabella to make Antony jealous. Dollabella tells Cleopatra she must resign both
Antony and her kingdom. Dollabella is touched with pity
for her. Ventidius uses this moment of tenderness to make

Antony jealous. Alexas confirms Ventidius's accusations. Antony is beside himself with passion, when Dollabella and Cleopatra enter they are accused of falsehood and banished.

Act V Cleopatra's apartments. Alexas points out that Antony is jealous rather than out of love. He can still be Cleopatra's. News is brought that the Egyptian fleet has gone over to Caesar. Alexas tries to comfort his queen by suggesting that she should abandon Antony and make peace with Caesar. Antony and Ventidius enter. Alexas tells them that Cleopatra has committed suicide within her monument. News is brought that Caesar is at the gates:

> What should I fight for now? My queen is dead.
> I was but great for her; my power, my empire,
> Were but my merchandise to buy her love;
> And conquered Kings, my factors. Now she's dead,
> Let Caesar take the world, –
> An empty circle, since the jewel's gone.
> Which made it worth my strife: my being's nauseous;
> For all the bribes of life are gone away.

Ventidius and Antony take their own lives. Before Antony has died Cleopatra enters. Alexas has falsely reported her death. Cleopatra and Antony are reconciled. Rather than grace Octavius's triumph, Cleopatra, dressed in her queenly robes, sitting by Antony dies by snake bites. Caesar is too late.

Critical commentary

It is impossible to consider *All for Love* without comparing it with *Antony and Cleopatra*. The first impression is that Shakespeare's poetry is more exciting and spontaneous but Dryden applies greater order. This leads us to the questions posed by Bonamy Dobrée (*Restoration Tragedy 1660–1720*, 1929):

If *Antony and Cleopatra* is better than *All for Love*, is this
due to advantages of method or mind? And if to the latter,
whether the genius of Shakespeare itself would not have
benefitted from the more austere discipline?

This is to presume that both plays are similar in aim and
that the response of their audiences allows an ideal treatment. They are not and it did not. Dryden's audience
were remarkably familiar with the history of Rome. They
applied to themselves the term Augustans, freely compared themselves to Brutus, Cato and Cicero and had
themselves sculpted and painted in costumes suggestive of
Roman grandeur. It is possible therefore for him to begin
the story as the tragedy reaches its climax. Shakespeare's
audience are less familiar with the story. It is necessary to
set the scene. Hence there are thirty-eight episodic scenes
in *Antony and Cleopatra* and the tragedy is confined to
the last two acts. Shakespeare's form is more informative
than Dryden. He makes remarkably little change to the
story as he found it in North's *Plutarch,* his sole original
creation being the role of Enobarbus. The form Shakespeare uses is the circular, wheel of fortune structure. We
see Antony rise to the pinnacle of greatness and then fall.
All contrasting aspects of life are shown, the comic and
the tragic, in a series of vividly contrasting pictures that
leave a disturbing sense of waste and destruction. Dryden's
aim is to clarify the emotions and finish in a settled manner To achieve this he selects from and alters his sources.
He wishes us to admire his heroes, thus Antony is more
heroic and Cleopatra more tragic than in either North or
Shakespeare. Their petty inconsistencies are distilled to
fit a stage convention, Ventidius, a mere cipher in Shakespeare, possibly borrowing a little from Enobarbus, is
built up into the representative of Roman virtue. Pity is
much more an important emotion for Dryden and his
audience than it had been in the theatre of Shakespeare's
time. The true answer to the question which is the better

play must be that *All for Love* would have failed for Shakespeare's audience, as *Antony and Cleopatra* failed for Dryden's.

One must finally suggest that many actors, embued with a false idea of tragedy, have brought an attitude of mind more suited to Dryden than to the acting of Shakespeare's play. A comparison between the two speeches describing Cleopatra on Cydnus will clarify the above. Shakespeare, in spite of the beautiful phrases, allows Enobarbus to burlesque Antony's appetite for Cleopatra, note for example that the passage begins with the phrase, 'Antony being barbered ten times o'er' and ends:

> for vilest things
> Become themselves in her, that holy priests
> Bless her when she is riggish.

Dryden uses the same passage for tender reminiscence.

King Lear

Altered and revised from Shakespeare

Nahum Tate (1652–1715)

Born in Dublin and educated at Trinity College, Dublin, Tate succeeded fellow dramatist Thomas Shadwell as Poet Laureate. He has been unfairly reviled in most theatrical reference books for his honest reflection of the taste of his age in his alteration of *King Lear*. Dryden collaborated with him in the second part of *Absalom and Achitophel*. His best work is his collaboration with Nicholas Brady in a metrical version of the psalms. His other dramatic works are: *Brutus of Alba* (1678); *The Loyal General* (1680); *Richard II, or The Sicilian Usurper* (1681); *The Fall of Coriolanus* (1681); *Cuckold's Haven* (1685); *A Duke and No Duke* altered from Cockain's *Trappolin*; *The Island Princess* (1687); and *Injured Love* (1707).

DATE 1681

CAST

King Lear
Gloster
Kent
Edgar, son to Gloster
Edmund, bastard son to Gloster
Cornwall, husband to Regan
Albany, husband to Goneril
Burgundy
Gentleman-usher

Goneril
Regan
Cordelia
SCENE England

Plot

Act I,*i* The play opens with the Bastard's soliloquy,
'Thou nature art my goddess.' The quarrel between Edgar
and his father, Gloster, has already taken place. As Lear
and the court enter, Edgar pleads with Cordelia not to
accept Burgundy. The scene then follows Shakespeare
with Lear dividing his kingdom between his daughters.
He requires that they state their love for him. Regan and
Goneril satisfy him with suitable fluency but Cordelia is
unable to match their flatteries and is disinherited. Kent
is banished for defending Cordelia. Burgundy rejects the
hand of the now dowerless princess and Edgar is left in
possession of Cordelia.

Cordelia, suspicious after her treatment from Burgundy,
rejects him. The Bastard warns Edgar to fly from their
father's rage and then allows the forged letter incriminating his brother to fall into Gloster's hands. The disguised
Kent gains service with Lear. Lear strikes Goneril's gentleman-usher for impertinence. Goneril accuses him and the
hundred knights, which are the sole remnant of kingly
state that he has retained, of turning her house into a
riotous inn. She cuts his following by half. Lear exits curs-
ing her to seek lodging with her sister Regan.

Act II,*i* Gloster's house. The Bastard again urges Edgar
to fly. When Edgar has gone he wounds himself with his
sword to support his story that Edgar has attacked him.
Kent is put in the stocks for chastising Goneril's servant.
On Lear's entry Regan releases Kent but after the arrival
of her sister reduces his following still further. Lear's wits
begin to crack.

Act III,*i* A desert heath. This is Shakespeare's storm

scene with Lear raging against the elements but with the Fool removed. Thus the scene is severely truncated, scenic effect replacing poetry. *ii* Gloster's Palace. Edmund has noted that both the sisters are attracted to him:

> The storm is in our louder revelings drowned.
> Thus would I reign, could I but mount a throne.
> The riots of these proud imperial sisters
> Already have imposed the galling yoke
> Of taxes, and hard impositions on
> The drudging peasant's neck, who bellows out
> His loud complaints in vain – triumphant queens!
> With what assurance do they tread the crowd?
> Oh for a taste of such majestic beauty,
> Which none but my hot veins are fit t'engage;
> Nor are my wishes desperate, for even now,
> During the banquet, I observed their glances
> Shot thick at me; and, as they left the room,
> Each cast by stealth, a kind inviting smile,
> The happy earnest ... ha!

From both sisters he receives letters confirming this. Gloster, still unsuspecting of his son's villainy, confides his disgust at Regan's and Goneril's behaviour. He gives him letters to an enemy of Cornwall's requesting assistance to overthrow the Queens. Cordelia begs Gloster to assist her father. The sisters have decreed instant death to any who shall help Lear. Edmund plans to follow Cordelia and his father and thus betray them both. *iii* The desert heath. A hovel in the background. Kent persuades Lear to enter the hovel of Poor Tom, the disguise assumed by Edgar. Gloster and Cordelia try and persuade the King to find better shelter. They are surprised by ruffians. Cordelia and her gentleman are captured. Edgar rescues them and makes himself known to Cordelia. He has proved his love and they exchange vows. *iv* The palace. Gloster's letter has come to light. Edmund is made Duke of Gloster. Cornwall puts out Gloster's eyes.

Act IV,*i* A grotto. Edmund and Regan are making love.
He accidentally drops Goneril's letter. Blind Gloster leads
a revolt of the peasants against the palace. *ii* A field.
Edgar meets Gloster led by an old man. He is so overcome
with grief at his father's condition that he sustains the
character of Poor Tom. They are met by Cordelia and
Kent. Kent prepares to lead the peasant rebellion. *iii* The
palace. Cornwall has died from a wound received from a
servant during the blinding of Gloster. Edmund is
general of Regan's forces. *iv* The field. Edgar deludes
Gloster into thinking he has committed suicide by jumping from the cliffs of Dover. Mad Lear enters railing
against the world and authority as in Shakespeare. Gentlemen sent from Cordelia to find him arrive and Lear runs
off with them following. A murderer sent by Goneril to
kill Gloster is himself killed by Edgar. On the body Edgar
discovers a letter which reveals Goneril's plot to kill her
husband and marry Edmund. *v* A chamber, Lear asleep
on a couch. Lear wakes and is reconciled to Cordelia. The
incongruous scene of kneeling and counter kneeling between father and daughter which Shakespeare had inherited from the old *King Lear* is not retained in this version.
In the distance the drums of Kent's peasant army are
heard.

Act V,*i* Goneril's camp. Edmund is general of her forces
as well as those of Regan. *ii* A valley near the camp. Edgar
settles his father who is still unaware of his identity. He
leaves to join the battle. The blind man tries to follow the
battle from the off-stage noises. Edgar re-enters with the
news that Kent has lost and that Lear and Cordelia are
prisoners. The successful army enters. The still disguised
Edgar accuses Edmund of plotting Albany's life. Lear
recognizes Kent and is led off to prison. Goneril dispatches
a guard to murder Cordelia and Lear. Edgar and Edmund
fight. Edgar kills Edmund. The two Queens quarrel over
his dying body and learn that each had plotted against the
other. *iii* A prison. Soldiers enter to kill Lear and Corde-

lia. Lear kills two with a partition, the rest run away.
Edgar and Albany enter and remove Lear and Cordelia's
chains. Regan and Goneril are condemned. Albany re-
stores Lear who resigns the throne to Cordelia who accepts
Edgar's hand.

Critical commentary

The fact that this emasculated version of Lear held the
stage for a century and a half seems hardly comprehen-
sible to us today. Of the eighteenth century critics only
Addison stood out against the happy ending. This is consistent with his views on poetic justice as demonstrated in
Cato. Even Samuel Johnson lent the ponderous weight of
his authority to the Tate version:

> I was many years ago so shocked by Cordelia's death, that I
> know not whether I ever endured to read again the last
> scenes of the play till I undertook to revise them as editor.

In the nineteenth century critical opinion reversed the
judgement of its fathers. Hazlitt and Lamb took up the
cudgels on behalf of the original. The moral aim of
Restoration tragedy is to elevate by presenting an ideal
world for the admiration of audiences. Thus tragic characters take on the simplified characteristics almost reminiscent of Jonson's 'humours'. Lear, Gloster, Edgar and
Kent are all elevated from their Shakespearean originals.
Edmund, Goneril, Regan and Cornwall are all more
clearly villainous. This idealized, elevated characterization aims to strip away the inconsistencies of reality. The
Restoration tragic world is peopled not by persons as they
are or might have been but persons such as the author
wished them to be. We no longer share the same ideals
but we must respect them if we are to understand Restoration tragedy.

Admiration is a settled emotion which negates the tur-
bulence of Elizabethan and Jacobean tragedy. Tragedy

now comes, as we have shown in our other examples from this period, to rely more and more on pity. The commonest form of dramatic pity is produced by the trials and tribulations of love hence the necessity for introducing the love plot between Edgar and Cordelia. The happy ending is the result of the application of the rules of poetic justice which dictate that the blameless must be rewarded and the guilty punished. What Restoration Tate has missed is Shakespeare's condemnation of Lear surrendering his kingly obligations against the natural order. Both an anarchic and a low comedy fool have no place in the tidy world of Restoration tragedy. By 1800 plays such as *The Iron Chest* and *The Castle Spectre* have prepared the audiences for the inclusion of low comic characters, and the romantic death of blameless innocents, and the dominance of pity has been considerably reduced.

Venice Preserved, or A Plot Discovered
Thomas Otway (1625–85)

Otway was born in Sussex, his father a clergyman. He was educated at Winchester, going on to Christ Church, Oxford in 1669. He left the University in 1672 without taking a degree. He made the acquaintance of Mrs Aphra Behn and in 1672 he appeared as the old king in her *Forced Marriage*. He suffered badly from stage fright and this was his one and only appearance. Three years later at the same theatre, the Dorset Garden, his first play *Alcibiades* was presented. This was written in heroic couplets and only saved from complete oblivion by superb acting. In 1677 he made two remarkable adaptations from the French *Titus and Berenice* (from Racine) and *The Cheats of Scapin* (from Molière). He had by this time fallen desperately in love with the actress Mrs Barry. Six of his letters to her survive. She was unwilling to lose the protection of Lord Rochester and gave Otway little encouragement. In desperation he enlisted for service in the Netherlands. A year later the troops were disbanded and Otway returned to London in poor straits. Like Dryden, he abandoned heroic couplets to produce his two masterpieces, *The Orphan* (1680) and *Venice Preserved* (1682) in blank verse. These plays were to be continually revived until the end of the nineteenth century and both have been played with success during the twentieth century. They were particularly attractive to actresses. Monimia in *The Orphan* and Belvidera were, with the heroines of

Rowe, to become obligatory tests of an actress's quality, in the same way that *Richard III* and *Hamlet* were to be for male performers. In spite of these successes he slipped deeper and deeper into poverty. The story of his death, recounted by Theophilus Cibber in *Lives of the Poets*, is probably apochryphal but he certainly did die in extreme want. According to Cibber he was begging in the street when a passer-by discovered who he was and gave him a guinea. Otway took this treasure to a baker's shop and, being so ravenously hungry, choked and died. He was buried on 16 April 1685 in the churchyard of St Clement Danes.

His main dramatic works are: *Don Carlos* (1676); *Titus and Berenice* (1677); *Cheats of Scapin* (1677); *Friendship in Fashion* (1678); *The Orphan* (1680); *Caius Marius* (1680); *The Soldier's Fortune* (1681); *Venice Preserved* (1682); and *The Atheist* (1684).

DATE 1682

CAST

Duke of Venice
Priuli, father to Belvidera, a senator
Antonio, a fine speaker in the Senate
Jaffier
Pierre
Renault
Bedamar, the Spanish ambassador
Spinosa
Theodore
Eliot
Revillido   conspirators
Durand
Mezzana
Brainveil
Ternon
Retrosi
Brabe

Belvidera
Aquilina
SCENE Venice

Plot

Act I A street in Venice. Three years before the beginning
of the play Jaffier has secretly married Belvidera, after
rescuing her from drowning. He has spent what little
fortune he possessed maintaining her in suitable state. At
the opening of the play he begs help from Belvidera's
family but is scornfully turned aside with advice to live
within his means. Pierre finds Jaffier in a state of righteous
indignation against his father-in-law. He feeds this by
recounting how he discovered his mistress Aquilina in the
arms of the old senator Antonio. Pierre uses these mutual
private wrongs to sweep Jaffier into conspiracy against the
Venetian Senate. Pierre is further justified by the fact that
he had taken the matter into his own hands and driven
'the rank old bearded Hirco stinking home', only to have
Antonio bring the matter before the Senate. The act closes
with an exchange of love between Belvidera and Jaffier.
Act II,*i* Aquilina's house. Pierre rejects Aquilina's offer
to let him share her bed that night. He despises her for
having sold herself to Antonio and this is the night that
he must meet the other conspirators. He warns her to keep
Antonio out of the way. *ii* The Rialto. Pierre secures
Jaffier to the conspiracy. *iii* Aquilina's house. The conspirators assemble. Pierre introduces Jaffier to the plotters
who, led by Renault, with the sole exception of Bedamar
the Spanish ambassador, greet him with suspicion. As a
pledge of good faith he delivers Belvidera into Renault's
charge. He also presents Renault with a dagger to employ
against Belvidera should he prove faithless. Belvidera
begs for an explanation and is hustled off stage.
Act III,*i* Another room in Aquilina's house. Aquilina
entertains the gruesome old senator Antonio, who crawls

about on his hands and knees pretending to be his 'Nicky Nacky's' dog:

> Ay with all my heart: do kick, kick on, now I am
> under the table, kick again – kick harder – harder
> yet, bow wow wow, wow bow – 'odd, I'll have a snap
> at thy shins – bow wow wow, wow bow – 'odd she
> kicks bravely.

Antonio is forcibly ejected by Aquilina's footmen for refusing to stop barking. *ii* Another room in the same house. Belvidera enters to tell us that Renault, instead of guarding her as a pledge of honour, has offered to rape her. When Jaffier appears Belvidera alternately hurls reproaches at and demands explanations from him. Under such pressure Jaffier betrays the conspiracy. Now Belvidera, using the immediate hurt of Renault's treachery in the same way that Pierre had used Priuli's scorn in the opening scene, works on Jaffier to undermine his oath to the conspiracy. She is so far successful as to achieve his setting aside his oath to the extent of agreeing to meet her at midnight. Pierre shares his friend's outrage at Renault's behaviour but begs him to wait for his revenge until the conspiracy has succeeded. The conspirators assemble. Renault advocates a general slaughter which will spare neither age nor sex but totally exterminate the senators and their families. Jaffier hears this with horror. Renault noticing this remarks scornfully 'You droop Sir'. Jaffier excuses himself but shortly after leaves the meeting. The conspirators, led by Renault brandishing Jaffier's dagger, are immediately suspicious. Pierre defends his friend and snatches the dagger from Renault.

Act IV,*i* The streets of Venice. Belvidera leads Jaffier to the Senate to betray the plot. *ii* The Senate house. Priuli has already had knowledge of the conspiracy from an unknown hand. Jaffier demands pardon for all as the price of betrayal. This is granted and he delivers the names and plans. The conspirators are arrested and brought on stage.

Pierre requests to be faced with his accuser. Jaffier enters. At first Pierre thinks he too has been arrested but when he discovers the truth he scorns mercy and his friend, only demanding 'Death, honourable death'. He brushes aside Jaffier's attempts to excuse his conduct, striking him on the face and flinging the dagger, the symbol of Jaffier's faith, on to the ground at his feet. The insult of a blow is something we tend to accept lightly in the modern theatre. It is the ultimate contempt that a gentleman should think another unworthy of his sword and this must be appreciated as one of the climaxes of the play. Pierre rails at Jaffier, who has accepted the blow, for a traitor. As Pierre is led off Jaffier picks up the dagger. Belvidera enters. Jaffier relives in his description, the humiliation of his meeting with Pierre. She begs him to forgive his friend since he is to be broken on the wheel. The senators have ignored their promise to spare the lives of the conspirators just as he broke his promise to the plot. He sees Belvidera as at once his pledge of good faith and the instrument that made him break that faith. Three times he fumbles for his dagger or 'offers to stab her' only to throw it from him and embrace her. He begs her to use her influence with her father to obtain a pardon for Pierre.

Act V,*i* The Rialto. Belvidera works on her father to plead with the Senate for the lives of the conspirators. He agrees to do this. Aquilina pleads with the goatish Antonio to intercede for Pierre, finally threatening to kill him if he is unsuccessful. It is too late for intercession. Belvidera and Jaffier meet. It is obvious he intends suicide. Priuli fears for his daughter's sanity. The flats open to discover the scaffold and wheel prepared for Pierre's execution. Jaffier begs Pierre's pardon for betraying him, Pierre begs Jaffier's pardon for the blow. Pierre whispers to Jaffier, miming a request to him to use the dagger to release his friend from the indignity of the wheel. As the executioner binds Pierre on to it, he calls out 'Now'. Jaffier stabs him and then stabs himself. The dying Jaffier curses the Senate and the scene shuts upon them. Priuli enters with a mad Belvidera. She sees the ghosts of Pierre and Jaffier and dies.

Critical commentary

This play was first performed in February 1682 just as the panic and hysteria of the Popish plot began to subside. The conflicting political issues in England as it was being written, to a certain extent explain the audience's confusion as to whether they should sympathize with the conspirators or the Senate. The plot is loosely based on Saint-Réak's, *History of the Spanish Conspiracy against the State of Venice*. This had already been associated, in pamphlets, with the Popish Plot disclosed by Titus Oates. When the original disclosures were made the country became violently Whig and anti-Catholic. It was rumoured that England was threatened by invasion from France, Spain and Ireland. The King was to be murdered, all Protestants were to be put to the sword and the Catholic Duke of York established on the throne. Unfortunately these disclosures came near to the truth in that there was intrigue between Louis XIV and Charles II. The King was isolated and the fortunes of the Whig leader, the Earl of Shaftesbury, in the ascendant. As the rumours began to clear it became obvious that the Whig Parliament of 1680 was an almost revolutionary body. A scheme was introduced for the King's divorce and the acknowledgement of the Protestant Duke of Monmouth as his heir. There was an even greater threat to peace from the Whigs than there had ever been from the Catholic minority and if there was any conspiracy then Shaftesbury and Titus Oates were not uninvolved. The clouds of rumour bunched around two main figures, Charles and Shaftesbury. Otway was a Tory but his audience were divided. *Venice Preserved* achieves topicality, even obvious political statement by, as we shall see, identifying both sides with the discredited and unpopular Shaftesbury. Any republicanism implicit in the fact that both the main characters are conspirators is clearly avoided by making their involvement the result of private feuds. Neither Pierre nor Jaffier are revolutionaries against the state but rather they are men, like Melantius in *The Maid's Tragedy*, caught up in political events to cleanse stains on their private honour.

It is a commonplace of criticism of Otway to point out how his work harps back to and echoes the Jacobeans and to some extent Shakespeare. Love has become such a fractured value in court life that Otway elevates it to an ideal which even excuses the betrayal of friends, family and kingdoms. No Elizabethan or Jacobean writer could have been as absurdly out of touch with their reality. Women, however beautiful or good, were of a lower order than mankind and this outlook does not change until after the Restoration. Certainly Otway echoes the best of the past in this play particularly in the third act where the exchanges between Belvidera and Jaffier seem to derive from those between Brutus and Portia in *Julius Caesar*:

> Tell me! Be just and tell me
> Why dwells that busy cloud upon thy face?
> Why am I made a stranger? Why that sigh,
> And I know not the cause? Why when the world
> Is wrapt in rest, why chooses then my love
> To wander up and down in horrid darkness,
> Loathing his bed and these desiring arms?

But this is no more than a pale echo of the good things of his predecessor. Any examination of parallel passages in the work of Otway and pre-Restoration dramatists demonstrates his familiarity with dramatic literature rather than a true kinship with the previous age. These passages show needless expansion of concise Jacobean thought together with a contraction and narrowing of ideas that reach beyond the restricted limits of the Restoration tragic

world. The only real achievement which we can grant
Otway is the genuine rediscovery of the merits of the
run-on line:

> When you, great Duke, shrunk trembling in your palace,
> And saw your wife, th'Adriatic, ploughed
> Like a lewd whore by bolder prows than yours
> Step't not I forth, and taught your loose Venetians
> The task of honour and the way to greatness.

Verse such as this comes as a great relief after the monotonous end stopping which echoes the rhythms of heroic
tragedy.

The political meaning of the play gives it a backbone
entirely absent from Otway's other work. It is here we find
the explanation of the curious 'Nick-Nacky' scenes which
seem so out of keeping with our expectations of the Restoration tragic world. It can be argued that in showing a
65-year-old senator crawling about on his knees barking
like a dog and allowing himself to be whipped by a prostitute, Otway is showing that the Senate was unsuited for
power and thus that rebellion is justified. This is an over
complicated interpretation. These scenes are superb
theatre, they are very funny. A modern equivalent would
be to dress an elderly politician as a schoolboy and have
him beg a prostitute to punish him. Swings in taste have
resulted in these scenes being left out and included by
turns. Their aim is biting satirical humour rather than
any higher moralistic purpose. Antonio is an obvious
familiarity for Anthony Ashley Cooper, Earl of Shaftesbury. There are too many parallels between the known
preferences of the Whig leader and Antonio for there to
be any doubt as to Otway's intentions. It has been suggested that these scenes were included at the King's request. This may be so, for it would explain the remarkable
double appearance which Shaftesbury makes in the play,
for there is little doubt that the plotter Renault is also
intended for him. Here Otway has shown considerable

skill. He has divided the libertine and parliamentary sides of Shaftesbury between Antonio and Renault. The latter being as easily identified as the deep plotting Shaftesbury whom Dryden, three months earlier had drawn as Achitophel, 'turbulent, subtle, mischievous and bold', as is the former for the lecherous private man.

All in all *Venice Preserved* is a good play where we can study the changes which have taken place in the clichéd conflict between love and honour since Boyle penned *Henry V*, but it is exaggeration to offer it any title to greatness and despite the superficial dissimilarities in style Boyle is much closer to the spirit of the Jacobeans than is his successor.

Love for Love
William Congreve (1670–1729)

As all of Congreve's work appeared after the death of
Charles II he is more correctly described as a late seventeenth century rather than a Restoration playwright. His
genius often escapes the criticism levelled at Wycherley
and Etherege. Brilliant is the only word which fits his
technique. He is another in the long procession of British
playwrights with Irish connections. He was born near
Leeds, of good family but he was brought up in Ireland
and educated at the University of Dublin, where he was a
contemporary and friend of Swift. From Dublin he proceeded to the Middle Temple. His writings demonstrate
an easy familiarity with classical literature.

In London he quickly established himself in the best
circles as a wit and a conversationalist. His first literary
work was a pseudonymous novel of little importance.
His first play, a comedy called *The Old Bachelor* (1693),
was a complete success. The opening line: 'Vainlove, and
abroad so early!' demonstrates his ability to use his observation to arrest his audience's attention without attacking or satirizing them. It was the fashion for society to rise
late thus the play is immediately recognizable and familiar. Seven speeches later the audience are treated to a
comfortable, epigrammatic phrase which sounds like
truth:

> Ay, ay; wisdom's nothing but a pretending to know
> and believe more than we really do.

Followed by a truth delivered as if it were a joke:

> You read of but one wise man, and all that he
> knew was, that he knew nothing.

Yet Congreve displays less obvious moral purpose than Wycherley. He observes the life of his time without making any violent attempt to reform or better it. He affects a certain cynicism but in all his plays there are representatives of the 'honest man' to provide an example of the golden mean advocated by the classical writers. Whether this was a deliberate purpose or something instinctively adopted from his models is difficult to determine. In 1694 *The Double Dealer* was first performed. This was not an unqualified success, perhaps because it is too clear a picture of the audience for whom it was intended. One year later he wrote his most successful play *Love For Love*. He then turned to tragedy with *The Mourning Bride* (1697). He was involved, with mixed success, in defending the theatre against the attacks of Jeremy Collier. In 1700 he wrote his last play *The Way of the World*. This failed in its own age. Plot is never Congreve's strong point. The wit combats between Mirabell and Millamant are not only subtle and difficult to comprehend on the first hearing but they do not advance the plot to any great extent. There is a danger of the audience not only failing to gather exactly what is being said but being left with a feeling that the conversation has served no other purpose than to display wit.

DATE 1695
CAST
Sir Sampson Legend, father to Valentine and Ben
Valentine, fallen under his father's displeasure by his
expensive way of living, in love with Angelica
Scandal, his friend, a free speaker
Tattle, a half-witted beau, vain of his amours, yet valuing
himself for secrecy

Ben, Sir Sampson's younger son, half home bred and half
sea bred, designed to marry Miss Prue
Foresight, an illiterate old fellow, peevish and positive,
superstitious and pretending to understand astrology,
palmistry, physiognomy, omens, dreams etc, uncle to Angelica
Jeremy, servant to Valentine
Trapland, a scrivener
Buckram, a lawyer
Angelica, niece to Foresight, of a considerable fortune in
her own hands
Mrs Foresight, second wife to Foresight
Mrs Frail, sister to Mrs Foresight, a woman of the town
Miss Prue, daughter to Foresight by a former wife, a
silly awkward country girl
SCENE London

Plot

Act I Valentine's chamber. Valentine is discovered reading. He is considering ways of recovering his fortune
while holding the debt collectors at bay. Valentine receives a kind of reprieve when he learns that his father
has offered £4,000 to pay his debts on condition that he
resign his inheritance to his younger brother. Valentine
agrees to the terms because of his love for Angelica. Scandal sounds a warning note when he remarks that Angelica
has never given Valentine any assurance of returning his
love but Valentine brushes this aside, comforting himself that she has never given him any reason for despair
either. The bulk of the first act is taken up with introducing us to the humours of the town as presented by Scandal, Tattle and Mrs Frail. The conclusion is that Valentine's desperate chance of giving up his estate in order to
win Angelica is likely to bring him more harm than good.
Act II Foresight's house. Foresight is troubled by an old
prophecy that when all the women folk leave a house
its head is in danger of becoming a cuckold. Angelica

ridicules her uncle's prophecies. Sir Sampson calls on Foresight to make arrangements for the marriage between Miss Prue and Ben. He is greatly put out by old Foresight's concern about the suitability of the omen. However he recovers himself and jests Foresight into a better humour. Valentine calls to pay his respects to Angelica. He pleads with his father not to insist on the conditions of his gift but is rejected. Mrs Foresight in attempting to trap Mrs Frail into disclosing where she has lost a gold bodkin, reveals that she herself has found it at Tattle's. They become allies. Mrs Foresight promises to assist Mrs Frail in her designs upon Valentine's brother Ben, now the heir to Sir Sampson's fortune. This must be at the expense of Mrs Foresight's step-daughter Prue who is designed to be his wife. The two ladies contrive to leave Tattle with Prue and he proceeds to give the country girl her first lesson in gallantry:

> *Tattle* If I ask you to kiss me, you must be angry, but you must not refuse me. If I ask you for more, you must be more angry – but more complying; and as soon as ever I make you say you'll cry out, you must be sure to hold your tongue ... Well, my pretty creature; will you make me happy by giving me a kiss?
> *Prue* No, indeed, I'm angry at you. [runs and kisses him]
> *Tattle* Hold, hold, that's pretty well; – but you should not have given it to me, but have suffered me to have taken it.
> *Prue* Well, we'll do't again.

Act III Foresight's house. The nurse discovers Tattle with Miss Prue. Angelica refuses to admit to any *tendre* for Valentine and the scene dissolves into Tattle boasting of his conquests. News is brought that Ben is about to arrive. Valentine takes his leave lest his father press him to the immediate signing of the deed of conveyance of his estate. Sir Sampson is infuriated that Valentine will not stay to welcome his brother. Angelica continues to affect coolness to Valentine, much to Sir Sampson's relief for he was afraid that she had been in love with him and might have suffered from his disinheritance. Ben enters full of salty phrases. Left alone with Miss Prue on purpose by his father he behaves exceedingly boorishly to her and they end their scene abusing each other with such endearments as 'cheese curd' and 'tar barrel'. Mrs Frail cunningly contrives to serve her own ends by leading Ben into her chamber on the excuse of hiding the quarrel from Foresight and Legend. The marriage between Ben and Prue is arranged for ten o'clock the next morning. Scandal brings news to Sir Sampson that his son is sick. He then works the old fool into believing that he too is unwell thus clearing the way for his seduction of Mrs Foresight. They are interrupted by the entry of Mrs Frail and Ben who have arrived at an understanding.

Act IV Valentine's lodgings. Scandal and Jeremy have arranged it that Valentine shall pretend madness to the intent of softening Angelica and Sir Sampson. Angelica interrupts a wink between Scandal and Jeremy and realizes the trick. Sir Sampson arrives with the deeds conveying Valentine's estate to his brother. Valentine uses his pretended madness to avoid signing, chasing the lawyer out of his chamber. Ben boasts to Mrs Frail how he refused to marry Prue. Mrs Frail sees the danger of such a stubborn temper and their understanding is concluded by a quarrel. Mrs Foresight comes to her sister with another plan. Sir Sampson, angered at Ben's rejection of Prue is determined to reinstate Valentine. It is her intention to take advantage of Valentine's supposed madness and have him marry Mrs Frail for Angelica. Valentine falls in with their trickery and pretends to take Mrs Frail for Angelica. Tattle meanwhile makes love to Angelica. Angelica knowing Valentine's madness for a pretence refuses to believe that he is sane and their scene together ends with Valentine losing his temper with his servant.

Act V Foresight's house. Sir Sampson makes love to

Angelica and suggests rather than reinstate either of his
sons that his fortune should pass upon the issue male of
he and Angelica. Angelica pretends to consider this proposition and obtains possession of the deeds of conveyance. Tattle and Mrs Frail are tricked by Jeremy into
marrying each other in error for Angelica and Valentine.
Angelica now tears up the deeds against Valentine and
accepts his hand in marriage. Ben will return to sea and
Miss Prue has declared that it is her intention to marry
the butler.

Critical commentary

The satirical tone of the play is set in the first scene in
speeches such as Scandal's warning to Valentine against
becoming a playwright:

> No, turn pimp, flatterer, quack, lawyer, parson, be chaplain
> to an atheist, or stallion to an old woman, anything but
> a poet; a modern poet is worse, more servile, timorous and
> fawning than any I have named: without which you could
> revive the ancient honours of the name, recall the stage
> of Athens, and be allowed the force of open, honest satire.

The morality, or lack of it, of the age, upon which so
many critics have foundered is openly displayed. Among
Valentine's creditors is a nurse 'With one of your children
from Twitnam'. Money is sent to her from both Scandal
and Valentine with advice from Scandal:

> ... d'ye hear, bid Margery put more flocks in her bed,
> shift twice a week, and not work so hard, that she may
> not smell so vigorously.

There is an offensive reality here which contrasts with the
bawdy of speeches such as the description of Trapland's
widow later in the scene:

> Pretty round heaving breasts, a Barbary shape, and a jut

with her bum would stir an anchorite, and the prettiest
foot! Oh, if a man could but fasten his eyes to her feet,
as they steal in and out, and play bo-peep under her
petticoats'.

Congreve intends to be offensive and to show the truth.
Young men of breeding talked and behaved as Valentine
and it is the duty of a comic writer to truthfully depict
the manners of his time. The plot of the play is Valentine's change from his position of complete selfishness to
a man able to sign away his inheritance under the purify-
ing influence of love. Unless he starts the play as an un-
sympathetic character there will be no development and
no lesson. It is an inability in some critics to accept the
less pleasant aspects of humanity which has turned the
production of Restoration comedies into a stylized exercise instead of a mirror of life. The style is only the setting
for unpleasant and unpalatable truths, often this setting
is allowed to obscure the meaning, yet if comedy is to reform vice it must depict it at its least attractive.

At first sight Congreve would appear to be presenting
an altogether different world to that created in *The Way
of the World*. The characters are much less subtle and we
can understand a critical desire to couple him with Ben
Jonson. Many of them are pure 'humour', such as the
gullible astrologer Foresight who can even be brought to
believe in his fidelity; good old Sir Sampson Legend, a
particularly fine example of the stock Restoration old
man typically willing to try his hand or some other part of
his body for a new heir; Tattle whose humour to secrecy
betrays him into telling all; Prue the archetypal country
girl, ignorant but willing to learn; Mrs Foresight and
Mrs Frail as easy as Wycherley's Fidget and Squeamish
but infinitely better natured; and sailor Ben who, although he does not appear until two acts are gone, has
it in his power to steal the play. It is an incredible stroke
of daring to risk so many strong characters in the same

play. To bring them into such harmony with each other that they compliment rather than distract is a great achievement. If one looks closely at other plays, contemporary and modern, it will be seen that most authors allow themselves only one or two such characters in case they should take the attention from the hero and heroine. Thus Wycherley confines himself to Sparkish and the Fidgets in *The Country Wife*; Etherege to Sir Jopling and Lady Woodvill in *The Man of Mode*; and Vanbrugh to Lord Toppington and Sir Tunbelly in *The Relapse*. It is this diversity of characterization which is the secret of *Love for Love*'s stage success over *The Way of the World*, for while its dialogue may be a little inferior and its aims more careless, although even here we find a touch of the new sentiment when Valentine offers to abandon his inheritance should Angelica marry his father, it is all in all a funnier play and in spite of literary critics, audiences will prefer it. True it employs such well worn theatrical clichés as pretended madness and mock astrology but it uses them because of their proven success with a deliberate precision which is altogether successful.

The Relapse, or Virtue in Danger
Sir John Vanbrugh (1664–1726)

Vanbrugh was of Dutch extraction; his grandfather had
come to England during the reign of James I. The
family was driven from London where Vanbrugh was
born and he was brought up in Chester, being educated
at the King's School in that town. At the age of nineteen
he was sent to France to study the arts. Two years later he
returned to England and obtained a commission in the
army. We next hear of him being arrested by the French
on a charge of spying on the information of a lady. He
spent some time in the Bastille where he wrote the first
draft of *The Provok'd Wife*. He returned to England and
inspired by the success of Cibber's *Love's Last Shift* wrote
The Relapse. This was followed almost immediately by
Aesop (1696) which was a failure but the success of *The
Relapse* brought about the production of *The Provok'd
Wife* in 1697. This was a triumph although it brought the
main brunt of Jeremy Collier's attacks on the theatre as
a source of immorality upon Vanbrugh's head. In 1700 he
adapted Beaumont and Fletcher's *Pilgrim*. Most of his
later writing consisted of English versions of French
plays: *The False Friend* from Le Sage's *Traître Puni*; *A
Country House* from Dancourt's *Maison de Campagne*;
Confederacy from Dancourt's *Bourgeoises à la Mode*;
Squire Treloolsy from Molière's *Monsieur de Pourceaugnac*; and *The Mistake* from Molière's *Dépit Amoureux*.
His last play survived only as a fragment *Journey To*

London and was finished by Colley Cibber as *The Provok'd Husband* (1728).

It is possible that it was Collier's attack which turned his attention from the stage to architecture. His most famous building is Blenheim Palace, still one of the largest domestic buildings in England. Besides this he built many other country mansions: notably Castle Howard for the Earl of Carlisle; Duncombe Hall in Yorkshire; Oulton Hall in Cheshire and in 1716 became architect to Greenwich Hospital. He died in March 1726 at his London House, now the site of the Ministry of Defence.

DATE 1696

CAST

Sir Novelty Fashion, newly created Lord Foppington
Young Fashion, his brother
Loveless, husband to Amanda
Worthy, a gentleman of the town
Sir Tunbelly Clumsey, a country gentleman
Sir John Friendly, his neighbour
Coupler, a matchmaker
Bull, chaplain to Sir Tunbelly
Serringe, a surgeon
Lory, servant to Young Fashion
La Verole, valet to Lord Foppington
Waterman
Shoemaker
Tailor
Mend-legs, a hosier
Foretop, a periwig-maker
Amanda, wife to Loveless
Berinthia, her cousin, a young widow
Miss Hoyden, a great fortune, daughter to Sir Tunbelly
Nurse, her governess
SCENE London and the country

Swellfoot the Tyrant

P. B. Shelley

DATE 1820

CAST

Tyrant Swellfoot, King of Thebes

Iona Taurina, his queen

Mammon, arch-priest of famine

Pyrganax ⎫
Dakry ⎭ wizards, ministers of Swellfoot

Laoctonos, a general

The Gadfly

The Leech

The Rat

The Minotaur

Moses, the sow-gelder

Solomon, the porkman

Zephaniah, pig-butcher

SCENE Thebes

NOTE The tragedy of *Swellfoot the Tyrant* must be read in the light of the events of the comedy of the trial of Queen Caroline staged at the House of Lords in 1820. Princess Caroline had married the Prince of Wales in 1795. A year later they separated. Queen Caroline then became a much enjoyed national embarrassment. In 1806 she survived what was to become known as the Delicate Investigation. From 1814 onwards she toured Europe with a supporting cast of vulgar eccentrics leaving behind her subtle attentions of Mr Worthy. She confesses an attraction for the latter to Berinthia.

Act III,*i* Lord Foppington's lodgings. Lord Foppington refuses to lend money to his brother. The way is now open for Young Fashion to accept Coupler's offer. *ii* A garden adjoining Loveless's lodgings. Loveless makes love to Berinthia. Worthy, whom we discover is an ex-lover of Berinthia's, enlists her aid on his designs on Amanda. Amanda, unaware of her cousin's real relationship with her husband and Worthy, confides in her that she suspects Loveless of a mistress. Berinthia, while concealing the true state of affairs, encourages her in this view. *iii* Before Sir Tunbelly's house in the country. Young Fashion, pretending to be his brother, arrives armed with letters of introduction from Coupler. *iv* Miss Hoyden's chamber within the house. The bride to be, ripe for a husband, welcomes the news of her supposed fiancé's arrival. *v* Another room in the house. Sir Tunbelly arranges the marriage for a fortnight hence. Young Fashion attempts to hurry matters lest his masquerade be discovered before that date but Sir Tunbelly is insistent that his daughter's wedding should be surrounded with suitable ceremony.

Act IV,*i* A room in Sir Tunbelly's house. With the help of the nurse Young Fashion exploits Miss Hoyden's eager anticipation of the pleasures of marriage to arrange for an immediate private ceremony. *ii* Loveless's lodgings. Berinthia insinuates Worthy's suit to Amanda. *iii* Berinthia's chamber. Loveless enters in the dark to wait for her. He hides in a cupboard. Berinthia opens the cupboard and takes him for a ghost. Loveless violently presses his suit and the scene ends with her being carried off stage crying out, very softly so as not to waken her maid:

Help, help, I'm ravished, ruined, undone! O Lord
I shall never be able to bear it.

iv Sir Tunbelly's house. Bull has just married Miss Hoy-

den and Young Fashion. Only just in time for news is
brought of Lord Foppington's arrival. Young Fashion
attempts to brazen it out by pretending his brother is an
imposter. *v* The gate. Lord Foppington is lured into the
house by Sir Tunbelly. *vi* Sir Tunbelly's hall. Sir Tunbelly interrogates Lord Foppington. Young Fashion im-
pudently refuses to recognize him. In desperation Lord
Foppington appeals to Sir Tunbelly to send for Sir John
Friendly, a mutual acquaintance. Sir John arrives and
identifies Lord Foppington. Realizing that discovery is
imminent Young Fashion and his servant have made a
hasty exit. The act ends with Miss Hoyden, Bull and the
nurse deciding to deny the secret marriage, after all as the
chaplain explains:

> . . . to take two husbands for the satisfaction of the
> flesh is to commit the sin of exorbitancy, but to do
> it for the peace of the spirit is no more than to be
> drunk by way of physic; besides to prevent a parent's
> wrath is to avoid the sin of disobedience; for when
> the parent's angry the child is forward.

Act V,*i* Coupler's lodgings in London. The matchmaker
has learnt from Lord Foppington that it is his intention
to return to London with his bride to be for the marriage
ceremony. The chaplain and the nurse have maintained
their silence about the previous wedding and there may
be difficulties in establishing Young Fashion's claim.
ii Berinthia's chamber. Worthy begs Berinthia to inform
Amanda that Loveless is unfaithful and thus remove the
last resistance against himself. This Berinthia does, still
managing to keep her own part in the affair secret from
her cousin. *iii* Young Fashion's lodgings. Young Fashion
bribes Bull and the nurse with the promise of a rich living, which will lie within the gift of him who is proved
husband to Miss Hoyden, to help establish the legality of
his marriage. *iv* Loveless's lodgings. Although now fully
aware that her husband has suffered a relapse Amanda

resists Worthy's attentions and even works some kind of moral reformation on that gentleman. *v* Lord Foppington's lodgings. The whole cast are invited to a bridal mask to celebrate Lord Foppington's wedding. This is interrupted by Young Fashion with proofs of his prior claim. Lord Foppington accepts his disappointment philosophically, Miss Hoyden accepts hers eagerly and Sir Tunbelly retires to the country.

Critical commentary

The Relapse owes its inspiration to Colley Cibber's *Love's Last Shift* (1676), a piece written mainly to provide Cibber himself with a superb acting vehicle in Sir Novelty Fashion, but also brilliantly calculated for the taste of the time. The hard cynical view which darkens so much of the comedy of the first two decades of the Restoration is now giving place to a softer more sentimental outlook. The main plot of *Love's Last Shift* recounts the intrigues of the virtuous Amanda to regain her husband Loveless who had deserted her after six months of marriage and gone abroad. Loveless is now returned to London penniless. The play is technically moral in that Amanda's aims are unimpeachable, but the strategy employed is pure bawdy.

Amanda pretends to be a stranger and regains Loveless by the highly questionable means of the old familiar Jacobean bed-trick. She finds virtue where she wants to find it and manoeuvres her husband to the desired repentance. After boasting in his epilogue that 'There's not one cuckold made in all this play,' Cibber apologizes for his hero's reformation stating that he ends the play thus to please the ladies and that the gentlemen must be content with the fact that he is 'lewd for above four acts'. This statement has led to a superficial judgement of *Love's Last Shift* as a piece of four acts of Restoration intrigue with a sentimental ending tacked on. As Clifford Leech has pointed out the moral idea is cultivated throughout the play.

Similarly, it can be seen from *The Way of the World* that a new moral strain entirely lacking in the plays of Etherege and Wycherley is becoming more and more intrusive. Vanbrugh and Cibber still seem to be juggling with two conflicting sets of values but it is superficial to accept the view of Cibber's work as displaying vulgarity, casuistry and irresponsibility or to see *The Relapse* simply as a rejection of Cibber's moral ending. Both men are faced with the problem of satisfying a revolution in audience taste and the success of both pieces justifies any seeming moral ambivalence. There can be no suggestion of any quarrel between Vanbrugh and Cibber. The latter eagerly repeated his performance as Sir Novelty in the new play which, very far from being a rejection is rather an exploitation of the success of its parent. Vanbrugh admits in his prologue that he wrote *The Relapse* in under six weeks and this shows in its rather careless structure and uneven style. Three of the Amanda – Loveless – Worthy scenes are written in a rather curiously old fashioned blank verse reminiscent of Caroline drama. So carelessly are these printed that editors are still uncertain as to which lines are intended as verse and which as prose. They presumably reflect the play's hasty composition. His obvious intention is by the use of verse to intensify the emotion of these scenes leaving common prose for the more farcical portions of the play. It should be noted that Worthy was at its first creation a breeches role.

There is hardly a line of true wit in the play yet it stands out as seminally representative of the drama of the century's end for two reasons. The first, which we have already discussed, is the change in the moral outlook of comedy. We shall examine Steele as the dominant advocate of sentimentalism but beneath Steele's allegedly altruistic concern for the moral well being of others lies a certain snobbishness and condescension. Vanbrugh is more humanly opportunistic: libertinism and reform interact honestly in *The Relapse*, Worthy making no exaggerated claims for the length of his reformation. In spite of the satire on Lord Foppington and Sir Tunbelly Clumsey the play takes an optimistic view of human nature. Amanda is confident that Loveless has suffered no more than a relapse and both Lord Foppington and Sir Tunbelly Clumsey are allowed to retain at least the shreds of their dignity.

The Mourning Bride
William Congreve

DATE 1697

CAST

Manuel, King of Granada

Gonsalez, his favourite

Garcia, son to Gonsalez

Perez, captain of the guards

Alonzo, an officer, creature to Gonsalez

Osmyn, a noble prisoner

Heli, a prisoner, his friend

Selim, a eunuch

Almeria, princess of Granada

Zara, a captive queen

Leonora, chief attendant on the princess

SCENE Granada

NOTE The printed text is set out in the classical manner with each alteration of the number of characters on stage marking a new scene. For the synopsis given below this is ignored.

Plot

Act I A room of state in the royal palace at Granada. The play opens with the line, 'Music has charms to sooth a savage breast'. Almeria is a poor pawn in the hereditary feud between the kings of Granada and Valentia. She recounts to her maid Leonora how she was for a while the

captive of Anselmo, King of Valentia, who was killed by
her father and whose tomb lies near the royal palace.
While a captive she fell in love and married Alphonso,
Prince of Valentia. When her father attacked the city her
father had her smuggled aboard a ship, which was wrecked
before she returned home. Now she has heard that Alphonso is dead and her father returns in triumph from the
war. It is his intention to marry her to Garcia the son of
his favourite. The King has brought back among his captives Zara, a queen with whom he is in love and the
mysterious Osmyn in whom he suspects a rival with Zara.
Act II An island with a temple upon it, containing the
tomb of Anselmo. To this tomb comes Almeria calling in
grief upon Alphonso. Osmyn rises from the tomb. He is
Alphonso. The lovers are reunited only to be sundered
again by the jealousy of Zara who, ignorant of his true
identity, loves Osmyn. She accuses him to Manuel of
making love to her.
Act III Osmyn's prison. Osmyn learns that the King's
troops are ripe for rebellion, because Manuel has refused
to share his plunder, retaining all for his own use. Zara
visits Osmyn. He at first takes her for Almeria and calls
her his love. She arranges to help him to escape, but when
she returns to free him he is with Almeria. Her jealousy
starts up anew and she orders the guards to redouble their
vigilance:

> Heaven has no rage, like love to hatred turned,
> Nor hell a fury, like a woman scorned.

Act IV A room of state. The mutiny against the King has
begun. Zara learns that Alphonso is still alive and at last
realizes Osmyn's true identity. Manuel discovers that his
daughter has visited Osmyn. As he questions her she becomes distracted. She admits that Osmyn is Alphonso and
that he is her husband. The King attributes this confession
to the ravings of a madwoman but Gonsalez recognizes its
truth and arranges to kill Osmyn.

Act V A room of state. The King discovers a letter involving Zara in the plot to free Osmyn. He decides to disguise himself as the moor and face Zara with her treachery when she comes to release him. The scene changes to the prison. Osmyn has escaped. Gonsalez has in error killed the King. Alonzo cuts off the head so that the body may still appear to be Osmyn's. Zara discovers it and thinking it that of her beloved drinks poison. Almeria is about to follow suit when Alphonso enters. The mistakes are discovered and the harsh laws of poetic justice served.

Critical commentary

Every critic has a blind spot and Bonamy Dobrée, the great pioneer of serious study of late seventeenth-century tragedy, reveals *The Mourning Bride* as his when he writes in *Restoration Tragedy*:

> It is not hard to understand why *The Mourning Bride* was hailed as a great work, and why Dryden could write of Congreve: 'Heaven that but once was prodigal before,/ To Shakespeare gave as much, she could not give him more,' if a stringent course of average Restoration drama has first been undergone. There really is a richness of thought and feeling in Congreve's work which marks it out strongly from all the plays written since *All for Love*.

He goes on to claim that Congreve's blank verse is better than Dryden's, adding that the lines are internally constructed in a way that neither Lee's nor Otway's nor Rowe's come within sight of being. A comparison between the number of end stopped passages in this play and *Venice Preserved* seems to directly refute such claims, and overall there is a sameness about the play's Gothic morbidity not immediately apparent to the reader but precluding its ever being seriously considered for revival. The verse and tone are monotonous and though one might quote

single passages to great effect there is insufficient variety
for any of these to be memorable at first hearing.

The play's importance derives from its utter disregard
of the dramatic conventions of its time and this must have
given it a freshness at its first presentation. Firstly, even
allowing for the obligatory happy ending dictated by the
rules of poetic justice, it is truly neither a tragedy nor a
heroic play. We have seen that one of the main requisites
of heroic drama is that it should appeal to our sense of
wonder. Even in the character of Osmyn there is little or
no pretence at admiration. Distressed love is the theme
but this love is more nearly passionate than heroic; the
noble torture of Otway and the pathos of Rowe are wanting. This is to the play's advantage and in the second reading we discover a Gothic adventure story not unlike those
which will begin to dominate the stage one hundred years
later and without the tongue in cheek clowning demanded
by the change in audience. When Zara, having taken
poison beside what she believes to be the headless corpse
of Osmyn, caresses the stump we are very close to *The
Castle Spectre* and *A Tale of Mystery*:

> O friendly draught, already in my heart.
> Cold, cold; my veins are icicles and frost.
> I'll creep into his bosom, lay me there;
> Cover us close – or I shall chill his breast,
> And fright him from my arms – see, see, he slides
> Still further from me; look he hides his face,
> I cannot feel it – quite beyond my reach.
> O now he's gone, and all is dark ... [*Dies*]

This is much closer to nineteenth-century drama than it is
to the excesses of Webster or Tourneur, only the supernatural element being wanting, although this is suggested
when Osmyn–Alphonso rises out of his father's tomb in a
manner which forestalls the celebrated entry of the vampire Ruthven in J. R. Planché's *The Vampire* (1820).

It will be noted that although the play is given a background setting of inter-state feud, the court intrigue is minimized and we can just discern the beginnings of the new domestic flavour which will characterize the work of Rowe.

All these differences between *The Mourning Bride* and the heroic drama which precedes it serve to disguise the fact that the situations are all stock theatrical clichés: the noble prisoner in disguise, secretly married to a princess whose father designs her for another; the captive queen beloved by the King but in love with the prisoner; the villain the author of the accident which brings about his own death and so on. These devices are all to be found in the plays of Dryden, Lee and others and there is no doubt that Congreve has given them new life so that in his strange setting, shorn of heroics, we hardly recognize them for what they are.

The Way of the World
William Congreve

DATE 1700

CAST

Fainall, in love with Mrs Marwood

Mirabell, in love with Mrs Millamant

Witwoud ⎫
Petulant ⎭ followers of Mrs Millamant

Sir Wilfull Witwoud, half-brother to Witwoud and nephew to Lady Wishfort

Waitwell, servant to Mirabell

Lady Wishfort, enemy to Mirabell, for having falsely pretended to love her

Mirabell, for having falsely pretended to love her

Mrs Millamant, a fine lady, niece to Lady Wishfort and loves Mirabell

Mrs Marwood, friend to Mr Fainall, and likes Mirabell

Mrs Fainall, daughter to Lady Wishfort, and wife to Fainall, formerly friend to Mirabell

Foible, woman to Lady Wishfort

Mincing, woman to Mrs Millamant

SCENE London. The time equal to that of presentation.

Plot

Act I A chocolate house. Mirabell and Fainall are playing at cards. Mirabell is bored. His mind is not upon the game. He is at the point of abandoning a life of fashionable libertinage for Millamant, an heiress, ward to Lady Wishfort. Without being introduced Millamant is discussed throughout the act, so that our expectations are high. The previous evening had seen her deliver a snub to Mirabell, under which he still smarts. Her aunt Lady Wishfort is Mirabell's declared enemy. In order to win her favour he pretended a courtship but was unable to carry this to its ultimate conclusion:

> I did as much as man could, with any reasonable
> conscience; I proceeded to the very last act of flattery with
> her, and was guilty of a song in her commendation.

Act II St James's Park. Lady Wishfort's daughter, Mrs Fainall, has been Mirabell's mistress during her widow-hood previous to her marriage with Fainall. Mrs Marwood would be his mistress in the present but is in fact mistress to Fainall. Jealous of Millamant she does all in her power to stir up trouble between her and Mirabell. Her alliance with Fainall is in part due to his intriguing against the pair. Should he cause Millamant to marry against her aunt's wishes the greater part of her fortune will revert to his wife. Millamant makes her first entry in the middle of the act. Mirabell describes it:

> She comes i'faith full sail, with her fan spread and
> streamers out, and a shoal of fools for tenders.

Millamant is not yet ready to make a public declaration of her feelings for Mirabell and there follows the first of the many exchanges of verbal steel which are the play's especial delight. To assist his matrimonial schemes, Mira-bell has invented an uncle, Sir Rowland. This creation is to be portrayed by his servant Waitwell, that day married to Lady Wishfort's maid Foible, thus providing them with an ally in the Wishfort household.

Act III Lady Wishfort's house. Lady Wishfort is about her toilet. The progress of this endeavour is seriously hindered by the absence of Foible. When the maid arrives she is accused by Lady Wishfort of intriguing with Mira-bell. She evades the accusation with news of the arrival of

Sir Rowland and advises her mistress to marry Sir Rowland and thus disinherit Mirabell. Lady Wishfort's nephew, Sir Wilfull Witwoud arrives from the country. It is Lady Wishfort's plan that he shall marry Millamant, thus preserving her fortune to the family. Fainall plots with Mrs Marwood to cheat Mirabell out of Millamant and himself into a fortune. He will threaten to make public the earlier liaison between Mrs Fainall and Mirabell and use the threat of disgrace to attach himself to his wife's fortune and Lady Wishfort's fortune.

Act IV Lady Wishfort's house. Sir Wilfull subjects Millamant to some country wooing. This is contrasted with the exchange between Mirabell and Millamant known as the 'proviso' scene:

> *Millamant* Positively, Mirabell, I'll lie abed in a morning as early as I please.
> *Mirabell* Then I'll get up in a morning as early as I please.
> *Millamant* Ah! Idle creature, get up when you will – And d'ye hear, I won't be called names after I'm married; positively I won't be called names.
> *Mirabell* Names!
> *Millamant* Ay, as wife, spouse, my dear, joy, jewel, love, sweetheart, and the rest of that nauseous cant, in which men and their wives are so fulsomely familiar – I shall never bear that – Good Mirabell, don't let us be familiar or fond, nor kiss before folks, like my Lady Fadler and Sir Francis: nor go to Hyde Park together the first Sunday in a new chariot, to provoke eyes and whispers; and then never to be seen there together again; as if we were proud of one another the first week, and ashamed of one another ever after. Let us never visit together, nor go to a play together, but let us be very strange and well bred: let us be as strange as if we had been married a great while; and as well bred as if we were not married at all.

Mirabell lays down his provisos as well and agreement is reached. This happy accord is interrupted by Mrs Fain-

all's warning that Lady Wishfort approaches. The three
fools Witwoud, Petulant and Sir Wilfull are all drunk
and have to be hurried out of sight before the entrance of
Waitwell disguised as 'Sir Rowland'. He is a suitably impatient lover. Dancers are called for. This revelry is cut
short by the delivery into Lady Wishfort's hands of a
letter from Marwood exposing 'Sir Rowland' as a fraud.
Foible's quick wit suggests that Waitwell should deny all
and maintain that it is an evil device of his supposed
nephew. Lady Wishfort accepts these explanations.
Act V Lady Wishfort's house. Between the acts all has
been discovered. Lady Wishfort is in the process of ex-
pelling Foible from the house, Waitwell has already been
delivered over to the constables. Mrs Fainall comforts
Foible with the assurance that Mirabell has gone to give
security for her husband. Marwood and Fainall have
brought about this discovery. Lady Wishfort accuses her
daughter of being among those plotting against her. Mrs
Fainall denies the accusation. Fainall presses home his advantage. He will publish his wife's earlier misconduct with
Mirabell if Lady Wishfort does not agree to hand over
Millamant's fortune. Fainall leaves to have articles formally drawn up. To Lady Wishfort come Millamant and Sir
Wilfull. Millamant seeming to accept him and he to
accept her. Thus when Fainall produces the document
for Lady Wishfort's signature she is able to refuse him.
Mirabell exposes Fainall's liaison with Marwood. He follows this up by producing a deed which protects Mrs Fainall's estates from her husband's depredations. Fainall is
thoroughly exposed and thwarted. Sir Wilfull resigns
Millamant to Mirabell.

Critical commentary

The reigns of Charles II and James II saw a reaction
against the Puritanism of the previous generation, which
made anything resembling preachment detestable. Lib-

ertinage was flaunted and affected, the court almost lending support to an atmosphere of witty decadence. Actual morals were probably no worse than in any other period but such was the antipathy towards the hypocrisy of the Commonwealth that dissipation was displayed almost as a virtue. Our examination of the drama of this period has shown that dramatic writers reflected rather than supported such behaviour. With the coming of William and Mary libertinism became less fashionable and moderation began to assert itself. *The Way of the World* is an exposure of false wit. Appetite is outwitted by reason. There is far less burying of the moral elements in sexual fooling and witty frivolity. The characters held up for our admiration and disapproval are much more certain in their beliefs than those of Etherege and the playwrights of the reign of Charles II. Like Dorimant, Mirabell is a reformed rake, but this reformation has taken place before the play's beginning and his libertinage has been more exclusive. His refusal to satisfy Marwood, although such action would have been to his advantage, and his inability to carry his flattery of Lady Wishfort to its ultimate conclusion argue a discrimination above that of Dorimant and his fellows. His affair with Mrs Fainall was in the past when that lady was herself a widow, and thus excusable under the prevailing moral code. There is nothing more than a firm friendship and respect between them during the action of the play.

The lightness of touch in the characterization of Millamant looks forward to a more idealized femininity. Her affectation is presented as charming fancy and as a shield assumed for the world. Her affection for Mirabell is real but it does not please her to reveal it before she is ready.

Fainall is a more old fashioned wit. His attitudes are not very different from those of Horner in *The Country Wife* and Dorimant yet the play is an indictment of these attitudes. His way is 'the way of the world', a way of marital infidelity and treachery and it is defeated by the honesty and reason of Mirabell and Millamant. The idea that basic good nature and reason go together which lies at the heart of this play acts as a prologue to the sentimental comedy of the next 150 years.

Clifford Leech in his article 'Congreve and the Century's End' compares the work of Congreve, Cibber and Steele to draw the same basic conclusion as is discovered above in terms of Vanbrugh's *The Relapse*. Congreve anticipates the optimistic concern with hard-pressed virtue which was to dominate eighteenth-century comedy but his work is a truer summation of what has gone before than either Vanbrugh or Cibber. Where they juggle with conflicting moral standpoints, Congreve is able to fashion a world where the villainy of Fainall and Lady Wishfort can be exposed calmly and without the animus of Etherege and Wycherley and at the same time include Mirabell's thoroughly believable reformation. His wit is tempered by consideration and there is nothing defensive or apologetic about his seriousness. He is however sufficiently rooted in the traditions of the decades which preceded him to have a distinction and authority which the more ephemeral work of Cibber and Vanbrugh lacks.

Congreve was born ten years after the Restoration and all his work dates from after the Revolution. He is the John the Baptist of the Age of Reason but the Age of Reason was yet to come. His exquisite lightness of tone, which even that arch-enemy of late seventeenth-century comedy Macaulay was forced to admire, serves to obscure a dramatist as concerned as Jonson and Wycherley. Yet unlike most writers of serious comedy one never feels that he hates or despises the foolish or their folly, rather he shares with Chekov an immense capacity for pity. It is this sensitivity which is sometimes overlooked in too much attention to his style. It is worth considering the idea that

Congreve's brilliant precision is a deliberate cloak for a seriousness perceived perhaps only by Hazlitt when he wrote of *The Way of the World* that it was:

> . . . an essence almost too fine, and the sense of pleasure evaporates in an aspiration after something that seems too exquisite ever to have been realised.

The Funeral, or
Grief à la Mode
Richard Steele (1672–1729)

Steele is probably best known today for his contributions to the *Tatler* and the *Spectator* but his position in the history of English theatre is equally significant. Born in Dublin in 1672 he is yet another in the large list of Irish contributors to the English stage. He started his association with Joseph Addison when they were pupils together at Charterhouse in the late 1680s. They were both educated at Oxford. In 1694 he enlisted as a private in a Guards regiment. Private soldiers in such regiments were the sons of gentlemen and by 1700 we find him referred to as 'Captain' Steele, on terms of intimacy with the leading dramatists of the day such as Vanbrugh and Congreve. A soldier engaged in guard duties at the Tower of London was almost automatically involved in a mildly debauched life. Steele was a man of high principles which he enjoyed breaking. To remind himself of these same principles he wrote a tract, called *The Christian Hero* 'an argument proving that no principles but those of religion are sufficient to make a great man'. The effect of this work was to make Steele very unpopular with his friends. They had thought him an agreeable bottle companion, a good man to go whoring with and here he had turned preacher. To regain the good opinion of his literary friends Steele wrote his first comedy, *The Funeral, or Grief à la Mode* (1701).

The convenient labelling of authors who produced the

bulk of their work prior to the century's end as Restoration is not simply an accident of date. 1700 was the year of Dryden's death and it was the year of Congreve's last play, *The Way of the World*. Two years earlier Jeremy Collier, a non-juring clergyman, had published his *Short View of the Profaneness and Immorality of the English Stage*. This had led to replies from Congreve, Dennis and others but there were many who accepted a great deal of Collier's criticism, Steele among them.

Steele followed *The Funeral* with *The Lying Lover* (1703) and *The Tender Husband* (1705) before turning his energies to essay writing. He remained in touch with the theatre supplying prologues for the plays of other authors. In 1719–20 he produced the first English theatrical journal *The Theatre*. This appeared twice a week. His last play *The Conscious Lovers* (1722) is an adaptation of the *Andria* of Terence. Steele himself said that his main purpose in writing it was to work in the duel scene in the fourth act, which condemns duelling and ridicules the contemporary standards of honour: '... decisions a tyrant custom has introduced, to the breach of all laws both divine and human'. That Steele should attack something so sacred as society's concept of honour shows his courage and individuality but it also indicates the return of sensible middle-class attitudes. The play sparked off controversy. Dennis, one of the opponents of Collier twenty years earlier, led the opposition. It was quickly translated into German and French and contributed to the European vogue for *comédie larmoyante*. Steele completed nothing more for the stage although he left two further fragments, *The School of Action*, which has for its scene a theatre, mistaken by a lady's guardian for an inn and *The Gentleman*, the beginnings of a dramatized version of a paper in the *Spectator* on how servants ape their masters. The former may well have given Goldsmith the idea for *She Stoops To Conquer*.

DATE 1701

CAST

Lord Brumpton
Lord Hardy, son to Lord Brumpton, in love with Lady
Sharlot
Mr Campley, in love with Lady Harriot
Mr Trusty, steward to Lord Brumpton
Cabinet
Mr Sable, an undertaker
Puzzle, a lawyer
Trim, servant to Lord Hardy
Tom, the lawyer's clerk
Lady Brumpton
Lady Sharlot ⎫   orphan sisters left in ward
Lady Harriot ⎭   to Lord Brumpton
Madamoiselle D'Epingle
Tattleaid, Lady Brumpton's woman
Mrs Fardingale
Kate Matchlock
SCENE Covent Garden

Plot

Act I Lord Brumpton's house in Covent Garden. Lord
Brumpton is recently supposed to have died and Cabinet
and Sable are making the arrangements of mourning.
They discuss the fashionable affectations of grief with the
gravedigger, layers out and others. This atmosphere of
exaggerated grief is shattered by the entrance of the supposed corpse, Lord Brumpton, and his steward Trusty.
Trusty has persuaded his master to take advantage of his
seeming death to test his wife's fidelity. One conversation
overheard between Lady Brumpton and Tattleaid her
maid in which she boasts how she cleverly persuaded her,
as she believes, late husband to disinherit Lord Hardy his
son by a former marriage, is enough to prove the truth of
the steward's assertions. In this conversation it is also re-

vealed that Lady Hardy has been enjoying an affair with
Cabinet a creature of the town. Trusty reasons Lord
Brumpton from immediately speaking out promising if
Lord Brumpton be patient to set all to rights.

Act II,*i* Lord Hardy's lodgings. Lord Hardy lies under
the obligatory penury of all young men of the drama of
this period, but his fortune has been dispersed not so
much by rakehelly behaviour as from generosity and misfortune. He is a captain in the army and his recruits have
eaten his last guinea. He and his friend Tom Campley
discuss their love for the ladies Sharlot and Harriot, the
wards of Lord Brumpton, placed by Lady Brumpton
under the care of a Mrs Fardingale, an elderly female
relative of Campley's. By her the young men shall have
access to the ladies. Campley contrives to give Trim a note
for £300, sensitively frightening Hardy from the room by
offering to read him verses, and thus sparing him the
embarrassment of receiving the money in person. His
purse full, Hardy is still generous. He sends Trim to pay
his debts, ordering him should he meet with any needy
officers to send them to him for help. *ii* Lord Brumpton's
house. Lord Brumpton and Trusty bribe the undertaker
to keep their secret. *iii* Another room in Lord Brumpton's
house. With the assistance of Mrs Fardingale, Campley
and Hardy woo and win their mistresses. This is not
achieved until after Campley has chased Harriot around
the stage. The lovers are interrupted by Lady Brumpton
and the young men exeunt precipitously. A confrontation
and declaration of war between Lady Brumpton and her
wards follows.

Act III Lord Hardy's lodgings. Campley has received a
letter from Harriot informing him that the widow has
designs on the fortunes of the girls. They persuade Trim's
friend Madamoiselle D'Epingle to insinuate Campley into
Lord Brumpton's house dressed as her maid. Hardy's
nature is again demonstrated when Trim requests that his
master should treat him as a familiar rather than as a

servant in front of Madamoiselle to which Hardy good-naturedly agrees:

> Pish is that all. I understand you; your mistress does
> not know that you do me the honour to clean my shoes or
> so, upon occasion. Pr'ythee, Will, make yourself as
> considerable as you please.

ii Lady Brumpton's room. That good lady enacts the grief stricken widow for the benefit of her society friends, while the reputations of their acquaintance are ruthlessly destroyed by scandal. Campley in his woman's weeds gains footing inside the house. He persuades Harriot to change clothes with Madamoiselle and thus disguised escape from the house. The conventions are fully observed, for when Madamoiselle offers to undress then and there, Harriot restrains her and the ladies exit to effect the change.

Act IV,*i* Lord Brumpton's house. Lady Brumpton thinks she has won Trusty to her side by assurance of bribes. Trusty will not yet reveal the truth to Hardy lest that young man act in passion and dishonour his father by a scandal. *ii* Lord Hardy's lodgings. Trusty comes to Hardy with the strange proposal that the young man should employ his recruits to seize his father's coffin as it is borne out of the house. Such is Hardy's confidence in the steward that he agrees to this plan without question, accepting it as being in his own and Sharlot's interest. *iii* Covent Garden. Hardy reviews the company he has raised for the French war.

Act V,*i* Lord Brumpton's house. The last remnants of Lord Brumpton's feeling for his wife are stripped away when he intercepts a letter from her to her brother instructing him to rape Sharlot. Trusty can now begin to initiate the final series of reconciliations and exposures. *ii* Covent Garden. Trim instructs the recruits for their assault upon the coffin. *iii* Lord Brumpton's house. The audience are given a final reminder of the depth of Lady

Brumpton's grief when she suffers the additional loss of a
pet squirrel which affects her much more nearly:

> *Tattleaid* Alas! alas! we are all mortal. Consider
> madam, my lord's dead too.
> *Widow* Ay, but our animal friends do wholly die; an
> husband or relation, after death, is rewarded
> or tormented.

The announcement of the seizure of the coffin sends her
post haste to Hardy's lodgings. *iv* Lord Hardy's lodgings.
Sharlot is discovered inside the coffin and reunited with
Hardy. Cabinet has seen Lord Brumpton and believing
him to be a ghost confessed that Lady Brumpton was
secretly married to him six months before she married
Lord Brumpton. This not only ties her and Cabinet together but conveniently removes the horns from the brow
of the worthy peer and places them on Cabinet's own. The
play ends with a suitably patriotic song.

Critical commentary

Although Congreve is less bawdy than many of his predecessors he still addresses himself to a restricted minority.
Steele's approach is more consciously popular. At this time
the Restoration play-going élite had been joined and even
in part replaced by the socially aspiring, a strata of society
one rung below those who made up the bulk of theatre
audiences twenty years previously. This newer audience
was in turn beginning to find itself sharing the auditorium
with the middle classes. Citizens and their wives for the
main part lived a life of flagrantly open morality and the
result was the playwrights were forced to remove much of
the bawdy element from their work. Steele is different
from his contemporaries because he, almost alone, cam-
paigns for a new kind of comedy. The basic theory of
comedy was that it showed low characters, as opposed to

tragedy which portrayed high and noble characters. Tragedy, as we have seen, aimed to evoke admiration. Comedy by exposing the follies of the low evoked scorn. It was to be hoped if the comedy was truly successful that the spectator might at a later date take the lesson which he had so scornfully received in the playhouse and apply it to himself. If comedy fulfilled its theoretical aims it was a form which could evoke discomfort. This should have satisfied Steele's rigidly moral ideals but it did not and he continually argues in his critical writings that common popular comedy feeds the self-esteem and pride of the spectator. Even the discomfort which he allows it capable of imparting he finds offensive to virtue.

At this time there are three kinds of comedy being written, together with an indeterminate number of mixtures of these types. The most popular and successful type of comedy prior to Steele is basically critical, with a main aim to reform 'low' characters. Ideas are important but they are never allowed to distract from the action and entertainment. Into this broad class fall the comedies of Shakespeare and Jonson, together with the works of Etherege, Wycherley, Congreve and Farquhar. The second type of comedy is exemplary, it relies on high ideals misunderstood. The characters are presented as either good or beyond reform. The world is benevolent and the ideas openly didactic. The third type of comedy is that written for instant consumption. To conveniently label these three types they are: (i) critical comedy (ii) comedy of ideas (iii) popular comedy.

In *The Funeral* Steele, almost but not quite, invents the comedy of ideas. Although there had been attempts in the work of lesser writers such as Shadwell, D'Urfey and Ravenscroft to forestall Steele's theories, he alone had the reforming vigour to establish them on the stage. *The Funeral* is a seminal discovery of a viable formula where intrigue, humour and satire make benevolent moral pur-

pose and serious characters acceptable to an audience
whose basic desire, whatever moralists and essayists may
have told them, was to be entertained.

Steele to a far greater degree than Shaw, whose work he
to large extent forestalls, has too fine an instinctive sense
of theatre to ever totally follow his own theories, although
these do interfere in his free creation. One reads with sad
amusement in number 51 of the *Spectator* how Steele
altered the dialogue at the beginning of Act II between
Sharlot and Campley lest it offend delicate modesty. The
text as first performed and as we now have it reads:

> *Campley* O that Harriot! To embrace that Beauteous ...

and Campley is interrupted by Hardy's comment that his
mind runs too much on the wedding night and that
marriage is something purer. Hardy's moralizing makes
much more sense in answer to the original speech:

> O that Harriot! to fold these arms about the waist
> of that struggling – and at last yielding fair!

We have to this point circumvented any use of the term
most commonly applied to Steele's work – 'Sentimental.'
This is because there is as yet no agreed critical definition
of the term, although for most of us it has strong negative
connotations. The term 'exemplary comedy' more truly
captures the positive reforming zeal which underwrites
Steele's achievements as a dramatist. 'Sentimental' implies
an enjoyment of tears which more properly belongs to the
comedy in vogue half a century later. Unfortunately much
that is written in the next fifty years is not so much a development of Steele's ideas as a compromise with them.

This play signals the clear emergence of a set of stock
comic characters which will survive almost unchanged
into the twentieth century. The first pair of lovers are
often less interesting than their secondary foils, for the
first pair are limited by a need to be noble and worthy, if
very often victims of adversity. The second pair have

greater freedom; this is clearly demonstrated here where Campley and Harriot are infinitely more human than Sharlot and Hardy. The last generation reacted against and mocked their elders, often holding them up to ridicule as slaves of old fashioned passion in an age of reason. There now enters into the drama, in the person of Lord Brumpton, the stock old man, the embodiment of solid virtue, and his companion the faithful old retainer. With *The Funeral* comedy takes a sharp right turn. Its importance as a seminal influence on the development of English comedy cannot be overstressed.

The Recruiting Officer
George Farquhar (1677–1707)

Another Irish contributor to the English theatre, Farquhar was born in Londonderry where he was educated at the grammar school. His father was a Protestant clergyman who is said to have died of grief when James II's troops burnt down his rectory in 1688. Two years later the orphan, then thirteen years old, marched with William III's troops to the battle of the Boyne.

At seventeen he went to Trinity College, Dublin. He left without a degree. It was during this period that he first became friends with the actor, Robert Wilks, who was to create most of the leading roles in Farquhar's plays, including Plume, in *The Recruiting Officer*. After leaving university Farquhar became an actor at the Theatre Royal, Dublin. He was not a distinguished actor, and he finally abandoned this career after accidentally wounding a fellow actor in a fight scene during Dryden's *The Indian Emperor*. The actor recovered but Farquhar stuck to his decision to retire from acting. The company gave him the proceeds of a benefit. He used this to start himself in London. For the first two years of his London career Farquhar hung around the fringes of the literary circle which frequented Will's coffee house. Under the chairmanship of John Dryden this included all the well known playwrights of the time. His first play *Love In a Bottle* (1699) was favourably received and he followed this with *The Constant Couple*, with Wilks as Sir Harry Wildair. This

had an unprecedented run of fifty-three performances at
Drury Lane. Although this made Farquhar an acknowledged theatrical success it did not give him financial
security. A playwright made a certain amount from the
sale of his play to the booksellers. If the piece ran for three
nights he received a benefit which could amount to as
much as £100, after six performances he was granted a
second benefit. Any further payment was unusual, although Farquhar himself received a third benefit for *The
Recruiting Officer*. Farquhar married a widow, ten years
older than himself with three children, presumably for a
fortune he supposed her to possess. She was in fact without
any money and Farquhar's life became a constant struggle
against debt. He secured a commission as a Lieutenant of
Grenadiers which brought him just over fifty pounds a
year. This took him on recruiting duty to Lichfield, the
scene of his last play *The Beaux Stratagem* and to Shrewsbury, the scene of *The Recruiting Officer*. His superior
officers were not opposed to his writing a comedy about
recruiting procedures, even going so far as to give him
leave to go to London to arrange for the production of
The Recruiting Officer (1706). Its outstanding success was
not enough to rescue his failing finances. By this time he
was also suffering from tuberculosis. Wilks gave him
twenty guineas to tide him over. The dying Farquhar
wrote his last play *The Beaux Stratagem* and this was presented on the 8 March 1707, seven weeks later Farquhar
was dead. His friend Robert Wilks paid for his funeral at
St Martin-in-the-Fields. It is extraordinary to think what
he might have achieved if he had lived, considering that
all of his work was written before he was thirty.

DATE 1706
CAST
Mr Balance ⎫
Mr Scale   ⎬   three justices
Mr Scruple ⎭

Mr Worthy, a gentleman of Shropshire
Captain Plume $\Big\}$ two recruiting officers
Captain Brazen
Kite, sergeant to Plume
Bullock, a country clown
Coster Pearmain $\Big\}$ two recruits
Thomas Appletree
Pluck, a butcher
Thomas, a smith
Melinda, a lady of fortune
Silvia, daughter to Balance, in love with Plume
Lucy, Melinda's maid
Rose, a country wench
SCENE Shrewsbury

Plot

Act I The market place. The drums beat and Sergeant
Kite exhorts the locals of Shrewsbury to join the army.
Captain Plume enters. Kite reports to him that recruiting
is going well, even if he has accidentally enlisted a lawyer.
This must be put right and the fellow discharged, as a
man in the ranks who can write is a man in the ranks who
can draw up petitions. A further recruit is obtained when
Plume learns that one of his mistresses has given birth to
a son. This is taken care of by Kite agreeing to marry the
wench and add her to a long list of wives, while Plume
engages to enter the boy upon the roll as Francis Kite,
absent on furlough and allow him full pay. After all it is
a maxim among recruiting officers to leave as many recruits in the country as they carry out of it. We are then
told how Kite uses the disguise of a fortune teller to boost
recruitment. Plume's friend Worthy is much cast down.
He had been making good progress in his siege of Melinda.
She was about to capitulate on terms of marriage until she
inherited £20,000. Now she has become proud and
haughty towards Worthy. Plume repays his friend's con-

fidences by admitting that he himself is more than half in love with Silvia. Kite comes to them with the news that Silvia has heard about the boy and sent the mother ten guineas. The scene closes with the news that there is a second recruiting officer in the town. This officer is Captain Brazen, Worthy's rival for Melinda. *ii* Melinda's apartment. Silvia is the ideal, understanding woman and obviously has great spirit. In contrast Melinda is exploring a certain languid affectation. Silvia chides her cousin for turning this against Worthy. The result is a quarrel and Silvia leaves.

Act II,*i* An apartment in Justice Balance's house. Justice Balance tries to draw Plume into military reminiscence but tolerantly abandons him to Silvia when he sees his mind is elsewhere. Silvia brings up the subject of Plume's bastard but there seems nothing to prevent Plume, Balance and Silvia coming to an agreement. But Balance receives news that Silvia's brother is dying and as this will make her his heir Plume's pretensions are no longer welcome. *ii* Another apartment. The boy dies and Balance extracts a solemn promise from Silvia that she will not dispose of herself without his consent. *iii* The street. Kite tricks two countrymen into enlisting. They deny the enlistment but pretended kindness from Plume secures them for his sergeant and they march off singing.

Act III,*i* The market place. Kite detains Bullock with military stories while Plume carries his sister Rose off to his lodgings. Bullock becomes worried that Plume intends to 'press' his sister. Balance intervenes to ask Kite to restore Rose. Balance is concerned to help Plume fill up his quota of recruits and to speed him from the country before he becomes, literally, the father of his company. The extraordinary Brazen makes his first appearance:

> . . . his impudence were a prodigy were not his ignorance proportionable. He has the most universal acquaintance of any man living; for he won't be alone, and nobody will

keep him company twice. Then he's a Caesar among the women, *Veni, Vidi, Vici*, that's all: if he has but talked with the maid, he swears he has lain with the mistress. But the most surprising part of his character is his memory, which is the most prodigious and the most trifling in the world.

It is absurd that Worthy should pay him the compliment of supposing that Melinda entertains him for any other purpose but to arouse Worthy's jealousy. He, Worthy and Balance exchange amusing trifles to introduce the character. He leaves to meet Melinda. Rose enters and innocently shows Balance the gifts she has received from Plume. Plume, following her, realizes that Balance will have correctly interpreted his designs on the girl and hastily makes himself scarce. *ii* The walk by the Severn side. Brazen woos Melinda. She is more irritated than amused by his effrontery until Worthy enters, when she walks off with her arm on the captain's in the most familiar manner. Plume enters slightly drunk and on the re-entry of Brazen can only contrive to look as sober and demure as a whore at a christening. After accepting Brazen's kiss, Plume pretends to favour Melinda. Brazen challenges him. The quarrel is avoided by the entrance of Silvia in man's clothes, calling herself Jack Wilful. The two officers vie with each other to enlist the supposed youth, Plume even offering to share his bed with him.

Act IV,*i* The walk by the Severn. Silvia in her character as a rake takes Rose from Plume. He is quite willing to let the girl go provided Silvia enlists with him. The bargain is struck. Plume repeats his offer to let the youth share his bed but is reminded that he/she already has a bedfellow in Rose. *ii* The same. Melinda has visited the fortune teller (Kite) where she learnt she is in grave danger of dying a maid. Coupled with this, following the advice of Plume, Worthy pretends to ignore her. Brazen enters and seizes her round the waist. Thinking, or pretending to think, that it is Worthy that so presumes, she cuffs him. Seeing this Worthy begins to think that Plume has given him bad advice and is only half reassured when Plume maintains that all goes well and another visit to Kite·will secure the lady for him. *iii* A chamber. Kite in the disguise of an astrologer promises two countrymen that they will make their fortunes if they enlist. Melinda and Lucy enter. Kite convinces Melinda that a gentleman (Worthy) will call on her at about ten the next day preparatory to leaving for abroad. It is important that she should not let him go.

Act V,*i* An anteroom adjoining Silvia's bedchamber. Rose is disappointed after an uneventful night, but Silvia is arrested at Bullock's suit on the charge of seducing his sister. She is delighted at the chance of being brought before Justice Balance and surrenders her sword. *ii* Justice Balance's house. Silvia, her disguise undiscovered, is most insolent to her father and Justice Scale. *iii* Melinda's apartment. She and Worthy are reconciled and she sets out for Justice Balance's house to make up her quarrel with Silvia. *iv* The market place. Worthy discovers that Melinda may yet be false as it would appear Brazen has a letter from her. *v* A court of justice. In order to teach 'Jack Wilful' a lesson the justices hand her over to Plume. Thus has Silvia kept her promise to her father to give herself to no man except upon his order. *vi* The fields. Brazen's letter was from Lucy and but for Worthy's interruption he would have found himself duped into marrying the maid. *vii* Justice Balance's house. Silvia's absence has been discovered and a suit of her brother's clothes is also found to be missing. Balance realizes that 'Wilful' was Silvia. His thought is that Plume and Silvia have arranged the deception between them. He soon discovers that Plume is ignorant of the identity of his recruit. Plume writes 'Wilful's' discharge. Balance redelivers the discovered Silvia to Plume. Melinda begs pardon for slandering Plume to Balance after her quarrel with Silvia. Plume commands her to make reparation to Worthy. Even Brazen is satisfied for Plume declares his intention to resign his commission and makes a free gift of all the recruits he has gathered to his brother officer.

Critical commentary

The Recruiting Officer offers us a chance to consolidate our attitudes to that group of comedies written between 1660 and 1710 which custom and practice has loosely and confusingly labelled 'Restoration'. As we have already complained the taking of the year 1660 as a starting point is misleading for the Restoration dramatists inherited an established dramatic structure from their Caroline predecessors, but for all the obvious absurdities of starting at 1660 it is something we must accept as imposed upon us by traditional course structure. Our problems in understanding the links between the drama of the first half of the seventeenth century and the drama after the Restoration of the monarchy stem from the fact that we have over distilled the study of this period into a selection of too few authors. In comedy we examine only the work of Etherege, Wycherley, Vanbrugh and Congreve supporting this with Dryden, Otway and Rowe in tragedy. This is to exclude a vast amount of diverse writing and give us an atypical view of the period. We have over the years refined our study to exclude all but the very best but the very things which attract us to some writers over others are their refusal to conform to a contemporary pattern.

Farquhar is such a writer. All his work is certainly atypical of the early eighteenth century and studied alongside that of the four comic writers selected above, he appears to be the inheritor of a tradition established by them. Such a simplistic view is to ignore the irreversible process which had begun with Steele. The obvious difference between the plays of 1660–70 and the plays written at the end of the century is one of exclusiveness. If we lump Farquhar in with his predecessors we ignore an audience revolution which had taken place. To a certain extent Congreve does this and this is why *The Way of the World* failed in 1700 while Steele succeeded with *The Funeral* in 1701. Farquhar would appear to follow Steele and not Congreve in that he rejects the Restoration–Caroline theory that the aim of comedy was to recommend virtue and discourage vice by realistically copying the characters and manners of the time. Certainly he makes little use of the main seventeenth-century comic weapons, irony and scorn. Rather, he is genially realistic and the coming of sentimental comedy is prophesied in the basic good nature of his plays. Farquhar, unlike Steele, is not a reformer or dramatic theorist. There is no sense in his work of seeking to renew comedy's moral purpose by any deliberate following of Steele's theory of exemplary comedy, but at the same time his work is always sensitive to a growing audience impatience with satire, which is by its nature the ridicule of the many by an exclusive few. Farquhar mellows the vintage of Etherege and Wycherley by an enjoyment of uninhibited burlesque. Thus Brazen is celebrated rather than criticized as someone who makes our lives the brighter by his existence.

With burlesque replacing satire *The Recruiting Officer* can retain the realism of the previous generations. It is however a much more genial realism. Although the characters and plot situations are of an older vintage than those of Steele they are startlingly fresh and new in comparison with Restoration or Caroline drama. Farquhar, without attempting the drastic theoretical upheavals of Steele, succeeds in making an alternative jump into the Augustan age which Congreve for all his posthumous success had failed to make. His work must be understood as making a forward move and the careless assumption that he harps back to earlier periods ignored. It is to belittle him to consider him an Etherege or Wycherley *manqué*.

What then are the changes? The simplest but in many ways most blatant difference between Farquhar and his predecessors lies in his preference for rustic settings over the tired pleasures of the town. This allows him in spite of an appearance of realism to create a comic world requiring a certain suspension of belief. In fact Lamb's famous apology for Restoration drama, which claims that as the world of comedy was artificial and unreal normal moral judgements cannot be applied to it, would seem to a great extent true when applied to Farquhar's comic world. This is borne out by Farquhar's own statement on the problem of realism in 'Discourse upon Comedy'. In this he condemns 'unnaturalness' but also argues against 'verisimilitude':

> The poet does not impose contradictions upon you because he has told you no lie; for that is only a lie which is related with some fallacious intention that you should believe it for a truth; now the poet expects no more that you should believe the plot of his play, than old Aesop designed that the world should think his eagle and lion talked like you and I ... If you are so inveterate against improbabilities you must never come near the playhouse at all; for there are several improbabilities, nay, impossibilities, that all the criticisms in nature cannot correct; as for instance in the part of Alexander the Great ... we must suppose that we see that great conqueror ... yet the whole audience at the same time knows that this is Mr Betterton who is strutting upon the stage and tearing his lungs for a livelihood.

Farquhar then has a very real appreciation of the unreality of the theatre which helps him to rework timeworn theatrical devices so that we scarcely recognize them for the clichés that they are: Silvia's trick upon her father and Plume is no more than a romanticized version of the Jacobean bed-trick, we could not possibly believe it outside the context of the play. It is justified by convention rather than reality.

The characterization suggests the eighteenth rather than the seventeenth century. This is most clearly apparent in the treatment of the ladies who are appreciably elevated, even Rose being treated with a good natured sympathy entirely alien to the previous generation. The old men have also radically altered. Thirty years before, age had been presented as a senile contrast to the new reason but now in Balance we discover the first stirrings of the stock good old man character who will become such a respected figure in eighteenth and nineteenth century drama. In spite of the appearance of realism man's basic good nature is exalted at the expense of his other side. Thus, remarkably when one remembers Farquhar's own unhappy marriage, the main plot exalts marriage for love over marriage for fortune by the simple device of having Plume start his advances to Silvia *before* he learns that she has become an heiress. Even the treatment of recruitment is affectionate and in its way as idealized as Steele's portrait of the soldier who had saved Campey's life at the battle of Steinkirk re-enlisting after being whipped from constable to constable all the way from Cornwall to London.

The sexuality of the Restoration wits is replaced by acceptable bawdy behaviour. Comparison between the implied homosexuality in Brazen and Plume's attraction to Jack Wilful and Coupler's pawing of Young Fashion in *The Relapse* underlines the change.

One notes finally a subtle encroachment of bourgeois values in the gentle raillery at the expense of Melinda's assumption of fashionable airs and graces.

Cato
Joseph Addison (1672–1719)

Addison was educated at Charterhouse and Queen's College, then Magdalen College, Oxford. This was followed by a period of continental travel by embarking on a political and literary career. He was the author of three dramatic works: *Rosamund* an opera (1707); *Cato* (1713); and a moral comedy called *The Drummer* (1715). With Steele he contributed to dramatic theory and criticism in the *Tatler* and the *Spectator*. The *Tatler* number 42 (1709) gives an amusing satirical inventory of the properties owned by the Drury Lane Theatre.

DATE 1713
CAST
Cato
Lucius, a senator
Sempronius, a senator
Juba, Prince of Numidia
Syphax, general of the Numidians
Portius ⎫
Marcus ⎭ sons of Cato
Decius, ambassador from Caesar
Marcia, daughter to Cato
Lucia, daughter to Lucius
SCENE A large hall in the governor's palace of Utica.

Plot

Act I,*i* The sons of Cato talk together. We learn that
Caesar has defeated Pompey and Cato is pent up in Utica
with a remnant of the Roman Senate. Both brothers are
in love with Lucia. Portius has concealed his love from
his brother. He urges Marcus to suppress passion. Marcus
exits lest the entering Sempronius should discover this
weakness. *ii* Sempronius enters to Portius. He announces
that Cato has called a meeting of the Senate. Privately he
expresses a desire to marry Marcia. Portius puts him off
with the argument that a time of civil danger is not a time
to talk of love. Sempronius is revealed in Machiavelian
soliloquy. Cato has refused him his daughter Marcia, so it
is Sempronius's intention to claim her from Caesar as a reward for betraying the city. *iii* Syphax, Sempronius. The
Numidians are about to revolt to Caesar. Only Juba, their
prince, is incorruptible. *iv* Juba, Syphax. Syphax tries to
corrupt Juba. Juba is in love with Marcia but he admires
Cato's stoicism and ability to conquer passion. *v* Juba,
Marcia and Lucia. Marcia reproves Juba for allowing her
presence to slacken his resolve to fight. He accepts the
justice of the rebuke. *vi* Marcia, Lucia. Lucia chides
Marcia for being too severe on the prince and is answered
with the rebuke that this is no time for love. Lucia prefers
Portius over Marcus.

Act II,*i* The Senate. Sempronius urges that their choice is
death or slavery. Lucius speaks for peace. Sempronius
accuses him of treachery. Cato takes the middle way.
Marcus enters with the news that Decius demands to speak
with Cato. *ii* Decius, the Senate. Decius brings an offer of
friendship from Caesar. Cato rejects this in the name of
liberty. *iii* The Senate. Sempronius and Lucius bicker.
iv Juba, the Senate. Juba offers Cato an asylum in Numidia. He urges that the Kings of Africa would flock to his
standard. Cato rejects this offer considering that to fly
from Caesar would admit defeat. He asks the young prince

if there is any favour he can grant. Juba mentions his love for Marcia and is again sternly rebuked that this is not the time for private emotion. *v* Syphax, Juba. Syphax suggests that the Numidians should carry Marcia off. Juba is appalled at this insult to his honour. He calls Syphax a false old traitor. Although the pair seem reconciled by the end of the scene, Syphax is now wholly Caesar's. *vi* Syphax, Sempronius. The plot to betray Cato and Juba.

Act III,*i* Marcus, Portius. Marcus asks Portius to plead his suit with Lucia. Portius begs to be excused but Marcus insists. *ii* Portius, Lucia. Lucia asks why Marcus flies her presence. Portius explains his brother's love, also telling her of Marcus's request. She is appalled at the anguish she is causing the brothers during such a time of national need. She vows to cast out any thoughts of love for either of the brothers. *iii* Portius, Marcus. Returning, Marcus learns that Lucia feels only pity for him. *iv* Sempronius with the leaders of the mutiny. The mutineers feel safety from the friendship of Sempronius. *v* Cato, Sempronius, Lucius, Portius, Marcus and the leaders of the mutiny. Cato harangues the mutineers to such good effect that they submit. Sempronius asks that the leaders be given into his charge for execution. *vi* Sempronius and the leaders of the mutiny. The mutineers' confidence in Sempronius is rudely shattered when he orders their summary execution. *vii* Syphax, Sempronius. Syphax urges Sempronius to fly to Caesar. They devise that Syphax, dressed in Juba's clothes, will trick the guards into admitting him to Marcia's apartments. Once inside they will seize her and fly to Caesar.

Act IV,*i* Lucia, Marcia, Lucia laments the problem of being loved by two men. Marcia speaks of her two lovers, Juba and Sempronius, leaving us with no doubt of her contempt for Sempronius. *ii* Sempronius, dressed like Juba with Numidian guards. He is interrupted by the entry of Juba. Juba kills him. *iii* Lucia, Marcia. Marcia thinking the body is that of Juba, addresses it as the best of men. Juba entering and overhearing at first thinks she is praising Sempronius. When he realizes that Marcia is speaking of himself he steps forward. *iv* A march at a distance. Portius brings Cato and Lucius news of Syphax's treachery. Lucius again begs Cato to make peace with Caesar. He refuses. Juba enters ashamed of his countryman's treachery. Cato comforts him by pointing out that Rome has had her Caesars. Marcus has died fighting against the traitors. His body is brought in. Cato's total subjugation of emotion is almost inhuman:

> Welcome my son! Here lay him down, my friends,
> Full in my sight, that I may view at leisure
> The bloody corpse, and count these glorious wounds.
> – How beautiful is death, when earned by virtue!
> Who would not be that youth? What pity is it
> That we can die but once to serve our country!
> Why sits this sadness on your brows, my friends?
> I should have blushed if Cato's house had stood
> Secure and flourished in a civil war.
> – Portius, behold thy brother, and remember
> Thy life is not thy own, when Rome demands it.

This provokes from Juba the exclamation, 'Was ever man like this!' Cato resolves to commit suicide rather than submit to Caesar.

Act V, *i* Cato, in his hands Plato's book on the immortality of the soul. He soliloquizes on the hereafter. *ii* Cato, Portius. Portius tries to dissuade him from his resolve. Cato takes some comfort and sleeps. *iii* Portius, Marcia. They both wish for a sound sleep for their father. *iv* Lucia, Marcia. Lucia hopes to obtain Cato's consent for her to marry Portius. Lucius and Juba enter followed by Portius. Cato has fallen on his sword. He is brought out dying to give permission for Marcia to marry Juba and Portius, Lucia. Cato dies.

Critical commentary

At first sight this piece must appear little more than a
rag-bag of clichés, both of character and situation. We
have not one but two heroines of the uncomplaining,
submissively noble Indamora, Jane Shore type. Military
heroes in Portius and Juba, the latter also presenting us
with a noble savage, as ever, more noble than savage,
except presumably in his costume. Two brothers love one
woman, the nobler (we are told rather than shown that
this is so) concealing his love for impeccable motives.
There are reconciliation scenes, sound moral precepts and
'Romanism' carried to its extreme. Perhaps the greatest
absurdity for the modern reader is Cato's near happiness
at his son's death. That Addison's audience accepted his
intended value of Cato is proved by the now unthinkable
popularity of the play for the next eighty or so years.

Criticism of the above type is just the sort of reaction
we must put behind us. It is our duty to seek the virtues
of the play, to understand why it is written in the way
it is and appreciate Addison's positive attempt to achieve
something with the drama of his age. This play is certainly no pot-boiler climbing on to a Roman band wagon.
The plea for a middle road uninfluenced either by emotion, caution or party interest is sincerely put forward
and this aspect of the play seen in the context of the Peace
of Utrecht and the national fear of Bolingbroke and the
nonconformity bills must be acknowledged as sound
achievement. The contemporary political aspect of the
play is far from being its sole achievement. Addison is
trying to free tragedy from the growing shackles of poetic
justice. That this is definitely his intention is confirmed
by his essay in *Spectator* number 40. Poetic justice had
come to mean that virtue and innocence were rewarded
and the guilty punished, as in Tate's version of *King Lear*.
Addison's argument is that this removes terror from
tragedy. There is no doubt that he is correct and that the

drama of poetic justice almost totally replaces terror and fear with pity and anguish. *Cato* is potentially a more unsettling play than anything written by Dryden, Otway or Rowe. Addison has reduced the importance of love and although we have all the stage clichés of love, these serve no real dramatic purpose and are certainly not used to wet our handkerchiefs. The play is blatantly anti-love and anti-pity, hence Cato's extraordinary behaviour over the body of his son.

If he could have freed himself from the extreme classicism of the scenic arrangement and the syllabic competence of the verse, Addison might have achieved a startling, almost Shavian prose drama. His idea is the tragedy of the pointless death of a worthy hero rather than a dramatic effect manipulated through unfortunate love. In other words the destruction of an idea. Pope summarizes his intentions in the prologue:

> A brave man struggling in the storms of fate,
> And greatly falling with a falling state!

The failure for us is that Addison is unable to inspire us with real sympathy for his hero. He is not in sufficient command of his medium to achieve his intention. His means often appear pastiche, even imitation. He is obviously not a professional playwright, thus he can only imitate the dramatic form from great familiarity with the classical theatre and a more than working knowledge of the drama and dramatic theory of his own age; this is never more apparent than in his handling of blank verse. The utterly predictable end stopping gives the play a monotony which the recitative acting of the eighteenth century could exploit and even turn to advantage but which is an insuperable bar to any revival of the play outside the limits of early eighteenth century acting conventions. This is not to damn Addison as monotonous – very few users of blank verse during this period are better. His short end stop lines achieve a precision which more fluent blank verse often lacks. We have noted how heroic drama employed rhyme for this purpose and Addison's verse seems still to be conceived in couplets or at the best quatrains. It is very much of its time but a dramatic writer must use the method, vocabulary, and thought processes of his time. Even if he can see beyond this his audience cannot and it is poor criticism to be insensitive to general trends and blame a particular author for what at our privileged distance of time we should be able to recognize as weaknesses in the dramatic form of a whole period.

Cato is unsatisfactory for the modern reader but it contains the seeds that will lead to the break up of blank verse as the sole means of dramatic expression and it strikes a well intentioned but unsuccessful blow at the theatrical dominance of the anguish of fractured love and pity for star-crossed heroines.

Jane Shore
Nicholas Rowe (1674–1718)

Rowe was educated at Westminster. He entered the
Middle Temple in 1691. His father had been a barrister
and serjeant-at-law, and so one presumes that Rowe's
legal studies were somewhat less superficial than those of
other dramatists of the Caroline and Restoration period.
He abandoned the law when his father died leaving him
a competence. His first play *The Ambitious Stepmother*
was first presented in 1700 and two years later he followed
it with *Tamerlane*. Tamerlane stands for William III,
while Bajazet, steeped in vice and villainy, is Louis XIV.
The piece is full of topicality which makes it difficult
reading at this distance of time, yet it held the stage,
particularly on the anniversary of William III's landing.
It was with *The Fair Penitent* (1703) that Rowe wrote
himself into the repertory. Calista is, arguably, the best
vehicle for a tragic actress written in the English language.
The morals and manners of the play are totally alien
today but the opportunities it shows for an actress to
display a variety of moods, from petulance to pathos, are
unsurpassed. Richardson based Clarissa Harlowe on
Calista and Lovelace on the rake Lothario. *The Fair
Penitent* held the stage into this century. Then came the
unsuccessful comedy, *The Biter* (1704), *Ulysses* (1706) and
The Royal Convent (1707). There is a long gap before
Jane Shore (1715). This had an initial run of nineteen
performances and like *The Fair Penitent* continued in
the repertory into the early twentieth century. His last

play was *Lady Jane Grey* (1715). In 1715 he succeeded his fellow dramatist, Nahum Tate, as poet laureate.

Rowe's greatest contribution was as the first editor of Shakespeare. His edition was printed in 1709 in six volumes but his familiarity with Shakespeare is obvious as early as *The Fair Penitent*. His text, based on the corrupt fourth folio, has been discarded but his division into acts and scenes and the clarification of entries and exits remains the basis of modern texts. The biographical essay which introduces this edition was compiled from traditions collected by the actor Betterton who was able to draw on pre-Restoration traditions, and modern scholarship has added little to this statement.

DATE 1714

CAST

Richard, Duke of Gloster	Bellmour
Lord Hastings	Dumont
Catesby	Alicia
Sir Richard Ratcliffe	Jane Shore

SCENE London

Plot

Act I,*i* The Tower. The Lord Protector, Gloster is poised to usurp the crown. To him comes the Lord Chamberlain Hastings to speak on behalf of Jane Shore the late King's mistress. Richard hints that Hastings is rather too courteous to the lady to be entirely disinterested in his pleas on her behalf. Hastings protests that his attentions to her are no more than tender hearted charity but we are left in no doubt but that he intends to succeed his late master in her bed and that Richard intends to use Hastings' lack of control over his lusts to further his schemes. *ii* An apartment in Jane Shore's house. We are introduced to Jane, fallen on hard times and thus repentant. Her repentance has been aided by her loss of fortune but it is no less sincere for that. The age of reason would hardly have

accepted a heroine who repented purely on moral
grounds. Her neighbour Bellmour introduces her to her
own husband disguised as Dumont. Dumont in his first
speech declares, 'all my answers must be my future truth'
and then goes on to give a totally fictitious description of
his own funeral in Flanders. Jane is appropriately moved
and accepts Dumont as her servant. She explains that this
will entail becoming the partner in her misfortune for
there is little hope of lavish wages. The two men take
their leave as her supposed friend Alicia is announced.
Jane confides to Alicia that Hastings has promised to
plead for her cause. This immediately awakens Alicia's
jealousy for she is in love with Hastings. With no suspicion of this change in Alicia's feelings Jane entrusts her
few remaining jewels to her.

Act II Outside Jane Shore's house. Alicia takes her leave
of Jane as Hastings arrives. Hastings tries to persuade her
that his interest in Jane is avuncular. Disbelieved he dismisses her as a shrew. She leaves the stage threatening
revenge. Hastings now enters Jane's house. (Some explanation of early eighteenth-century staging may well explain
the slight confusion in the heading 'scene continues' at
the top of this act in most printed editions. At the start
Jane is visible to the audience in her apartment. Alicia
enters through the proscenium doors confronting Hastings on the apron. After her exit he goes out through a
proscenium door to re-enter Jane's apartment. Thus although this scene employs an inside and outside location
there is no break in its continuity.) Jane thanks him for
his efforts on her behalf. He hints that her thanks should
take a sexual form. His hints become more obvious until
finally he makes to drag her into the bedroom. Dumont
enters. He and Hastings fight, Hastings is disarmed and
leaves swearing vengeance. Dumont comforts Jane suggesting that she should retire into the country. The act
ends on a note of hope that she will escape both Alicia's
and Hastings' vengeance.

Act III The court. Before Dumont could convey Jane
to safety he was arrested at Hastings's instigation. Jane is
homeless and her only hope is to petition Richard. She
meets Alicia in an antechamber. Alicia substitutes for
Jane's petition a letter she herself is carrying to the Duke
accusing Jane of influencing Hastings against his plans
to usurp the throne. (It may be that in this act also the
two areas of the apron and of the stage itself are employed
to stand for two locations, the first an antechamber, the
second the court itself.) Richard dismisses Jane and sounds
Hastings as to how he would receive any attempt to
disqualify the young king. Hastings patriotically opposes
any suggestion of alteration in the succession.

Act IV The court. Richard tries to persuade Jane to
work Hastings round to his party. In spite of promises of
comfort and plenty if she bend to his will she refuses.
Richard orders that she be turned out into the street and
that it be proclaimed that if anyone offers her comfort,
shelter or food they will die. What follows closely parallels
Shakespeare's *Richard III*. In the council Richard accuses
Hastings together with Jane of working witchcraft against
him:

> Then judge yourselves, convince your eyes of truth,
> Behold my arm thus blasted, dry and withered,
> Shrunk like a foul abortion, and decayed,
> Like some untimely product of the seasons,
> Robbed of its properties of strength and office.
> This is the sorcery of Edward's wife,
> Who in conjunction with that harlot Shore,
> And other like confederate midnight hags,
> By force of potent spells, of bloody characters,
> And conjurations horrible to hear,
> Call friends and spectres from the yawning deep,
> And set the ministers of hell at work,
> To torture and despoil me of my life.

Hastings is condemned to death, as he is hurried out of
the council chamber to re-enter through the proscenium
doors into the antechamber he is confronted by a despair-
ing Alicia. She confesses how she changed Jane's petition
for her own letter of accusation. Her guilt and the sight
of her lover being conducted to his death sends her mad.
Act V The street. Old Bellmour and Dumont-Shore search
the streets for Jane. At least two days have passed since
Richard's decree. Jane must be close to starvation. They
are unsuccessful in their search and leave the stage. Jane
now enters and finds herself outside Alicia's house. She
begs help but is refused by the servants. The mad Alicia
appears to rail at Jane. Alicia is forcibly removed by her
servants. Jane begins to feel faint and collapses on the
ground. She is discovered by Bellmour who prepares her
for the entrance of her husband. Jane is unable to eat and
dies in her husband's arms. The touching reconciliation
is heightened by the brutal interruption of Gloster's
guards to tear him from her dead arms to carry him off
to his death for having disobeyed the order that she was
to receive no succour.

Critical commentary

As in comedy the work of Steele clearly marks our entry
into the eighteenth century, so Rowe in tragedy. There
are superficial similarities with Dryden and Otway, in
that the plays are written in blank verse and he still
favours comparatively exotic settings but the distance between Rowe and his predecessors is immense.

We have noted in Otway the first tentative moves towards domesticity but his subjects are still essentially
heroic. Eighteenth century and Restoration tragic theory
is for the most part confusing, much of the talk about
the unities and French models is irrelevant confusion and
examples are employed rather as sticks with which to
beat rivals than as genuine models. We can safely narrow

the argument to one concerning the definition of nature. Dryden and other late seventeenth-century exponents of tragedy had claimed to be imitating nature in the sense that they were representing *la belle nature*, things as they should be, heightened reality. The result is that they select in order to exalt. In contradiction to this Steele had expounded in the *Tatler* number 172, that our fortunes are too humble to be concerned with the fate of princes and that:

> ... it would be of great use to lay before the world such adventures as befall persons not exalted above the common level.

This is analogous with Rowe's significant announcement in the prologue to *The Fair Penitent* (1703):

> Long has the fate of kings and empires been
> The common business of the tragic scene,
> As if misfortune made the throne her seat,
> And none could be unhappy but the great.
>
> Stories like these with wonder we may hear,
> But far remote, and in a higher sphere,
> We ne'er can pity what we ne'er can share.
>
> Therefore an humbler theme our author chose,
> A melancholy tale of private woes:
> No princes here lost royalty bemoan,
> But you shall meet with sorrows like your own.

This break with tradition may in part be due to an ideological difference between Rowe and the previous generation. The earlier writers had used tragedy as a vehicle to express Tory monarchical principles while Rowe is most decidedly Whig, primarily interested in the liberty of the individual. This contributes to the shift in emphasis from grandiose heroic subjects to something more recognizably domestic. Tragedy previous to Rowe relies on the soliloquy, Rowe discovers a new spontaneity and much greater intimacy by substituting quasi-domestic exchanges between confidants. Another significant reformation is his reduction in the number of characters, the normal number employed by Rowe being eight as in *Jane Shore* as opposed to the fifteen or more common to his predecessors, and the fact that he seldom employs more than three of these in any one scene. This neo-classic economy of casting helps to replace declamation with diction and almost for the first time since the beginning of the seventeenth century we feel characters are speaking to each other rather than at each other.

'Pity' and 'pathetic' are the words most used in connection with Rowe's tragedies. It is often suggested that 'pathetic' is opposite to 'heroic'. This is to overclarify the change marked by Rowe's work. We are still basically concerned with admiration and wonder. We do not simply feel sorry for Jane in the present play, for simultaneously we admire the nobility which she discovers in her adversity; thus it is intended that we should be moved by the greatness to which she rises because of her predicament rather than by the predicament itself. Pity is almost an unsatisfactory term because it still coexists with admiration. There is more muscle behind Rowe's attempt to make us regret Jane's tragedy than the present critical condescension behind terms such as 'pity' and 'pathetic' would imply.

Another commonplace of critical statement to be made in connection with Rowe is to credit him with the invention of She-tragedy and the partial dismissal of this as something following on the replacement of the Caroline boy player by the actress. Here again over simplification leads us very close to error. The increase in women in the audience is more significant to the drama's greater feminine orientation in the first decade of the eighteenth century than the introduction of actresses forty years previously. Swift observed in his *Thoughts on Various*

Subjects that: '... it is observable that the ladies frequent tragedies more than comedy'. Again it should not be overlooked that women were considered a less elevated species than men. It would have been impossible to centre a heroic drama around a woman. The domestication of drama increases their importance but it is wrong to think of Rowe deliberately creating a female repertory.

Domestic tragedy being less selective of events than its heroic counterpart allows for greater complexity of characterization by contrasting the private with the public. Thus in *Jane Shore* Hastings makes several revealing shifts from gaiety to brutality, from mockery to sentiment and from plausibility to seriousness. This gradual revelation of character provided the actor with a superb vehicle to express variety of passion. There can be no doubt that it was the recognition by actors of the opportunities which Rowe provided which led to his retention in the repertory almost to the twentieth century.

Jane Shore is professedly 'written in imitation of Shakespeare's style'. It would be more correct to say that it is written in the style of the Restoration Shakespearean imitations. It is Shakespeare without poetry; it has the sound but not the substance. What many critics have failed to recognize is that Rowe, by introducing more complex characters, has provided the actors with ample material to supply that substance. A few scenes are lifted and crudely embellished from Shakespeare's *Richard III*, and any comparison between Act IV,*i* and the parallel passages in the former play will bear out the remarks on improvement already made above in our entry dealing with *Venice Preserved*. The main interest and strength of the play lies in the triangle presented by Jane, Hastings and Dumont. The Shakespearean portions simply serve to place the discovery of domestic virtue in a contrasting context of ruthless tyranny.

Our distance from the play traps us into falsely elevating what is mundane, particularly in the character of

Jane herself. Her excuse must be folly. This was the reason for her treatment of her husband, a difficult hurdle for Rowe to surmount and which he rightly chooses to play down as much as possible by consigning it to the past long before the play starts. Examples of her folly, which clarify it as excessive simplicity, are shown in her inability to read the true motive behind Hastings' assistance. The character has to be interpreted with a naïve charm which will exploit this and make her unsuspecting of Richard's true character, while putting her trust and her jewels in the hands of such a friend as Alicia. If this is realized then she becomes too good for the world and we truly regret her tragedy. In such a light the play's relationship to *George Barnwell* is exposed; like him she is a character of the same clay as ourselves who falls from excessive vulnerability rather than from basic evil, and we should recognize a strong didactic element which raises this above being a mere exercise in the inducement of pity.

The Beggar's Opera
John Gay (1685-1732)

Gay was born at Barnstaple and educated at the Grammar
School. He was apprenticed to a London silk mercer, but
soon abandoned this and returned to Barnstaple. When
exactly he reappeared in London and the details of his
early literary career are uncertain. He himself complains
in *Rural Sports* (1713) that he had wasted considerable
energy and gained nothing but unkept promises looking
for patronage. His first dramatic work was a comedy called
The Wife of Bath (1713). By this time he was on friendly
terms with all the leading literary figures of the day, such
as Pope, Swift and Arbuthnot. It was through Swift's
influence that he obtained the position of secretary to the
British Ambassador to the Court of Hanover. The death
of Queen Anne ended his hopes of government employment. Possibly with assistance from Pope he wrote a burlesque of contemporary tragedy, with particular reference
to *Venice Preserved*, called *What D'ye Call it?* (1715). In
January 1717 his comedy *Three Hours After Marriage*, in
which he was almost certainly helped by Pope and Arbuthnot, was unsuccessfully presented. Gay lost everything
in the South Sea affair but thanks to the efforts of his
friends received the sinecure of lottery commissioner, with
a salary of £150 a year in 1722 and between 1722 and
1729 he had lodgings in the palace of Whitehall. In spite
of this he felt himself neglected. In 1724 he produced a
tragedy called *The Captives*.

In 1727 he wrote for Prince William, later the Duke of Cumberland, his *Fifty-One Fables in Verse*. He was offered the post of gentleman-usher to the Princess Louisa but, considering this beneath his dignity, rejected it. *The Beggar's Opera*, which was first produced on 29 January 1728, ran for sixty-two nights bringing him four benefits. It was presented by John Rich at Covent Garden. The idea is said to have originated from Swift and Pope. Arbuthnot was also consulted during its composition but there is no question of divided authorship. The sequel *Polly* was suppressed through the influence of Walpole, but this suppression led to Gay making more than £1,000 from its printing in 1729. The Duchess of Queensberry was dismissed from court for canvassing subscribers. In 1732 his pastoral opera, with music by Handel, *Acis and Galatea* was produced at the Haymarket. He was buried in Westminster Abbey. Three further dramatic pieces, an opera *Achilles* (1733), *The Distressed Wife*, a comedy, and a farce, *The Rehearsal at Goatham* were published after his death.

DATE 1728

CAST

Peachum, a police spy and receiver of stolen goods
Lockit, a jailor
Macheath, a highwayman
Filch, servant to Peachum
Jeremy Twitcher ⎫
Crook-Fingered Jack ⎪
Wat Dreary ⎪
Robin of Bagshot ⎬ Macheath's gang
Nimming Ned ⎪
Harry Paddington ⎪
Mat of the Mint ⎪
Ben Budge ⎭
Beggar
Player

Mrs Peachum, wife to Peachum
Polly Peachum, her daughter
Lucy Lockit, daughter to Lockit
Diana Trapes
Mrs Coaxer
Dolly Trull
Mrs Vixen
Betty Doxy　　　　　　women of the town
Jenny Diver
Mrs Slammerkin
Suky Tawdry
Molly Brazen
SCENE London

Plot

There is an introductory conversation between the beggar author and a player. By means of this the Beggar tells us he has introduced all the right similes for an opera: such as the swallow, the moth, the bee, the ship, the flower etc. He also promises a prison scene which he trusts the ladies will find pathetic; and he hopes that he may be forgiven that there is no recitative, prologue or epilogue as in all other ways his piece conforms to all the conventions of opera.

Act I Peachum's house. Peachum considers himself an honest man; working on the one hand on behalf of the law as a police spy and on the other in the interest of cheats, whom we should, he maintains, protect as we live by them, as a receiver of stolen goods. He aptly compares this balance of interest with the legal profession. The fair way he maintains the scale between his dual roles is shown by the way he helps to mitigate the evidence against an active and industrious thief while letting the lazy go hang. His great care for the future is also demonstrated for, like a wise gamekeeper, he takes care to protect breeding females over the males of the species. Mrs Peachum informs him that their daughter Polly is in love with the highwayman Macheath. Peachum would indulge the girl as far as prudence and business will allow but marriage would place them in Macheath's power. He is not a little concerned that Polly should take it upon herself to imitate the airs and graces of the gentry in this way. He and Mrs Peachum have never bothered with such formalities. He instructs his wife that it is her duty to warn Polly against such an action. Mrs Peachum questions the boy Filch as to whether he knows of anything that may have passed between her daughter and Macheath, while her husband does likewise with Polly. Polly is actually married to the man, and to make matters worse did not marry for honour or money – but for love. Mrs Peachum faints at the news of her daughter's unnatural behaviour. When she comes round Peachum comforts her by outlining a scheme for turning this seemingly disastrous situation to their daughter's advantage. While the married state has little to recommend it, widowhood is an old, honourable and profitable institution. Macheath shall be peached at the next assizes thus making Polly a rich widow. When Polly expresses doubts upon the scheme her mother calls her a shame to her very sex. Both parents feel it is their duty to provide for their daughter in this way and Peachum exits to prepare matters for the Old Bailey while his wife undertakes to manage Polly. Polly warns Macheath of her father's plans and the lovers take a suitably fond farewell.

Act II A tavern near Newgate. Macheath informs his gang that Peachum and he have quarrelled. He must for a while keep out of the way, he advises his fellows not to let his private affairs interfere with business, but that it were best if they let it be thought that he had left the gang. Macheath shows great understanding of the fine motives behind Peachum's action and in no way displays any unreasonable ill will towards his father-in-law. Mrs Coaxer and her girls join Macheath. The girls persuade the good captain to surrender his pistols to them, then sign to Peachum and the constables to arrest him. Newgate: Macheath is confined. Lucy Lockit, the jailor's daughter to whom Macheath once promised marriage, leaving her as a sign of good faith pregnant, comes to upbraid him with his cruelty in marrying Polly. Although there is little significance in a promise to a woman, for man in marriage itself promises a hundred things he never means to perform, Macheath takes a businesslike advantage of the situation to try and effect his escape. He soothes her by repeating his promise of marriage to her, after all what signifies another wife more or less? Lucy is mollified and accepts his denial of Polly. Lockit is something the reverse of Peachum, having a humour to an unbusinesslike suspicion in the same way that Lucy's jealousy is contrasted to Polly's reason. All is smooth between the two fathers when Peachum agrees to share the reward for Macheath's capture. They fall out over another prisoner only to realize that they need each other and make friends. Lucy comes tearfully to her father to plead for her lover. She is given the sound advice that although it is her duty to go and moan over her dying husband she cannot have the man and the money too. At the very moment that Lucy promises to Macheath to help him escape Polly enters. Macheath disowns her and Peachum carries her off. Lucy touched by Macheath's behaviour agrees to steal her father's keys when he is drunk.

Act III Newgate. Macheath has escaped. Lockit upbraids his daughter for helping him. Lucy is now fully convinced after all that Macheath is married to Polly. Both father and daughter suspect the Peachums of planning to cheat them of their rightful share in the reward money. A gaming house. Macheath is at play. In spite of the recent activity in his life Macheath is still able to order his gang with businesslike efficiency. Peachum's warehouse. Lockit, Peachum and Mrs Trapes plot to catch Macheath in a brothel. Newgate. Lucy is unnaturally civil to Polly, insisting that she drink with her. It is a plot to poison her rival from which Polly escapes only because she drops the glass when a recaptured Macheath is led in. Macheath for his part is appalled to find both women waiting for him and is almost relieved to be led off to the Old Bailey for his trial. The prisoners perform a dance of chains. The condemned cell. Macheath is ordered immediate execution for having broken prison. Polly and Lucy visit him and were that not enough four more 'wives' appear, each nursing an infant. Macheath is only too willing to face his execution. It is intended by the Beggar that, in accordance with strict poetic justice, Macheath should be hanged but on the insistence of the Player he has Macheath brought back on stage to receive a reprieve:

... for you must allow that, in this kind of drama, 'tis
no matter how absurdly things are brought about.

Polly
John Gay

DATE 1729

CAST

Mr Ducat, a West Indian planter

Macheath, alias Morgan, captain of the pirates

Vanderbluff ⎫
Capstern   ⎪
Hacker   ⎪
Culverin   ⎬ pirates
Laguerre   ⎪
Cutlace   ⎭

Pohetohee, an Indian king

Cawwawkee, his son

Polly Peachum

Mrs Ducat

Diana Trapes

Jenny Diver

Flimzy   ⎫
Damairs ⎬ servants to Trapes

SCENE The West Indies

Plot

Act I Ducat's house. A shipload of girls has arrived from
England. Mrs Trapes convinces Ducat that it is barbar-
ously colonial of him not to keep a girl and persuades him
to buy one of the new girls, about whom she has heard

particularly high reports and whom she has ordered to have brought to the house as soon as she is disembarked. The girl, when she is brought in, turns out to be Polly Peachum. Macheath was transported after the events dealt with in *The Beggar's Opera*, and in the intervening space of time her father has been hanged. After this happening she decided to emigrate to the West Indies and search for Macheath, but her fortune was stolen from her during the voyage and until her remaining funds can be sent out from London she is in great difficulties. Mrs Trapes recognizes her. She has further bad news. About eighteeen months previously, Macheath robbed his master, escaped from the plantation and turned pirate, with him escaped a transported female slave, one Jenny Diver whom he has married since coming to the West Indies. Mrs Trapes pretends great concern to help Polly, offering to obtain her a post as maid to Mrs Ducat.

Polly is sent out of the room while Mrs Trapes sells her to Ducat for a hundred pistols. Only just in time for Mrs Ducat returns to upbraid her husband for keeping company with Mrs Trapes. She becomes even more incensed when he attempts to pacify her by telling her he has bought her a pretty maid. They quarrel and she instructs her servant to watch the master closely. Ducat attempts to seduce Polly and is rejected. She realizes the extent to which Mrs Trapes has betrayed her when Ducat threatens that if she will not play in the bedchamber then she must work in the fields among the planters. She is a slave. They are interrupted by news of an Indian rising. This turns out to be a false report and we learn that the Indians have armed themselves for protection against the depredations of the pirate band now led by the fierce negro Morano, who has succeeded Macheath, who is presumed dead, as captain. Mrs Ducat accuses Polly of being her husband's mistress but she softens after hearing her story and helps her to escape in a suit of her nephew's clothes.

Act II A view of an Indian country. The disguised Polly
seeks news of Macheath. She is tired and lies down to
sleep. Some pirates enter and fall to quarrelling as to who
shall be emperor of Mexico when they have conquered
South America. The noise awakes Polly. They take her
for the son of a rich planter and thus a potential ransom
so they carry her off to their leader. Another part of the
country. We learn that Morano is Macheath who has disguised himself at his new wife Jenny's request in order to
hide from the numerous women who lay claim to him
wherever he goes. The disguised Polly is hauled before
him. He leaves Jenny to question her. Finding her a
pretty youth Jenny tries to seduce Polly, when Polly returns her advances with indifference Jenny reacts in the
classical Potiphar's wife manner and is much put out
when Macheath refuses to show any jealousy, remarking
that it is the way of the town when a man would have the
favour of the husband to pay court to the wife. The
pirates have also captured the Indian prince, Cawwawkee. Macheath questions him but he refuses to betray his
friends. Macheath orders his torture and he and Polly are
hustled off to share captivity. Jenny suggests to Macheath
and Vanderbluff, the second in command of the pirates,
that the three of them steal the ship and its store of
treasure and abandon the other pirates. This plan is cut
short by the entry of a sailor with the news that the way to
the ship is blocked by the plantation militia. A room in a
poor cottage. Polly persuades Cawwawkee to bribe their
jailors. The pirates are prepared to believe the prince's
word because being an Indian he knows no better than to
keep it.
Act III The Indian camp. The Indians have been joined
by Ducat in his capacity as a colonel of militia. He is
brave by European standards but has more substance
to lose than an Indian, although it is a well known fact
that an Englishman would rather part with his life than
his money. Then again he carries his wife's heart with

him and he is under her orders to quit should things come to a battle. Cawwawkee returns with the disguised Polly. She is to fight by his side in the coming fray. The field of battle. Some of the pirates have mutinied. They are distracted in their flight by a convenient drum head and sit down to enjoy a game of dice. This soon breaks up in a fight. Vanderbluff and Macheath enter and persuade the men to return to the fray at pistol point. The Indian and pirate armies face each other across the stage. The pirates are beaten off. Ducat comes in à-la-Falstaff at the battle of Shrewsbury. He explains that while private soldiers must content themselves with fighting, officers run away and get most pay. The Indians are victorious but Macheath has escaped and Polly is missing. She returns safe and sound having captured Macheath, neither has recognized the other. He is tried and sentenced to death. The Indian king asks how he may reward Polly and is astonished when she, a European, declares that the pleasure of having served an honest man is reward in itself. Cawwawkee questions her further and her sex is discovered. She tells them her story and how she is searching for her husband. Her tale is interrupted by the entrance of Jenny to plead for her husband's life. She lets slip that Morano is Macheath. It is too late, the execution has been carried out. Cawwawkee offers to marry Polly and is accepted. The play ends with a victory dance by the Indians.

Critical commentary

Gay's work has been more properly esteemed by students of the history of music than by literary critics. The former have seized on both the pieces described above as a seminal reservoir of late seventeenth- and early eighteenth-century music. Gay suffered both in his own age and succeeding ones from being both popular and successful, two attributes which tend to scare critics away from any ex-

pression of delight lest it be supposed that they share the
common taste of ordinary mortals. In spite of the dis-
appointments in his political career he was a remarkably
gentle and kindly man. His acquaintances in the over
mature Augustan age treated him as an untypical irre-
sponsible child. Swift repeatedly advised him to write
something of weight that would be the result of several
years research. Gay seems to have taken this advice to
heart for he wrote to Swift, 'I remember your prescription,
and I do ride upon the downs, and at present I have no
asthma'. Nothing can be less conducive to building an
artistic reputation than to be generally liked. The cutting
edge of critical controversy rusts in such a climate.

The most damaging judgement we have inherited is
that of Dr Johnson. Johnson betrays time and time again
the total absence of any leavening sense of humour and a
morbid fear that anybody might accuse him of vulgarity.
At the beginning of his account of Gay and his work he
declares that Gay cannot be rated as of much worth as
he had once heard a lady remark that he was 'of a lower
order'. He then proceeds to draw up a damning balance
sheet of his literary vices and virtues, drawing the conclusions that he is 'never contemptible, nor ever excellent'
and again that he is to be 'neither much esteemed, nor
totally despised'.

Thus was dismissed the man who out of burlesque,
popular music, pantomime and drama had fashioned an
entirely new form which we now call 'ballad opera', which
became so popular that it merits discussion as something
higher than merely reference under the slightly dismissive
term irregular drama. Ballad operas could be either main
pieces or after pieces: if main pieces of three acts, if after
pieces of one or two. They are often used as a vehicle for
satire or burlesque but they can also be either farcical
or pastoral. The dialogue is spoken, not sung in recitative
as were the Italian operas. The music was almost always
fitted to already popular ballad tunes, rather than speci-

ally composed. The topicality of the tunes often adds another dimension and meaning to the songs in the play. Thus in *The Beggar's Opera*, Gay uses sixty-nine airs, none of which were specially composed. The bulk come from a six volume collection of songs collected by D'Urfey, called *Pills to Purge Melancholy*. All the others are borrowed from the contemporary stage. Gay capitalizes on the popularity of the tunes by modelling all his songs on their original versions. Thus Macheath's, 'If the heart of a man is depressed with cares,' closely follows a song in D'Urfey's *The Modern Prophets* (1709):

> Would you have a young virgin of fifteen years,
> You must tickle her fancy with sweet and dears,
> Ever toying and playing, and sweetly, sweetly,
> Sing a love sonnet, and charm her ears:
>> Wittily, prettily talk her down,
>> Chase her, and praise her, if fair or brown,
>> Sooth her, and smooth her,
>> And tease her, and please her,
> And touch but her smicket, and all's your own.

Much more subtle is his use of this song from Thomas Doggett's *The Country-Wake*, which tells how man's freedom is curtailed after marriage:

> We're just like a mouse in a trap,
> Or Vermin caught in a gin:
> We sweat and fret and try to escape,
> And curse the sad hour we came in.
> This was the worst plague could ensue
> I'm mewed in a smoky house;
> I used to tope a bottle or two,
> But now 'tis small beer with my spouse.

There is much parody of the contemporary Italian opera, particularly those of George Frederick Handel which were enjoying considerable vogue among the upper classes. This would appeal to the philistine instinct always

present in popular English theatrical taste, which consistently rejected the pseudo-artistic from Elizabethan days
to the first years of this century:

> I have introduced the similes that are all in your celebrated
> operas: the swallow, the moth, the bee, the ship, the
> flowers etc. Besides I have have a prison scene, which the
> ladies always reckon charmingly pathetic. As to the parts,
> I have observed such a nice impartiality to our two ladies,
> that it is impossible for either of them to take offence. I
> hope I may be forgiven, that I have not made my opera
> throughout unnatural, like those in vogue; for I have no
> recitative; excepting this, as I have consented to have neither
> prologue nor epilogue; it must be allowed an opera in all
> its forms.

The line 'I have observed such a nice impartiality', does
not refer to Polly and Lucy but to a recent quarrel between
two Italian sopranos, thus further underlining that the
piece is a burlesque of Italian opera. Another feature of
the opera that is mocked are the dances, particularly in
the grotesque dance of the prisoners in chains.

The word 'parody' is used advisedly in place of the
term 'satire' more commonly applied to Gay. It is difficult
to find any corrective intention in Gay's work, rather
there is a huge enjoyment of literary and theatrical absurdities: one notes especially the heroine narrowly rescued from accidentally poisoning herself in *The Beggar's
Opera* (cf *The Mourning Bride*) and the use of the noble
savage in *Polly* (cf Juba in *Cato*), and the list could be
endlessly extended. Nor should we allow our preoccupation with the drama to blinker the fact that contemporary
popular biographies of criminals are also burlesqued:
with low life scenes, narrow escapes, amorous intrigues
and even if we take, as Gay intended, *Polly* as a sequel of
The Beggar's Opera the hero-villain meeting his just
deserts at the hands of the woman he had betrayed as a
climax.

If the play is in any way satirical it is socially and politically so rather than literary or theatrical satire. Even here we can take too heavy a line on the play's enjoyment of topical scandal. Walpole, in public life first minister and in private life a compulsive lecher, is of course Macheath. We never see Macheath actually commit a crime, in the same way Walpole's alleged peculations were always carried out under the cloak of his official position. He is also Peachum and it is not impossible that this duality of character owes as much to Otway's treatment of Shaftesbury in *Venice Preserved* as to any desire to attack Sir Robert, to whom other glancing references are made in 'Robin of Bagshot, alias Gorgon, alias Bluff Bob, alias Carbuncle, alias Bob Booty'. Walpole himself was in the audience for the first night and seems to have taken no offence.

The social jokes are similarly lacking in vice. True the heroes behave in parody of businessmen, Peachum being constantly confronted by decisions that affect the lives of others. His wife has a well developed maternal sense and a care for her family's reputation. Polly is basically a steady and prudent creature, while their servant Filch is loyal to the family interest. Macheath is, at least in the first play, generous and gallant. Lockit is a slightly lesser Peachum, while his daughter Lucy is a tender tempest and one not easily slighted. The humour lies in the way that all these virtues are applied to their rascally and scandalous way of life. It is reading too much into the lines of the play to suggest a social message, or to suggest that Macheath's gang are simply correcting the unjust distribution of wealth. When we examine the conduct of the thieves and pirates we find that they are no better than their superiors and are, like them, governed by self interest.

In 1727 when *The Beggar's Opera* was first written, Gay and his friends were doubtful of its reception. According to Boswell, the Duke of Queensberry, Gay's patron, remarked after reading it: 'This is a very odd thing, Gay; I am satisfied that it is either a very good thing or a very bad thing.' The early rehearsals are illuminating to the student. Gay wanted the songs sung unaccompanied but, after making a start thus, Rich insisted on instrumental support. It would appear that neither play has ever been performed without accompaniment as Gay intended. The modern musical can be said to have derived from this original fusion of music, dance, drama and spectacle.

The Tragedy of Tragedies, or The Life and Death of Tom Thumb the Great
Henry Fielding (1707–54)

Fielding was educated at Eton and the University of
Leyden. His first two plays, *Love in Several Masques*
(1728) and *The Temple Beau* (1730), are conventional
artificial comedies. The second of these was presented at
the Goodman's Fields Theatre. When this was closed in
April 1730 Fielding fell back on the Little Theatre in the
Haymarket where *Hurlothrumbo, or The Supernatural*
by the other Samuel Johnson, a Cheshire dancing-master,
had had a great success. He was persuaded to write in a
similar burlesque style and *The Author's Farce* (1730)
was the result. From this point on he concentrated on
satirical drama. The ballad-opera, *The Welsh Opera, or
The Grey Mare the Better Horse* (1731) openly attacks
both political parties and brings the Royal Family in
thin disguise on to the stage. This play is better known
under its later title, *The Grub Street Opera*. The reper-
cussions were sufficient for him to drop politics for three
years till the outcry at the Excise Bill and the announcement of Parliamentary elections inspired *Don Quixote in
England* (1734). The success of this encouraged Fielding
to take over the management of the Haymarket Theatre
but the production of *Pasquin* (1736) and *The Historical
Register* (1737) led to Walpole introducing the Licensing
Act. This may have influenced Fielding to abandon the
drama for the novel. His best known works are the novels
Tom Jones and *Joseph Andrews*.

DATE 1730

CAST

King Arthur, a passionate sort of king, husband to Queen
Dollallolla, of whom he stands a little in fear, father to
Huncamunca, of whom he is very fond, and in love with
Glumdalca

Tom Thumb the Great, a little hero with a great soul,
something violent in his temper, which is a little abated by
his love for Huncamunca

Ghost of Gaffer Thumb, a whimsical sort of ghost

Lord Grizzle, extremely zealous for the liberty of the subject,
very choleric in his temper, and in love with Huncamunca

Merlin, a conjuror, and in some sort father to Tom Thumb

Noodle and Doodle, courtiers in place, and consequently
of that party that is uppermost

Foodle, a courtier that is out of place and consequently of
that party that is undermost

Bailiff, and follower of the party of the plaintiff

Parson, of the side of the church

Queen Dollallolla, wife to King Arthur, and mother to
Huncamunca, a woman entirely faultless, saving that she is
a little given to drink, a little too much a virago towards her
husband, and in love with Tom Thumb

The Princess Huncamunca, daughter to their Majesties King
Arthur and Queen Dollallolla, of a very sweet, gentle and
amorous disposition, equally in love with Lord Grizzle and
Tom Thumb, and desirous to be married to them both

Glumdalca of the giants, a captive queen, beloved by the
King but in love with Tom Thumb

Cleora and Mustacha, maids of honour in love with Noodle
and Doodle

SCENE The court of King Arthur and a plain thereabouts

Plot

Act I Noodle and Doodle open the play with suitable
remarks on the weather:

Sure such a day as this was never seen!
The sun himself, on this auspicious day,
Shines like a beau in a new birthday suit:
This down the seams embroidered that the beams,
All nature wears one universal grin.

(Corneille had recommended some very remarkable day
wherein to fix the action of a tragedy. English authors had
generally interpreted this to mean a fine summer's day).
They go on to talk of the glories of Tom Thumb who
has just saved the kingdom from giants. The King and
Queen are so grateful to Thumb that all are commanded
to cry for joy. Apart from the echo of Shakespeare's 'Uncle
me no uncles' there is a general enjoyment of the way
tragic heroes are drunk with death, blood, grief, love etc.
When Tom Thumb enters with the captive Glumdalca,
King Arthur falls in love with her. Tom Thumb requests
as his reward to be allowed to marry Huncamunca. The
King agrees. Dollallolla is passionately angry at it. Grizzle
is jealous. The Queen and Grizzle plot to prevent the
match. The Queen is in love with Tom Thumb.
Act II Tom Thumb confides to Noodle how his grand-
mother has warned him against marriage. A bailiff and his
follower attempt to arrest Noodle for debt and are sum-
marily killed by Tom Thumb for their presumption. In
the Princess Huncamunca's apartments the Princess
orders sad music as fitting background for her love: O
Tom Thumb! Tom Thumb! wherefore art thou Tom
Thumb? The King brings her the welcome news that he
intends for her to marry Tom Thumb. He goes off to tell
Thumb that all is agreed. Her other lover Grizzle beside
himself with love successfully pleads his suit, but Huncamunca again changes her mind after an altercative scene
between her and Glumdalca which parodies the scene
between Cleopatra and Octavia in *All for Love*. Asked to
choose between Glumdalca and Huncamunca, Thumb
chooses Huncamunca. King Arthur woos the rejected

giantess. Meanwhile a parson marries Tom Thumb and
Huncamunca. Grizzle learning of this swears to kill Tom
Thumb.

Act III The ghost of Gaffer Thumb enters. He tells the
King that Grizzle is in rebellion and the state in danger.
Noodle enters with news that Grizzle demands that
Huncamunca and the headless body of Tom Thumb be
delivered up to him or he will attack the palace. Thumb
has already sallied out alone to attack the rebels. Grizzle
having been unopposed is up to this point victorious. In
thunder and lightning Tom Thumb and Glumdalca are
met by Merlin who prophesies that Tom Thumb's end
shall be so glorious that future ages shall write a play
about him. (The lines are reminiscent of the conspirators
in *Julius Caesar*.) The army of Grizzle encounters Tom
Thumb and Glumdalca, and a bloody battle follows.
Grizzle kills Glumdalca. Thumb kills Grizzle.

King Arthur bids, in celebration of this victory, that
the prisons be opened and debts paid by the treasury. All
dance. This rejoicing is cut short by the entry of Noodle
to relate that Tom has been accidentally eaten by a cow.
The King orders the prisons to be shut up again and
everybody hanged, guilty or not.

	Kill my cows!
	Go bid the schoolmasters whip all their boys!
	Let lawyers, parsons and physicians loose,
	To rob, impose on and to kill the world.
Noodle	Her majesty the queen is in a swoon.
Queen	Not so much in a swoon but I have still the strength to reward the messenger of ill news. [*Kills Noodle*]
Noodle	Oh! I am slain.
Cleora	My lover's killed! I will revenge him so. [*Kills the Queen*]
Huncamunca	My mama killed. Vile murderess beware. [*Kills Cleora*]

Doodle	This for an old grudge to thy heart. [*Kills Huncamunca*]
Mustacha	And this I drive to thine, O Doodle! for a new one. [*Kills Doodle*]
King	Ha! Murderess vile, take that. [*Kills Mustacha*] And take thou this [*Kills himself and falls*] So when the child, whom nurse from danger guards, Sends Jack for mustard with a pack of cards, Kings, queen, and knaves, throw one another down, Till the whole pack lies scattered and o'erthrown; So all our pack upon the floor is cast, And all I boast is – that I fall the last.

The footnote to the printed edition summarizes this ending:

No scene, I believe, ever received greater honours than this. It was applauded by several encores, a word very unusual in tragedy. And it was very difficult for the actors to escape without a second slaughter. This I take to be a lively assurance of that fierce spirit of liberty which remains among us, and which Mr Dryden in his essay on Dramatic Poetry, hath observed. 'Whether custom,' says he, 'hath so insinuated itself into our countrymen, or nature hath so formed them to fierceness, I know not; but they will scarcely suffer combats and other objects of horror to be taken from them.' And indeed I am for having them encouraged in this martial disposition; nor do I believe our victories over the French have been owing to anything more than to those bloody spectacles daily exhibited in our tragedies, of which the French stage is so entirely clear.

Critical commentary

This is not the old joke against bombastic tragedy which
we have already enjoyed in *The Knight of the Burning
Pestle* and *The Rehearsal*. It is freed from the interruptions, comment and diversification provided by author,
friends and critics. The idea is not so much theatrical
satire *per se* as the adaptation to the stage of the mock
heroic humour of *The Rape of the Lock* and *The Dunciad*. It takes a trivial theme and applies to it the full
honours of tragedy. No one poet is being given the treatment, for although from the notes Lee would seem to
suffer more than most, Rowe and Shakespeare provide as
many unnoted parallels. The notes themselves by Scriblerus Secundus, added to the published version of the play
following the example of the 1729 edition of *The Dunciad*,
with its 'Prologema of Scriblerus and Notes Variorum',
point us to parallels taken from over forty plays. These
notes are not so much a satirical expression as a magpie's
collection of enjoyable absurdities. The whole is a patch-
work of theatrical souvenirs enjoyed for their own sake.
Although the couplet and the simile remain the staple of
the mock heroic, exaggerated blank verse with its tendency to bathos is the main target. This is never better
expressed than in Fielding's treatment of the tragic oath.
It would seem impossible to top the absurdities of 'Hell!
Scalding lead! and Sulphurs!' in Bank's *The Innocent
Usurper* or 'Night, Horror, Death, Confusion, Hell and
Furies!' in Lee's *Oedipus* yet it is not beyond the power
of a good tragic actor to express the author's intention
in the atmosphere of their proper context. The inclusion
of one word of shattering incongruity in Glumdalca's
oath: 'Confusion, Horror, Murder, Guts and Death' puts
the line beyond the reach of any actor. Excessive slaughter, one man armies and ghosts are all enjoyed with an
energetic lack of malice which accounts for the continued
playing of the piece well into the nineteenth century.

The London Merchant, or George Barnwell
George Lillo (1693–1739)

Lillo was born in London, the son of a Dutch jeweller. He was brought up to his father's trade. The family was nonconformist and his contemporaries speak of his strict morals. Fielding wrote thus of him in *The Champion* (26 February 1740):

> He had a perfect knowledge of human nature, though his contempt of all base means of application, which are the necessary steps to great acquaintance, restrained his conversation within narrow bounds. He had the spirit of an old Roman, joined to the innocence of a primitive Christian; he was content with his little state of life ...

Much of Lillo's work is second rate. He is certainly not a poet nor does he display the literate facility of his more formally educated contemporaries but he demonstrates a love and knowledge of the drama that was to have considerable influence on the future. He left an unfinished version of *Arden of Faversham* which was completed by John Hoadley and first presented in 1759. The catalogue of the auction for the sale of his library in 1739, lists 'Four very old plays', '144 plays bound in fourteen volumes', and '129 ditto stitched', which are further described as 'Many of them scarce'. It is fair to presume that he had made some study of the drama and was deliberately trying to return to less exhalted heights. He succeeds in this with *The London Merchant or the History of George Barnwell*

(1731) and *Fatal Curiosity* (1736). In the latter an old couple murder a young man whom they later discover to be their own son.

Lillo's first dramatic work was the ballad opera *Sylvia* (1730) and his other work includes a masque devised to celebrate the marriage of Princess Anne and William IV of Orange, called *Britannia and Batavia* (1734), *The Christian Hero* (1735) based on the life of Scanderberg, *Marina* a version of *Pericles* (1738) and *Elmerick* (1740). These are pedestrian pieces lacking the authenticity of his work in the field of domestic tragedy.

DATE 1731

CAST

Thorowgood, a London Merchant

Uncle to George Barnwell

Barnwell ⎫
Trueman ⎭ clerks to Thorowgood

Blunt, servant to Millwood

Jailor

Millwood, Barnwell's mistress

Lucy, her maid

Maria, Thorowgood's daughter

SCENE London one hundred years ago

Plot

Act I,*i* A room in Thorowgood's house. Thorowgood's honesty, and by implication the honesty of all English merchants, is established. It would give Thorowgood great pleasure if his daughter Maria would marry one of the young lords who visit his house. Maria who is secretly in love with his clerk George Barnwell promises that while she will not marry where she cannot love, love will never make her act contrary to duty. *ii* A room in Millwood's house. It is a general maxim among the knowing part of mankind that a woman without virtue like a man without honour is capable of any action. Millwood having had her honour stolen by man makes it her creed to prove the truth of this maxim. She sets her lures now to ruin George Barnwell, insisting that he stay and sup with her rather than attend to the duty of his master.

Act II,*i* A room in Thorowgood's house. Thorowgood pardons Barnwell for spending the night away from home. *ii* Another room in Thorowgood's house. Millwood and Lucy call purporting to be two ladies sent by his uncle in the country. After Thorowgood's patience with him in the previous scene Barnwell opens this scene with the resolve never to see Millwood more but Lucy and Millwood work on his sympathy. It is pretended that Millwood's protector hearing that Barnwell spent last night at her house determines to ruin her. Accepting responsibility for his mistress's supposed ruin Barnwell embezzles a bag of money from his master.

Act III,*i* A room in Thorowgood's house. Trueman discovers a letter from Barnwell confessing the embezzlement. He has run away. Trueman and Maria attempt to cover up his absence, Maria replacing the money. *ii* Millwood's house. From a scene between Blunt and Lucy we learn that Barnwell on being called by his master to make up his accounts applied to Millwood for help and was rejected. She then suggested that he murder his rich uncle as a way out of his difficulties. The servants try and prevent the deed by reporting its intention to the authorities. *iii* A walk at some distance from a country house. Barnwell lies in wait to murder his uncle. *iv* A cut wood. Barnwell murders his uncle who, recognizing his attacker, dies blessing his nephew and calling on him to pardon his murderer.

Act IV,*i* A room in Thorowgood's house. Lucy has told Thorowgood of his apprentice's intention at her mistress's instigation of robbing and murdering his uncle. Thorowgood attempts to prevent the murder. *ii* Millwood's house. Barnwell enters bloody from the deed. Millwood demands

he give her what gold or jewels he has taken from the
body:

> Think you I added sacrilege to murder? Oh! had you
> seen him as his life flowed from him in a crimson flood, and
> heard him praying for me by the double name of nephew
> and of murderer; alas, alas! he knew not then that his
> nephew was his murderer; how would you have wished as I
> did, though you had a thousand years of life to come, to have
> given them all to have lengthened his one hour.

Afraid that his remorse will betray them both Millwood
hands him over to the law. Thorowgood enters to upbraid
her with destroying Barnwell and charge her with being
an accessory to the murder. She exultantly defends her
behaviour as just revenge for the crimes men have committed upon her sex.
Act V,i A room in a prison. Thorowgood, Blunt and
Lucy describe Barnwell's repentance at his trial. ii A
dungeon. Barnwell resigned for death takes leave of
Thorowgood, Trueman and Maria. iii The place of execution. The gallows and the ladder at the farther end of
the stage. Millwood utters a characteristic speech of de-
fiance and flouts Barnwell's advice that she should make
her peace with God. She goes to death, in contrast to
Barnwell's repentance, encompassed with horror, loathing
life and yet afraid to die.

Critical commentary

If one takes a broad view of the English dramatic tradition
then *The London Merchant* comes exactly midway between Elizabethan domestic tragedy of the *Arden of
Faversham, A Yorkshire Tragedy* type and Victorian
domestic melodrama. If on the other hand one studies
this play alongside more characteristic tragedies of the
age such as the plays of Rowe, Addison's *Cato* and Home's
Douglas it seems almost eccentric. Its complete disregard

for the orthodox procedures of neo-classic tragedy is in part explained by Lillo's biography, his background being strikingly different from the general run of eighteenth century playwrights. It would be all too easy to impose this background on to *The London Merchant* and interpret the play as a narrow moral tract eulogizing the virtues of the middle class by a second-rate writer. After all, although it was popular throughout the eighteenth century, it was mainly produced as a Christmas and Easter holiday piece, since, as Theophilus Cibber records it was:

... judged a proper entertainment for the apprentices,
as being a more instructive, moral, and cautionary drama,
than many pieces that had usually been exhibited on those
days with little but farce and ribaldry to recommend them.
The Lives of the Poets of Great Britain and Ireland.

We have already drawn attention to Lillo's extensive knowledge of Elizabethan drama and using such plays as *Arden of Faversham* and *A Yorkshire Tragedy* as his models he manages to answer a basic English delight in stage crime which has continued through to the present in the undoubted stage appeal of Agatha Christie and others. The bulk of Elizabethan crime plays (and indeed their 19th century melodramatic counterparts) were hastily composed works often exploiting a local sensation. Their sources are mainly ballads (in the nineteenth century crime journalism replaces the ballad as the main source). Following the Elizabethans Lillo also derived his plot from an old ballad. Here we have an often overlooked concession to eighteenth century tragic practice for Lillo's play is set in the seventeenth century and therefore distanced by time from its audience. It would appear that eighteenth century practice updated the dresses in the play but that distance is Lillo's intention seems to be indicated by the prologue.

Although this work did not change the accepted standards of tragedy, it left an impression that was to become a major influence on European drama. Lessing employed it as the model for *Sara Sampson* and through him an idea is passed on, albeit increasingly overstressing the elements of fate and moral retribution, until it reaches Ibsen and re-emerges as a truly tragic strain. For *The London Merchant* is something far deeper than mere moral statement. True the history of George Barnwell is exemplary rather than tragic, but Millwood in the 'powerful magic of her wit and form' is first cousin to Cleopatra and Hedda Gabler, and she comes close to Lady Macbeth in her reception of Barnwell after he has committed the murder. Is there not great strength in her speech upbraiding him as a coward, beginning 'Ridiculous! ... No more of this stuff!' after he has entered with bloodied hands and the remorseful exclamation 'Here's a sight to make a statue start with horror', and does not the real tragedy lie in her misuse of this strength? Further are we not all implicated in this tragedy by her great speech on man's injustices to women? The many questions which the play poses are obscured by its frequent *longeurs* and general tendency to moralistic rant but it undeniably rises above mere sensationalism or appeals to the handkerchief and while we feel little sorrow for Barnwell, the fate of Millwood approaches true tragedy.

It would appear that Millwood's tragedy was obscured by performance for no contemporary critic enlarges upon it. It may be because the part is contrary to the English acting tradition which until the end of the nineteenth century tended to flatter actresses. The role must draw on the unpleasant and unromantic; English actresses preferred to be pathetic so that much of the real bite of the part was removed. The theatre did not free itself from the romantic and the pathetic until the nineteenth century novel, unshackled by the interpretation of actors, developed the aims of *The London Merchant*, nursing the tale of private woe so that it could be reintroduced to the theatre by Jones and Pinero.

Take away the character of Millwood and we find *The London Merchant* anticipating all the main features of melodrama except the happy ending. Even the comic relief is suggested by the opening scenes between Millwood and Lucy which mark a sincere attempt by Lillo to lead the comic and tragic worlds out of their eighteenth century estrangement. The characters such as the good old man, the spotless heroine, the woman with a past and the faithful friend will become old favourites while prison scenes and murders in dark woods become too common for us to need to record further examples.

This extraordinary play seems to offer English drama an opportunity to anticipate the realism we associate with Ibsen and other European writers. It would appear that this opportunity was missed not so much because of a lack of critical appreciation but because the players themselves rejected the theatre of the unpleasant for there is not a leading eighteenth century actor or more significantly actress who records a role in this play as among their favourite parts.

The Gamester
Edward Moore (1712–57)

Moore was the son of a dissenting minister in Abingdon.
In his early life he was a linen draper. He turned to letters
at a comparatively mature age in 1744 with *Fables for
the Female Sex* written after the manner of Gay. His first
play, *The Foundling*, was presented in 1748. This was
followed by *Gil Blas* which dramatizes the story of Aurora
from Le Sage's novel. *The Gamester*, which owes something to the assistance of Garrick, is his only significant
work:

DATE 1753
CAST
Beverley
Lewson, in love with Charlotte
Stukely
Jarvis, faithful old steward to the Beverleys
Bates, Stukely's agent
Dawson, a creature of Stukely
Waiter
Mrs Beverley
Charlotte, Beverley's sister
Lucy
SCENE London

Plot

Act I,*i* Beverley's lodgings. It is the day following the sale
of Beverley's house and effects because of Beverley's gambling. Beverley himself has been absent from home the
whole night. His young wife hardly seems to need the
support of her sister-in-law who offers comfort and promises of aid. They are joined by Jarvis who offers to
continue to serve the family without pay. He even offers
his savings. Stukely calls seeking Beverley. Charlotte
blames his example and encouragement as the cause of
her brother's ruin. Stukely evades the charge. He seems
at some pains to draw attention to Beverley's absence over-
night insinuating another cause than gambling. A violent
knock is heard. It is a creditor whom Jarvis persuades to
leave. A second knocking is heard. They again fear a
creditor but Lewson enters. It is obvious that he dislikes
and distrusts Stukely who leaves soon after his arrival.
Lewson and a friend have purchased items at yesterday's
sale which he presses Mrs Beverley to accept. A further
fear is mentioned during this scene that Beverley may
have embezzled his sister's fortune. *ii* Stukely's lodgings.
Any doubts as to Stukely's character are swept away as he
informs us:

> This Beverley's my fool; I cheat him, and he calls me friend.
> But more business must be done yet – his wife's jewels are
> unsold – so is the reversion of his uncle's estate: I must have
> these two, and then there's a treasure above all – I love his
> wife ...

Bates enters and his master's plans are set in motion.
Their creature Dawson, with a set of cogged dice is ready
to entrap him. It is Stukely's plan to lend Beverley money
till he believes Stukely has beggared himself on his behalf.
Act II,*i* A gaming house. Jarvis tries to persuade Beverley
to return home. Stukely enters. He sets in motion his plot
of the previous scene. Beverley determines to ask his wife

to give him her jewels. *ii* Beverley's lodgings. Charlotte inquires for her fortune but Beverley puts her off. Beverley and Lewson almost quarrel when the latter suggests that Stukely is a villain. A letter is brought from Stukely. It states he is leaving England to escape his debts. In order to settle these Beverley obtains possession of the jewels.

Act III,*i* Stukely's lodgings. Stukely supplies Bates with funds with which to purchase Beverley's rights in his uncle's fortune. He tells Beverley that Lewson has been openly accusing him of embezzling his sister's fortune. *ii* Beverley's lodgings. Charlotte suggests to her sister that she has been tricked out of her jewels. Lewson enters. He tells Charlotte that he has information from Bates that her fortune has indeed been embezzled. He insists that she marry him. *iii* A room in a gaming house. Beverley has lost the jewels. He sells the reversion of his uncle's estates. He is now completely beggared. *iv* Beverley's lodgings. It only remains for Stukely to seduce Mrs Beverley for his plans, as outlined in the second scene, to be complete. To this end he suggests that Beverley has given the jewels to a mistress. He presses his suit only to be scornfully rejected.

Act IV,*i* Stukely's lodgings. Lewson breaks in on him with violent accusations of deliberately destroying Beverley. Lewson has guessed all. Stukely persuades Bates to murder him. *ii* A street. Lewson and Beverley meet. Beverley accuses him of spreading the tale of the embezzlement of Charlotte's fortune. They quarrel. Beverley is violent and distracted but Lewson persuades him to put up his sword, promising to provide him with proofs that Stukely is his enemy. Jarvis and Bates have witnessed the quarrel. Jarvis leads his old master, still carrying his drawn sword, home. *iii* Stukely's lodgings. Stukely provides Dawson with a warrant to arrest Beverley for debt.

Act V,*i* Stukely's lodgings. Bates reports that Lewson has been killed. The blame will fall on Beverley. Jarvis is a witness to the quarrel between the two men. *ii* Beverley's

lodgings. Beverley has been imprisoned for debt. Jarvis
brings news that Beverley's uncle is dead. Unaware that
the right of inheritance has been sold Mrs Beverley and
Charlotte hurry to the prison with the news. *iii* The
prison. In despair Beverley drinks poison. Stukely enters
and accuses him of murdering Lewson, but Lewson is not
dead. Bates had seemed to fall in with Stukely's plan in
order to prevent it. Lewson, warned by Bates, had kept
aloof until sufficient evidence had been gathered to un-
mask Stukely, who is now led off presumably to arrest and
punishment. Nothing can stay the action of the poison:
Beverley dies.

Critical commentary

In selecting *The Gamester* and placing it in such close
proximity to *The London Merchant* we are guilty of the
same kind of misleading critical selectivity of which we
have repeatedly accused others throughout this survey.
Such a position seems to imply a development of the type
of domestic tragedy initiated by Lillo, when in fact it is a
comparatively isolated example. This play and Home's
Douglas have quality in their own right and are worthy
of individual study but it cannot be too strongly underlined that they are atypical of the period, which is more
properly represented by tragedies such as Murphy's
Orphan of China (1759), Robert Dodsley's *Cleone* (1758)
and Whitehead's *The Roman Father* (1750).

The first of these is drawn from Voltaire's *Orphelin de
la Chine*. Apart from its exploitation of things Chinese
it is typical of the neo-classicism of the period, being in
everything but dress a roman drama. Zamti, a mandarin
and his wife Mandane, rear the prince Zaphini as their
son, sacrificing their own son Hamet in his place to the
barbarian usurper Timurkan. Timurkan conquers all
China and brings about the deaths of Zamti and Mandane
only to be killed by Zaphini. It offers plenty of oppor-

tunity for pathetic emotion. There is the customary conflict between love and duty particularly for the mother of
Hamet. The scene where Mandane commits suicide just
before she is about to be rescued is another situation
familiar to all readers of eighteenth-century tragedy, while
Timurkan's pangs of conscience before he is killed by
Zaphini are hardly a surprise.

Cleone is similarly pathetic though more domestic in
its setting. The villain Glanville slanders Cleone the
general's wife. She is forced to fly into the forest with her
child where Glanville's creature bungles her murder so
that she recovers after a suitably pathetic display of madness over her murdered child whose death she refuses to
accept. The pathos of the situation is worked to the
highest pitch but the tears that we shed are tears for others
and the piece never touches ourselves.

The Roman Father is based on the quarrel between the
Horatii and the Curatii which Corneille employed for
Horace. It is such a play as we would expect from an
eighteenth century Poet Laureate, over subservient to the
unities and consciously striving after poeticism.

The pseudo-classical formalism of the representative
pieces described above is contrary to real tragedy and it
is no accident that of the tragedies which stand out from
the period, *Douglas* and *The Gamester* both attempt in
their different ways to find a new road. *The Gamester*
applies the benevolent view of humanity familiar to us
from eighteenth-century comedy to tragedy. It is written
in prose, albeit a heightened prose fashioned from an
original blank verse version. Contemporary critics felt
that this lessened the play's dignity but they could not
deny its tragic effect on the audience. Beverley is a man
driven by his fate, his death is brought about by his
despair rather than as a simple retribution. The play is
much more than a simple warning against the evils of
gambling. This was a national vice. Young men were
being despoiled of fortunes in circumstances not so very

different from those depicted. The story was infinitely possible. Beverley, however, is a truly tragic character within this sordid everyday story. He is not so very far removed from Cato in the way he is unable to avoid his end. For this reason we prefer *The Gamester* over *The London Merchant*. Moore is obviously aware of the earlier play. The morality is less openly the main aim of the play and the climax, which comes in the earlier piece in the fourth act with the arrest of the central character for murdering his uncle, is sustained in *The Gamester* till the final scene. Suspense is to a very great extent lacking in eighteenth-century tragedy. The reunion with certain elements of comedy leave us with the hope of a happy ending till virtually the final curtain. One notes certain stock characters: Lewson is a remarkably successful portrayal of a good man; Jarvis is the faithful old retainer; Mrs Beverley is the uncomplaining virtuous woman. These characters look backwards, Mrs Beverley having a certain sisterhood with Melesinda in *Aureng-Zebe* and Jarvis and Lewson dividing between them the virtues of Ventidius in *All For Love*. *The Gamester* is the ancestor of the feeble temperance dramas and the anti-vice plays of the nineteenth century but we should not confuse the outline with the substance. This is a very real tragic achievement.

Douglas
John Home (1722–1808)

Distantly related to the Earls of that name, Home was
born at Leith and educated at Leith Grammar School and
Edinburgh university, where he graduated an MA in
1742. Although he wished to be a soldier he studied
divinity and was licensed by the presbytery of Edinburgh
in 1745. He fought as a volunteer against the Jacobites
and, in 1746, was taken prisoner at the battle of Falkirk.
He was imprisoned in the castle of Doune in Perthshire,
from where he escaped. Later in 1746 he became minister
of the parish of Athelstaneford, Haddingtonshire. It was
during this period that he became friendly with his kinsman, David Hume, the philosopher, historian and political economist, who encouraged his literary ambitions. His
first play, *Agis*, was rejected as unsuitable for the stage. He
then spent five years writing *Douglas*. The play was presented in Edinburgh in 1756, where it had an enormous
success, a voice from the pit exclaiming on the first night:
'Whaur's yer Willy Shakespeare noo?' It was further publicized by the controversy stirred up by the Church of
Scotland's opposition. An incredible number of pamphlets were produced, such as: *An Argument to prove
that ... Douglas ought to be Publicly Burnt at the Hands
of the Hangman*. The play gained the full support of the
Edinburgh audience and also of literary figures such as
Adam Smith, David Hume and others. It was performed
at Covent Garden in March 1757. Home made some slight

revisions for the London production, the most notable being to change Lady Barnard to Lady Randolph. The play remained a stock drama for the next hundred years. Home resigned his parish after *Douglas* had raised him to literary consequence. In 1758 he became private secretary to Lord Bute. He became tutor to the Prince of Wales. Garrick produced *Agis* in 1758, *The Siege of Aquileia* (1760), and *The Fatal Discovery* (1769). Home had tried to repeat the romantic success of *Douglas* with *The Fatal Discovery*, taken from Macpherson's *Ossian*.

The Fatal Discovery might have succeeded better thirty years later when romantic settings and costumes were coming into their own. Home wrote two other plays *Alonzo* (1773) and *Alfred* (1778). The latter was so coolly received that he never wrote for the stage again. From 1767 he lived in Scotland writing a *History of the Rebellion of 1745* which was published in 1802. In 1778 he joined a regiment formed by the Duke of Buccleuch but a fall from horseback permanently injured his brain. He died at Murchiston Bank, near Edinburgh, on 5 September 1808.

DATE 1756–7

CAST

Lord Randolph	Lady Randolph
Glenalvon	Anna
Young Norval	Servants
Old Norval	

SCENE Lord Randolph's castle and the woods surrounding it

Plot

Act I The court of a castle surrounded with woods. Lady Randolph enters bewailing the death twenty years ago of her first husband and infant son. Her present husband, Lord Randolph enters but is unable to change her mood.

He leaves her with her maid Anna to whom she describes
her secret marriage to Lord Douglas, his death in battle
and the supposed death of her infant son by drowning.
Although she cannot love him she acknowledges the
nobility of Lord Randolph but has nothing but scorn and
contempt for his heir Lord Glenalvon. Glenalvon is in
love with Lady Randolph and has planned to have Lord
Randolph murdered.

Act II The scene continues. A wounded Lord Randolph
is carried in escorted by a stranger. The stranger introduces himself as Young Norval in a speech beginning:

> My name is Norval: on the Grampian hills
> My father feeds his flocks a frugal swain ...

and continuing for a further thirty lines of alliterative
blank verse. This was one of the most famous speeches of
the nineteenth-century theatre and was quoted in every
recitation book from the play's first production to the end
of the nineteenth century. Norval it was who rescued
Randolph from the villainous attack of Glenalvon's hire-
lings although his part in the affair remains unsuspected.
Lady Randolph, imagining her own son had he lived
would have looked thus, feels strangely drawn to Young
Norval. Glenalvon has not only failed to do away with
Lord Randolph but he has introduced a rival into the
household.

Act III The scene continues. Lord Randolph's men enter
with a prisoner (Old Norval) whom they have found lurk-
ing in the wood. At first they suspect the man of being
one of Lord Randolph's erstwhile attackers. The prisoner
has jewels about him which Lady Randolph recognizes
as having belonged to her dead first husband. She dismisses the servants. In questioning the prisoner she discovers that Young Norval is her son. Before this news can
be imparted beyond the maid Anna, news is brought that
the Danes have landed and the men are called away to
repel the invasion.

Act IV The scene continues. Randolph and Glenalvon
return for a brief pause in the fighting. Lady Randolph
informs Norval of his true rank while Glenalvon sows the
seeds of jealousy in Lord Randolph's mind. Inspired with
pride after discovering his true identity Norval rather
haughtily rebuffs Lord Randolph. This seems to suggest
that there is truth in Glenalvon's insinuations and Randolph begins to suspect Norval of being his wife's lover.

Act V A wood. Young Norval meets first his foster father
and then Lady Randolph. Randolph and Glenalvon surprise Norval off stage. Glenalvon wounds him. He enters
to die in his mother's arms. She rushes off stage to commit
suicide while Anna informs Lord Randolph of the true
relationship. Glenalvon has died, killed by Norval, and
Lord Randolph resolves to return to battle where the man
that makes him turn aside must threaten more than
death.

Critical commentary

Douglas is one of the few mid-eighteenth century tragedies
to be passed on into the nineteenth century. The reason
is that in spite of its external neo-classicism in that it
observes the unities, confines its scenes to two or three
performers and culminates with an off stage catastrophe
it marks the beginnings of the Gothic phenomenon. Almost certainly this is accidental and outside Home's intention but we note marked changes in the playing and
presentation of the play during its hundred years of
popularity. The engraving at the head of the text, as
printed in the 1825 *The London Stage*, shows cut out
trees with a suitably romantic castle in the background.
The costumes illustrated are contemporary nineteenth-
century for the women and kilts with semi-classical boots
for the men. This is very far removed from the eighteenth-
century court dress in which the play was first performed.
What *Douglas* does is to anticipate some of the main

features of melodrama: such as the stronghold, almost
always a castle, although sometimes a robber's cave or a
forest lair within which the villain exercises unfettered
power. Of course this is not so on this occasion where
Lady Randolph carries with her such an all pervading
air of destructive gloom that one almost overlooks the
role of the mechanical villain Glenalvon, nor is the castle
properly equipped with sliding panels, torture chambers
and the rest of the Gothic paraphernalia we will encounter
when we examine *The Castle Spectre* but the play is
dominated by its two romantic settings of a medieval
castle and a dark forest, twin favourites of melodrama. It
also provided scope for the introduction of the romantic
pseudo highland costumes so beloved of the romantics.
Thomas Dibdin in his *Reminiscences* describes the process
of alteration, recalling how *Douglas*:

> ... without omitting a single line of the author, made a
> very splendid melo-drame, with the additions of Lord
> Randolph's magnificent banquet, a martial Scotch dance,
> and a glee, formed from Home's words – 'Free is his heart
> who for his country fights, &c &c', exquisitely set by
> Sanderson, and delightfully sung, together with an expensive
> processional representation of the landing of the Danes:
> besides all this, as a Surrey Theatre gallery audience
> always expects some ultra incident, I had a represesentative
> of Lady Randolph in the person of a very clever boy, by
> whose good acting and fearless agility, the northern dame,
> at the conclusion of the tragedy, was seen to throw herself
> from a distant precipice into a boiling ocean, in a style
> which literally brought down thunders of applause.

But *Douglas* could not have succeeded from external
appeal alone, its true power lies in the suppressed Scottish-
ness with which it deals with dark and forbidden things.
Although uncorroborated the suggestion of incest looms
large and it touches on the inner world of the psyche.
Much of the eighteenth-century tragedy is destroyed by

the concept of poetic justice which grants, albeit after heavy trials, the good man or woman their due. Not so here where there is no benevolent providence to heal Lady Randolph's wounds or bring a sudden reconciliation between her and Lord Randolph.

Eighteenth-century critics, Goldsmith in particular, were struck by Home's use of language, and although modern readers may not be so enthusiastic it does contain many fine descriptive passages and there is a variety of pace lacking in the bulk of eighteenth-century dramatic verse. Compared with Shakespeare the verse is pedestrian, the speeches too long and there is excessive use of alliteration and other decorative figures, but when one places it alongside representative eighteenth-century tragedies such as Dodsley's *Cleone* its true quality is appreciated. It owes much to its extra-national origins for it combines Home's study of the classical drama with a Scottish romanticism which anticipates the novels of Sir Walter Scott. It is noticeable that after the success of *Douglas* and his introduction into London literary society. Home became affected by the prevailing tragic mode and *The Fatal Discovery* (1769) is a worthy but undistinguished piece which entirely fails to recapture the romance of his earlier success.

The Way to Keep Him
Arthur Murphy (1727–1805)

Murphy was educated at St Omer and began life as a merchant's clerk. Later he published *The Gray's Inn Journal* (1752–4). He became a barrister and then, on the encouragement of Samuel Foote, an actor. At the latter profession he was never particularly successful. From 1756 he became a farce writer and in 1759 his adaptation of Voltaire's *The Orphan of China* established him as a serious dramatist. His later tragedies include *The Grecian Daughter* (1772) and *Alzuma* (1773). Many of his comedies were based on French plays but it would be wrong to dismiss him as a writer without originality. He shares with many Anglo-Irish dramatists a natural gift for dialogue and his work helps to erode the domination of sentimental comedy. His best comedies are *The Way to Keep Him, All In the Wrong* (1761), *The School for Guardians* (1767) and *Know Your Own Mind* (1777).

DATE 1760

CAST

Lovemore

Sir Brilliant Fashion

William, servant to Lovemore

Mrs Lovemore

The Widow Bellmour

Muslin, waiting-woman to Mrs Lovemore

Mignionet, maid to Mrs Bellmour

Pompey, a black boy belonging to the Widow
Jenny, maid to Mrs Lovemore
SCENE London

Plot

Act I,*i* The servants' hall in Lovemore's house. William
and a brother servant are playing cards, aping the vices of
their betters. Muslin enters to demand when Lovemore
returned home. We learn that he has been visiting a rich
widow that he met at Bath. Muslin is jealous of William's
relationship with her maid. William hints at further complications as the scene ends. *ii* Mrs Lovemore's apartment.
Muslin advises Mrs Lovemore that marriage is old fashioned. Sir Brilliant Fashion enters and continues in this
strain. Mrs Lovemore accuses him of misleading her husband with similar advice and introducing him to the
Widow Bellmour. Sir Brilliant denies that Lovemore is
acquainted with the lady. Lovemore enters and is very
civil and restrained with his wife, suggesting they meet
that night. Both affect to believe that for a husband and
wife to meet together would be 'gothic to the last degree!'
Lovemore exits. Sir Brilliant describes the widow. He
again denies that Lovemore visits her. He was himself her
suitor till cut out by Lord Etheridge who has recently returned from the continent. He suggests that as he himself
is disappointed in his address to the widow and Mrs Lovemore neglected by her husband that 'the least they can do
is both heartily to join to sweeten each other's cares.' Mrs
Lovemore desires him to quit the house. She resolves to
pay a visit to the widow.
Act II,*i* A room at Bellmour's. The widow is talking with
Mignionet of Lord Etheridge. Mrs Lovemore is announced. Mrs Bellmour denies being acquainted with
Lovemore, and gives Mrs Lovemore advice on marriage.
Lord Etheridge is announced and Mrs Lovemore takes her
leave. Lord Etheridge turns out to be Lovemore. They

gossip on fashionable topics until Mrs Bellmour is called away. Sir Brilliant enters and Lovemore who has assumed the disguise in order to cheat his friend, makes an embarrassed exit quickly followed by a now suspicious Sir Brilliant. Mrs Bellmour and Mrs Lovemore re-enter. Mrs Bellmour has a scheme to turn Lovemore's deceit to his wife's advantage and insists on her staying to dine.

Act III,i An apartment at Mr Lovemore's. Mrs Lovemore and Mrs Bellmour await the two men. The Widow has had Lovemore denied entrance to her house and we learn he 'went off as sulky as a Russian General when a garrison refuses to capitulate.' Sir Brilliant has been lured by a message from Mrs Lovemore stating that she is alone. As Lovemore is heard returning Mrs Bellmour retires. Lovemore is amazed to find his wife entertaining but has no reply when she turns his own words of the first act back at him:

> ... for a married couple to interfere and encroach on each other's pleasures – oh hideous! It would be gothic to the last degree. Ha! Ha! Ha!

Muslin enters with a letter from Sir Brilliant to his wife. He then observes the two flirting, but the bubble of the outraged husband is pricked by Mrs Bellmour entering and greeting him as Lord Etheridge. After the exposure it is agreed that Mrs Lovemore will strive to be a more entertaining wife and the two men will be more honest in their dealings with each other.

Critical commentary

Most people familiar with this play are aware of it as one of the best five act comedies of manners written in the second half of the eighteenth century, indeed Allardyce Nicoll goes so far as to link it with the best of Sheridan and Goldsmith in *A History of English Drama*. It was, however, first performed as an after piece, and it is the

earlier and less well known version which we have sum-
marized above.

The strength of the period 1660–1900 lies in the sheer
bulk of diverse material, of which a large portion of the
most significant is visual or theatrical rather than instantly literary in its appeal. The tradition of studying
English drama as an offshoot of English literature has led
to a serious and misleading underestimation of the dramatic importance of irregular forms and the interrelationship between main piece and after piece drama. The strict
division between the comic and tragic worlds inherited
from the Augustans led to tragedy dealing only with such
aspects of life as admiration and pity, while comedy, as we
have seen, in spite of a pretended division between laughing and sentimental was essentially good hearted. Elizabethan drama had managed to maintain three contrasting
worlds in the one play: a heroic world, a benevolent
world and a vigorous low world. We need look no further
than *A Midsummer Night's Dream* for an example of this:
Oberon and Titania provide a high plot; the lovers a
sentimental plot; while coarse commentary on both is
provided by Bottom and his fellows. Augustan regularity
had only superficially altered this by confining these separate elements to separate plays, but the practice of multiple bills meant that these elements were all available in
the one evening. The main difference between Elizabethan
and eighteenth-century drama is that while in the Elizabethan theatre you were simultaneously provided with
soup, meat and pudding the eighteenth century divided
these into separate courses.

This division between tragedy, comedy and farce derives from French neo-classical dramatic theory where the
practice was to include contrasting genres in a multiple
bill, the worlds of tragedy and comedy allowing no over-
lap. Dramatic theory was helped by theatrical fact. In the
late seventeenth century there was a practice of exacting
'after money' from late comers. These were numerous and

'after money' an important source of revenue. In the reign
of Charles II the entertainment started at 2 p.m., by the
end of the century the starting time was 5 p.m. and by the
time of Garrick 6 p.m. Even this was too early a start for
the business and working classes who were now beginning
to demand theatrical entertainment. The theatre found
the answer in an average programme of four or five hours
duration divided into a main piece (either comedy or
tragedy), an after piece (either melodrama, farce, ballad
opera or dramatic satire), and a pantomime. Half price
was accepted after the main piece. The more obvious
theatricality and broader tones of the half-price material
reflects the less elevated nature of the audience but it is
quite wrong to see this material as lesser, indeed the reverse is probably the case. Even in 1785 critics were recognizing the general vigour of after piece drama, and it was
noted that playhouses were often fuller for the second
half of the entertainment. Yet literary criticism remains
biased towards main piece comedy, neglecting the shorter
plays.

The Way to Keep Him is a tightly constructed petite
comédie and not a farce. The lack of sub-plot makes every
scene essential and we are never in danger of losing the
moral aim of the play as we are even in Sheridan and
Goldsmith, nor does the moral statement on married life
become obsessive and morality swamp comedy.

The five act version dilutes this tautness. Of the example of expansion given below, R. W. Bevis notes in his
introduction to the edition from which this summary is
taken: '(It) is indicative of one respect in which a main
piece was expected to differ from an after piece.' In the
first scene of the second act, when the widow Bellmour
denies knowledge of Lovemore, in our text she simply
says: 'May I beg to know who the gentleman is?'
Mrs Lovemore replies with a straightforward description
of her husband's recent coldness to her. In the five act
version the following lines are inserted:

Mrs Lovemore The story will be uninteresting to you, and to me it is painful, My grievances ...
[*Puts her handkerchief to her eyes*]
Mrs Bellmour [*aside*] Her grief affects me.
[*Looks at her till she has recovered herself*]

The handkerchief is out and tearful sympathy is looked for from the audience. In our present era where serviceable tissue has replaced decorative linen the after piece comedies are much more to our taste.

The Country Girl
David Garrick (1717–79)

Garrick is usually hailed as being one of the great origin-
ators and reformers of the English Theatre. Charles
Macklin should probably be more correctly credited with
initiating a more natural manner of speech but Garrick's
incredible success established this. How natural both
Garrick and Macklin were is a matter of debate, they were
close enough to the declamatory performers, as typified by
James Quin, to be able to appear side by side with them.
Drawings of Garrick depict large gestures and formal
poses. His restoration of Shakespeare's text was, to say the
least, tentative. He was himself a successful adapter of
Shakespeare's plays, producing farcical versions of *The
Taming of the Shrew* (*Katherine and Petruchio*, 1756)
and *The Winter's Tale* (*Florizel and Perdita*, 1756) which
held the stage for many years. A version of *Hamlet*, unique
to him, totally altered the fifth act, yet he became the
great upholder of Shakespeare's genius. One of his most
publicized achievements was the Shakespeare Jubilee at
Stratford, in 1769. This took the form of odes, songs,
speeches and tableaux of Shakespeare's characters by
David Garrick but seems to have included little by William Shakespeare. His best writing is in the field of farces,
such as *Miss in her Teens* (1747) and *Bon Ton, or High
Life Above Stairs* (1775) and as an adapter and collaborator. From 1747 he was manager of Drury Lane. It is to his
credit that he had enough confidence in his art to appear

with all the leading actors of his time. He had a remarkable talent for recognizing and employing the talents of
others. He is responsible for introducing the scenic de-
signer Philip Jaques de Loutherbourg (1740–1812) to
Drury Lane. Loutherbourg introduced many new devices,
some of which we will explore in our description of *The
Castle Spectre*. The most significant alteration was the use
of a series of lights directly behind the proscenium, which
had the result of forcing the actors back into the stage
picture and thus increasing the importance of scenery.
De Loutherbourg brought the beginnings of naturalism to
scenery which complimented Garrick's own more restrained playing. Garrick quarrelled with or used his contemporaries unmercifully. He brought Sarah Siddons to
London in 1775 in order to frighten his regular actresses
into greater obedience. His brother George was virtually
his servant for years and dying only a few days after him
it was said by the wits of the time because 'Davy wanted
him!' Garrick's farewell appearance was as Felix in Mrs
Centlivre's *The Wonder, a Woman Keeps a Secret* in June
1776. He retired to Hampton where he died three years
later. He is buried in Westminster Abbey. His greatest
achievement was to establish the theatre as a social form
and it is his sensitivity to the manners of his time which
is apparent in all his writings.

DATE 1766
CAST

Moody	Miss Peggy, ward and
Harcourt	supposed wife to Moody
Sparkish, engaged to Alithea	Alithea, sister to Moody
Belville, nephew to Harcourt	Lucy, her maid
SCENE London	

Plot

Act I, Harcourt's lodgings. Belville confesses to his uncle

that he is in love with a country girl, Peggy. Harcourt in
his turn is in love with Alithea who is about to be married
to Sparkish. Sparkish calls with news that Moody suspects
Belville of making sheep's eyes at Miss Peggy. He inquires
of Harcourt whether he knows of a clergyman who can
tie the knot between him and Alithea. Harcourt quickly
responds by inventing a twin brother who will he claims
be in town that day and only too proud to attend to Sparkish's commands. Sparkish accepts the offer further informing them that Moody has a mind to marry Miss Peggy at
the same time. Moody has been spurred to this resolve by
an old raking acquaintance who saw him with Miss Peggy
skulking and muffled up at the play. This acquaintance
took her for Moody's wife and swore to cuckold him. Harcourt was under the impression that Moody had been
married to the girl already and questions Sparkish further.
It now comes to light that because of a clause in her
father's will Moody was unable to marry her in the
country but in order to keep the girl for himself he went
through the country ceremony of breaking a sixpence with
her and she is under the impression that he is her husband.
Belville is delighted with this news. Moody calls to warn
Belville away from his women folk and Harcourt contrives to suggest that it is Alithea and not Peggy that has
caught the youth's fancy.
Act II,*i* A chamber in Moody's house. Peggy questions
Alithea about the town. Moody enters and accuses his
sister of teaching Peggy where men are to be found. Peggy
praises the players and begs Moody to take her to the
theatre a second time. Sparkish, Harcourt and Belville
call. Moody warns Belville not to make eyes at his wife,
while Sparkish behaves with odious self sufficiency by
allowing Harcourt to flirt with Alithea:

> ... Go, go, with her into a corner, and try if she has wit;
> [*He puts Harcourt over to Alithea*] talk to her anything,
> she's bashful before me – take her into a corner.

Moody returns and upbraids Sparkish for allowing Harcourt such freedom but Sparkish disdains to seem jealous like a country bumpkin. Sparkish and Harcourt carry Alithea off to the theatre. Sparkish promises that Harcourt shall stay in the box to entertain her, for his own part if he were to remain throughout the play he might be thought no critic. *ii* Another room in Moody's house. Peggy confesses to Lucy that she is greatly attracted to Belville while Lucy relays a message to her from that gentleman. Peggy begs Moody to take her for a walk in the park. At first he refuses but at Lucy's suggestion he agrees provided she wear a suit of clothes he has bought for his godson and pretends to be a youth.

Act III,*i* The park. Belville walks in the park in the hope of meeting Peggy. Harcourt accompanies him in the hope of meeting Alithea. Sparkish enters and rallies Harcourt with having offended his mistress by making love to her. Alithea is seen approaching. Sparkish has another engagement and would avoid her. Harcourt persuades Sparkish to leave Alithea in his company that he might make his peace with her. Moody enters with the disguised Peggy. Harcourt and Belville pretend not to recognize her and in spite of Moody's suspicions Harcourt contrives that his nephew should show 'the young gentleman' Rosamond's pond. *ii* Another part of the park. Belville explains to Peggy that there is no law on earth that can compel her to marry a man she does not like. If she marries without Moody's consent she loses half her fortune. The young couple are on the point of elopement when Moody re-enters and repossesses himself of his 'godson'.

Act IV,*i* Moody's house. Lucy advises Alithea against going through with her marriage to Harcourt. The lines are Wycherley's:

> Can there be a greater cheat or wrong done to a man, than to give him your person without your heart?

ii Another chamber in Moody's house. Moody compels

Peggy to write to Belville;.as in the original play she substitutes her own love letter for that dictated by Moody.
iii Belville's lodgings. Lucy and ·Belville are plotting
Peggy's elopement when they are interrupted by the arrival of Moody with her letter. Lucy hides in a closet.
Sparkish enters most put out. He was on the point of being
married by Harcourt's twin brother when Alithea took an
aversion to the parson, and swore 'twas Harcourt himself.
She walked up within a pistol shot of the church, then
twirled round upon her heel, called Sparkish every name
she could think of and left him in the middle of a laughing
crowd. Moody and Belville, and even Lucy in her closet
all burst out laughing. Sparkish exits to the sound of
their ridicule.

Act V,*i* Moody's house. Moody catches Peggy writing
another love letter to Belville. She tricks him into believing that she writes upon Alithea's behalf. Moody escorts
Peggy disguised as Alithea to Belville, taking great comfort from the belief that it is his sister that Belville pursues
and not his 'wife'. *ii* The park before Belville's house. A
drunken Sparkish intercepts the disguised Peggy, whom
he takes for Alithea on the way to Belville's house. Moody
intervenes and delivers Peggy into Belville's care with instructions that he is to marry her without delay. Harcourt
comes on the scene with Alithea whom he has married
within the hour. Moody demands to know whom it was he
delivered to Belville, but he is too late, Belville and Peggy
have obeyed his commands and are now man and wife. It
is Sparkish's turn to laugh at Moody and he is more than
prepared to give evidence that Moody gave his consent to
the match and thus secure all Peggy's fortune to the young
couple.

Critical commentary

Study of *The Country Girl* offers a chance to reconsider

and consolidate our attitude to Georgian comedy. Before
the Second World War it was a commonplace of literary
dramatic criticism to view Sheridan and Goldsmith as of
a different species to the other comic writers of their age
and it was often suggested that Sheridan marks a return
to something approaching the style of Congreve while
Goldsmith reintroduces the vitality of the Elizabethans.
Such statements only reveal that those uttering them have
an insufficient knowledge of Georgian drama as a whole
and the work of Garrick, George Colman the elder,
Murphy and Cumberland in particular, for there can be
no doubt that when Sheridan is read in the context of the
work of these authors it is clearly apparent that he makes
no changes in comic theory or dramatic structure. The
comparative critical silence about Sheridan in the past
thirty years seems to indicate a growing realization that
his work has perhaps been overvalued.

The presiding genius of the start of the Georgian era
was David Garrick. During the period of his domination
theatrical development tended to be in the arts of acting
and stage presentation rather than in dramatic composition. Actors were judged not so much on new plays but on
radically altered performances of established favourites.
What is 'new' almost always conforms to established
themes and techniques and just as the new plays were
written to adhere to accepted theory and structure so the
old was revised upon identical lines.

The close relationship between Garrick and Sheridan
as authors is often overlooked owing to lack of familiarity
both with the work of Garrick and with Sheridan's minor
work. The revision of *The Country Wife* to *The Country
Girl* is analogous to Sheridan's alteration of *The Relapse*
into *A Trip to Scarborough* and there are also a great
number of parallels between Garrick's rehearsal burlesque
A Peep Behind The Curtain and *The Critic* but most significantly the code of *The Country Girl* is identical to that

of *The Rivals* and *The School for Scandal*: sex was not inadmissible at this time provided its treatment conformed to certain standards.

The Country Girl is by custom overlooked as a mere bawdlerized reworking of Wycherley's *The Country Wife*. The loss of the overt sexuality of the original results in our over emphasizing its sexual blandness at the expense of other typically Georgian omissions. Restoration and Augustan drama is often political and almost always social. It reflects the upheavals and lack of stability contemporary with it. In direct contrast Georgian drama totally avoids any reference to social dislocation in spite of the fact that the starting date for what we term the Industrial Revolution is usually given as 1760. Nor does the drama of this period reflect in any way such political issues of its time as the constitutional problems raised by Wilkes, attempts to institute electoral reform or even the regency crisis. The plays all conform to the taste and attitudes of a London society utterly disinterested in persons of lower rank. Thus even in plays like *The West Indian* requiring a heroine beset by poverty, she will be presented as a lady. The lack of attention to social and political themes would seem a far more serious omission than genuine attempts to refine theatrical sexuality. It can be argued that sexual relations are essentially of a private nature and that to rely for laughs on the bawdy is hardly proof of wit.

The refinements of *The Country Girl* go too far for the taste of the 1970s but it should be noted that it was preferred in the theatre not only in its own time but for the next 150 years, for even after *The Country Wife* was acknowledged the better play it was for many years considered too broad for public presentation. Today we will deplore the moral 'improvements' but at the same time we must acknowledge the fact that Garrick has given the play greater unity.

The original contains three plots: The Fidget incidents, the Alithea–Harcourt–Sparkish triangle and the cuckolding of Pinchwife. While Pinchwife's jealousy is contrasted to Sparkish's self-sufficiency apart from this and certain dramatic techniques, such as the dialogue of one scene serving as an ironic echo of another and the parallel device of both Harcourt and Margery disguising themselves as their twins, there is little link between the plots save Horner's tenuous acquaintance with all the other characters and the fact that Alithea is Pinchwife's sister.

Garrick's reorganization is extreme and along the lines he sets out eleven years later in the prologue he wrote for Sheridan's revision of *The Relapse, A Trip to Scarborough*:

> As change thus circulates throughout the nation,
> Some plays may justly call for alteration;
> At least to draw some slender covering o'er
> That graceless wit, which was too bare before:
> Those writers well and wisely use their pens,
> Who turn our wantons into Magdalens.

Audience taste dictated perhaps to an even greater extent than the attitude of the examiner of plays that cuckoldry, the central theme of the original, be banished. This meant that in spite of its noble pedigree from *The Eunuch* of Terence, Garrick had to dispense with Wycherley's starting point of Horner's stratagem of pretended impotence. Shorn of this device Horner is truly impotent and thus the linking character of *The Country Wife* disappears and Garrick is faced with the problem of creating a totally new frame plot which will still allow him to retain the bulk of the episodes and character relationships of the earlier play.

His solution is to return to Wycherley's own inspiration, Molière's *L'École des Femmes*. From Molière Garrick borrows the idea of transforming Pinchwife into an English version of Arnolphe, now called Moody, who has deliberately kept his rich country ward ignorant so that she will in the fullness of time make him the more obedient wife. Because Moody, unlike Pinchwife in the earlier play, is not yet married but only pretending to be so the element of cuckoldry is removed and Belville's pursuit of the girl utterly honourable in that its ultimate conclusion is marriage. The young men of Georgian comedy are allowed to suggest libertinage but we seldom see them at anything more rakish than a supper party, but even allowing them a certain status as reformed rakes the essential difference between them and their late seventeenth-century counterparts is that while the Mirabels and Dorimants are reformed by good sense their successors owe their alteration to their good hearts. By making Belville nephew to Harcourt the two plots are drawn together. Of course the Fidgets have to go and with them the famous china scene but while we must regret this loss we cannot claim that they were essential even to the original play.

What remains are the old man's devices to keep his country girl from the young man, such as the hilariously unsuccessful ploy of disguising her as a boy and his attempts to manipulate the letters and the entire Sparkish–Harcourt–Alithea plot. The overt homosexuality of the scenes between Horner and the disguised Margery are prettified in those between Peggy and Belville and similarly the vicious threats of Pinchwife are reduced to senile fumblings, but a surprising amount of the original does remain. A scene that is certainly drawn more closely into the play is that in which Moody delivers Peggy's letter to Belville, for its observation by Lucy flows more naturally out of the intrigue which has gone before than does Horner's device of hiding Quack in order to demonstrate the success of his stratagem.

The deliberate ambiguity of Wycherley's last act is replaced by an obligatory ordering which is entirely satisfactory in the new context.

The Clandestine Marriage
George Colman (1732–94)

George Colman is usually called 'The Elder' to distinguish
him from his son, also a dramatic and miscellaneous
writer. The elder Colman was born in Florence where his
father was attached to the court of the Grand Duke of
Tuscany. His father died within a year of his birth and
his upbringing was paid for by Lord Bath whose wife was
the sister of Colman's mother. He was educated at a private
school in Marylebone, Westminster and Christ Church,
Oxford. He left Oxford in 1755 without taking a degree.
He was entered at Lincoln's Inn being called to the bar in
1757. He continued to practise as a barrister until the
death of Lord Bath in 1764. Previous to this he had
formed a close relationship with David Garrick and begun
to write plays. His first was the after piece *Polly Honeycombe* (1760) which satirizes the trends in contemporary
fiction. This was a great success. A year later his comedy
The Jealous Wife, partly based on *Tom Jones*, established
his reputation. He published a verse translation of the
comedies of Terence. *The Clandestine Marriage* (1766)
written in collaboration with Garrick resulted in a
quarrel between the collaborators. Garrick refused to play
Lord Ogleby, although the part was to become a favourite
of leading actors. It was instead created by King who was
later to be the first Sir Peter Teazle. In the next year
Colman purchased a share in Covent Garden thus setting
himself in direct opposition to his former friend. He was

manager of Covent Garden for seven years. In 1768 he
was elected to the Literary Club, then nominally consist-
ing of twelve members. In 1774 he sold his share in Covent
Garden. In 1777 he bought the Little Theatre in the Haymarket from Samuel Foote. He was the author of numerous adaptations of Elizabethan and Stuart drama, including versions of *Epicoene*, *Bonduca* and *Comus*. He
edited the works of Beaumont and Fletcher in 1778. His
knowledge of both classical and old English drama is
revealed in *The Clandestine Marriage* in which he seems
responsible for the larger share.

DATE 1766
CAST
Lord Ogleby
Sir John Melvil, his nephew
Sterling, a rich merchant
Lovewell, a kinsman of Lord Ogleby
Canton, Lord Ogleby's secretary, a Swiss
Brush, valet to Lord Ogleby
Serjeant Flower
Traverse
Trueman
Mrs Heidelberg, Sterling's sister
Miss Sterling
Fanny, her younger sister
Betty, Fanny's maid
Trusty
SCENE Mr Sterling's country house and its environs

Plot

Act I,*i* A room in Sterling's country house. From a scene
between Fanny and her maid Betty we learn that Fanny
has recently contracted a secret marriage with the impecunious Lovewell, forced by circumstances, in spite of
good connections, to earn his bread as her father's clerk.

Lovewell enters and assures Fanny that in a few days he hopes, after her elder sister has becomes engaged to Sir John Melvil, to announce their marriage. This note of optimism is smashed when Sterling ridicules Lovewell's pretensions towards his younger daughter and makes him promise that he will carry the matter no further without his consent. Sterling leaves Lovewell to make the most of some sound materialistic advice that would not have been out of place in *George Barnwell*:

> You're not rich enough to think of a wife yet. A man
> of business would mind nothing but his business ...
> Get an estate, and a wife will follow of course – Ah!
> Lovewell! an English merchant is the most respectable
> character in the universe, 'Slife, man, a rich English
> merchant may make himself a match for the daughter of
> a Nabob.

ii Another room in the house. Miss Sterling boasts to Fanny of the comforts she will enjoy after she is married to Sir John Melvil. Mrs Heidelberg enters busy with the final preparations to receive Sir John and Lord Ogleby who are expected within the next quarter of an hour. Miss Sterling confides to her aunt that Sir John pays much more attention to Fanny than to herself. She also remarks that the old lord his uncle has ten times more gallantry about him. 'He is full of attention to the ladies, and smiles, and grins, and leers, and ogles, and fills every wrinkle in his wizen old face with comical expressions of tenderness.' Canton, the Swiss gentleman that lives with Lord Ogleby, arrives to announce that his master follows at his heels.

Act II,*i* The antechamber to Lord Ogleby's bedroom. Brush the valet makes love to a chambermaid. This is followed by Lord Ogleby's transformation, with the help of medicines and make-up from a decrepit dried up shell to an elderly roué. *ii* The garden. Sir John Melvil confides to Lovewell that he had agreed to marry Miss Sterling out of duty to his family which is, despite its nobility, in desperate need of her money, but that now after seeing Fanny he is desperately in love with the younger sister. He begs his kinsman's assistance in advancing his new suit. Sterling proudly displays his garden complete with ruins which cost a thousand pounds to repair while Mrs Heidelberg tries to tempt the old lord to visit her little gothic dairy to take a dish of tea with her. The act ends with Miss Sterling interrupting Sir John on his knees declaring his passion to Fanny. She accuses her sister of trying to filch Sir John's affections.

Act III,*i* The hall. The lawyers gather for the important business of drawing up the marriage settlement. As this is something not to be passed over lightly the lawyers are given a certain amount of time in which to establish themselves. Into these contracts Sir John Melvil drops the bombshell of the change in his affections. Sterling's fury is abated when after some hard bargaining Sir John agrees to take a smaller portion with the younger daughter. The change of plan is conditional on Sterling's gaining the consent of Mrs Heidelberg. *ii* Another apartment in Sterling's house. Miss Sterling complains to her aunt about what she takes to be Fanny's perfidy. Sir John and Sterling come as ambassadors for the new arrangements and are disdainfully rejected. Both sides determine to appeal to Lord Ogleby.

Act IV,*i* A room in the house. It is determined that Fanny shall be sent to London. This will entail a separation from Lovewell and make the disclosure of their secret marriage more difficult. *ii, iii* The garden. She has naïvely misinterpreted Lord Ogleby's partiality for her. On Lovewell's advice she appeals to him and in trying to explain her situation leaves him with the impression that his own suit would not be unwelcome. On the strength of this misunderstood encouragement he proposes to Sterling that he and not his nephew should marry into the merchant's family. Such is his vanity that when Sir John asks his per-

mission to change from the elder to the younger sister he
says:

> I look upon women as the *ferae naturae* – lawful game –
> and every man who is qualified has a natural right to
> pursue them; Lovewell as well as you.

Act V,*i* Fanny's apartment. Matters have come to such a
pass that Lovewell is determined to announce his and
Fanny's marriage the next day. *ii* A gallery which leads to
several bedchambers. Miss Sterling has overheard voices
in her sister's room. She and Mrs Heidelberg presume that
Sir John Melvil is within. They are forced to retreat by
the entry of a half drunk Brush trying to seduce the
chambermaid. They interrupt this revelry when Brush
tells the girl that if she is not more compliant such is his
humour he will break down a door and ravish Mrs Heidelberg. Brush runs off and Mrs Heidelberg instructs the girl
to fetch her brother. This activity brings the whole household upon the scene, including the lawyers. Mrs Heidelberg is so relieved to discover that it is Lovewell and not
Sir John with Fanny that she is prepared to accept their
marriage. Lord Ogleby declares himself to be annihilated
but rises sufficiently to the occasion to offer the young
couple a home should Mr Sterling still refuse to accept the
match. But Sterling accepts the match and even Sir John
apologizes to Lovewell declaring his infatuation for
Fanny to be over. The piece is followed by a brief farcical
epilogue written by Garrick. Several people of society
discuss in rhyming couplets over cards what they have
heard of the play. They are unanimous in their judgement that it should be damned and they end with a song:

> Would you ever go to see a tragedy? Never, never.

Critical commentary
Theatre is strongly influenced if not controlled by the
things an audience takes for granted but future judge-

ments, often passed without the benefit of a continuing performing tradition, rely all too often on critical comment rather than direct relationship between student and text. The problem with Georgian comedy is that it has been to a very great extent ignored. It was impossible with the study of English drama relegated to a subsidiary of English literature to pay full attention to the volume of work which must be read before the diversity of the period can be fully understood, and many scholars tended to follow each other in a mass condemnation of the bulk of the comic writing of the period as artificial and sentimental. The first scholarly attempt to reinstate eighteenth-century comedy came in the 1930s with Allardyce Nicoll's *History of English Drama* but even to this day many tutors seem incapable of recommending work outside that by Sheridan and Goldsmith. There remains with us an inflated idea of a division between 'laughing' and 'sentimental' comedy which can be traced back to Goldsmith's essay 'On the Theatre' and Richard Cumberland's reply to this in his dedicatory epistle attached to the first edition of *The Choleric Man* (1775). Goldsmith had called main piece comedy:

> ... a kind of mulish production, with all the defects
> of its opposite parents and marked with sterility.

He had proceeded to say that:

> ... a new species of dramatic composition has been
> introduced under the name of *Sentimental* comedy, in
> which the virtues of private life are exhibited, rather than
> the vices exposed; and the distresses, rather than the faults
> of mankind make our interest in the piece ... In these
> plays almost all the characters are good, and exceedingly
> generous: they are lavish enough of their tin money on the
> stage, and though they want Humour, have abundance of
> Sentiment and Feeling.

It is always fascinating to listen to a writer justifying

his work, the more so because Goldsmith himself is not
entirely free from the faults he condemns in others. Cumberland chose to interpret these remarks as a personal
attack on his own *The Fashionable Lover* (1772), a piece
which certainly comes close to a tragic conclusion. The
distressed heroine Miss Aubrey is on the receiving end of
the unwelcome attentions of Lord Abberville and the unjust oppression of the merchant Mr Bridgemore and his
family, in whose house she resides. She is driven out of the
Bridgemore household after having been placed in a compromising situation by Lord Abberville, unfortunately
taking refuge with a woman in league with that peer. She
is only rescued from this overwhelming combination of
disasters by the good offices of the warm hearted Scotsman
MacLeod and the timely return of her father who reveals
that Mr Bridgemore has been embezzling her fortune. The
formula is recognizably similar to Cumberland's *The
West Indian* in its exploitation of passive characters in
adversity.

The Clandestine Marriage is superbly representative of
the middle way in comedy (others of this school being
Benjamin Hoadly's *The Suspicious Husband,* which with
the character of Ranger gave the Georgian stage its closest
approximation to a Restoration rake, and Colman's own
The Jealous Wife) being undeniably a laughing comedy
but one cast within the acceptable conventions of the
sentimental school.

It is perfectly justifiable to view the predicament of
Lovewell and Fanny as a distressing situation and the
attempts at manipulation by Sterling and Ogleby are not
so terribly far removed from those of Lord Abberville and
Bridgemore in *The Fashionable Lover*. Certainly all the
characters, once we arrive at the final exposure, demonstrate or discover a good heartedness that is sentimentally
moral. The play tends to be uncritical in its celebration
of the manners of the time. The vulgarity of Sterling and
Mrs Heidelberg are enjoyed as facts with no attempt at

reformation. The authors make no attempt to create or feed potential social antagonism between the rising merchant class and the distressed aristocracy. Sterling has a shrewd appreciation of his abilities but lacks polish. On the other hand Lord Ogleby's affectations do not make him a fool. Even his battle with age is merely a superficial battle with externals and he never allows his pretence at vigour to cloud the judgement of his experience. Even Mrs Heidelberg is rescued from ridicule by being depicted as a lady of considerable will and decision, something after the manner Wodehouse will employ for his aunts. We recognize in her a worthy ancestor of Lady Bracknell, formidable indeed. Sir John Melvil is an unrewarding part. He tends towards affectation without the violent exaggerations of the Froths and Foppingtons of the drama of the turn of the century. Here good nature is detrimental to good theatre for it is the muting of the character preparatory to his reformation in Act V which gives it a blandness to the point that we are neither sympathetic to nor revolted by him. In this field of exaggerated foppery Restoration and late seventeenth-century writers have a distinct edge over their eighteenth-century successors who seem almost afraid that too rich a characterization in a minor part might detract from the actor manager's role. The lawyers, traditional theatrical targets though they may be, come lightly off in comparison with their counterparts in Steele's *The Funeral*. A minor example this of increasing respect paid throughout eighteenth-century drama to middle-class opinion. Although the prologue makes reference to Hogarth's Marriage-à-la-Mode the only satirical target would appear to be the valet, Brush. In him is given a comparatively harsh picture of the opportunist servant aping the manners of his betters. The pretension of servants was a popular if dangerous target as is shown by the reception offered to James Townley's farce *High Life Below Stairs* (1759), at which some footmen rioted during the second performance, the play only proceeding after the intervention of their masters.

The treatment of love as a justification for marriage is sentimentally escapist, for the Georgian era was still very much an age when marriage was a means to alliances between classes and families. Few members of the original audience would have been allowed to consider a possibility of marrying for love. Contracts and settlements had to be considered. The authors show a shrewd respect for reality in confining the love interest to the younger sister, who is by her position less immediately involved in matters of inheritance.

Even allowing for the play's distinctly eighteenth-century tone and comparatively bland characterization it still seems to answer many of the requisites of laughing comedy and knowledge of it and its fellows must surely temper any view that Sheridan and Goldsmith are unique in their efforts in this direction. Indeed Garrick should be understood to be a much more significant influence on Georgian drama, dominating the theatre from his position as manager of Drury Lane from 1747 to 1776, than his successor R. B. Sheridan who dissipated much of what he inherited. With hindsight we can see the Garrick and Colman decades as too commercially careful to leave us any revolutionary dramatic literature. Garrick's attitude to Shakespeare typifies the age. He was for example personally attracted to the mingling of tragedy and comedy in Shakespeare but he did not trust it on stage. Garrick and Colman both allow popular taste to limit their own intellect and the result is that they display great talent as dramatic writers rather than genius. Elegant, accomplished and ingenious are the adjectives most in use when describing the work of this period but with it is established secure conventions for laughing comedy which remain unchanged to the era of Pinero and Shaw. The next generation of comic writers could only continue in the same vein, sometimes better, sometimes worse, and any impression of arresting improvement in comic technique in the work of Goldsmith and Sheridan stems from a lack of knowledge of the comedy which immediately precedes it, rather than genuine critical insight.

The West Indian
Richard Cumberland (1732–1811)

Cumberland has a distinguished literary pedigree. On his mother's side he was the grandson of Richard Bentley while both his father and grandfather were bishops. He was educated at Bury St Edmunds Grammar School and Westminster, where he was a contemporary of George Colman, the elder. At the age of fourteen he proceeded to Trinity College, Cambridge, where he took his degree in 1750 as tenth wrangler. He was both a fellow of Trinity and private secretary to the Earl of Halifax. These two posts subsidized his earliest efforts. In 1761 he accompanied his patron, Lord Halifax, who had been appointed Lord Lieutenant, to Ireland as Ulster secretary. He offended Halifax by refusing a baronetcy offered for his Irish services. He continued in public office being appointed to the Board of Trade and Plantations from 1775 until that board was abolished in 1782 by Burke's economical reform. He was what we would describe today as a trusted civil servant; in 1780 he had been chosen to negotiate peace with Spain. We learn that he was well received by Charles III and his ministers, although even his tact could not overcome the obstacle of Gibraltar and the coincidental outbreak of the Gordon riots brought about his eventual recall in 1781. This was the beginning of Cumberland's troubles, he had been advanced £1,000 towards his expenses in Spain and on his return the government refused to refund the difference, so that he was

nearly £4,500 in debt. Both Lord North and his secretary
Robinson who had made the original promise ignored his
claims, and at the same time he lost his post with the
Board of Trade. His compensation was less than half and
he became dependent on his son for the last years of his
life. He died on 7 May 1811 and was buried at Westminster Abbey.

With Richard Cumberland's background it was natural
that he should write and he wrote all his life. Essays, art
criticisms, pamphlets, novels, and poetry all came from
his pen but it is only as a dramatist that he had any real
claim to fame. Not all his plays, even to this day, have
been published. He himself claimed that no English
author had written as many which supposes a much
greater number than the fifty-four usually ascribed to him.
Of these only a little over two-thirds are regular plays, the
rest being farces, operas, burlesques and other dramatic
trivia. It was in the genre that he himself called 'legitimate' comedy that he particularly excelled. He says in his
Memoirs that he made his plays from 'homely stuff, right
British drugget', avoiding 'the vile refuse of the Gallic
stage.' Apart from *The West Indian*, his best plays were
The Natural Son (1785) in which Major O'Flaherty again
appears, *The Impostors* (1789) a comedy of intrigue, *The
Jew* (1794) a serious play which in spite of heavy dialogue
may well yet find itself revived on the modern stage, and
The Carmelite (1784) a romantic blank verse play something after the manner of Home's *Douglas*. He also
altered *Timon of Athens*, Massinger's *The Bondman* and
The Duke of Milan in versions that held the stage into the
twentieth century.

DATE 1771
CAST
Stockwell, a merchant
Belcour, recently returned from the West Indies
Captain Dudley

Charles Dudley, his son
Major O'Flaherty
Stukely, Stockwell's head clerk
Fulmer
Varland, a lawyer
Servant to Stockwell
Lady Rusport
Charlotte Rusport
Louisa, daughter to Captain Dudley
Mrs Fulmer
Lucy
Stockwell's housekeeper
SCENE London

Plot

Act I,i Stockwell's counting house. Stockwell is discovered reading a letter which appears to move him greatly. Thinking it concerns business matters Stukely questions his master and learns that Mr Belcour, a young gentleman who has inherited estates in the West Indies, is Stockwell's son by a secret marriage. Stockwell resolves to discover the true character of his son before acknowledging the relationship. *ii* The same. A sailor and several black servants enter with Belcour's luggage which includes two green monkeys, a pair of grey parrots, a Jamaica sow and pigs, and a mangrove dog. Stockwell's confusion is ameliorated by the fact that the sailor speaks well of his son, declaring he might have brought the whole island with him had he so desired. *iii* The drawing room of Stockwell's house. The servants are surprised by the amount of trouble Stockwell is going to, to entertain this West Indian. *iv, v* The scene continues. Stockwell and Belcour meet for the first time. Belcour admits that the hazards of his journey were as nothing to the difficulties he has found in England. He has already embroiled himself in a fight with the boatmen. But he declares all's one for that and

now that he has arrived at the fountain head of pleasure
it is his intention to enjoy himself. Stockwell reprovingly
reminds him of the responsibilities of capital. Belcour responds generously. He is himself he admits the offspring
of distress and therefore he considers it his duty to help
the needy. Belcour's greatest fault would appear to be
that he is too easily governed by his passions. *vi* A room
in Lady Rusport's house. We are now introduced to the
grasping old dowager Lady Rusport; the second heroine
Miss Rusport her step-daughter; the impecunious Ensign
Charles Dudley, her nephew; and Major O'Flaherty whose
strong stomach enables him to undertake a campaign
against the dowager and her fortune. Charles is refused
money on his father's behalf and dismissed.

Act II,*i–viii* A room in Fulmer's house. The introduction
of new characters continues with the first appearances of
the ensign's father, Captain Dudley, together with his
landlord and landlady Mr and Mrs Fulmer. The scheming
Fulmers are waiting like spiders for the chance to ensnare
a fortune and the impetuous Belcour seems to offer them
a God-sent opportunity. Belcour has seen Louisa Dudley
in the street and mistaking her quality followed her, he
loses her but overhears that Captain Dudley is in need of
two hundred pounds. The generous side of his nature
responds to the officer's need and he promptly supplies
him. *ix–xi* Louisa Rusport's dressing room. Louisa and
Charles come close to a quarrel because, on account of his
poverty, Charles refuses to allow himself to love her. She
accuses him of having another mistress. This he denies
and they are reconciled. Lady Rusport enters with Major
O'Flaherty. When the Major hears that the dowager has
refused to help his brother officer, Captain Dudley, in
spite of his pretensions towards the dowager he leaves us
in no doubt as to his disgust. This is typical of the stage
Irishman who must be irascible, generous, foolish and
wise by turns.

Act III,*i* A room in Stockwell's house. Stockwell entrusts

to Belcour the returning of Louisa's jewels. These she had sent the merchant as security for a loan she wishes to raise to help Captain Dudley. Belcour is about to undertake the commission when he receives a note from Mrs Fulmer informing him that she has traced the girl (Louisa Dudley) whom he followed that morning. *ii–iv* The Fulmers' house. Mrs Fulmer attempts to use Belcour's infatuation for Louisa Dudley to part him from his fortune. She is so far successful as to obtain supposedly on Louisa's behalf, Charlotte's jewels. *v–x* Lady Rusport's house. Belcour confesses to Charlotte that he has given her jewels to Louisa. He is still unaware of her identity, supposing her to be Charles Dudley's mistress. He begs Charlotte to accept others in their place. She is charmed by his honesty. Louisa then enters and denies any knowledge of the jewels, as well she might seeing that they have been retained by the Fulmers.

Act IV,*i–v* The Fulmers' house. In an interview between Belcour and Louisa arranged by Mrs Fulmer he suggests that she should become his mistress. This is overheard by Charles. The two men quarrel and fight only to be interrupted in their turn by O'Flaherty. The Major rebukes Charles for drawing his sword in front of a woman but is only too willing to arrange a formal duel for a later date. *vi–ix* Lady Rusport's house. The fortunes of the Dudleys begin to improve as Lady Rusport is informed by the lawyer Varland that a second will of her husband's has been discovered which leaves his fortune to his nephew Charles Dudley. Varland's conscience is for sale and Lady Rusport may well hold what she has. Major O'Flaherty has overheard the lawyer's statements. He keeps watch over Lady Rusport while Charles and Charlotte enjoy a *tête à tête*, the gist of which is that Charlotte tries to persuade Charles to elope with her while he maintains that his lack of money must ever part them. She prevails and persuades Charles to leave her in Belcour's care. In the light of Charles's previous quarrel with Belcour her in-

sistence that he is the most generous and honourable of
men is particularly ironic. Before this can be debated the
major returns to warn them that Lady Rusport is coming.
Charles is hustled into the elopement before he knows
what he is doing. The major now persuades the lawyer
who has accepted a bribe of £5,000 to destroy the will to
surrender it to him:

> I am a soldier, this is not the livery of a knave; I am an
> Irishman, honey; mine is not the country of dishonour.
> Now, sirrah, begone; if you enter these doors, or give
> Lady Rusport the least item of what has passed, I will
> cut off both your ears, and rob the pillory of its due.

x Stockwell's house. Stockwell has heard of Belcour's
generosity to Captain Dudley. He is about to disclose their
relationship when Belcour enters full of confessions.
Prime among these being of his duel with Ensign Dudley.
He assures Stockwell that the quarrel is over a most un-
common beauty but of whom he has the report that she is
'an attainable wanton'. Imagine then his horror when the
major, while making the final arrangements for the meeting, lets slip that Louisa is the ensign's sister. It now comes
out that Belcour's information derives from the Fulmers
who have already been discovered trying to sell Charlotte's jewels.
Act V,*i* The London Tavern. The information discovered
in the last scene serves to cheat the major out of his duel,
Charles accepts Belcour's apology and the two are reconciled. The Fulmers are handed over to the law. *ii–viii*
Stockwell's house. Belcour now makes honourable pro-
posals to Louisa and is accepted. O'Flaherty produces the
will which by making Charles rich removes any impedi-
ment to his marriage with Charlotte. Lady Rusport is
exposed and Belcour acknowledged as Stockwell's son.

Critical commentary

The differences between 'laughing' and 'sentimental' comedy have been outlined above in our discussion of *The Clandestine Marriage*. There is no doubt that Cumberland accepted the role of champion of the latter school, claiming with arguments anticipated half a century before by Steele to be following the strictest classical precedent. To these Goldsmith replied with 'Retaliation: A Poem Including Epitaphs on Some of the most Distinguished Wits of this Metropolis':

> Here Cumberland lies having acted his parts,
> The Terence of England, the mender of hearts;
> A flattering painter, who made it his care
> To draw men as they ought to be, not as they are.

Thus were people asked to take sides in a literary division which never really existed outside the minds of the original protagonists and they have been taking sides ever since. *The West Indian* is certainly sentimental but any comparison between it and the work of Sheridan demonstrates the close affinity between sentimental and anti-sentimental comedy. Belcour is a good-natured innocent owing something, as several critics have pointed out, to Tom Jones. His libertinism is confined to a statement to Stockwell that he intends to sample the pleasures of London, and his eagerness to make Louisa his kept mistress. The idea of a man making advances to a respectable woman at the instigation of sharps who have told him she is for sale derives from Farquhar's *The Constant Couple*, which is hardly a sentimental comedy, nor is this motif terribly far removed from Tony's trick on Marlowe which leads to him courting Miss Hardcastle under the impression she is the chambermaid. The sentimentalism lies in the insistence on Belcour's good nature but is this insistence on benevolence any greater than Sheridan's for Charles Surface? Sheridan too insists that his hero is a rake but the only example of this which we are shown is a harmless gentleman's party of extreme sobriety at which no women are present. The quality which most distinguishes Charles Surface is good nature. Nor is he exposed or ridiculed into reformation, rather his good qualities are finally appreciated by his uncle Oliver. There are other similarities between *The West Indian* and *The School for Scandal*, both plays sharing the motif of a wealthy relative seeking to test a young man's good nature before acknowledging him heir to a fortune. Lady Teazle's sudden 'cure' in Act V of the latter play is paralleled in many sentimental and mixed comedies and would certainly not be out of place in *The West Indian*.

The main difference is in choice of subject rather than in treatment, ideology, diction or characterization. Cumberland, both in *The Fashionable Lover* and the present play creates a series of situations which logically seem to propose a tragic ending. Passive innocent characters are manipulated by villains who are only thwarted by the intervention of benevolent providence in the form of the discovery of lost wills or the unexpected return of absent fathers. With this type of plot we are coming very close to melodrama as is shown by speeches such as Belcour's 'I cannot invent a lie for my life, and if it was to save it I couldn't tell one.' The relationship between melodrama and exemplary comedy is further underlined by the use of comic relief in both forms. The more serious and pathetic 'comedies' such as *The West Indian* found it necessary to graft on comic characters if not a comic sub-plot to provide relief to the main story.

The diction of *The West Indian* falls into two categories. Characters such as Stockwell and Louisa Dudley utter incredible strings of moral clichés, although to be fair it should be pointed out that they are not dissimilar to passages in Dickens and elsewhere and it was an accepted convention that the virtuous expressed their emotions thus. In sharp contrast are the speeches of Belcour and

O'Flaherty. It is interesting in the light of our earlier remarks on the blandness of Georgian characterization to observe Cumberland's explanation of the use of such characters in his 'Advertisement' to *The Fashionable Lover*:

> The level manners of a polished country, like this, do not
> supply much matter for the comic muse, which delights
> in variety and extravagance; wherever therefore I have made
> any attempts at novelty, I have found myself obliged
> either to dive into the lower class of men, or betake myself
> to the outskirts of the empire; the centre is too refined
> for such purposes.

Later in his *Memoirs* he expanded on this, explaining that such characters were 'usually exhibited on the stage as the butts for ridicule and abuse' but that he had tried to 'present them in such lights as might tend to reconcile the world to them'. That he succeeded is a matter of fact and we learn from the *Critical Review* that Moody's playing of O'Flaherty 'filled the theatre with repeated convulsions of laughter'.

It is the characters of Belcour and O'Flaherty that give this play its vigorous appeal. For the rest of the characters the good are good and the bad obnoxious and one must suppose that the play's audience appeal derived as much from the fun and burlesque of Belcour and O'Flaherty as from its exemplary portrayal of a moral. The question is must we be compelled to take sides? Are we not entitled to enjoy Cumberland as well as Goldsmith and Sheridan without getting drawn into a hypothetical argument about the merits and demerits of comic theories to which neither side appear wholly to adhere?

She Stoops to Conquer
Oliver Goldsmith (1728–74)

Goldsmith is yet another writer with an Irish connection.
Although Protestant and English by descent his upbringing was Irish. His first teacher was a poor relation called
Elizabeth Delap and he passed from her care into that of
the village schoolteacher at Lissoy. This gentleman was a
retired quartermaster who interspersed the disciplines of
the three *R*s with an inexhaustible store of Irish stories.
He left this school at the age of nine to attend a succession
of grammar schools before at the age of sixteen, in 1744, he
entered Trinity College, Dublin, as a sizar. A sizar had
free food and tuition and paid only a nominal sum for
lodging in exchange for menial duties. These duties and
the humiliations of his position may have contributed to
his poor academic performance. He did, however, obtain
his bachelor's degree in 1749. His father had by this time
died leaving very little. Goldsmith's life at this point becomes a little complicated by anecdote. We gather he attempted several careers with striking lack of success. His
relations scraped together thirty pounds to help him emigrate to America but he returned home broke, his ship
having sailed when he was drinking in a tavern. He
studied medicine for eighteen months at Edinburgh from
where, still nominally studying physic, he proceeded to
Leiden. Three years after starting his abortive medical
career he left Leiden without a degree, possessing, it
would appear, nothing but his flute and the clothes he

stood up in. Playing Irish airs he learnt from his village
schoolmaster he begged his way around Europe. He returned to England in February 1756 absolutely penniless. His flute was of little use to him in England. He
scraped an existence as a druggist's assistant and even,
according to some accounts, as a strolling player. He was
an usher in a school, a bookseller's hack, then a schoolmaster again. He tried to obtain medical employment
without success. At the age of thirty he was again an unsuccessful literary drudge. The anonymous translations,
pamphlets and hack compilations he produced during
this time began to win him a certain reputation. Goldsmith was later to compile a *History of Rome*, a *History
of Greece*, a *History of England* and an *Animated Nature*,
all of which are a graceful reorganization in simple language of the work of well known authorities. They incorporate error and absurdity but, as well as demonstrating
Goldsmith's lack of application, research and care they
show his easy, readable, gentle style. It is easy to sneer at
this aspect of Goldsmith's career but this work made
learning easier for children throughout the nineteenth
century. Success did not come until almost the end of his
life. His novel *The Vicar of Wakefield* was completed and
sold in 1762 (the proceeds kept him out of debtors' prison)
but was not published until 1766. In 1767 he completed
The Good Natured Man, and it was presented at Covent
Garden in 1768. It was received with reservations, the
public preferring Hugh Kelly's *False Delicacy* produced
the same year. He followed this with *She Stoops to Conquer*, staged in 1773 with great success. Goldsmith was
also the author of a farce *The Grumbler* (1772).

DATE 1773
CAST

Sir Charles Marlow	Hastings
Hardcastle	Tony Lumpkin
Young Marlow	Stingo

Diggory   Tom Tickle
Roger   Jeremy
Ralph   Mat Muggins
Gregory   Mrs Hardcastle
Tom Twist   Miss Hardcastle
Jack Slang   Miss Neville

SCENE An old fashioned house in the country and an inn nearby

Plot

Act I,*i* A room in Hardcastle's house. Mrs Hardcastle complains to her husband that she is cramped by country society. She upbraids her husband for calling her old, claiming she was but twenty when her twenty-year-old son Tony was born. Hardcastle quietly adds twenty and twenty and makes it fifty-seven. According to Mrs Hardcastle Tony is a delicate youth with a fine sense of humour, according to her husband he needs throwing in the horse-pond. In contrast to Tony and Mrs Hardcastle, is Hardcastle's daughter by his first marriage, Kate. She, too, is almost affected by the fashions of the times, being as fond of gauze and French frippery as the best of them but bowing to her father's preference for country simplicity she has arranged with him to have the morning to receive and pay visits and to dress in her own manner, while in the evening she puts on a housewife's dress to please him. Kate's contrasting costumes will contribute to the deception around which the plot revolves. Her father informs her that it is his hope that she will marry Young Marlow, the son of his old friend Sir Charles. Young Marlow is expected that very night. He leaves her to digest this information as her cousin and confidante Constance Neville enters. Marlow is the most intimate friend of Hastings, Miss Neville's admirer. She is able to warn Kate of the singular duality of his nature. Among women of reputation and virtue he is the modestest man alive; but his acquaintances give him a very different character among creatures of another stamp. Miss Neville's romance is hindered by the fact that her fortune which is in the form of jewels is controlled by Mrs Hardcastle. In order to try and keep these jewels within the family she is trying to force Constance to marry Tony. Neither Tony nor Constance wish this and are thus allies against the old lady.

ii An ale-house. Tony's convivial evening with the country lads is interrupted by the arrival of Marlow and Hastings seeking directions to Hardcastle's house. Tony, in questioning them, discovers that they have heard him described as an awkward booby, reared up and spoiled at his mother's apron strings. Taking offence he tells them they have no hope of reaching their destination that night and then directs them to Mr Hardcastle's house telling them that it is an inn. He elaborates by describing the landlord as a rich man on the point of retiral and thus eager to be thought a gentleman. He warns them that he will insist on inflicting his company upon them.

Act II A room in Hardcastle's house. Hardcastle instructs his servants in preparation for Marlow's arrival. Their host, corresponding to Tony's description, is ignored by Marlow and Hastings. Hardcastle becomes nearly beside himself with suppressed rage, particularly when his guests criticize the available food and express doubts as to whether the beds have been properly aired. Marlow insists on seeing after this himself and he and Hardcastle exit. Constance enters. She realizes that it is one of Tony's tricks but plots with Hastings to sustain Marlow in the deception as, were he to discover his mistake, his embarrassment would make him leave immediately. This would remove Hastings's excuse for remaining in the house and thus all chance he and Constance have of eloping together. Marlow on his return is introduced to Kate. He is led to believe that she has accidentally stopped at the inn, a coincidence which her walking dress seems to support. His bashfulness with ladies of quality prevents his looking directly at her, thus making it possible for us to accept his later mistaking her in her country dress for one of the servants. Hastings makes up to Mrs Hardcastle, flattering her unmercifully. He then enlists the assistance of Tony upon his elopement plans.

Act III A room in Hardcastle's house. Kate and her father discuss Marlow. This conversation begins at complete cross purposes because of the different sides of his character they have each experienced. Agreement is reached that if Hardcastle discovers him to be less impudent and Kate finds him more importunate he may yet prove acceptable to both. Tony has stolen Constance's jewels in order to give them to Hastings. At the same time Constance is importuning Mrs Hardcastle for them. Mrs Hardcastle assures her they are lost. Constance plagues her to such an extent that she agrees to fetch them. Her horror at discovering that they are really lost is hardly mitigated by Tony pretending to believe that she is play acting for Constance's benefit. By this time Kate has been informed of the trick that is being maintained upon Marlow. She resolves, in her housekeeper's dress, to break through his bashfulness. The scene that follows, full of suggestion and flirtation, contrasts with their first meeting. Indeed so forward does he become that Hardcastle surprises him kissing his daughter; when Kate assures her father that she can yet prove Marlow's modesty the old man is totally confused.

Act IV A room in Hardcastle's house. Hastings and Constance have very little time left to finalize their plans. Sir Charles Marlow is expected later that night which will mean the discovery of Tony's trick. Hastings has given Constance's jewels into Marlow's keeping, ironically he has in turn entrusted them to the 'landlady' or in other words returned them to Mrs Hardcastle. In his belief that he is lodged at an inn Marlow has ordered his servants not to spare the cellar. Following their instructions they all become drunk and turn the house upside down. This is the final straw and Hardcastle throws the whole pack of them out. Marlow begins to realize his mistake, but even as he discovers the truth he still manages to accept Kate as a poor relation in a semi-menial position, thus he is able to take leave of her unhindered by an embarrassment. Tony and Constance, by pretending to be reconciled to each other, smooth Mrs Hardcastle into believing that the confusion over the jewels was a mistake on the part of the servants. Just as harmony is achieved the servant Diggory enters with a letter for Tony. Unable to read it for himself Tony gives it to his mother. It is from Hastings and reveals the elopement plans. Mrs Hardcastle resolves that Constance shall go to her Aunt Pedigree's. She leaves to organize the journey. Hastings and Marlow almost quarrel, each blaming the other for his misfortunes. Tony assures them he has a plan which will secure all.

Act V,*i* A room in Hardcastle's house. Sir Charles has arrived. He and Hardcastle have discussed the mistake and are prepared to forgive. It still remains for Marlow to learn that Miss Hardcastle and the supposed poor relation are one and the same person. Thus his continuing denial that anything has passed between him and Kate presents him in a bad light. *ii* The bottom of the garden. Hastings keeps his appointment with Tony. Far from escorting her to Constance's Aunt Pedigree, Tony has driven his mother in circles round the house. There is not a pond or slough within five miles that they haven't driven through and he has now fairly lodged the coach in the horse-pond at the bottom of the garden. Mrs Hardcastle, in a blind panic, believing herself to be lost upon Crackskull Common forty miles away, mistakes her husband for a highwayman. Her fright makes her controllable. *iii* A room in Hardcastle's house. Kate confesses that Marlow was unaware of her identity and that she assumed a lower station to reform him. Hardcastle is reconciled to a match between the two. He exploits Mrs Hardcastle's condition to engineer her agreement to Constance marrying Hastings.

Tony's real age has been kept from him. He is of age and free to reject Constance. This he does and she is free to marry as she wishes while Tony, we presume, can now find solace in the arms of that Bet Bouncer to whom he has constantly referred.

Critical commentary

Goldsmith would appear to have written *She Stoops to Conquer* in 1771, for he alludes to having written a play in a letter written in September of that year and he is known to have spent the bulk of 1772-3 trying to place it. Goldsmith's difficulties in getting a performance reflect the tyranny of the Patent System at its worst and we must ever wonder whether unknown budding reformers were withered by the similarity of outlook of the two houses, neither of which was prepared to take a commercial risk, and abandoned playwriting altogether.

Even with the play's acceptance Goldsmith's problems were not over. A new type of play requires a reformation in the prejudices of actors. Luckily the established players refused to act in it. It is significant that the new stars created by *She Stoops to Conquer* became the first creators of the leading roles in the comedies of Sheridan. Acting conventions had inhibited the growth of the drama and but for the success of this work might have robbed us of *The Rivals* and *The School for Scandal*.

We have to this point dealt very favourably with the theatrical establishment of Garrick and Colman and it certainly did much to establish the theatre for a brief period as a respectable social institution but in the unadventurous treatment of Goldsmith we see the beginnings of the managerial and the professional arrogance which contributed to the split between men of letters and the stage at the beginning of the nineteenth century. There is no doubt that actors saw playwrights as providers of parts and had no desire to risk their reputations in anything new.

Critical surveys tend to be rather bland about this work, marking it as casting off the dreary cloak of sentimentality and then moving decorously on. The reason is that it is such a good play and so entirely right in its context that the guns of criticism are silenced. The plot may hinge on an improbable mistake but it is well within the bounds of possibility (Goldsmith claimed that it was based on a true story) and it is clearly sustained. Perhaps Tony's pretence of driving his mother forty miles is a little far-fetched but there is never any question of an audience rejecting its reality. The characters are brilliant. They tend towards Jonsonian humour, in that each displays an exaggerated character trait, but the exaggeration never descends into caricature. Hardcastle is sentimentally wrapped up in the past but otherwise shrewd and level-headed. The faults of his good lady stop short of absurdity. Tony, although he has suffered at the hands of bad actors, is an unsubtle person rather than an unsubtle character. This reality reaches right through the play so that even minor characters are brought vividly to life for the brief time they are on stage, as for example the Third Fellow at the Three Pigeons:

> What though I am obligated to dance a bear, a man may be a gentleman for all that. May this be my poison if my bear ever dances but to the very genteelest of tunes – *Water Parted*, or the minuet in *Ariadne*.

Or, when Hardcastle, trying to make a motley gang of country servants behave like smart footmen, forbids them to laugh if he should tell a joke at dinner:

> Then, ecod, your worship must not tell the story of Old Grouse in the gunroom: I can't help laughing at that – he! he! he! – for the soul of me. We have all laughed at that these twenty years – ha! ha! ha!

In an age when minor characters are usually little more than perfunctory cogs in the mechanism of a play such attention to detail coupled with restraint so that it is carried so far and no further – we are for instance spared the actual story of Old Grouse – helps to create a reality beyond anything contemporary to it. It is this sense of truth which makes it impossible for us to doubt any of the happenings presented.

The least satisfactory character, for the modern reader, is Marlow the man of sentiment. Such characters are now, even at their best, only intermittently amusing. Sheridan's Faulkland appears to us a neurotic and even Goldsmith's previous creation, Honeywood in *The Good Natured Man*, does little more than irritate. Marlow rises above the means of such characters because we recognize his affliction. His lack of self-assurance which leaves him a trembling jelly in the presence of 'good women' but which disappears when sexual opportunities are provided with barmaids and below is a subject touched on within recent memory by Mary McCarthy and others. Here Goldsmith shows himself very much of his age for the sexual potential of this problem is ignored and it is used simply as a means of complicating the plot.

Even the criticism that Goldsmith has borrowed rather than invented the best things in his play is hardly valid. It must be admitted that the idea of mistaking a gentleman's house for an inn seems to owe something to Steele's fragmentary *The School for Action* (which has for its scene a theatre, mistaken by a lady's guardian for an inn); that Steele also provides, in Humphrey Gubbin in *The Tender Husband* the model for Tony Lumpkin; and that the idea of a lady pretending to be of a lower station derives from Nabbes's *Tottenham Court*; but Goldsmith has thoroughly assimilated his models. If some critics may express disappointment or even surprise at the discovery that Kate and Tony are not as inimitable as they appear at first sight they reveal by this their lack of understanding of the evolutionary nature of English drama, for our greatest playwrights are seldom truly original but rather re-expressors of a totally assimilated tradition. It is almost impossible to discover points of revolution in English drama and it is dangerous to try and force parallels between historical upheaval and theatre evolution. Thus 1660 sees the Restoration of the monarchy but the drama continues along an evolutionary path which begins around 1600. The French influence so blandly claimed by would-be simplifiers as representing the newly acquired tastes of exiled courtiers being much more prevalent in the reign of Charles I. Again *Pygmalion* is written in 1913 when one might expect the approaching European conflict to be beginning to influence the theatre, but the play shows no formal advance over those written in the 1890s. Sheridan, Goldsmith, Shaw and others are sufficiently in tune with the problems of dramatic writing to accept the current theatrical conventions and use them in a highly individual manner thus contributing to their evolution. The art of the theatre is the art of working with others and of serving audience expectations. A great dramatist suggests and leads towards improvement, a poor one blames the restrictions of his age for his inability to work with others. To criticize a dramatist of plagiarism is only relevant when the models are not assimilated and the result lacks spontaneity. Goldsmith's work is above such attack as is proved by the continuing popularity of this play which above all other English comedies continues to delight.

The Rivals
R. B. Sheridan (1751–1816)

Richard Brinsley Butler Sheridan has an unimpeachable literary and theatrical pedigree. His grandfather, Dr Thomas Sheridan, was the friend and confidant of Swift. He was noted for his wit and good humour. His father was Thomas Sheridan, the Irish actor. As far as we know Thomas Sheridan was the author of only one play, *Captain O'Blunder, or The Brave Irishman*. This seems never to have been printed though it was for a while a stock piece. From 1760 onwards Thomas Sheridan acted under Garrick at Drury Lane, being counted second to him in ability, although no way admitted as a rival. This move to London accounts for his third son's (R. B. Sheridan) basically English background. Here, yet again, we have an English playwright with strong links with Ireland. From eleven to seventeen Sheridan was educated at Harrow where, it is said, with no cause for us to question the truth of the information, that he had 'the esteem and even admiration of all his schoolfellows'. After leaving Harrow his education continued with a private tutor, supplemented by elocution lessons from his father and daily fencing and riding lessons at Angelo's. His earliest literary efforts were in collaboration with a school friend who had gone up to Oxford, N. B. Halked. With him he published a verse translation of Aristaentus in 1771. A year later the pair offered a farce called *Jupiter* to both Garrick and Foote. It was doubly rejected. Like *The Critic* this play uses the device of a rehearsal. The Sheridan family moved to Bath in 1770. They became intimate with the family of Thomas Linley the composer. The Linleys' eldest daughter was, on the authority not only of report but of Gainsborough's portrait, exceedingly beautiful. The story of Sheridan's elopement with Anne Linley is recounted below in the context of discussion of *The Rivals*.

A tradition has it that *The School for Scandal* was hurriedly written; a second tradition, while essentially confirming the first, states that the basic idea of a play about a group of scandalmongers first occurred to Sheridan in Bath, during the tittle-tattle aroused by this incident. According to the second tradition Sheridan attempted several versions of the play, none of which provided a sufficiently substantial plot. The play as it was finally written is said to be a combination of two of these preliminary ideas. During the period immediately following the elopement Mr Linley forbade Sheridan access to Anne, hardly considering him an eligible match. He was packed off to Waltham Abbey to continue his studies. In 1773 he was openly married to Anne Linley. The young couple took a house in Portman Square and entered fashionable society.

The School for Scandal (1777) continues the vein of wit exposed in *The Rivals* but Sheridan himself helped to stifle the growth of English drama by his execrable management of Drury Lane. In 1776 Sheridan, together with his father-in-law and Dr Ford, had purchased Garrick's share in the Drury Lane patent. Two years later, the partners purchased the other half. Sheridan became the manager of the theatre. He carried out this post with singular selfishness. He was averse to paying either the tradesmen or actors, a habit only mellowed by his extraordinary personal charm and the loyal stage management of J. P. Kemble, until Kemble, virtually forced from Drury Lane, became in his own right the manager of Covent

Garden. Sheridan allowed the scenery, wardrobe and theatre fittings to deteriorate to such an extent that his management must in part be blamed for the decline of the patent theatres, although the rot was well advanced before he took over. After he became a member of Parliament in 1780 he virtually abandoned playwriting. The only finished dramatic work of his mature years being his tragedy *Pizarro*, adapted from the German of Kotzebue in 1799.

As a politician he had a distinguished career, being considered one of the best speakers in the House and holding several significant minor offices. He particularly distinguished himself during the trial of Warren Hastings. His speeches on that occasion are among the finest in our parliamentary history. With Fox, he advocated non-intervention in the French Revolution, opposing the pyrotechnical speeches of Burke. When Napoleon came to power he argued for war. One of his most effective orations supported the measures taken against the Nore mutineers. An intimate friend of the Prince Regent he used this royal purse to keep him in Parliament after he had lost the membership for Westminster. Finally after a quarrel with the Prince he lost his seat in 1812, as he could not raise the necessary funds to purchase Stafford, his original borough. His position as an MP had made him immune from arrest for debt. His latter years were plagued by bailiffs. He died in 1816 and was buried in Westminster Abbey with great state.

It is difficult in a brief introductory biography of this kind to give a true impression of Sheridan's life. Problems are created by the sheer volume of conflicting but fascinating anecdotes which surround his life. From the theatrical point of view he divides into two personalities. On the one hand the genius which left us *The Rivals* and *The School for Scandal*, on the other the misapplication of his managership of Drury Lane to pay for his extravagances. He thus is perhaps best described as a theatrical figure who was never truly a part of the theatre. Perhaps it was this lack of commitment to the stage which makes his work something apart from the main stream. Had he dedicated and controlled his genius to theatrical reform it is not unlikely that the strength of his talent would have moved English comedy along a totally different course. Unhappily he was content to give the public what it thought it wanted – pantomime and spectacle flourished under his influence.

DATE 1775
CAST
Sir Anthony Absolute
Captain Jack Absolute, his son
Faulkland
Acres
Sir Lucius O'Trigger
Fag, the captain's servant
David
Thomas
Mrs Malaprop
Lydia Languish, her niece
Julia, ward to Sir Anthony
Lucy, Lydia's maid
SCENE Bath

Plot

Act I,*i* A street. Captain Absolute's man Fag and Thomas, his father's coachman, meet. Each is astonished to find the other in Bath. From their exchange of news we learn that the captain is at present passing under the alias of Ensign Beverley. This is to better facilitate his courtship of Lydia Languish, a lady much addicted to sentimental novels and thus much more approving of a poor ensign than the son and heir of Sir Anthony Absolute, a baronet of £3,000 per year. *ii* A dressing room in Mrs Malaprop's lodgings.

Lydia is a lady determined, in the true spirit of romantic
fiction, to sacrifice her fortune on the altar of her love for
Beverley. Her aunt, Mrs Malaprop, has interrupted one
of the ensign's letters. The interruption is opportune as
Lydia had decided it was time they quarrel and had herself written a letter to herself informing herself that
Beverley was paying court to another lady. She signed
this letter 'a friend unknown' and on the strength of it
(for the time being) swore never to see Beverley more.
This then was no time for Mrs Malaprop to interfere.
Sir Anthony's ward and Lydia's friend Julia is equally
beset by problems of the heart. The smooth passage of
her love for Faulkland is complicated by that swain's
determination to suffer all the torments of extreme sensibility. Mrs Malaprop is negotiating with Sir Anthony
with a view to his son paying court to Lydia, about whose
education she is suitably concerned:

> ... but above all, Sir Anthony, she should be mistress
> of orthodoxy, that she might not misspell, and
> mis-pronounce words so shamefully as girls usually do;
> and likewise that she might reprehend the true meaning
> of what she is saying.

Mrs Malaprop herself has formed a *tendre* for Sir Lucius
O'Trigger, to whom she has been writing under the
pseudonym of Delia. Sir Lucius is maintained in this correspondence by the maid Lucy under the impression that
his understanding is with the niece and not the aunt.
Indeed Lucy and the other servants find all this amorous
activity very profitable.

Act II,i Captain Absolute's lodgings. Faulkland is tormented by worry over Julia's health. Reassurance from
Bob Acres that she is enjoying all the pleasures of country
society only results in the additional exquisite torture of
jealousy. Bob Acres is a further pretender to Lydia's hand.
He has been at pains to veneer his country honesty with
town polish with which to impress her. Apart from train-

ing his hair out of its natural course and wearing new clothes, he is experimenting with a sentimental or referential method of swearing that is most genteel. Thus, referring to his journey, he exclaims 'Odds whips and wheels!', of Julia's health 'Odds blushes and blooms!', and of Ensign Beverley 'Odds triggers and flints!', The young men having left, Jack's father calls to tell him of the proposed marriage. The Captain's cool manner infuriates his father who leaves without revealing the name of the lady of his choice who he promises shall be as ugly as he chooses, have only one eye and a hump, but in spite of this to whom he will force his son to write sonnets. *ii* The North Parade. Sir Lucius O'Trigger receives a letter from Delia via Lucy. Fag interrupts this business and is surprised to learn that Beverley has a new rival in Captain Absolute.

Act III*i* The North Parade. The good captain, now primed to the true state of affairs, assures his father that in spite of his hints about humps and other graces of that kind he is prepared to accept his choice of a wife. *ii* Julia's dressing room. Faulkland and Julia continue to quarrel. *iii* Mrs Malaprop's lodgings. Jack Absolute in his own character calls on Lydia. She believes that her clever ensign has deceived Mrs Malaprop into believing he is the captain. Mrs Malaprop interrupts their idyllic lovemaking, but having misheard their exchanges, upbraids Lydia with taunting Absolute with her love for Beverley. *iv* Acres' lodgings. Bob finds his true English legs reluctant to learn French dance steps. Sir Lucius calls to incite Bob to challenge Ensign Beverley to a duel for presuming towards Lydia.

Act IV*i* Acres' Lodgings. To Jack's consternation Acres asks him to be his second in this affair. Jack refuses on the grounds that it would not be quite proper but agrees to terrify Beverley with reports of Acres' courage. *ii* Mrs Malaprop's lodgings. Sir Anthony insists on accompanying Jack on a visit to Lydia. Lydia is almost able to persuade herself that Beverley is clever enough to deceive Jack's own father, but Sir Anthony and Mrs Malaprop force him to confess. His letters in the character of Beverley have used such choice epithets in reference to Mrs Malaprop as 'old weather-beaten she-dragon' so that it takes a super-human effort from Sir Anthony to calm her, but Lydia is outraged at having been made ridiculous and it seems impossible that she and Jack can ever be reconciled. *iii* The North Parade. In this mood Jack is only too willing to entertain a challenge from Sir Lucius. At six o'clock the next morning at Kings-Mead-Fields, Jack will, as Beverley, fight Acres and then as himself engage Sir Lucius. Faulkland is to be his second.

Act V,*i* Julia's dressing room. Faulkland's excessive jealousy causes an apparently final rift with Julia. Mrs Malaprop, Lydia and Julia hear of the duel and hurry to Kings-Mead-Fields to prevent a catastrophe. *ii* The South Parade. Sir Anthony meets Jack on the way to the duel. Jack almost deludes him into believing he is carrying his sword with the intention of drawing it in front of Lydia and swearing to fall upon its point if she will not accept him, but he is tricked for the last time and he too makes for Kings-Mead-Fields. *iii* Kings-Mead-Fields. All is resolved. Bob Acres, ever reluctant in spite of promptings from Sir Lucius flatly refuses to fight Beverley when he discovers he is his friend Jack Absolute, to whom he resigns his claims to Lydia. Jack and Sir Lucius draw swords and prepare for their engagement. Sir Anthony, Mrs Malaprop, Lydia and Julia interrupt the duellists. Mrs Malaprop announces that she and not Lydia is Sir Lucius's Delia, thus removing the cause of the fight. Sir Lucius, generously, not only resigns his claims in Lydia to his rival but throws in the aunt for good measure. Sir Anthony helps settle Julia and Faulkland's misunderstandings, while Lydia, brought to her senses by the sight of the swords, accepts Jack.

Critical commentary

It is possible that the fact that both his parents were playwrights and his father a respected actor and theatrical
personage, bred in Sheridan a rather ambivalent attitude
to the stage. He had his dramatic inheritance at his finger-
tips but he never quite appreciated it with fit Georgian
seriousness. Where Garrick strove to become a great man
in society on the strength of his theatrical success, Sheridan
used his early theatrical achievement to find a way into
Parliament and his position as a patentee of Drury Lane
to pay for his excesses.

The Rivals is all the better because Sheridan has to a
certain extent used it to perpetrate a literary joke. One is
never more aware of this than when one attempts to
classify the piece. The plot is pure comedy of intrigue,
as any comparison between it and *The Duenna* demonstrates. The laughter in both plays stems from characters
being unaware of the assumed identity of others, the
Absolute-Beverley device being essentially the same as that
of Clara and Louisa. Yet *The Rivals* is a comedy of character where the action of the plot is subordinate to the
opportunities offered for displaying the humours of the
characters. In *The Duenna* with the exception of Isaac
and that pale echo of Faulkland, Ferdinand, there is no
distinct characterization: Clara and Louisa are interchangeable and Jerome and the Duenna perform their
functions in pale contrast to their opposites in *The Rivals*
Sir Anthony and Mrs Malaprop. Although it is a comedy
of character *The Rivals* is not a comedy of manners. Such
a classification would deny it the essence of burlesque
which distinguishes it from the general run of Georgian
comedy. It is almost a Jonsonian comedy of humours, for
with the exceptions of Julia and Jack Absolute every
character in the play exhibits some exaggerated trait. No
author since Congreve had dared to place so many absurdities in the same play.

Robertson Davies suggests in *The Revels History of Drama in English VI* (1975) that *The Rivals* is carelessly plotted. In support of this he marshals the fact that it was withdrawn for repairs after two performances: '... ten days later it returned to the stage decidedly improved, but still with signs of hasty workmanship'. This is a standard view which inclines to underestimate the bulk of Sheridan's work along with that of his Georgian contemporaries and then exaggerates the achievement of *The School for Scandal*. How can the adjective 'careless' possibly be applied to dramaturgy that has so appositely positioned opposites such as Sir Lucius and 'Fighting' Bob Acres; the wordy Mrs Malaprop and the concise Sir Anthony ('If you have the estate, you must take it with the live stock on it, as it stands!'); the sensible Julia and the neurotic Faulkland; Lydia with Jack Absolute? In each of these pairings of characters the one compliments the other so that there is never any need for directional arbitration as to which should have the attention in a scene. The play contains its own built-in safeguards against the vagaries of egotistical actors and this is stagecraft at its very best. Similarly in an age which literally tended to leave the business of acting to the performer Sheridan exercises great control over the visual aspects of his play. His intrigue plot calls for a pleasing variety of indoor and outdoor settings without that variety undermining an essential unity of place. More precisely Sheridan supplies his actors with natural business derived from the text, such as Bob Acres's tentative dance steps in Act III,*iv* and Lydia's business with the library books on her first appearance. One need look no further than the long passages of undiluted conversation in Shaw, where directors and actors are called upon to underwrite the text with gratuitous movement and business, to appreciate Sheridan's keen visual sense.

The heavy characterization and the concern for dramatic business are rather more in the tradition of the farcical after piece than that of main piece comedy of manners.

Here is much of the complicated machinery which we associate with farce: a truncated time scale containing an incredible series of coincidences, characters accidentally meeting who should at all costs have been kept apart and complicated physical business. The only nineteenth-century farce characteristic which is not present is the use of doors and hiding places. All this is employed to burlesque the standard sentimental view that the tyranny of the older generation over the younger contained at the best the seeds of humiliation (*Pride and Prejudice*) and at the worst tragedy (*Clarissa*). That it is burlesque and not satire is established by the clear respect shown to prudent marriages. Lydia's willingness to elope with a penniless ensign is ridiculed and while the attractive Jack is to be preferred over the booby Bob there is no question of either being financially unsuitable. The targets of the play, mild parental tyranny, the neurosis of love, romantic indifference to reality, intellectual pretentiousness and duelling, are all celebrated as part of life's rich pattern and any sense of social reform or satirical criticism is rigidly excluded.

The play's refusal to take anything very seriously is reflected in the relationship between this play and Sheridan's biography. The audience must have hoped that it would throw some light on the interesting scandal behind his own marriage with Elizabeth Linley. At the age of sixteen Elizabeth had been betrothed to a wealthy old man Sir Walter Long and although the marriage was broken off with Elizabeth receiving £3,000 as compensation this whole rather curious business would seem to parallel in reality the complete disregard for Lydia and Jack in the treaties of Mrs Malaprop and Sir Anthony. Further parallels exist between *The Rivals* and the Sheridan-Linley romance in that in 1773 he escorted his future wife to France in order to remove her from the attentions of a married army officer called Thomas Mathews. Sheridan returned to England and fought two duels with

Mathews. The audience must have hoped that Jack's military position and Sir Lucius's pugnacity would throw some light on this part of the scandal. It does not. If Sheridan recalled his own experience at all it is done with such a keen sense of propriety that there can be no identification of O'Trigger with Mathews. Indeed in his fierce Irishness there is if anything a touch of self-parody, similar to that which several critics have recognized in Faulkland's neurotic possessiveness, for according to Sickel's 1909 biography the exchanges between Julia and Faulkland draw on Sheridan's letter to Elizabeth prior to their marriage. Sheridan has whetted the audience's appetite for scandal and then politely frustrated it.

It is impossible to treat of *The Rivals* without some acknowledgement of the accusations of plagiarism levelled at it. *The Rivals* is a play which draws on the whole gamut of English comic tradition. The plot, in spite of the personal relevance to Sheridan noted above, is one told a hundred years before: the conflict between the generations over the relative importance of love and property as a basis of marriage. Sheridan, after the manner of the age, looted the existing repertory for suggestions from which to compile his play. Biddy Tipkin in Steele's *The Tender Husband*, the title role in *Polly Honeycombe* and Biddy Bellair in Garrick's *Miss in Her Teens* all contribute to the creation of Lydia Languish. The conclusion to Garrick's piece where Fibble the fop and Flash the braggadocio fight a duel at long distance somewhat resembles the final scene of *The Rivals*. All this borrowing is a critical irrelevancy excepting as far as it demonstrates the continuity of Georgian dramatic tradition. Originality of material was not expected, rather the public desired the old familiar refashioned in a fresh and lively manner. These borrowings are of most use to us not as weapons of degeneration but as a yardstick to the author's position in the dramatic tradition. Comparison between *The Rivals* and the more overtly satirical *Polly Honeycombe* illuminates the degree of Sheridan's opposition to sentimentality. Colman's Polly, like Lydia, has cultivated her views on life in the circulating library. This leaves her vulnerable to the advances of a quite unsuitable young man employing the devices and sensibility of a novel, while at the same time alienating the affections of a suitor of solid worth, if rather lacking in imagination. Polly ends the play unmarried if wiser, a markedly less sentimental conclusion than Sheridan's ordered pairings off.

The Duenna
R. B. Sheridan

DATE 1775
CAST
Don Ferdinand
Don Jerome, his father
Don Antonio
Don Carlos
Isaac Mendoza, a rich Jew
Father Paul
Father Francis
Father Augustine
Lopez, servant to Ferdinand
Donna Louisa, sister to Ferdinand
Donna Clara
The Duenna
SCENE Seville

Plot

Act I,*i* The street before Don Jerome's house. The servant Lopez, as he waits outside a darkened house, complains that his master Ferdinand is much too gallant to eat, drink or sleep. Antonio enters with masqueraders to serenade Ferdinand's sister Louisa. *ii* A piazza. Lopez complains to Ferdinand that he is allowed no rest while Ferdinand answers that rest is forbidden him by Clara's cruelty. He tells his friend Antonio that tomorrow is the day fixed by Clara's stepmother for her to enter a convent. Made desperate by this Ferdinand had bribed the maid to provide him with a key and entered her chamber only to be very coldly received. Antonio comforts him with the conviction that Clara will use the key to escape on her own account. Antonio's own circumstances are not so very different. For him tomorrow is the day when Ferdinand's father will force Louisa to marry the rich Portuguese Jew Isaac Mendoza. The situation is further complicated by Ferdinand's suspicion that Clara may love Antonio. *iii* A room in Don Jerome's house. The Duenna, content in the Jew's riches, has agreed to substitute herself for her mistress. Louisa herself plans to elope with Antonio. Jerome asks his daughter to marry Mendoza and is refused. He gives orders that she shall be locked in her chambers. He then discovers a letter seemingly betraying Louisa's whole plan to elope leaving the Duenna in her place. He orders the Duenna from the house. Louisa takes her place while, as planned, the Duenna prepares to play her part. *iv* The court before Don Jerome's house. Louisa, disguised as the Duenna, is thrust out of doors. *v* The piazza. Louisa and Clara both having escaped confinement meet. Clara intends to seek temporary refuge in a convent. Louisa is determined to find Antonio. To this end, borrowing Clara's name, she seeks the help of the very Isaac she is to have married, he having never seen her : courting her ducats and not her person. Mendoza, having heard a report that Antonio rivals him with Louisa, is delighted to agree to take 'Clara' to him.

Act II,*i* A library in Don Jerome's house. Jerome and Mendoza indulge themselves in mockery of Clara's father for allowing himself to be duped. *ii* Donna Louisa's dressing room. Isaac courts the Duenna in mistake for Louisa. It is well that his affections are fixed upon her purse and not her person for he is surprised at her age. *iii* A library in Don Jerome's house. Ferdinand begs his father to consider Antonio's suit. Jerome is a little taken aback when

Isaac criticizes his daughter's charms. Ferdinand realizes
that there must have been an exchange but his father,
having as he thinks locked Louisa in her room, is confident that the Jew means to insult him. The quarrel
between the old men is averted. *iv* Isaac's lodgings. Isaac
enters to Louisa with Antonio. Isaac advises Antonio that
since he cannot have Louisa he may as well secure the
good that is offered him. The Jew is delighted and considers himself a very Machiavel when Antonio accepts the
girl. Isaac then tells them that he is to carry off the
Duenna that very evening.

Act III,*i* A library in Don Jerome's house. Jerome learns
that his daughter has eloped with Isaac. At the same
time a letter asking forgiveness for eloping with Antonio
is received from the real Louisa. No names are mentioned
in the second letter and, thinking the references to her
lover mean Isaac, Jerome sends back his free consent for
her to marry. *ii* The new piazza. Ferdinand hears from
Isaac that Clara has eloped with Antonio and now waits
at a convent preparatory to her marriage. *iii* The garden
of the convent. Louisa receives her father's permission to
marry Antonio. Ferdinand arrives sick with jealousy
against Antonio. The veiled Clara is delighted that she
has the power to make him so unhappy. She sends him
after Louisa and Antonio but follows to be present at
his surprise when he is undeceived. *iv* A court before the
priory. Isaac and Antonio both seek priests to marry them.
Isaac suggests that they will save time if they are married
together. Antonio accepts his offer. *v* A room in the
priory. In a gratuitously anti-catholic scene the priests are
discovered drinking. *vi* The court before the priory. Ferdinand interrupts Antonio's marriage. Louisa and Clara
identify themselves. *vii* A grand saloon in Don Jerome's
house. It is now discovered that Isaac has been tricked into
marrying the Duenna. Antonio makes his peace with
Jerome by betraying how the Jew had intended to overreach his nearly father-in-law by getting Louisa's fortune

without making any settlement in return. Isaac blames the mistake on Jerome:

> ... you would be so cursed positive about the beauty of her you had locked up, and all the time I told you she was as old as my mother, and as ugly as the devil.

Hearing this the Duenna abuses Isaac and he replies in kind. Antonio and Louisa show Jerome his written consent to their wedding but Antonio scorns to obtain her fortune by a trick and asks only Jerome's blessing. The old man is put in a good temper when he hears that Ferdinand has married the rich Clara and all ends with a wedding celebration.

Critical commentary

Samuel Johnson referred to *The Rivals* and *The Duenna* as the two best comedies of the age and Hazlitt confirms the high contemporary opinion of the latter play:

> *The Duenna* is a perfect work of art. It has the utmost sweetness and point. The plot, the characters, the dialogue are all complete in themselves, and they are all his own; and the songs are the best that ever were written, except those in *The Beggar's Opera*.

The Duenna became established in the eighteenth and nineteenth century as a more popular musical comedy than Gay's, a decision reversed by our own age. The difference between the beginning and end of the eighteenth century are again clearly demonstrated for although Sheridan has the more neatly contrived plot there seems an almost total lack of the burlesque dimension and its lack of originality of treatment makes *The Duenna* rather remote reading. The success or failure of a musical lies in its songs, today most composers, compilers or authors of musicals will admit that the book is of secondary importance to the numbers, for while the plot is important, the reality of characterization is established in the songs. This is not the case with *The Duenna* as a critic noted after the first performance (the *Morning Chronicle*, 22 November 1775):

> The fable of *The Duenna* is infinitely more substantial than that of any other musical performance we remember. – It is in fact so full of business and plot, that the piece might very aptly, after the manner of the managers of this theatre, be styled a comedy interspersed with an opera.

The songs are too often overlooked, they originate something after the manner of those of *The Beggar's Opera* and *Polly Honeycombe* being partly compiled and partly composed, the Linley family into whom he had married being pressed into service for the arrangement of the music. They are for the most part dramatically appropriate fitting easily into the scenes as where Isaac's attitude to his mistress and her money is underwritten by the song:

> Give Isaac the nymph who no beauty can boast,
> But health and good humour to make him his toast;
> If straight, I don't mind whether slender or fat,
> And six feet or four – we'll ne'er quarrel for that.

Nor are all the songs comic but varied from the lyrical numbers of the lovers to the rousing drinking song of the friars in Act III.

Even so the songs are something of a bonus and we must look at *The Duenna* in the context of Georgian retreatment of Restoration themes and conventions. The story is a very fine example of what Dryden called the Spanish plot, what we now critically term comedy of intrigue. With only fifty titles to describe there must be gaps in a survey such as this and we have not fairly represented the development of this kind of drama, confining it to a brief outline of *An Evening's Love*. It is the mirror image to the type of comedy represented by *The*

Rivals, for where the former play is comedy of character with the action, though intricate and well contrived, entirely subordinate to the humours of the characters, here the characters are little more than stock puppets in the elaboration of intrigue. Only Mendoza is a truly individual character in *The Duenna*, the lovers are interchangeable only being rescued from utter banality by Ferdinand's jealousy which we instantly recognize as a retreatment of Faulkland's successful humour in *The Rivals*. Don Jerome almost stands for Pantalone in *comedia* and it is a typical convention of the form that the older generation should be represented by the father and not the mother for mothers imply a continuity and seriousness diametrically opposed to the world of comic intrigue. To the same end the Duenna is represented as a grotesque but this is achieved rather by make-up and external effect than through any overriding humour as in the case of Mrs Malaprop.

If we compare the opening of *The Duenna* with the opening of *An Evening's Love* we must be struck by the similar use of a nocturnal scene common to many Spanish plays. The servant Lopez, although never fully exploited, demonstrates here, in his complaints about his master, his relationship with Sancho Panza and a host of *graciosos* in Spanish drama. The use of disguise, the mistakes in identity and the intrigue employed by the younger generation to trick their elders are at once common to *An Evening's Love* and Spanish cape and sword plays.

The most popular play of this type previous to *The Duenna* was Mrs Centlivre's *The Wonder: A Woman Keeps a Secret* (1714). In *The Wonder* Felix and Isabella correspond to Ferdinand and Louisa, while Violante like Clara is on the point of being forced to become a nun. An English colonel replaces Antonio. The main difference between the two plays is that Sheridan pays less attention to the reverence for family honour which inspirits Spanish drama, by having Don Jerome choose for Louisa the grotesque Jew Isaac Mendoza, while Susanna Centlivre chooses a man who is high born as well as rich. Sheridan has taken over a popular dramatic formula without taking over its animating spirit. Once more one is struck by his ability to write for his audience and while it would be comparatively simple to expose him for plagiarism and lack of innovation in that the plot situations, if not the moral principles which control the character's actions, are a composite of existing stage favourites derived from the intrigue plays of Dryden and others through popular successes such as *The Wonder*, his borrowing is no greater than that of any other Georgian writer. What the play lacks is anything provocative. It could be argued that it makes some comment on the power of wealth to corrupt human relationships, but when one considers Sheridan's autobiographical experience of parental tyranny in his own courtship of Elizabeth Linley, contracted at the age of sixteen to the sixty-year-old Walter Long, one is disappointed that neither in *The Rivals* nor in this play is the antagonism between the generations taken beyond the conventions traditionally established in comedy. Only perhaps in the character of Ferdinand does Sheridan allow his own personality to peep through for we can allow ourselves to suspect that his jealousy which differentiates him from the other lovers reflects the author's own melancholic strain.

A Trip to Scarborough
R. B. Sheridan

DATE 1777

CAST

Lord Foppington

Sir Tunbelly Clumsy

Colonel Townly

Loveless

Tom Fashion, younger brother of Lord Foppington

La Varole, valet to Lord Foppington

Lory, servant to Fashion

Probe, a surgeon

Mendlegs

Jeweller

Shoemaker

Tailor

Amanda, wife to Loveless

Berinthia

Miss Hoyden, daughter to Sir Tunbelly

Mrs Coupler

SCENE Scarborough and its neighbourhood

Plot

Act I,*i* The hall of an inn. Tom Fashion arrives at Scarborough with the intention of wheedling money out of his elder brother Lord Foppington. From his friend Colonel Townly he learns that his brother is about to

marry the rich daughter of Sir Tunbelly Clumsy who
lives in the neighbourhood of Scarborough. The match
has been arranged by Mrs Coupler. The Colonel tells him
that his brother has quarrelled with this good lady which
gives Tom the notion of trying to cut his brother out. In
this the Colonel will be delighted to assist for Lord Foppington has been his rival in an affair of the heart. Tom
presumes that his brother has been paying court to
Townly's mistress Berinthia but Townly corrects this mistake. Berinthia was indeed supposed to meet him a month
since but kept him cooling his heels without explanation.
Out of boredom Townly turned his attentions to Amanda,
the wife of his friend Loveless. It is for this lady that Lord
Foppington has proved a rival. *ii* Lord Foppington's
dressing room. Lord Foppington instructs La Varole his
valet to postpone paying his respects to Miss Hoyden as
he wishes to sacrifice a day or two more to the pursuit of
his friend Loveless' wife. The tailor, shoemaker and others
prepare Lord Foppington to face the day while he keeps
his brother waiting. This treatment strengthens Fashion's
resolve to cheat his brother if he can. Mrs Coupler tells
him that no one in Sir Tunbelly's family have met Lord
Foppington and supplies him with a letter of introduction
which will enable him to take his brother's place.

Act II,*i* Loveless' lodgings. Loveless confesses to Amanda
that he is greatly taken with the looks of a lady he saw at
the theatre the night before. The lady in question, Berinthia (but recently admired of Colonel Townly) arrives on
cue. She, it turns out is a cousin to Amanda who invites
her to lodge with them. Lord Foppington makes open
love to Amanda. Loveless draws on him and wounds him.
Lord Foppington is carried off for repairs by the conveniently handy Probe. Amanda confesses to her cousin that
Townly has paid discreet addresses to her. Berinthia resolves to be revenged on Townly and Amanda at the same
time by encouraging Loveless a little.

Act III,*i* Lord Foppington's lodgings. Tom tries once

more to borrow from his brother and is refused with the
result that any last scruples about cheating him in the
matter of the heiress are removed. *ii* A garden behind
Loveless' lodgings. Berinthia leads Loveless into paying
court to her. Townly surprises them. Berinthia rebukes
him for making love to his friend's wife while he accuses
her of keeping him waiting a month without any explanation. Amanda confides to Berinthia that she suspects
her husband of an interest elsewhere. Berinthia advises
her to make him jealous in turn. *iii* Outside Sir Tunbelly
Clumsy's house. Tom arrives to impersonate his brother.
iv A room in Sir Tunbelly Clumsy's house. Miss Hoyden
confesses that it is 'as well she has a husband a-coming or
ecod she'd marry the baker'. She is delighted when her
nurse tells her that 'Lord Foppington' has arrived.

Act IV,*i* A room in Sir Tunbelly Clumsy's house. Tom
persuades Miss Hoyden to marry him secretly the next
day. The chaplain is bribed with the promise of a fat living and all is arranged to Tom's satisfaction. *ii* Amanda's
dressing room. Amanda complains to Berinthia that Loveless follows some flirt for variety. Townly calls and is
detained by Amanda until her husband's return. *iii* Berinthia's dressing room. Loveless hides in a closet and is
mistaken by Berinthia for a ghost, but when her maid
appears in response to her scream she bundles Loveless
back into the closet and gets rid of her. She makes an
assignation to meet Loveless later that night in the garden and, as Amanda is heard coming, back into the closet
goes Loveless. From this point of vantage he overhears
that Townly has been paying court to his wife.

Act V,*i* Loveless meets Berinthia in the garden at the same
time that Amanda meets Townly. The resulting reconciliation is rather after the manner of the last scene of
The Way to Keep Him with the wife and husband and
lover and mistress all acknowledging equal guilt. *ii* A
room in Sir Tunbelly Clumsy's house. Tom and Miss
Hoyden are married just in time for Lord Foppington

arrives to claim his bride. He is arrested by Sir Tunbelly's
yokels. Loveless, Townly, Amanda and Berinthia arrive
but continue the joke by pretending he is an impostor.
Tom comes to his rescue by admitting the deception and
the secret marriage. Lord Foppington loses the support
of Sir Tunbelly when upon being untrussed he calls him
a clod and sneers at his brother's poverty. Sir Tunbelly
remarks that he could mend his beggary:

> Ay, old fellow, but you will not do that – for that would
> be acting like a Christian, and thou art a barbarian,
> stap my vitals.

This is enough to make Sir Tunbelly forgive his daughter.

Critical commentary

It is a commonplace to dismiss this piece as a tawdry
reworking of *The Relapse* but to overlook it is to miss
a valuable chance to come to direct grips with the major
differences between the attitudes of Sheridan and his
late seventeenth-century predecessors. To admit a preference for the original does not negate the possibility
of excellences in Sheridan's play.

The major changes are of course sexual. The open
homosexuality of Coupler who makes advances to Young
Fashion in *The Relapse* are removed by the substitution
of a female arranger. Berinthia's ravishment, when she is
carried off stage crying out faintly so as not to alarm her
maid also goes, and the sentimental shuffling of the lovers
back to their original pairs without any suggestion of
anything more serious than coy flirtation is too bland
for modern taste but it hardly seems fair to censure Sheridan for bawdlerization when almost until our own age
Vanbrugh has been condemned for obscenity. Certainly
it is only within recent years that overt male homosexuality has been considered a legitimate means for theatrical
humour.

We must not allow our affectation of lack of moral prejudice to cloud our appreciation of Sheridan's very real achievements. *The Relapse* is, as we have seen, very closely linked with Cibber's *Love's Last Shift*, at times approaching close to being a gentle burlesque of its inspiration. This link no longer exists and Sheridan has succeeded in freeing the Amanda-Loveless portion of the play from its dependence on the original. Loveless, shorn of his reputation as a libertine, starts *A Trip To Scarborough* no different from any normal husband with a roving eye. Again at the end of Vanbrugh's play Worthy is rejected by Amanda and undergoes a sudden transformation which recalls Loveless' equally sudden repentance in *Love's Last Shift*. Without knowledge of the earlier play Worthy's reformation seems extravagantly sentimental rather than the gentle parody which Vanbrugh intends. Sheridan is right to omit this from his ending, which as we have noted conforms to eighteenth-century dramatic convention.

The great weakness of Vanbrugh's play is the lack of connection between the two plots. Sheridan takes much more care to create a unity of action. The locale is changed from London and the country to Scarborough in the service of this unity. There is no difficulty in bringing the London characters to this town and it is plausible to have Sir Tunbelly's country seat nearby. All the characters can be in approximately the same place at the same time. Thus they can become participants in both lines of intrigue.

Sheridan's opening scene carefully details the complications. Lord Foppington's attempt upon Amanda's virtue becomes motive enough for Loveless and Worthy (now called Townly) to help Tom Fashion in his masquerade. By bringing both sets of characters together it is possible to end the play much more quickly and smoothly without Vanbrugh's need to contrive all his characters in London for a final act of predictable discovery.

Foppington is the character that loses most in the

alteration; there is at the same time more fun and more dignity about the original than Sheridan achieves, lost too is much of the glorious confrontation between the rustic and the foppish which is in the original scenes between Sir Tunbelly and Foppington. But what Sheridan loses in farce and theatricality he gains in strategic structure. There can be no doubt that his play is the more articulate comic statement.

His aims seem not dissimilar to those which governed most alterations of Shakespeare. He refashioned an old play to make it conform to the unities. He explained ambiguities, removed what he considered to be the offensive passages and tightened the dialogue by removing the prose-like blank verse which Vanbrugh resorts to during portions of the Amanda-Loveless plot. These aims are entirely successful and, while we may consider the result muted, it would be very wrong to follow Allardyce Nicoll in dismissing it as 'nothing more than a genteel version of Vanbrugh's *The Relapse*'.

The Castle Spectre
M. G. Lewis (1775–1818)

Matthew Gregory Lewis was educated at Westminster
School and Christ Church, Oxford. In 1794 he became
attaché to the British embassy at the Hague. He only
remained in this post for a few months, finding time to
write in ten weeks his extraordinarily successful novel
Ambrosio, or the Monk, published in 1795. From this
combination of sex and gothic horror comes his nickname
'Monk'. Shortly after he was twenty-one Lewis entered
Parliament as member for Hindon, in Wiltshire. It appears that he never once spoke in the House and eventually gave up his seat to concentrate on literature. He
produced a second successful novel with *The Bravo of
Venice*, an adaptation from the German which appeared
in 1804. A knowledge of German drew him particularly to
Kotzebue, translating *Rollo* (1797), he also translated
Schiller's *Kabale und Liebe* as *The Minister* (1796). His
best known plays are *Timour the Tartar* (1811) and *The
Castle Spectre* (1797). Since they dropped from the repertory in the first half of the nineteenth century they have
been slightly regarded by critics, but they and all 'Monk'
Lewis's work provide opportunities for operatic acting,
lavish spectacle and incidental music which makes their
total much more than the bare script indicates. In 1815,
on the death of his father, he inherited large estates in
the West Indies. He visited these writing, during this first
trip, the posthumously published *Journal of a West*

Indian Proprietor (1833). He journeyed to Jamaica again in 1817 in order to better the condition of slaves. He died of fever on the homeward voyage on 14 May 1818.

DATE 1797

CAST

Earl Osmond

Reginald, his brother

Percy, son of the Earl of Northumberland

Father Philip

Motley, a fool

Kenric, Earl Osmond's creature

Saib ⎫

Hassan ⎬   black attendants on Osmond

Muley ⎬

Alaric ⎭

Allan

Edric

Harold

Angela, Reginald's daughter

Alice, her maid

The ghost of Evelina, her mother

SCENE Conway Castle and its environs, during the Middle Ages

Plot

Act I,*i* A dimly lit grove. The play opens with a comic exchange between Father Philip and Motley the fool. The purpose of this is to warm the audience up, rather than advance the plot of the piece. Father Philip is replaced by Percy and as if to make up for the irrelevancies of the opening this next exchange is crammed with information. We learn that Motley, who is now Earl Osmond's fool, was formerly in the employ of Percy's father and is thus prepared to assist Percy in any emprise. Percy has fallen in love with the ward of a simple villager. Afraid that she might be dazzled by the fact that he is the son of the Earl of Northumberland he has wooed and won her under the name of Edwy. Before he could reveal his true identity she was claimed by Kenric, a creature of Earl Osmond. We learn that Angela is now living in Conway Castle, it being given out that she is the daughter of a friend of Osmond's. Motley further warns Percy against Osmond. He is the very antidote to mirth, none dare approach him save Kenric and his four black attendants. Also it is rumoured that fifteen years previously Osmond murdered his brother Reginald and his wife and infant daughter. Certainly since that time Osmond has broken every tie of society, barring his gates against all strangers. Motley insists that it is not affection for Angela's father that has led to her introduction to the castle but rather affection for her father's child. *ii* The castle hall. We are introduced to Osmond's blacks. There is a short exchange between them and Kenric, in which Kenric suggests that he is about to betray Osmond, while the blacks hint that Osmond is about to betray Kenric. This gives place to a comic scene between Father Philip and Alice. Alice hysterically informs the priest how she has heard the ghost of Evelina, Osmond's murdered sister-in-law, singing a lullaby. Her description of the ghost is interrupted when a figure in white appears from the haunted room. This turns out to be Angela. The act concludes with a restatement by Alice of the events leading up to Osmond's inheritance of the castle.

Act II,*i* The armoury. Suits of armour are arranged on both sides upon pedestals, with the names of their possessors under each. Motley persuades Percy to hide in Reginald's armour. Osmond enters and forces his attentions on Angela. The armour comes to life and Angela's virtue is protected. *ii* The castle hall. That the last scene was intended as comedy is confirmed by Alice's first lines as she enters, which almost certainly refer to the hilarity of the audience:

Here's rudeness! Here's ill-breeding! On my conscience,
this house grows worse and worse every day!

Alice has been knocked over by Percy; not considering the
possibility that this figure in armour could be a ghost, she
rails against the rudeness. Father Philip warns Motley to
leave the house: Percy has been discovered and his part in
the affair is known. He promises the Fool that all shall
yet be well and Percy and Angela will be rescued from the
tyrant by means of movable panels, subterraneous passages
and secret springs. *iii* A spacious chamber: on one side
is a couch; on the other a table placed under an arched
and lofty window. Percy pretends to doze on the couch,
while the four blacks play dice on the front of the stage
for a bag of money with which Percy has unsuccessfully
attempted to bribe them. A song is heard outside the
window. Percy realizes that its repeated refrain is a message. His friends have prepared his escape. He creeps towards the window. One of the blacks looks round. He
throws himself back on the couch. He again creeps to the
window and jumps out.
Act III,*i* A view of the river Conway. Sunset. Percy is reunited with his friends. He has received a letter from the
priest promising to release Angela. *ii* The castle hall.
Osmond, furious at Percy's escape, attempts to stab Saib
but is prevented by Kenric. Saib repays Kenric by informing him that Osmond had planned to poison him that
night. We are now treated to a further block of information, much of which we had guessed. Angela is the
daughter of Reginald and Evelina. She is physically very
like her mother with whom Osmond was in love. In-
credibly Reginald was not murdered but has been kept a
prisoner in one of the castle's secret dungeons by Kenric.
The latter unknown to Osmond. *iii* The cedar room. In
the centre is a large antique bed with two full length
portraits on either side of Evelina and Reginald. The
female picture falls back and Father Philip enters from

a secret passage. Hearing a noise he conceals himself in the
bed as Osmond and Angela enter. The Earl insists that
Angela must become his wife. Left alone with Alice to
think over this demand Angela declares that she will take
her own life. This highly melodramatic moment is de-
flated by the collapse of the bed and the emergence from
it of Father Philip swathed in a sheet. Alice is again convinced that she has seen a ghost and exits screaming. The
audience laughter dies and Father Philip quickly demonstrates the secret passage to Angela.

Act IV,*i* The castle hall. Alice tells Father Philip how
she has a second time seen the ghost of Evelina. He assures
her her apparition was no more like Evelina than he is
and packs her off to bed. Osmond is in a state of frenzy.
He has had a terrible dream. In it he wandered among the
tombs of his ancestors. Suddenly he saw Angela. He em-
braced her only for her to turn into the dying Evelina who
promised to meet him again that night. Kenric enters on
his way to lead Angela to safety. *ii* Angela's apartment.
Osmond overhears Kenric tell Angela that her father lives.
He and the blacks seize Kenric. He offers Angela her
father's life if she will marry him. She produces a dagger
and offers to kill herself. Osmond recognizes it as the very
weapon that he used to stab her mother. He falls senseless
to the ground and is conveyed from the chamber by his
blacks. The ghost of Evelina appears and blesses Angela.

Act V,*i* A view of Conway Castle by moonlight. Percy and
his friends prepare to attack the castle. They have been
joined by Kenric and Saib. *ii* A dark vaulted chamber.
Angela and Father Philip are trying to escape through the
secret passages. They take a wrong turn which will lead
them into the dungeons. Osmond and the two blacks still
remaining faithful to him follow on their way to murder
Reginald. *iii* Reginald's dungeon. Raised at the back are
caverns with steps leading down to the stage level. Characters can thus be seen as they approach. The events of this
final scene are comfortably predictable. Angela is reunited

with her father. The Earl arrives and repeats his offer to
spare Reginald if she will marry him. News is brought that
Percy's men are attacking the castle. Reginald, surpris-
ingly strong after his long imprisonment, grabs a sword
and attacks the blacks. Reginald is just about to be stabbed by Osmond in spite of the help which we can see
arriving when the ghost of Evelina distracts him. Angela
takes this opportunity to plunge her dagger, the same that
killed her mother, into Osmond's bosom.

Critical commentary

The Castle Spectre received forty-seven performances in its
first season and remained a popular piece for the next
twenty-five years. It has more merit than the well known
anecdote of Lewis offering to stake the profits and Sheridan's reply (that he could not afford so much but that he
would be prepared to wager all that it was worth) suggests.

Native English melodrama is essentially domestic. It
originates from pieces such as *Arden of Faversham* and
A Yorkshire Tragedy: is resurrected in the mid-eighteenth
century with *The London Merchant*, *Fatal Curiosity* and
The Gamester, then makes a continental journey to re-
appear in its gothic-romantic shape which it throws off in
the second quarter of the nineteenth century, concentrating on domestic detail as exemplified by plays such as *The
Factory Lad*, *Luke the Labourer* and *Rent Day*. Critics
have a tendency to exaggerate continental influence on
English drama. On examination the so called French
influence on the drama of the second half of the seventeenth century can be shown to be very superficial, likewise the Spanish. The theatrical revolution, supposedly
credited to admiration of Ibsen, can be demonstrated as
beginning twenty years earlier. Even in our own time the
theories and models provided by Brecht have been anglicized out of all recognition. The English are notoriously

insensitive to foreign ideas and all continental models are always so radically altered that it is very dangerous to try to explain away a particular change of fashion as 'French', 'German', etc. Thus it is a dangerous oversimplification to explain the extravagances of *The Castle Spectre* as Schilleresque or Gothic. Rather they are part of a *fin de siècle* reaction against a growing boredom with the Age of Reason. Although Kotzebue is looted to provide parts of the plot, the play is solidly English. This shows particularly in the use of the supernatural. In Germany ghosts and spectres still retained some currency while in eighteenth-century England 'Tales of Terror' were beginning to have much the same muscular response as 'Broad Grins'. True it was still widely believed that deeds of darkness had, at least in the past, been revealed and punished thanks to supernatural intervention, but the more knowing were quick to point out that such a belief acted as a useful deterrent against those who, while careless of heavenly punishment, were fearful indeed of earthly discovery.

In this sceptical climate Lewis achieves a *tour de force* by pandering at first to the potential visibility of his subject with such hackneyed devices as moving suits of armour, panels which creak open mysteriously only for a comic character to emerge and several false alarms. Basically Lewis is exploiting his graveyard reputation derived from *The Monk*. The audience look forward to ghosts from him and he seems determined to frustrate this, as for example with Angela's entrance at the end of Act I, when the audience might reasonably expect a foretaste of horrors to come. As she opens the doors of the haunted chamber she is silhouetted against the light in that room, by shutting the doors she reveals herself in her own character! A simple theatrical trick but none the less effective for its simplicity. Having lulled the audience with brilliant tongue in cheek theatricality of this kind, the entry of the genuine ghost is a complete surprise.

Of course this scene is irrelevant to the organic structure of the play. It is commercial sensationalism but it is disarmingly honest commercial sensationalism and Lewis confounded his critics by admitting to such motives, going on to explain the anachronistic inclusion of four black slaves in North Wales in the Middle Ages as being simply to add 'pleasing variety':

> ... could I have produced the same effect by making my heroine blue, blue I should have made her.

Here he is possibly a little hard upon himself. Granted for the fashionable ladies, sitting in their boxes with their negro servants standing respectfully in the rear, Hassan's threats against mankind provide a titillating thrill, but we should also remember that Lewis was seriously disturbed by the treatment of West Indian slaves. His blacks are something more than a theatrical convention thrust in to pander to the exotic and the description of a black man torn from his native village and transported to foreign shores in the first act is the most moving passage in the play:

> *Hassan* ... Saib, I too have loved. I have known how painful it was to leave one on whom my heart hung; how incapable was all else to supply her loss. I have exchanged want for plenty; fatigue for rest; a wretched hut for a splendid bed. But am I happier? O, no! Still do I regret my native land, and the partners of my poverty. Then toil was sweet to me, for I laboured for Samba! Then repose ever blessed my bed of leaves; for there, by my side, lay Samba sleeping.
> *Saib* This from you, Hassan? Did love ever find a place in your bosom?
> *Hassan* Did it? Oh Saib! my heart once was gentle, once was good; but sorrows have broken it, insults have made it hard. I have been dragged from my native land; from a wife who was everything to me, to whom I was everything!

Twenty years have elapsed since these Christians tore me
away; they trampled upon my heart, mocked my despair,
and when in frantic terms I raved of Samba, laughed and
wondered how a negro's soul could feel. In that moment,
when the last point of Africa faded from my view, – when
as I stood on the vessel's deck, I felt that all I loved was to
me lost for ever – in that bitter moment did I banish
humanity from my breast. I tore from my arm the bracelet
of Samba's hair; I gave to the sea the precious token; and
while the high waves swift bore it from me, vowed aloud,
endless hatred to mankind. I have kept my oath; I *will*
keep it.

Melodramas use a basic three part structure from which
evolved the three act play which ousted the older five and
four act structures in the twentieth century. At its simplest
it is: Part one, heroine separated from hero; Part two,
heroine's chastity or life or both threatened by villain;
Part three, heroine saved from villain and rescued by hero.
In spite of its pretence at a five act structure *The Castle
Spectre* clearly conforms to the above formula, but Lewis
does initiate some interesting new developments. He is
relatively uninterested in his hero who he allows to be
conventionally impotent before the power of the villain,
but Angela shows the first beginnings of female self as-
sertion by stabbing Osmond to death in the final scene.
Osmond himself is not quite the straightforward villain he
at first appears. In him, in embryo, is the Byronic hero
tortured by a remorse a synopsis is unable to reproduce.
Remorse is the first stage in the humanizing of the villain
which will end with deep psychological characterizations
neither hero nor villain, such as Brand, Manders, and
Loveborg of Ibsen.

Pizarro
R. B. Sheridan

DATE 1799
CAST
Ataliba, King of Peru
Rolla, his kinsman and general
Orozembo, a Peruvian cacique
Orano
Alonzo, Pizarro's former friend, now fighting against him
Pizarro, leader of the Spaniards
Almagro ⎫
Gonzalo ⎬ Spanish officers
Davilla ⎭
Gomez
Valverde, secretary to Pizarro
Las-Casas, an old monk
Old Blind Man
Boy
Cora, wife to Alonzo
Elvira, Pizarro's mistress
Zuluga
SCENE Peru

Plot

Act I,*i* A pavilion near Pizarro's tent. From a conversation between Valverde and Pizarro's mistress Elvira, we learn that Pizarro is thirsting for revenge having been recently defeated by the Peruvians led by Rolla and his former friend and pupil Alonzo, who has turned against him because of his treatment of the Peruvians. Pizarro is particularly bitter against the latter for whose revolt he blames the 'canting precepts of humanity' of the old monk Las-Casas. Pizarro's force has been strengthened and he plans to wipe out the ignominy of defeat by massacring the Peruvians with a surprise attack planned to coincide with one of their religious festivals. Las-Casas begs Pizarro not to renew 'the foul barbarities which your insatiate avarice has inflicted' on the wretched unoffending Peruvians. Of the other Spaniards Elvira alone shows pity, lending her prayers to those of Las-Casas. Pizarro remains deaf to any appeals. He turns to his lieutenant Almagro and bids him give the order for their march. Almagro hails Pizarro as the future monarch of Peru. Pizarro replies that ambition must take counsel from discretion. It is his intention to allow Ataliba to retain the shadow of his sceptre but to prepare his way to the throne by marrying the daughter of the Peruvian King. Elvira overhears this but dissembles her jealousy. Orozembo, an old Peruvian cacique, who has been captured by Pizarro's soldiers, is dragged before the Spanish general. He remains firm in spite of bribes and threats, boldly refusing to betray his friends. When offered riches he answers that a pure heart is all the wealth he requires and when asked the number of the Peruvian host he replies that Rolla and Alonzo are themselves a host. He is brutally stabbed by Davilla and dies in Elvira's arms. Pizarro prepares for battle. Valverde and Elvira are left alone. Elvira has resigned her honour and family to follow Pizarro to the new world. Now Pizarro is on the point of rejecting her. Valverde loves her and is willing to kill Pizarro for her sake. Elvira dismisses Valverde disgusted with herself for momentarily listening to his offer to revenge her honour but in soliloquy she

confides to the audience that while virtuous women when
rejected may have the consolation of an unspotted fame
she has nothing left save despair and vengeance.

Act II,*i* A wood surrounded by a wild wood and rocks. In
contrast to the wild love of Elvira and Pizarro we are now
treated to a domestic scene where Cora shows Alonzo their
child. She refuses to leave him to go with the other Peruvian women to safety. Rolla enters, once in love with Cora
he unselfishly resigned his interest to that of his friend.
Alonzo has heard rumours of Pizarro's preparation but
Rolla assures him that all is prepared. *ii* The temple of
the sun. The Peruvians gather for a sacrifice. The Inca
Ataliba welcomes Rolla and Alonzo. Rolla addresses the
Peruvians in words which, for the English audience of
1799, directly identified the Spaniards and Pizarro with
the threat of a French invasion led by Bonaparte:

> They, by a strange frenzy driven, fight for power,
> for plunder and extended rule: we, for our country,
> our altars and our homes. They follow an adventurer
> whom they fear, and obey a power which they hate: we
> serve a monarch we love – a God whom we adore ...

The ceremony begins only to be interrupted by news of
the Spanish attack. *iii* A wood between the temple and
the camp. Alonzo and Rolla take leave of each other before the battle. Alonzo persuades the reluctant Rolla to
agree to marry Cora and bring up Alonzo's and her child
as his son if Alonzo should be killed in the battle. *iv* The
Peruvian camp. An old blind man and a boy wait for news.
The fortune of the day goes against the Peruvians. The
wounded Ataliba is carried in. The Spaniards renew their
attack and the King is captured. Rolla rallies the Peruvians and rescues the King, but news is brought that
Alonzo has been captured.

Act III,*i* A wild retreat among stupendous rocks. Cora
waits with the other wives and children. The Peruvians
enter singing a song of victory. Cora goes from man to

man seeking Alonzo. Rolla tells her of his capture. The
Peruvian women eagerly tear off all their ornaments and
offer them as contributions to Alonzo's ransom. *ii* The
wood. Rolla tells a distracted Cora Alonzo's last request.
Hysterically she accuses Rolla of deliberately letting his
friend be captured in order to gain her, exclaiming that
she would sooner link herself to the pallid corpse of the
meanest wretch that perished with Alonzo than that her
son should call Rolla father or she him husband. *iii* Elvira
brings Pizarro the news that Alonzo is captured. Pizarro
gives way to savage triumph. He orders the prisoner to be
brought before him. Elvira warns him that if he kills
Alonzo she is lost to him for ever. Pizarro begins to suspect
Elvira of loving Alonzo. He asks what Alonzo's fate is to
her. She replies that his fate is nothing, Pizarro's glory
everything. How could she, she asks, continue to love
Pizarro stripped of fame and honour? Pizarro condemns
Alonzo to death as a deserter. Alonzo answers this sentence
by maintaining that when Pizarro's soldiers, lured by a
lust for gold, forgot the honour of Castilians and forsook
the duties of humanity they deserted him. Elvira begs
Pizarro to act if not always justly at least greatly and suggests he settle his differences with Alonzo by single combat. Elvira is sickened by the meanness of Pizarro's vengeance but her pleas are ignored. Pizarro is adamant,
Alonzo is to die at dawn.

Act IV,*i* A dungeon. Rolla, seeking Alonzo, has entered
the camp disguised as a monk. The sentry will not accept
a bribe but he bends before Rolla's appeal to his humanity
and allows Rolla to visit his friend. Rolla persuades
Alonzo to change clothes with him, partly for the sake of
Cora and his son and partly because it is Alonzo's life
Pizarro seeks, and he allows himself to be persuaded that
the Spanish general will show mercy to Rolla when Rolla
threatens that if Alonzo refuses to go he will stay and die
with him. No sooner has Alonzo gone than Elvira enters.
Rolla admits to her that his motive for acting thus was his

love for Cora. She gives Rolla a dagger and offers to help Rolla kill Pizarro. He at first refuses but Elvira persuades him. She advises him to kill the sentry but, remembering how he refused gold only being bribed to admit Rolla by his own feelings, Rolla refuses. *ii* Pizarro's tent. Pizarro is tormented by foul dreams. Rolla cannot kill him in his sleep. Rolla cannot be an assassin. He wakes him to take him prisoner but, Elvira entering, Pizarro seizes the opportunity to call the guards. Elvira he condemns to torture and she is carried out shrieking curses at him:

> And when thy parting hour approaches – hark to the knell,
> whose dreadful beat shall strike to thy despairing soul.
> Then will vibrate on thy ear the curses of the cloistered
> saint from whom thou stolest me. Then the last shrieks
> which burst from my mother's breaking heart, as she died,
> appealing to her God against the seducer of her child!
> Then the blood-stifled groans of my murdered brother –
> murdered by thee, fell monster! – seeking atonement for
> his sister's ruined honour.

Pizarro cannot but admire Rolla and he sets him free.
Act V,*i* A forest. Cora lays her son on the ground. She hears Alonzo's voice and momentarily leaves the child. Two Spanish soldiers kidnap him. Cora's happiness at being reunited with Alonzo changes to an extreme of grief when she discovers the baby gone. *ii* An outpost of the Spanish camp. Rolla has been captured making his way out of the camp. Pizarro orders his release and gives him his own sword. The child is brought in and Rolla recognizes it as Alonzo's. Pizarro exults at this opportunity for revenge. Rolla throws himself at the Spaniard's feet offering himself in exchange. Pizarro refuses to listen. Rolla seizes the child and makes his escape but he is wounded to death. *iii* Ataliba's tent. Rolla enters with the child and gives it to Alonzo with the words 'For thee, and Cora', and dies. *iv* A recess among the rocks. The battle rages. Pizarro challenges Alonzo to single combat.

Alonzo is beaten down when, at what seems to be the moment of his death, Elvira enters habited as when Pizarro first beheld her. Thinking her executed at his order and therefore a ghost Pizarro staggers back and Alonzo kills him. The play ends with the bodies of Rolla and Pizarro being carried off.

Critical commentary

J. C. Trewin very rightly links *Pizarro* with *The Castle Spectre* in his biography of Macready, with a brief quotation from Osmond:

> An English baron loves you: a nobleman than whom
> our island boasts few more potent.

And a second from Rolla:

> On iron pinions borne, the blood-stained vulture
> clears the storm, yet is the plumage closest to her breast
> soft as the cygnet's down; and o'er her unshelled brood
> the murmuring ring-dove sits not more gently!

Apart from the lack of comic relief from servants or other characters *Pizarro* is a full-blooded melodrama. Cora's flight into the forest carrying her child was usually presented as taking place in the middle of a raging storm. Another cliché of melodramatic staging occurs when Rolla snatches Cora's child from the Spaniards and escapes across a narrow wooden bridge over a cataract hotly pursued by Pizarro's soldiers, while Pizarro's own end is almost an exact parallel of that of Osmond in *The Castle Spectre*. Spectacle and staging is everything in this play and it is significant that those that damn it as marking a senile decline in Sheridan's powers can never have seen it performed and by such dismissal reveal a total lack of visual imagination which must seriously undermine their right to pontificate with any authority on dramatic subjects. It is written twenty years after Sheridan had appeared to abandon playwriting for a parliamentary career, but he can hardly, at the age of forty-seven and at almost the height of his political success, be accused of senility.

The key to understanding *Pizarro* lies in an anecdote recounted by W. Oxberry in the introduction to his 1824 edition of the play:

> Pitt, having been to see the play, was asked by a friend his opinion of it. 'If you mean' said he, 'what Sheridan has written, there is nothing new in it for I heard it all long ago in his speeches at Hastings' trial.'

Sheridan and Burke had made themselves champions of the oppressed East Indians at this trial. Sheridan had also spoken out in the House against slavery and it is perhaps significant to note that William Wilberforce attended a performance of *Pizarro* although he had not previously visited the theatre for twenty years.

Before we condemn Sheridan's diction in this play let us glance at a selection of the phrases which gained him the reputation, in the era of Pitt, Fox and Burke, of being the finest orator in the House of Commons:

> For confident I am, that, as soon as one drop of English blood shall be shed by a Frenchman, on English ground, the English valour will that moment rise to a pitch equal to what its most sanguine friends can expect, or its warmest admirers can desire . . .

he had said on 26 April 1798, in a parliamentary speech referring to the threat of French invasion, going on:

> . . . They come for what they really want: they come for ships, for commerce, for credit and for capital. Yes; they come for the sinews, the bones; for the very marrow and for the very heart's blood of Great Britain.

This latter quotation seems to directly recall the section of Rolla's speech to the Peruvians in Act II,*ii* quoted above.

Sheridan's parliamentary oratory is hyperbolic and emotional, so too is that of Rolla. Taste has changed and we
now prefer understatement both in political oratory and
on stage but it is absurd to down language in the play
which is identical to that Sheridan has successfully used to
far more serious effect in the House. *Pizarro* is written in
the accepted stylistic convention of the period.

Having linked the play to Sheridan's political career it
would be wrong to leave any impression that its inspiration is anything but financial. A year before Sheridan had
assisted Benjamin Thompson with his highly successful
adaptation from Kotzebue *The Stranger*, which like
Pizarro anticipates many nineteenth-century themes such
as atonement, repentance and forgiveness. Sheridan
needed money. Drury Lane, his principal source of revenue, was suffering an extreme financial crisis. *The
Stranger* had been successful a year earlier, Kotzebue was
in fashion (according to one critic there were twenty-
seven translations or adaptations from his work in 1799
alone); thus the combined reputations of himself, Kotzebue, from whose *Die Spanier in Peru*, *Pizarro* is adapted,
and *The Stranger* guaranteed box office success.

In choosing to adapt *Die Spanier in Peru* Sheridan not
only chooses a vehicle which will allow him to follow
Voltaire and others in reiterating a humanitarian condemnation of European exploitation of a subject race, but
he also and perhaps more significantly writes to the
strengths of his company and theatre.

The new Drury Lane of which Sheridan as proprietor
had an intimate knowledge had a seating capacity of over
3,600. This destroyed subtle characterization but encouraged the style of declamatory acting, and, of course,
the new theatre had greatly increased resources for spectacle. Nearly all the reviews of the first presentation stress
the scenic contribution. *The True Briton* stating that it
was:

... highly magnificent. The *Tent of Pizarro*, the *Temple of the Sun*, various views of a romantic country, the forest illuminated by the fiery element and the subterranean retreat are admirable achievements of the period.

To the acting and the design must be added the expert contribution of Drury Lane's musicians. The play included songs and musical embellishment in the action, particularly in Act II,*ii*, Act III,*i*, (where the wives and children sang alternately, stanzas expressive of their situation, with a chorus in which all join) and Act V,*iv*, (the funeral dirge) and it was performed with musical intervals.

Pizarro then should be seen as entirely consistent with Sheridan's other dramatic work. It is exactly the kind of tragedy that one would expect from a leading dramatist in 1799. It shows the same appreciation of the visual as Sheridan has already demonstrated in *The Rivals*. Plagiarism is a meaningless critical term when applied to this period when plays were as much compiled as written. Sheridan always acknowledges his debt to Kotzebue, as the German's reputation greatly assisted the piece's commercial success.

Rob Roy Macgregor

Adapted from Sir Walter Scott by Isaac Pocock

Sir Walter Scott (1771–1832)
Isaac Pocock (1782–1835)

Scott was the son of a lawyer. He was educated at Edinburgh High School and Edinburgh University. At the
latter he studied law becoming an advocate in 1792. He
was appointed Sheriff-Depute of Selkirk in 1799 and Clerk
of Session in Edinburgh in 1806. His first book, a collection of Border ballads, was published in 1802 under the
title *Minstrelsy of the Scottish Border*. There was hardly
a branch of literature which he did not attempt. He himself valued his poetry and antiquarian publications above
his epic series of novels which began in 1814 with the
anonymous publication of *Waverley*. His first novels had
a distinctly Scottish flavour but in 1820 he turned to
English subjects with *Ivanhoe*, then came *Kenilworth*
(1821), *The Fortunes of Nigel* (1822), *Quentin Durward*
(1823), *Redgauntlet* (1824) and *The Talisman* (1825). He
was created a baronet in 1820.

He is remembered with especial gratitude by his
countrymen for his tireless work to preserve a distinct
Scottish identity, even in the early nineteenth century
threatened by English influences. It seems likely that in his
enthusiasm he may have invented some things but his
stage management of the Royal Visit to Edinburgh of 1823
was the starting point of a revival of interest in the clan
system and other aspects of Scottish life which had remained under a cloud since the '45. Another great
achievement was his share in the discovery in 1818 of the

Regalia of Scotland which had lain hidden since 1707.

Apart from *The Doom of Devorgoil* he wrote only one other play *Auchindrane, or, The Ayrshire Tragedy*, this is an even less successful production than the former, although there are passages in it, particularly where the murdered corpse floats upright behind the assassin's bark, of striking poetical merit. It was published early in 1830.

He died at his beloved Abbotsford where he had lived most of his life on 21 September 1832, and was buried at Dryburgh Abbey.

Isaac Pocock was the author of a number of farces, melodramas and adaptations from novels. It was his version of *Rob Roy* which first brought Macready into prominence as an actor. He is best remembered today for his melodramas. As an artist he was a pupil of Romney and exhibited at the Royal Academy. The best known of his many plays, his adaptations of Scott excepted, are: *Hit or Miss* (1810), *The Miller and his Men* (1813), *The Magpie or the Maid?* (1815), *Robinson Crusoe* (1817) and *The Robber's Bride* (1829).

DATE 1818

CAST

Sir Frederick Vernon	Saunders Wylie
Rashleigh Osbaldistone	Andrew Fairservice
Francis Osbaldistone	Lancie Wingfield
Mr Owen	Willie
Captain Thornton	Sergeant
Major Galbraith	Diana Vernon
Rob Roy	Martha
Bailie Nicol Jarvie	Mattie
Dougal	Jean McAlpine
MacStuart	Hostess
Jobson	Helen Macgregor

SCENE Mainly Scotland

Plot

Act I,*i* The interior of a village inn. Rob Roy, disguised as a north country grazier encounters Mr Owen, head clerk and junior partner in the London commercial and banking house of Osbaldistone and Company. Mr Owen is travelling north to visit Mr Francis Osbaldistone, the son of the head of the firm, who is absent on the continent, with bad news. By right Francis should be a partner in the firm but he preferred making poetry to making money and was disinherited by his father in favour of his cousin Rashleigh. This same Rashleigh is involved in Jacobite politics. He has taken advantage of his uncle's absence to steal certain bills bringing the firm to the brink of ruin. This is the news that Owen imparts to Francis. *ii* The library of Osbaldistone Hall. Although the Osbaldistones, with the dubious exception of Rashleigh, are adherents of the present government, not so their kin the Vernons. Diana, Francis' cousin, and her father are Catholics and Jacobites by conviction. Although Diana and Francis love each other, this is an insuperable barrier. Sir Frederick Vernon is hidden within the Hall, appearing either in antique costume identical to one of the family portraits or as Diana's confessor. He wishes to see Diana married to Rashleigh whom she has rejected. Francis comes to take leave of Diana. Her father is involved in Rashleigh's schemes. Torn between love for Francis and duty to her father she gives Francis a package instructing him to open it ten days before the bills fall due if all other means fail. *iii* A room in Bailie Nicol Jarvie's house in Glasgow. The good bailie is one of Osbaldistone and Company's two Scottish correspondents. He is brought news of the firm's impending ruin. Motivated partly by the fact that his rival correspondent MacVittie takes a contrary view, partly by a belief that the distress cannot be permanent, and partly by good nature, he decides to stand by the firm. In spite of the lateness of the hour he sallies forth to the tollbooth to bail out Mr Owen who has been imprisoned as a debtor on MacVittie's suit. *iv* The old bridge of Glasgow. Francis and a servant enter. Rob Roy muffled in a cloak appears at the back but seeing the servant exits. When the servant leaves he re-enters to warn Francis that he is in danger. He asks Francis to follow him. Suspicious, Francis demands his name, these suspicions are hardly allayed by Rob's refusal accompanied as it is by dark hints that were Rob to be recognized he would be arrested. Reluctantly, on the assurance that Rob is no enemy to him, Francis accepts his guidance. *v* The hall of the tollbooth of Glasgow. Dougal the jailor is an agent of Rob's. He admits Francis and the MacGregor. *vi* A cell in the tollbooth. Mr Owen at first thinks that Francis has also been arrested. Bailie Nicol Jarvie's arrival interrupts Francis' assurances to the contrary. He recognizes Rob but does not have him arrested partly because were he to cry out Rob would blow his brains out, partly because Rob is a remote kinsman and partly because of his basic good nature. There seems no solution to the problems of Osbaldistone and Company. It is ten days till the bills fall due. Francis remembers the package Diana entrusted to him. Inside is a letter to Rob. Rashleigh has sent the bills to the Highlands. Francis must visit Rob in the glens. The bailie agrees to guide him, partly on Rob's promise to repay £200 owing to him and partly because of his good nature.

Act II,*i* The old college gardens of Glasgow and a view of the spire of St Mungo's. Rashleigh enters with his associate Jobson. We learn that it was by his instigation that Mr Owen was imprisoned and that he now intends to revenge himself on Diana for rejecting him by betraying Rob and her father. Francis enters and demands the return of his father's papers. Rashleigh taunts him and after a short exchange of insults they draw swords and fight. Rob rushes between them and beats down their guard. He forcibly prevents Francis from following Rashleigh:

Would you follow the wolf to his den? Come, come, be
cool — 'tis to me you must look for that you seek.
Keep aloof from Rashleigh, and that pettifogging
justice-clerk Jobson; above all from MacVittie. Make
the best of your way to Aberfoil, and by the word of a
Macgregor, I will not see you wronged! Remember the
Clachan of Aberfoil.

ii The library at Osbaldistone Hall. Sir Frederick Vernon
receives a letter telling how Diana's rejection of Rashleigh has led to his betrayal of the Jacobite cause. Sir
Frederick determines to journey to Scotland in order to
regain the bills for the House of Osbaldistone and Company. He is still adamant that Diana should not marry
Francis. *iii* The interior of Jean MacAlpine's change-
house in the Clachan of Aberfoil. The Lennox troopers
under Major Galbraith and MacStuart are waiting to ap-
prehend Rob Roy and Francis on Rashleigh's information. Francis and the bailie seek shelter. The major, who
is very drunk, tries to turn them out. The bailie and he
fall to blows, the bailie being armed with a red hot poker.
This difference sorted, Francis receives instructions from
Rob to follow Dougal, before he can follow these Captain
Thornton arrives with a company of red coats. Francis is
searched and Rob's letter is discovered. *iv* The Clachan
of Aberfoil. Exterior of the inn. Dougal, Francis and the
bailie are brought out as prisoners. Rob, dressed for the
first time in Highland dress appears in the background.
He signs to Dougal who pretends to agree to guide the
troops to his master. The regular soldiers march off with
their prisoners. Rashleigh appears and calls on Galbraith.
Rob is captured.
Act III,*i* The pass of Lochard. Helen MacGregor, Rob's
warrior wife ambushes the regular soldiers. She treats the
bailie's claims to kinship with ferocious contempt and is
about to shoot Francis, in error for Rashleigh, until she
discovers her mistake. She contents herself with composing

a message to the authorities demanding Rob's release within twelve hours or she will send them Captain Thornton and the bailie each bundled in a plaid and chopped into as many pieces as there are checks in the tartan. To the Bailie's great relief Rob enters having escaped by jumping into a river. *ii* Rocks near Aberfoil. Diana takes leave of Francis after restoring to him his father's bills. *iii* Interior of Jean MacAlpine's inn. Francis learns that his father is in Glasgow. Examining the papers he discovers a will made by Rashleigh's father leaving everything to Francis. This explains Rashleigh's hostility. *iv* A distant view of the banks of Loch Lomond (this scene was usually omitted in performance) Dougal overhears Rashleigh and Jobson plotting to ambush Sir Frederick. *v* Rob Roy's cave, view of Loch Lomond by moonlight. Francis takes leave of Rob and the Highlanders march away. Sir Frederick and Diana are left. Rashleigh enters at the head of a party of soldiers. Sir Frederick is arrested as a traitor, Francis and Diana as aiders and abetters of treason. Rob re-enters and his Highlanders overpower the government troops. Rob kills Rashleigh. Acting on information from Dougal he had kept back half his force to frustrate Rashleigh. Sir Frederick withdraws his objections to Francis marrying Diana.

The Doom of Devorgoil
Sir Walter Scott

DATE 1818

CAST
Oswald of Devorgoil, a decayed Scottish baron
Leonard, a ranger
Durward, a palmer
Lancelot Blackthorn, a companion of Leonard in love with Kathleen.
Gullcrammer, a conceited student
Owlspiegle ⎱ maskers represented by
Cockledemoy ⎰ Blackthorn and Kathleen
Spirit of Lord Erick of Devorgoil
Eleanor, wife of Oswald, descended of obscure parentage
Flora, daughter of Oswald
Kathleen, neice of Eleanor
SCENE Castle Devorgoil

Plot

Act I,*i* An exterior of the decayed and partly ruined Castle Devorgoil, set in wild and hilly country on the Scottish borders. The lord of Devorgoil was once one of the proudest titles in Scotland but the present lord's grandfather, Lord Erick, drowned his English prisoners in the Solway in order to save a great treasure. Since then the fortunes of the family have sunk. Oswald the present lord lives like a peasant in the decayed castle of his an-

cestors. His wife is of peasant stock but his daughter Flora
has inherited all her father's pride. Eleanor wishes Flora
to marry the low born pedant coxcomb Gullcrammer. In
spite of the good sense of such a match and the ridiculous-
ness of Flora's pride considering her poverty, Gullcrammer is obnoxious to her.

Following a weapon show Oswald is to join a banquet
given by the King as if his family still retained its former
position. Gullcrammer has taken advantage of this and
sent Eleanor a gift of food. He intends to dine that night
at Devorgoil. A second gift, the carcass of a deer, is
presented to Flora by the forester Leonard Dacre. Leonard
is also in love with Flora. Gullcrammer is accosted by the
palmer, Bauldie Durward, once an abbot but now reduced
to beggary. Durward chides Gullcrammer for his presumption in loving Flora. Gullcrammer answers that although
he is technically low born his croft is worth much more
than Oswald's ruined estate. Durward warns him that
Oswald has left the banquet after a quarrel over a point of
precedence. Gullcrammer, fearing a confrontation with
Oswald, decides not to visit Devorgoil. Durward then
gives a similar warning to Leonard. He elaborates on the
curse of the house of Devorgoil. We learn that Erick's
ghost still haunts the castle. There are dark hints too that
Leonard is nobly born. *ii* A room in the castle. Oswald
returns from the weapon show. Eleanor suggests that his
concern over precedence is a dream, not worth a sane
man's care. Oswald rounds on her with fierce pride. It is
obvious that of all people Gullcrammer would be least
welcome in his halls.

Act II,*i* A chamber in an uninhabited part of the castle.
In a corner is a kist full of antique clothes. Kathleen has
coerced the peasant Blackthorn, who loves her, into joining her in a masquerade against Gullcrammer. As well as
Lord Erick the castle houses two further ghosts, those of
his barber Owlspiegle and his assistant Cockledemoy. According to legend a reverend hermit with a long beard had

taxed Lord Erick with the crime of drowning his prisoners. Lord Erick ordered Owlspiegle to shave the hermit. Since when visitors to Devorgoil have been liable to be seized and shaved by Owlspiegle and Cockledemoy. Kathleen's plan is that she and Blackthorn should dress up as these ghosts and shave Gullcrammer. *ii* Eleanor is about to serve a meal. Her preparations are interrupted by Gullcrammer calling without. Oswald proudly insists that the hospitality of Devorgoil, such as it is, be extended to the stranger as he takes Gullcrammer to be. He has heard of the pedant's pretensions to his daughter but does not recognize in his guest a 'certain whiffler, who hath dared to bait a noble maiden with love tales and sonnets'. Kathleen is sorely tempted to betray Gullcrammer but decides that there is more humour in her goblin plot. Gullcrammer almost betrays himself by replying to Oswald's apologies for the poverty of the coming supper with ill bred references to his gift to Eleanor. Attention is taken from him by the arrival of Leonard and Durward who have also lost their way. Leonard admires a gigantic suit of armour which adorns one wall. Oswald explains how the wall was once covered with the trophies of Devorgoil's greatness but that now all that remains is Lord Erick's armour about which there is a prophecy that it will fall during a feast fifty years after the date of Erick's death. Grimly he remarks that the date is arrived but such are his fortunes there is little likelihood of feasting. Durward and Oswald talk apart, such is the palmer's presence that though he is a beggar Oswald recognizes his quality and insists on setting him above Gullcrammer at the feast which is now spread. Oswald demands of his wife whence came the good food but allows himself to be distracted. At the height of the feast the storm breaks, lightning strikes the suit of armour and it falls crashing to the ground, bringing with it an old parchment. Gullcrammer pretends to translate it as Hebrew maintaining it is but a list of what they are eating but Durward recognizes the words as Saxon. It is a grim warning to Devorgoil to expect a further guest before morning. Oswald determines to watch for the promised visitation.

Act III,*i* A ruinous anteroom in the castle. Kathleen and Blackthorn, fantastically dressed as Cockledemoy and Owlspiegle, watch as Gullcrammer who, after his paltry attempt to translate the parchment, has been curtly dismissed by Oswald, is lit to the haunted chamber by Flora. *ii* Gullcrammer makes a feeble attempt to detain Kathleen. His advances cease when she informs him that the room is haunted. He almost decides to return to the hall but she points out that he has less to fear from Owlspiegle than Oswald in a rage. Gullcrammer again begs her to stay but she leaves. Gullcrammer discovers that she has locked him in. He tries to sleep. The bell strikes one. Cockledemoy and Owlspiegle enter and shave his beard and head. They give him a fool's cap with ass's ears to hide his baldness. *iii* A gothic hall. A real apparition dressed as a palmer appears to the recent fake ghosts. Blackthorn takes fright and rushes off. The palmer warns Kathleen to quit the castle. She refuses and he lets fall a key. Blackthorn returns ashamed at his loss of courage. *iv* The inhabited apartment. Gullcrammer rejoins the company, his brain affected by his recent experiences. The palmer enters and demands of Oswald the whereabouts of the trophies that once decked the hall of Devorgoil. When Oswald cannot satisfactorily reply the apparition reveals himself to be the ghost of Erick. He discovers a treasure chamber behind the wall and tempts Oswald with an offer of its contents if he will repudiate his low born wife. Oswald refuses the offer. Erick causes a portcullis to fall in front of the treasure. He leaves stating that it can only be opened by the rightful heir to those from whom the treasure was plundered. Durward reveals that Leonard is the heir, but neither he nor Oswald can open the gate. The storm has caused the lake to rise and they are in danger of drowning. Kathleen enters with the key. Oswald seizes it and tries unsuccessfully to open the gate. Leonard takes it from him and is successful. The flood subsides. Leonard and Flora are betrothed, the fortunes of Devorgoil restored and one presumes that Blackthorn attains his Kathleen.

Critical commentary

The dramatic works of Scott and Shelley highlight the great division between the popular and literary dramas over the greater part of the nineteenth century: the period 1800 to 1880 being at first sight richer in poets, novelists and essayists of outstanding achievement. All of these flirted with the drama only to turn back to other branches of literature. Whatever the literary achievements of these men they appear with hindsight too fastidious to communicate naturally with the vast new audience the early nineteenth century was beginning to attract.

The simplest explanation for the failure of the Romantic poets as dramatists is to suggest they were too concerned with self. The central character in the bulk of their work is 'I'. Their characters are given speeches provided by their authors rather than lines minted by the dramatic situation. All are too uncritically or mis-critically aware of the strength of seventeenth-century drama but their understanding is of the form rather than the essence. They are unable to see that the metaphysical and philosophical tone of their lyric writing lacks the concrete reality of even the poorest Elizabethan drama. It may also be advanced that the financial independence of the Romantics, of whom only Keats was forced to earn a living from his pen, allowed them too easily to avoid the possible indignity of the playhouse. Many early nineteenth-century writers were spoilt. They were revolutionary in an aristocratic sort of way and, while they sincerely examine themselves so that their individuality survives beyond their own age, they were often out of touch with the realities of their own time. Although achievements in poetry, novels and essays appear more dazzling it is wrong to denigrate the very real worth of nineteenth-century dramatists such as Holcroft, the Dibdins, Pocock, Planché, Moncrieff, Knowles, Buckstone, Fitzball and Jerrold which is now in great danger of being forgotten. Most of the novelists and poets who failed to make any theatrical impact, failed not because of the pitiful state of the nineteenth-century theatre but because they had no real appreciation of their contemporary theatre, little true dramatic talent and the wrong temperament.

Sir Walter Scott was certainly aware of the problems facing drama at the beginning of the nineteenth century – particularly the pseudo-Elizabethan artifice which was the main curse of poetic drama, but he nevertheless failed to come to terms with the theatre of his time. Where the Romantics are self-obsessed he shows a very real interest in others; where they are metaphysical or obscure his work displays a clarity of description and clear narrative line. The theatricality of the Waverley novels was acknowledged in his own time by the numerous dramas cobbled from them, and continues to be acknowledged in our own reasonably successful wireless, film and television adaptations. He proves himself with Wamba the Jester, Isaac of York, Redgauntlet and Bailie Nicol Jarvie, a master of dramatic characterization and dialogue. That he had a genuine sense of theatre seems to be further proved by his successful staging of one of the greatest theatrical events of the early nineteenth century, the Royal Visit to Edinburgh of 1822, for which he had to arrange and arbitrate on everything from the cut of a button or the sett of a tartan to the order of precedence of the various chiefs and chieftains. The achievement of this event does demonstrate that he is more of a romantic antiquarian than contemporary realist but there is a truth behind his nostalgia entirely lacking from the pastiche historical drama of his contemporaries. His interest in the British dramatic heritage is declared by his work as editor of Dryden and of the 1818 *Ancient British Drama*.

He was forty years ahead of his time in his recommendation of small middle-class theatres. Different audiences require different theatres, and by the 1820s the middle classes were abandoning the theatre to a mainly working-class audience. Scott, however, made the mistake of seeing the struggle as essentially one of class rather than taste. Unlike many of the ivory tower men of letters of this period he had a distinctly popular appeal which at second hand via adaptations of his novels did much to refine early nineteenth century sensationalism. This is clearly demonstrated by the remarkable restraint shown by Pocock in his treatment of the rescue of Diana and Frederick at the end of *Rob Roy*, in comparison to the climax of the same author's *The Miller and his Men*, where a robber band trapped in a mill are blown up with full stage management pyrotechnical ingenuity.

His appreciation of contemporary theatre problems is borne out by a letter of advice to Allan Cunningham, whose play, *Sir Marmaduke Maxwell* is poetic rather than dramatic. Scott tells him that the contemporary drama should be addressed chiefly to the eyes, advising him that as much as can be represented on the stage should neither be told nor described:

> Of the miscellaneous part of a large audience many do not understand, nay, many cannot hear, either narrative or description, but are solely intent upon the action exhibited. It is, I conceive, for this very reason that very bad plays, written by performers themselves, often contrive to get through and not without applause; while others, immeasurably superior in point of poetical merit, fail merely because the author is not sufficiently possessed of the trick of the scene.

The above offers some explanation for the inability of early nineteenth-century dramatists to reconcile character

and action. In *Devorgoil* there is a strong contrast between the integrated action of the Owlspiegle-Cockle-
demoy scenes and the scenic externals of the ghostly visitation, but Scott shows in the former scenes a real ability to
incorporate action within the plan of his play rather than
use it to decorate static dialogue. We will see later that
Boucicault succeeds in weaving the scenic resources of his
theatre into the fabric of his story so that with him a
sensation scene becomes the pivot of the narrative and not
something thrust in for novelty. Yet to a very great extent
Scott achieved this fifty years earlier both in *Devorgoil*
and his novels. The storming of the castle in *Ivanhoe* and
the rescue of the Vernons in *Rob Roy* are examples of this.
It is tragic that such an exact appreciation of the way to
write for the vast auditoria of Drury Lane and Covent
Garden should be undermined by a destructive literary
snobbery. Also worrying is Scott's surrender to the common distrust of men of letters for the acting profession,
especially as his expressed distrust would seem to be inter-
mittent rather than whole-hearted.

At the dinner of the Edinburgh Theatrical Fund (23
February 1827) when the Great Unknown at last threw
aside his useless incognito and publicly owned himself the
author of the Waverley novels, he drank to Mackay, the
Scottish Bailie Nicol Jarvie, as a perfect personification of
his character. One cannot help considering the possibility
that Scott's neglect of the theatre stemmed from its general
loss of favour in the world of letters and from the lack of
any real financial inducement rather than any deep-rooted
objections to it as a literary medium. His influence via the
adaptation of his novels was enormous. Pixérécourt,
France's Corneille of melodrama, from whom originate
most of the classic clichés of the genre, looted him for
plots, dialogue and situations and many a *coup de théâtre*
can be traced back to the Waverley novels, such as the
effect in *L'Évasion de Marie Stuart* (based on *The Abbott*)
where the faithful Catherine Seton thrusts her arm

through the staples of a door in place of a missing bolt in order to hold off pursuers. Scott himself had transferred this from another episode in Scottish history, but it was to be copied from Pixérécourt by Dumas in *Henri III et sa Cour,* by Ben Webster in *The Golden Farmer,* the anonymous author of *The Merchant's Daughter* and it was even used in *Davy Crockett* by F. H. Murdock.

The Cenci
P. B. Shelley (1792–1821)

Percy Bysshe Shelley was educated at Eton and University
College, Oxford. While he was still at Eton he published
Zastrozzi, followed in 1810 by *St Irvyne*. Both were gothic
romances reminiscent of 'Monk Lewis'. He was sent down
from Oxford in 1811 for his connection with a pamphlet
entitled *The Necessity of Atheism*. In the same year he
married the sixteen year old Harriet Westbrook from
whom he separated three years later to leave England with
Mary Godwin, the author of *Frankenstein*. He married
her two years later in 1816, after Harriet had drowned
herself in the Serpentine. This period 1816–17 marks the
beginning of his great friendship with Byron. In 1818 he
left England for Italy. The year 1819 saw the publication
of *The Cenci* and the composition of *Prometheus Unbound*, published in 1820. In 1819 the Shelleys moved to
Pisa and it was there that he wrote his greatest works *Ode
to the West Wind*, *To a Skylark*, *Adonais* and others. In
April he moved to Lerici on the shores of the bay of
Spezzia where he finished his dramatic poem *Hellas*
(1822). This was inspired by the Greek struggle for independence from Turkey. On 18 April 1821 he was
drowned sailing in the bay; his body was cremated, and
the ashes buried at Rome. He left an unfinished play
Charles I.

DATE 1819

CAST

Count Francesco Cenci

Giacomo ⎱ his sons
Bernardo ⎰

Cardinal Camillo

Orsino, a prelate

Savella, the Pope's Legate

Olimpio ⎱ assassins
Marzio ⎰

Andrea, servant to Cenci

Lucretia, wife to Cenci and stepmother of his children

Beatrice, his daughter

SCENE Principally Rome, but changes during the fourth act to
Petrella, a castle among the Apulian Apennines. The action
takes place in 1599

Plot

Act I,*i* An apartment in the Cenci palace. The opening
line 'The matter of the murder is hushed up' could not be
bettered as a matter of fact encapsulation of the decadence
of the old count, Francesco Cenci. In the opening scene
he pays a third of his estates to the Papal treasury as an
indulgence for a recent murder. This business transacted
he boasts of his cruelties to the Pope's representative
Cardinal Camillo. He admits he was happier when lust
was sweeter than revenge but though invention palls
there yet remains a deed to act whose horror might make
sharp an appetite duller than his. The object of this
culminating act of lust is his own daughter Beatrice. *ii* A
garden in the Cenci Palace. Beatrice walks with the
worldly prelate Orsino. Beatrice would have him present
a petition against her father to the Pope. She is presented
as fiercely loyal to her brothers and her stepmother. In the
past before Cenci's crimes and Orsino's ordination came
between them Orsino and Beatrice exchanged vows of

love. Orsino still covets Beatrice but she feels that even if
he was granted a dispensation there is no escape for her
from the hell created by Cenci. *iii* A magnificent hall in
the Cenci Palace. The Count welcomes the nobles of Rome
to a banquet, the purpose of which he announces as celebration of the death of two of his sons. Horrified, some of
the guests protest but all are too frightened of Cenci to
respond to Beatrice's appeal for rescue from this palace of
death on behalf of her stepmother and herself. There are
echoes of Macbeth in the disintegration of the feast followed by Cenci's gathering of resolution towards the rape
of Beatrice:

> Be thou the resolution of quick youth
> Within my veins, and manhood's purpose stern,
> And age's firm, cold, subtle villainy;
> . . . It must be done, it shall be done, I swear!

Act II,*i* An apartment in the Cenci Palace. Although
Beatrice is terrified by the looks Cenci throws at her at the
end of the feast she will not leave her brother Bernardo
and her stepmother. The Count enters and accuses them
of plotting against him. He orders Beatrice to her room.
Lucretia is to be imprisoned within his castle at Petrella.
ii A chamber in the Vatican. Beatrice's eldest brother
Giacomo has appealed to the Pope. He learns from Cardinal Camillo that the Pope refuses to take sides lest by
aiding a son against his father he weakens the paternal
power, being as it were the shadow of his own. Giacomo
cautiously suggests the assassination of his father to Orsino. As Orsino still desires Beatrice and marriage is impossible while Cenci lives, the two men reach agreement.
Act III,*i* An apartment in the Cenci Palace. Beatrice
enters after being raped by Cenci. She is interrupted in
her moans by the entry of Orsino. He suggests she accuse
her father to the Pope. She replies that he would only buy
another indulgence. He tells her that it is man's duty to

punish crime. Beatrice and Lucretia join his and Giacomo's scheme of revenge. Orsino tells her of two outlaws
Olimpio and Marzio who may be hired for their purpose.
An ambush is arranged. The description of the bridge over
the ravine is one of the few descriptive digressions which
Shelley allows himself in this work. Giacomo joins his
mother and sister to relate further wrongs wrought by his
father. Cenci has stolen his wife's dowry and when Giacomo demanded its return his father insinuated in front
of Giacomo's wife that he had wasted it in riot and only
accused his father as an excuse. Giacomo now finds his
wife and children turned against him. *ii* An apartment in
Giacomo's house. Giacomo waits for news of the conspiracy. Orsino enters to relate that Cenci has escaped the
ambush.

Act IV,*i* An apartment in the castle of Petrella. Cenci
summons Beatrice. His lust of the opening scenes has been
replaced by an overwhelming desire to do her and his
family an ultimate wrong. His bequest will be the memory of his deeds. It is his intention when all is done to pile
his silver, gold, tapestries, paintings and costly robes in the
Campagna and make a huge bonfire of them. Lucretia, although involved in the conspiracy, tries like a good
Catholic to make him repent and save his soul. Beatrice
refuses to obey his summons. Cenci flies into a rage, kneels
and, in words that resurrect in turn Lear, Iago, Othello
and Richard III calls down a blasphemous curse upon her
head, culminating in an evocation of Nature to make her
womb fruitful with some hideous likeness of herself, that,
as from a distorting mirror she may see her image mixed
with what she most abhors smiling upon her from her
nursing breast. *ii* Before the castle of Petrella. Beatrice
and Lucretia have drugged Cenci's wine. They meet the
murderers who enter to kill Cenci. Mother and daughter
wait listening intently. The ghost of Macbeth hovers
sepulchrally over the scene:

Olimpio Hark! Hark! What noise is that?
Marzio   Ha! Someone comes!
Beatrice Ye conscience-stricken cravens, rock to rest
          Your baby hearts. It is the iron gate,
          Which ye left open, swinging to the wind,
          That enters whistling as in scorn. Come, follow:
          And be your steps like mine, light, quick and bold.

iii An apartment in the castle. Nineteenth-century scenic
practice gives us this unnecessary change of location which
violates the intended tension. Beatrice and Lucretia continue to listen with further vampirical echoes of *Macbeth*:

Lucretia They are about it now.
Beatrice   Nay it is done.
Lucretia I have not heard him groan.
Beatrice   He will not groan.
Lucretia What sound is that?
Beatrice   List! 'tis the tread of feet about his bed.
Lucretia My God!
          If he be now a cold still corpse –
Beatrice   Oh fear not
          What may be done, but what is left undone.
          The act seals all.
          [*Enter Olimpio and Marzio*]
                    Is it accomplished?
Marzio   What?
Olimpio Did you not call?
Beatrice   When?
Olimpio ·   Now.

Olimpio has not had the heart to kill an old and sleeping
man. Marzio was about to stab when Cenci's mutterings
in his sleep made him remember his own father. Beatrice
snatches the knife and offers to kill Cenci herself. Horrified
Olimpio and Marzio take it from her and return to Cenci's
chamber. The deed is done. The murderers are rewarded

and Beatrice and Lucretia are about to counterfeit deep rest when, parallel to Macduff's knocking, a horn is heard and they hear the sound of the drawbridge being lowered. *iv* Another apartment in the castle. The Papal legate Savella arrives with a warrant for Cenci's arrest. Lucretia pretends that she dare not waken her husband. She points out his room. Savella enters and the murder is prematurely discovered. Search is made for the murderers. Olimpio is killed trying to escape. Marzio is arrested. Beatrice and Lucretia are incriminated by the gold he still clutches and a letter from Orsino. Savella gives orders that Beatrice and Lucretia be brought to Rome.

Act V,*i* An apartment in Orsino's Palace. Giacomo accuses Orsino of tempting him to involvement in the murder. Orsino calms him with assurances that he has arranged for his escape. Giacomo exits only to fall into a trap of Orsino's devising. Orsino uses the time thus gained to effect his own flight. *ii* A hall of justice. Marzio is summoned before the Court and confesses under torture that he was sent to Lucretia and Beatrice by Orsino and Giacomo and that he and Olimpio murdered Cenci for a thousand crowns. Lucretia, Beatrice and Giacomo are brought in to confront him. Beatrice does not deny her guilt but rather attempts to challenge the value of evidence gained by torture. Camillo is moved. Marzio recants his confession and for a moment it seems that Beatrice's equivocating declaration of her essential innocence will bring about an acquittal. The judges vote that she shall be tortured. *iii* A prison cell. Beatrice having convinced herself that she has nothing to confess has maintained her innocence even under torture but Lucretia and Giacomo have confessed. Beatrice still remains convinced that God will arrange for a reprieve knowing her wrongs. *iv* A hall of the prison. The Pope has rejected Camillo's intercession on behalf of the prisoners. With all hope gone Beatrice at last gives way to a fear of death which recalls Claudio in *Measure for Measure*, then in the second half of the

speech where she expresses a fear that she will meet her
father's spirit changes to an echo of Clarence's dream in
Richard III. Quickly she recovers herself as the guards
enter for the last time and is able to end on a note of calm
farewell to her younger brother Bernardo and her stepmother.

Prometheus Unbound
P. B. Shelley

DATE 1819

CAST

Prometheus	Asia
Demogorgon	Panthea
Jupiter	Ione
The Earth	The Phantasm of Jupiter
Ocean	The Spirit of the Earth
Apollo	The Spirit of the Moon
Mercury	Spirits of the Hours
Hercules	

Asia, Panthea, Ione } Oceanides

SCENE Mainly the Indian Caucasus

Plot

Act I A ravine of rocks in the Indian Caucasus.
Prometheus is discovered bound to the precipice as he has
been for three thousand years of sleep-unsheltered hours.
Here he nurses the secret stated in Aeschylus' *Prometheus
Bound*, upon which the first act is modelled, that if
Jupiter should marry Thetis he would beget a son more
powerful than himself who will eventually destroy him.
In his opening speech Prometheus tells us how at the beginning of his captivity he loathed Jupiter and called
down curses on his head but now he pities him as a
doomed tyrant unloved by his subjects. He ends the speech
with a request to be reminded of the curse he uttered. He

is answered equivocally by ghostly voices from the mountains, springs, air and whirlwinds and then by his mother, the Earth. She tells him that the elements dare not repeat a curse which she herself can only utter in the language of the dead. She then reminds him of the disasters which followed his well meant gift of fire to mankind. She takes upon herself the attributes of a living organism and it is her pain which she passes on to her parasites, men. She tells us there are a million inhabited worlds. She herself has a shadow world of death, which is inhabited by counterparts of all forms that think and live till death unite them and they part no more. Prometheus summons the Phantasm of Jupiter from this phantom world to repeat his curse. Hearing it Prometheus wishes to unsay it as he wishes no living thing to suffer pain. It is necessary for him to discover an ability to forgive and the reader does not share Earth's interpretation of this as weakness. To him now comes Mercury, with an offer from Jupiter that if he surrenders his secret he will live in luxury with the gods but if he refuses he will be handed over to the Furies who wait expectantly for his answer. Prometheus is not prepared to abandon mankind and rejects the offer, taking comfort from the fact that the destined hour will come. Mercury warns him that he may have a long time to wait. The Furies begin their work and Prometheus momentarily falters in his resolve but he is so inured to pain that he is able to endure their torments. The Furies now attempt to torture him mentally by telling him all the troubles in store for mankind. Another Fury goes on to further prophesy the impotence of wisdom and goodness:

> Many are strong and rich, and would be just,
> But live among their suffering fellow-men
> As if none felt: they know not what they do.

This echo of Christ's words from the cross ends the pressure of the Furies and the rest of the act is given up to the more hopeful prophetic lyrics of a chorus of spirits.

Throughout, commentary is provided by Ione and Pan-
thea, daughters of Ocean. Ione asks questions which are
answered by Panthea which literally translates 'all-seeing'.
The spirits end on a theme of love which recalls for
Prometheus his own love for a third daughter of Ocean,
Asia.

Act II,*i* A lovely valley in the Indian Caucasus. It is dawn.
Asia waits for her sister Panthea. The sisters discuss
dreams which hint at Prometheus' release. Their conversation is interrupted by echoes which summon them to follow. *ii* A forest intermingled with rocks and caverns. Asia
and Panthea are encouraged on their way by a chorus of
spirits and fauns. *iii* A pinnacle of rock among mountains.
This is the realm of Demogorgon and they are before:

> ... the mighty portal,
> Like a volcano's meteor-breathing chasm,
> Whence the oracular vapour is hurled up
> Which lonely men drink wandering in their youth,
> And call truth, virtue, love, genius or joy,
> That maddening wine of life, whose dregs they drain
> To deep intoxication.

Asia and Panthea are enveloped in mist and carried down
to Demogorgon's cave. *iv* The cave of Demogorgon.
Demogorgon himself is described as a mighty darkness
filling the seat of power. Asia questions him as to who
made the living world. Demogorgon answers God but refuses to name his name. Asia replies with a description of
the birth of civilization totally classical and therefore
identical with the Prometheus legend employed by Aeschylus. Demogorgon does not contradict her but he refuses to add to her story. Asia finally demands to know
when Prometheus will be released. Demogorgon answers
'behold' and shows Asia a procession of chariots drawn by
rainbow-winged steeds. The wild-eyed charioteers are the
immortal Hours. One of these tells Asia he is the shadow
of a destiny more dread than his aspect:

        Ere yon planet
    Has set, the darkness which ascends with me
    Shall wrap in lasting night Heaven's kingless throne.

He is the Hour of Jupiter's downfall and therefore of
Prometheus' release. Asia and Panthea enter his chariot
and are carried upwards. *v* The top of a snowy mountain.
Prometheus' voice in the air praises Asia in an image-
packed lyric which identifies love with light and fire. Asia
replies comparing her soul to a boat journeying to rejoin
the sea of the infinite.
Act III,*i* Heaven. Jupiter is enthroned. Thetis and the
other deities are assembled. Jupiter believes that his son
Demogorgon comes to trample out the soul of man after
which he will return to his own realm and leave Jupiter to
reign omnipotent. But Demogorgon has come not to succeed Jupiter, the tyranny of heaven none may retain, but
to carry him down with him to the bottomless void. *ii* The
mouth of a great river in the island of Atlantis. Apollo
describes Jupiter's fall to Ocean. *iii* Caucasus. Hercules
unbinds Prometheus. Prometheus-Man is reunited with
Asia-Nature, and from a cave, the imagery suggests the
neoplatonic idea of a cave of the mind, they intend to
instigate a new golden age. *iv* A forest. In the background a cave. The Spirit of the Earth has become a fair
and carefree child. She has wandered among the haunts
of humankind and discovered a new world of happy
anarchy. Thrones, altars, judgement seats and prisons are
empty and man is equal, unclassed, tribeless and nation-
less, exempt from awe, worship, degree, the king over himself. This is confirmed by the Spirit of the Hour. This
optimism is qualified by the continuation of chance,
death and mutability:

    The clogs of that which she might oversoar
    The loftiest star of unascended heaven
    Pinnacled dim in the intense inane.

Thus Shelley originally ended his symbolic description of an almost glimpsed platonic ideal and thus the play in many ways logically ends. The fourth act of 578 lines which is made up of two choric songs sung by bodyless spirits, separated by a further description of the Nature of Things from Ione and Panthea who return to their role of explanatory commentators of Act I abandons any attempt at the dramatic means of plot or character relying entirely on poetic virtuosity.

Act IV,*i* A part of the forest near the cave of Prometheus. In this amorphous poem, for it is more truly such rather than a final act to the drama, Shelley prophesies the advance of science and Man's conquest of the universe once freed from the tyranny of Jupiter, but he has Demogorgon return with a final summarizing warning that this tyranny will return if mankind abandons gentleness, virtue, wisdom and endurance. In spite of the obscurity of some of the syntax the message is very clear that men will get the world they deserve.

Plot

Act I,*i* Loveless's country house. Loveless, a reformed and happily married rake is confident that he can withstand the temptations of London. He and his wife prepare for a visit to town to sample its innocent pleasures. *ii* The Thames near Whitehall. Young Fashion, his sole remaining possessions the clothes he stands up in, decides to appeal for help to his brother. *iii* Lord Foppington's dressing room. Lord Foppington, late Sir Novelty, has recently bought a peerage in order to increase his appeal to the ladies. He has more time for his tailor and periwig maker than his brother as he rushes off to advertise his new dignity. Young Fashion is left alone with the matchmaker Coupler. Coupler has arranged for Lord Foppington to marry the rich Miss Hoyden, but having learnt that the peer intends to bilk him of his commission, he offers for a consideration to help Young Fashion to the lady. That gentleman is so far moved by conscience that he decides to sue once more to his brother for help. If this is denied he will accept Coupler's offer.

Act II Loveless's lodgings in London. Loveless is finding it hard to resist the temptations of London. His boasts in the opening scene seem about to be proved empty. He confesses to Amanda that he narrowly escaped a relapse when he saw a pretty woman at the playhouse and only maintained his reformation because the moral of the play lay near to his own case. Lord Foppington calls and presses his attentions on Amanda. Loveless draws on him and wounds him. Serringe, a surgeon, is conveniently near and the peer is carried off to be cured. Amanda's cousin Berinthia, an accomplished woman of society, turns out to be the woman so admired by Loveless at the theatre. He pretends a coldness towards her and Amanda invites her to live with them. In contrast to the heavy advances of Lord Foppington, Amanda receives the more a residue of scatological rumour. In 1818 the Milan Commission examined thirty-one Italian witnesses and came to the conclusion that she was an adulteress. It followed that when the Prince became King George IV in 1820 he and his Tory ministers ignored her existence when arranging the coronation ceremony. Caroline was not of the ilk to ignore such an insult and in June she returned to England to claim her rightful position. The Tory government retaliated by accusing her of adultery. This resulted in the Whigs taking the Queen's side and skilfully contriving that she became a popular figure. They had previously, in 1810, welcomed the royal matrimonial differences when they were disappointed of their expectancy of office at the beginning of the Regency and there was a sizeable Queen's party in existence. In 1820 Brougham led this group in her defence.

Her trial in the House of Lords took from August to November. A considerable amount of dirty linen was displayed by foreign servants who had probably blackened a deal of it themselves. The charges against the Queen were presented to Parliament in a green bag. Brougham defended the Queen brilliantly and the Bill was withdrawn when its third reading was passed with a majority of only nine.

The poor Queen, her entertainment value diminished, soon lost her popularity:

> Most gracious Queen, we thee implore
> To go away and sin no more;
> But if that effort be too great,
> To go away at any rate!

She turned up at Westminster Hall in July 1821 for the Coronation and was duly turned away. A fortnight later she died from an overdose of laxative.

The events up to her acquittal are the events dealt with in this satire. The association between Thebes and Great Britain is quickly established by the decoration of the

chorus of swine with crowns of thistle, shamrock and oak.
Shelley cunningly translates *Oedipus* literally as Swell-
foot, a very suitable designation for the gout plagued
George IV. The term 'swinish multitude' he adopts from
Burke. The Gadfly represents the Milan Commission of
1818 which was organized by Sir John Leach. The Rat
stands for the corrupt witnesses brought against the
Queen. General Laoctonos is Wellington; Mammon is
Lord Liverpool, Prime Minister for the whole of Shelley's
adult life and Pyrganax is Castlereagh. The persuasive
Dakry or *weeper* is meant for Lord Eldon, Lord Chancellor of England between 1807–27. Eldon gave judgement
against Shelley when he claimed the custody of his two
children by his first wife after her death. His deep feeling
of persecution is expressed in his bitter poem *To The
Lord Chancellor*.

Plot

Act I,*i* A magnificent temple, built of thigh-bones and
death's heads, and tiled with scalps. Over the altar the
statue of Famine, veiled; a number of boars, sows and
sucking pigs sitting on the steps and around the altar.
Swellfoot, whose graceful limbs are clothed in proud array
of gold and purple and whose kingly paunch swells like a
sail before a favouring breeze, enters to thank Famine for
providing him with such delicacies as turtle-soup and
brandy-devils. The pigs complain that they are starving
and oppressed. Swellfoot summons the Jews, Solomon the
court porkman, Moses the sow-gelder and Zephaniah the
hog-butcher. Since moral restraint, starvation, typhus-
fever and the royal example have no effect in keeping
down the numbers of the pigs they must be gelded and
butchered. The implication is that Swellfoot is obsessed
with food and only interested in his pig-people as a source
of bacon for his feasts. Mammon and Pyrganax enter,
They are troubled by the following oracle:

Boetia, chose reform or civil war!
When through the streets, instead of hare with dogs,
A consort queen shall hunt a king with hogs,
Riding on the Ionian minotaur.

They fear this verse may incite the absent queen Iona to imitate her ancestress Pasiphae's exploits with a bull. Pyrganax has taken certain steps: Iona is plagued by a Gadfly, a Leech and a Rat who have chased her all over Europe. The Gadfly enters to announce that Iona has arrived in Thebes. The Swine cry that they will no longer be pigs but bulls with horns and dewlaps (a neat joke at the presumed cuckoldry of the King). Swellfoot is greatly perturbed at the return of Iona and her popularity with the multitude. He orders Pyrganax to cut off her head. First a jury of Pigs must be impanelled and suitably flattered with ribbons, bits of tawdry lace and lustre glass. The military glory of Laoctonos and the rhetorical eloquence of Dakry are alike unable to keep Iona and the Swine apart. Mammon has prepared a mighty liquor, symbolic of the lies, fraud and calumny gathered as evidence against Caroline and sealed it in the Green Bag. This has the power to turn innocence to guilt. It is Mammon's plan to entice the Queen from the public sty, where she has taken refuge, by making the Pigs believe that the contents of the Green Bag are the true test of innocence and guilt.

Act II,i The public sty. The Boars in full assembly. Pyrganax persuades the richer pigs that the lean pigs, jealous of their fat, have tried to turn Iona against them and him. It is his desire, he claims, only to prove her innocent and suggests that this can best be achieved by submitting her to the test of the Green Bag. ii The interior of the temple of Famine. Iona seems impatient to undergo the test. Pyrganax unseals the bag but just as he is about to pour the liquor on her head she snatches it from him and empties it over Swellfoot and his supporters.

They are immediately turned into ugly animals. Some of
the Pigs eat the loaves intended to feast Swellfoot and his
courtiers and they turn into bulls. The Ionian minotaur
appears (with verbal casuistry Shelley translates this into
'plain Theban' as John Bull). Iona mounts John Bull and
chases the King and the animals out of the temple.

Critical commentary

We have already opened our investigation of the reasons
behind the failure of the Romantics and other early
nineteenth century men of letters to make any real impression on the theatre of their time. The early nineteenth
century saw a tremendous upsurge in the number of play
readers. Prior to the Commonwealth, in spite of the optimism of Ben Jonson, few people read plays, but with the
suppression of public theatre the habit began to grow.
Many who rarely attended the playhouse read plays.
Dryden certainly cultivated readership and by 1709 there
was a sufficient reading public for Rowe to publish the
first real reader's edition of Shakespeare. This was quickly
followed by those of Theobald and Pope. The history of
Shakespearian editorship demonstrates the graph of literacy and the growing gulf between stage and study, for
by the end of the century the most popular editions were
those of Dr Johnson, Stevens and Malone, whose critical
approach is often antipathetic to the theatre. Even
editions comparatively popular in appeal such as Bell's
Shakespeare are often accompanied by a companion set
of *Prefaces*. The attitude to Shakespeare in particular and
therefore the drama in general is typified by Charles
Lamb's essay 'On the Tragedies of Shakespeare, Considered with Reference to their Fitness for Stage Presentation.' Lamb describes the greater personal satisfaction he
obtained from reading rather than seeing the plays in
performance:

The Lear of Shakespeare cannot be acted. The contemptible
machinery by which they mimic the storm which he goes out
in, is not more inadequate to represent the horrors of the
real elements, than any actor can be to represent
Lear ... On the stage we see nothing but corporal
infirmities and weakness, the impotence of rage; while
we read it we see not Lear, but we are Lear, – we are in
his mind, we are sustained by a grandeur which baffles the
malice of daughters and storms.

Unfortunately we cannot ignore such absurdity as peculiar
to Lamb. Nor is it relevant to seek to excuse it as a reaction of sensitive souls to the growing simplicity of action
and more strident performance. Lamb is not reading with
an alternative theatre in mind but with an alternative to
the theatre. He and others are laying down alien criteria
for dramatic criticism which is the foundation of the
peculiar practice of studying English drama in a literary
context. From this stems the error and negative thought
which bedevils the study of plays to this day and was responsible for the emergence of a new type of playwright
who ignores the conventions of current stage practice. A
playwright who does not communicate with his audience
is no playwright. However some of this pseudo-dramatic
literature conceived in the vacuum of the study is not
without influence on the living theatre. A playwright freed
from the conventions of his time is sometimes able to
explore the forbidden. Actors and managers, in spite of
prejudice suggesting the contrary, were not either illiterate or insensitive, and the better part of the literary dramatic output was absorbed by popular playwrights. Thus
'Monk' Lewis owes a debt to Horace Walpole's experimentation with the forbidden subject of incest in *The
Mysterious Mother* (1768). In this play a mother beds her
own son. The result is a daughter who eventually marries
her father-brother. It is a dark exploration of the psyche
of quite extraordinary insight. Unacceptable beyond a

private readership it examines subjects the Gothic drama was to popularize. *The Mysterious Mother* is a genuine refusal to be bound by current stage convention and as such perfectly valid, but the plays of Lamb, Southey, Wordsworth, Coleridge and Byron seem to invoke the excuse that they are not intended for production to disguise inept dramaturgy. The first rule of drama is communication; obscurity is an inadmissible self-indulgence.

Shelley's *Cenci* is generally accepted as the most important and best written play of the romantic-literary school. When one examines these closet dramas their authors' professed abhorrence for the contemporary stage is revealed as nothing more than sour grapes, for the greater number of them were either rejected by or unsuccessfully produced at Drury Lane or Covent Garden.

What of the play as a practical stage proposition? Like most of the other poetic outpourings it is far too long, playing for approximately four hours without intervals. There are too many scene changes and the scenes themselves are too short, so that any early nineteenth-century production would have been dominated by the creak and crank of machinery rather than the virtuosity of the diction. The speeches are too long, particularly the soliloquies of which there are far too many, and there is an absence of real conversation; characters impart information to others without the cut and thrust of real dialogue.

It seems almost cruel to add to the already extensive criticism of his reliance on Elizabethan models. To do otherwise in a tragedy would have been to create a new dramatic idiom. Had he done this he would have ranked with Ibsen and Brecht in the development of world drama. While questioning then the validity of criticism which demands that he should with his first play have created a totally new form of tragic drama it is reasonable to examine his dramatic use of his models. His blank verse is eloquent, fluid and poetic and almost as far ahead of his contemporaries as Shakespeare is above him but it is impersonal and second hand, so that greatly inferior poets such as Lewis and Milman must be admitted to write better blank verse conversation. It is as if Shelley, having decided that the story of Count Cenci is suited to tragedy, suddenly realized that he didn't know where to start and looked around for the best models. He differs from the other Romantics in that he leavens his Elizabethanism with a strict attention to the dramatic rules, so that although the play deals with incest, rape, murder and torture we never actually see anything happen. Surely if we are to be horrified the horror must not be kept quite so much in the background? Even so he is a better classical than Elizabethan dramatist and one is constantly irritated by the echoes of Shakespeare and others. Every writer is firstly a reader. By his reading he acquires a vast storehouse of good things, which he assimilates and later uses as his own, but this defence does not apply to the echoes of Shakespeare in *The Cenci*. They seem to be thrust in to fill up a vacuum in the writer's theatrical technique. This gives Shelley's piece a lack of spontaneity which all critics have noted. The echoes of *Lear* (the persecution of Lear by his children is but a mirror image of Cenci's persecution of his and Lear's curse on his daughters exactly parallels Cenci's upon Beatrice) and of *Macbeth*, which is as we noted above looted for the murder scenes, are an irritating distraction and even the trial scene rewritten from the less familiar *White Devil* is decidedly second hand.

What Shelley does achieve in *The Cenci* is a clarity of expression which is lacking in much of his early poetry. The quality of the verse is undeniable. The characterization is mixed. Cenci himself rises well above being a mere cardboard tyrant. His cruelties are never funny. However Shelley seems to lack any real understanding of wickedness. He displays little curiosity as to its nature and causes, relying rather on attempting to share his fascination with its enormity which he seems to view as typical of the contemporary state of the world. This is confirmed by his approach to his main theme of incest which he handles with such undramatic delicacy that it seems almost an irrelevance. Yet he is sincere in his romantic desire to explore all forms of human experience.

Far more enthralling and equally controversial in the early nineteenth century is Shelley's presentation of a basically innocent human being forced to do an evil action by an evil world, where human justice is a mockery of the ideals it purports to serve. Unfortunately, possibly in the interests of clarity, he avoids making her defend her position. The tragic heroine by uttering a string of lies at her trial is reduced to a casuist. Against this fault should be set the true instinct which removes the self-seeking Orsino so ignominiously at the beginning of Act V. Had he remained, to either save his skin with lies or die with the other conspirators, he would have destroyed the few remaining traces of martyrdom to surround them.

So great is the conflict between Beatrice and Cenci that the other members of the family appear but shadows: Bernardo the querulous and weak-willed Giacomo, and Lucretia, the conventional oppressed wife. Of the other characters only Camillo enjoys a fitful life as a good man, but with him Shelley makes the mistake of trying to portray decency without humour with the result that Camillo is a bore.

The fable allows Shelley to explore his opposition to oppression and anthropomorphic religion. Cenci is deliberately presented as a practising Christian who trusts implicitly in the value of his purchased indulgences. Beatrice and her mother are presented as conventional rather than passionate in their beliefs. Shelley was inclined to enjoy being labelled as an atheist. In fact his atheism proves rather to be a disbelief in the scientific accuracy of Biblical history and a dislike of a power-seeking Church which he sees as oppressing the poor to the end of preserving established order. Had he lived in the 1860s during the Darwinian controversy his essential belief in the ideals of the New Testament might have been recognized. This ideal of a world regenerated by universal love is urged in *Prometheus Unbound*, which applauds passive resistance, forgiveness of wrongs and goodwill towards men, while the references to Christ suggest and intend identification with Prometheus.

Most of the criticism of *The Cenci* does not apply to *Prometheus*. The standard critical position is to treat it either as a poem or in that rarified class of unstageable dramatic poems which includes Goethe's *Faust* and *Under Milk Wood*. In fact it proposes an entirely new dramatic form with the potential lacking in *The Cenci*. Granted it is at its worst a series of episodes which serve as pretexts for lyric poetry but these poems have tremendous cumulative power. It is closer to a symphony than a drama. In a symphony a movement expressing one emotion can be followed by another expressing a contrasting one without a need for any explanation of the change of mood – thus *Prometheus*. The starting point is Aeschylus' *Prometheus Bound*. This was part of a trilogy concluded by a lost *Prometheus Unbound* which is known to have depicted a reconciliation between Zeus and his victim, Prometheus buying his freedom by discovering to Zeus the secret that his empire is threatened should he consummate his marriage with Thetis. Such a capitulation from Prometheus would not have suited Shelley's purpose. As he himself admitted:

> I was averse from a catastrophe so feeble as that of reconciling the champion with the oppressor of mankind. The moral interest of the fable ... would be annihilated if we could conceive of Prometheus as unsaying his high language, and quailing before his successful and perfidious adversary.

The Greek names are altered to their Roman equivalents, as these were more familiar to nineteenth century readers.

In Shelley's poem, Jupiter, the representative of celestial tyranny, is overthrown and Prometheus, the goodness of man, is freed. It is a simple and clear statement. The arch rebel is the hero and the play is a triumph for passive revolution. It expresses the new ideas of the age of revolution. If *Lear* is, as John F. Danby cogently argued, a dramatization of the Elizabethan world order, a similar case could be advanced for *Prometheus* being representative of the best in early nineteenth century intellectual rebellion. It is Shelley's personal restatement of the radical political view typified by Godwin's *Political Justice* of 1793. Godwin suggested that the human animal was capable of considerable moral improvement and that eventually men could live happily, rationally and peacefully together, without government or class distinctions. Shelley shows how man can improve his status by acquiring the New Testament virtues of love and forgiveness and by the marriage between Asia and Prometheus bring himself into greater harmony with nature. The central idea that the world is suffering from an organic disease due to celestial tyranny is of course peculiar to Shelley.

The main argument against its consideration as a play is the question mark which hangs over its stageability. Nothing 'happens'. The only 'event' is the fall of Jupiter and that is abrupt and relatively undramatic, for the rest of the characters drift about led by amorphous spirits or fly around in magic cars. Yet in spite of this seeming absence of conventional dramatic action, the varied dancing rhythms give the piece sufficient movement to justify claiming that this is a play. Where the Elizabethans had fused ideas and action, Shelley fuses emotion and idea by comparing the real with the ideal. When these are at odds, as in the first act, we have discord which even if it is intellectual rather than visual is intensely dramatic. In the last act when the real and the ideal are in harmony this harmony is underlined with exquisite pain, by the remembrance of the past

Swellfoot the Tyrant is a curious appendage to Shelley's other dramatic efforts. Burlesque and satire are the business of the stage and a healthy society allows their free expression but, as we have stated earlier, from Georgian times onwards the English theatre neglected specific social or political problems, either indulging in generalized sentimental comment or uncritical burlesque. In spite of the claims of several writers, from Samuel Foote to W. S. Gilbert, biting Aristophanic satire virtually died with Fielding and the introduction of censorship. *Swellfoot* is a clever if slightly undergraduate satire on the trial of Queen Caroline. It is the dramatic parallel of the anti-George IV cartoons of Rowlandson, Gilroy and others. It has a rumbustuous life of its own which deserves better than the casual dismissal it is given in many studies of Shelley's work. Although because of its subject it could not have been staged at the only time when it would have had meaning, it is eminently suited to pantomime presentation. 'Big heads' made out of *papier-maché* easily cope with the required transformations, which themselves suggest the climax of a pantomime opening.

Shelley left one other significant piece of dramatic writing. This is the fragmentary and unfinished *Charles I*. Unfortunately he returned to Shakespeare, particularly *Lear* and *Richard II*. An improvement over *The Cenci* is the introduction of the clown Archy, a near relation of Lear's fool. Here he shows that superiority over his fellow romantics who attempt their imitations without 'low' scenes or characters. The verse of *Charles I* promises much and it cannot be doubted that had Shelley been able to woo his public as a dramatist must he could have been a major influence on British theatre, but as it is his dramatic work remains a sterile digression from the mainstream of English drama.

Virginius
James Sheridan Knowles (1784–1862)

Knowles was born in Cork on 12 May 1784. He was a first
cousin of R. B. Sheridan. His father was the lexicographer
James Knowles. Thus his background was literary and not
as some nineteenth-century reports have it illiterate. In
1793 the family settled in London. Hazlitt took Knowles
under his wing, introducing him to Lamb and Coleridge.
He was for a time a soldier. He then studied medicine,
took the degree of MD but refused an offer to become a
partner of his tutor Dr Willan in favour of becoming an
actor. His first success as a playwright was a play written
for the Belfast theatre in which Edmund Kean attracted
notice. In spite of a second play he found it hard to exist
on his theatrical earnings and he became a school teacher
at the Belfast Academical Institution. In 1817 he moved
to Glasgow where he ran a school and continued to write
for the stage. His first significant success was *Caius
Gracchus* (1816) followed by *Virginius* (1820). *William
Tell* (1825) was one of Macready's favourite parts. His best
play was *The Hunchback* (1832). In his last days he became a Baptist preacher attracting large crowds at Exeter
Hall and elsewhere. For many years he received a pension
of £200 per annum from Sir Robert Peel. He died on 30
November 1862 and was buried in Glasgow. Knowles was
something of a character. Edward Stirling, who was responsible for dramatizing many of Dickens' novels, tells
how Knowles was chairman of various convivial societies

called after animals, birds, fishes and the like. He quotes an invitation that Knowles once sent him to join a group known as 'The Owls' which used to meet in a tavern near Drury Lane:

> Come to our Nest next Tuesday; I shall mount
> my perch at nine sharp. All our old Owls and
> several unfledged Owlets will be there Jolly whooping
> and woo-wooing, depend ... Nine, Tuesday –
> Woo-woo.
> *Old Drury Lane* (1881)

On another occasion Knowles received an anxious letter from his wife complaining that £200 he had promised to send her had not arrived. Knowles wrote a strong letter of protest to the head of the Post Office, Sir Francis Freeling. Freeling wrote a very polite answer which started by saying that although he and Knowles had not met he looked upon him as a valued friend. He continued that Knowles was correct in stating that he had posted a letter containing banknotes to the sum of £200 on such a day but that he had omitted either to sign the note, which had simply said 'I send you the money', or to address the package. Knowles apologized and his wife received her £200.

DATE 1820

CAST

Appius Claudius	
Spurius Oppius	} decemvirs
Vibulanus	
Honorius	} patricians
Valerius	
Caius Claudius	} clients to Appius
Marcus	
Dentatus, a veteran	
Virginius, a centurion	
Numitorius, his brother-in-law	
Icilius, in love with Virginia	

Lucius, brother of Icilius
Publius ⎫
Decius ⎬ soldiers
Sextus ⎭
Titus ⎫
Servius ⎬ citizens
Crieius ⎭
Virginia, daughter of Virginius
Servia, her nurse
SCENE Chiefly Rome

Plot

Act I,*i* A street in Rome. We learn from the conversation
between Virginius, Icilius and others that the patrician
Appius Claudius has laid down the consulate only to be
elected a decemvir, one of the ten magistrates governing
Rome. Appius has a reputation for honesty but Virginius
suspects these protestations. *ii* A room in Virginius' house.
Virginius teases his daughter with her liking of a painting
of Achilles' parting from Briseis in which Achilles bears a
striking resemblance to Icilius. Although Icilius now
shares the concern of Virginius and other thinking men
about the decemvirs he has been all too recently one of
their strongest supporters and was instrumental in their
election. By the end of the act Virginius' remaining suspicions are dispersed and it is certain that Icilius will
soon be formally engaged to Virginia with her father's
consent.
Act II,*i* A street. The Sabines are in force upon the borders of Rome. The legions have been mustered to oppose
them. All the decemvirs but Appius have taken the field.
He, who remains behind in Rome to keep good order, is
the violater of all order. *ii* Virginius' house. This war
serves to postpone the marriage between Icilius and Virginia. They are, however, betrothed. Virginius and Icilius
have to join the legions. *iii* Appius' house. Appius plots to

be free of his chief critic, the veteran Dentatus, by placing him in command of the army. *iv* The forum. News has arrived of Sabine victory. Appius tricks Dentatus into accepting his commission. He sees Virginia and immediately desires her.

Act III,*i* Appius' house. Appius has tried to buy the good offices of Virginia's maid. Claudius brings him Servia's scornful refusal to lend herself to his schemes. Appius conceives the plan of having Claudius claim that Virginia is not Virginius' daughter, but the child of a slave passing as his issue only to conceal his wife's barrenness. Claudius will then claim Virginia as his rightful property. *ii* A street. Claudius seizes Virginia. Servia summons help. The dispute is to be taken before Appius. *iii* The forum. The case is brought. Icilius and Virginius' friends intervene and there is a near riot. Appius gives way and agrees that upon security Virginia shall remain with her uncle, Numitorius, until Virginius can be brought before the court. *iv* The Roman camp. The decemvirs with the army have had Dentatus murdered and then killed the actual killers, giving out that Dentatus and a small body of men were killed in an enemy ambush. *v* A mountainous pass. Virginius sees through the lies and prepares a revolt against the decemvirs. News of the happenings in Rome strengthens his resolution to act against tyranny.

Act IV,*i* Numitorius' house. Virginia waits for her trial to begin. Virginius returns mad with passion against Appius. His daughter warns him to be prudent, eliciting from him the reply 'I never saw you look so like your mother in all my life!' *ii* The forum. The trial begins. The people have heard rumours of Dentatus' murder. Appius surrounds himself with guards. On the bought and forced testimony of a female slave belonging to Claudius, Appius bends the laws of Rome to give judgement in favour of Claudius. The people make a show of resistance in favour of Virginius, but upon the advancing

of the soldiers, retreat and leave Icilius, Virginius and
Virginia in the hands of Appius and his party. Virginius
seems to control himself and accept the judgement but
requests and is granted leave to speak aside with his
daughter. He promises not to leave her and then as she
tearfully blesses him seems at a loss what to do. He looks
anxiously around the forum. His eyes fall on a butcher's
stall with a knife upon it. He edges Virginia towards the
stall. Appius asks if he is satisfied. Virginius flares up:

> I am –
>   I am – that she is my daughter!

Appius orders the lictors to seize the girl. Virginius
snatches up the knife and stabs Virginia. The soldiers fall
back in horror and Virginius exits.
Act V,*i* A street. The revolution has taken place. Virginius is named tribune. Appius is arrested by the lictors.
ii Virginius' house. Virginius has gone mad and believes
his daughter is still living. He hears Appius is in prison
and misunderstanding interprets this as meaning Appius
holds Virginia in prison. He rushes out to rescue her. *iii* A
dungeon. Appius in prison despairs and is about to swallow poison. He changes his mind when his friends enter
with news that the fickle people are already being persuaded to return him to office. Virginius enters demanding
his daughter. He chases Appius out as Numitorius and
Icilius enter. *iv* Another dungeon. Virginius is discovered
kneeling beside the dead body of Appius. In an attempt
to bring Virginius back to the reality of his daughter's
death Icilius places an urn in the hands of the kneeling
man. Virginius at last notices the mourning worn by his
friends. He bursts into a passion of tears and the curtain
drops.

Critical commentary

Sheridan Knowles enjoyed an enormous reputation in his

own life time. Hazlitt considered *Virginius* the best modern tragedy and its author 'the first tragic writer of the age'. The price that Knowles paid for this acclaim was to be hustled unceremoniously from his throne by the advocates of the new drama. Even Pinero cannot resist a dig at 'the immortal works of Sheridan Knowles' in *Trelawny of the Wells*. Yet with hindsight we can see in his work significant steps towards social drama.

Virginius is a practical play about the virtues of Victorian family life. It advocates a virtually identical code to that employed by Pinero and Jones. R. H. Horne observed rather slightingly in *A New Spirit of the Age*:

> The costumes, the settings, the decorations are heroic.
> We have Roman tunics, but a modern English heart, the
> scene is the Forum but the sentiments those of the
> Bedford Arms.

This is not a weakness but rather the secret of the play's success. Unlike most blank verse offering of the period this is a modern play. The success of Elizabethan drama lies not in the playwright's evocation of historical subjects but in their ability to give the past contemporary life and relevance: *Gorboduc* mirrors and commentates on the doubtful succession of the English throne; *Richard II* is dangerously parallel to the Essex rebellion; and plays such as *Edward III* discuss the vexed question of the limits to the sovereign's power. *Virginius* is almost the first popular tragedy since *Cato* to attempt to use the past to mirror the present. It is written at the height of Chartist activity and one year before the Manchester massacre takes place. It was the year of the Cato Street conspiracy and George IV's accession to the throne. Many people considered England to be on the point of revolution. The answer was thought to be reform, in the sense of enlargement of the franchise and the greater involvement of the people in government. This is the main theme of *Virginius* where the security of the individual and the family are threatened by tyranny.

There are two plots: one revolving round the family, the other the state. The father of the family is treated ideally, the father of the state as a tyrant. The politics thus expressed are in no way inflammatory, rather are they calculated, as are those of Bulwer's *The Lady of Lyons* after them, to appeal to the majority of the audience. Having given the play a mildly radical political tone, Knowles concentrates on the conservative values of English family life. The relationship between Virginius and his daughter is believably enhanced by his widowhood which has strengthened the bond between them. Although the theme of honour might tempt to the contrary we are never treated to abstract polemics on the subject. Indeed we can see now that the tragedy is diluted by Knowles' insistence on reducing everything to a domestic level. Thus the, to us, incongruous ending, which might be likened to that of *Lear* tempered by the rational nineteenth-century mind, which prefers the neatness of an urn to a decaying corpse. So careful was Knowles to avoid controversy that even the killing of the tyrant Appius is excused, as he himself explained in his preface:

> After having excited such an interest in Virginius
> it would have been indecent to represent him in the
> attitude of taking the law into his own hands. I
> therefore adopted the idea of his destroying Appius
> in a fit of temporary insanity, which gives the
> catastrophe the air of a visitation of providence.

There is little real poetry in the play and many of Virginius' speeches, particularly those of the joys of fatherhood, are over long but in the context of the theatre of 1820 such faults are, if not virtues, at least highly competent professional construction. In the large patent theatre auditoriums, poetry was out. What worked was muscular stentorian acting with the stars given every opportunity to demonstrate their craft.

It may appear at first reading difficult to accept any

proposal that this is a step towards a twentieth century
theatrical voice but it should be remembered that the
dead hand of Elizabethan rhetoric still lay on the theatre
forcing it to spawn such ghosts as *The Cenci*. Macready
who as the play's arranger was as much collaborator as
actor sensed the domestic and realistic tone of the play
and presented it accordingly. We gather something of the
beginnings of the stage management revolution credited
to Robertson from his insistence, against contemporary
practice, on full company rehearsals. These were resented
by older actors who objected to one of the youngest of
their number 'taking on him to order and direct his
elders'. Even so the play's success guaranteed a continuation of this practice and from the first production of *Virginius* dates the institution of modern rehearsal pro-
cedure and thus the protection of the author from the
vagaries of the actor.

The Lady of Lyons
Edward Bulwer (1803–73)

Under the terms of his mother's will Bulwer became
known as Bulwer-Lytton in 1843. Later he was elevated to
the peerage as 1st Baron Lytton. Thus he is confusingly
referred to as either Bulwer, Bulwer-Lytton or Lytton. As
his work as a dramatist all comes before 1843 he is in this
context more correctly styled Bulwer. He was the youngest
son of General Bulwer and Elizabeth Lytton. His father
died when he was four years old. He was a spoilt child
attending a succession of boarding schools before settling
to one at Ealing run by a Mr Wallington. This master
encouraged him at fifteen to publish a volume of juvenile
verse entitled *Ishmael and other poems*. At the same time
Bulwer fell passionately in love, both families intervened
to separate the pair. The girl died four years later and
Bulwer was always to claim that this episode shadowed
his whole life. In 1822 he proceeded to Trinity College,
Cambridge, transferring shortly afterwards to Trinity
Hall. He took his degree in 1825. During this period he
published several immature volumes of poetry. He was an
active participant in society, being a noted dandy, acting
as a second in a duel and enjoying all the intrigues of
fashionable life. In 1827, against his mother's wishes, he
married the beautiful Irish girl Rosina Doyle-Wheeler.
His mother withdrew his allowance and Bulwer was
forced to use his pen to earn a living. His first novel
Falkland (1827) met with a moderate reception but a

year later *Pelham*, a study of fashionable society, was a
brilliant success. Other novels followed. In 1831 he was
elected a member of Parliament. His marriage broke up
during this period. Initially he neglected his wife for his
work but later passive neglect changed to active infidelity.
They were legally separated in 1836. In 1839 she published
a novel called *Chevely, or the Man of Honour* which was
a brilliant caricature of her husband. She took to appearing at his election meetings and denouncing him as a
hypocrite. The weakness which she exposed was the
theatricality of many of his moral stances. This flamboy-
ant, over decorative style for a novelist and politician was
particularly suited to the theatre. To his active careers as a
novelist and MP, Bulwer had added journalism and
dramatic writing. As a journalist he edited the *New
Monthly* (1831-2) and a semi-scientific magazine called
the *Monthly Chronicle* (1841). His plays promise much
and had the drama not been in a state of transition Bulwer's contributions would probably rank higher than they
do. In 1838 he wrote *The Lady of Lyons* discussed below.
He followed this in 1839 with *Richelieu* which opens with
the famous line 'Here's to our conspiracy!' This is something of a return to the Shakespearean, yet there are fine
moments of originality, as for instance when Richelieu
protects his ward from Baradas:

> Thus wakes the power which in an age of iron
> Bursts forth to curb the great and raise the low
> Mark where she stands! Around her form I draw
> The awful circle of our solemn Church!
> Set but a foot within that holy ground
> And on thy head – yea, though it wore a crown –
> I launch the curse of Rome.

This is an actor's play revolving round the title role, part
Iago part Wolsey. It has great power but it is hardly a
dramatic advance. The year 1839 also saw the production
of his only theatrical failure *The Sea Captain* which he

revised in 1869 under the title *The Rightful Heir*. His
most original play was *Money* (1840). The central character, Evelyn, is left money and uses it to test the affections
of the two girls, the ambitious Georgina and the devoted
Clara. The high points are the will reading which opens
the play and the gambling scene where Evelyn pretends to
lose his money. The play is a serious comedy of manners
and from it grows the drama of T. W. Robertson and
even the social dramas of Maugham, Galsworthy and
Priestley. Here at last the nineteenth century seems to be
finding a modern drama and a new voice. Macready never
felt comfortable in the part of Evelyn, although it had
been specially written to give him a chance to appear in a
modern play. Bulwer caught some of Macready's dis-
satisfaction with his performance and never wrote another
important play. That plays of this type were needed seems
to be proved by its fantastic success, a run of eighty
nights, so that the Haymarket season had to be extended
until 13 March 1841. Such a run was unprecedented for
those days.

DATE 1838

CAST

Beauseant, a rich gentleman of Lyons, in love with, and
refused by, Pauline Deschappelles
Glavis, his friend, also a rejected suitor to Pauline
Colonel, afterwards General Damas, cousin to Madame
Deschappelles, and an officer in the French Army
Monsieur Deschappelles a Lyonese merchant, father to
Pauline
Landlord of the Golden Lion
Gaspar
Claude Melnotte
First officer
Second officer
Third officer
Madame Deschappelles

Pauline, her daughter
The Widow Melnotte, mother to Claude
Janet, the innkeeper's daughter
Marian, maid to Pauline
SCENE Lyons and the neighbourhood in the years 1795 and 1798

Plot

Act I,*i* A room in the house of M Deschappelles. Old and
young, rich and poor do homage at the shrine of Pauline
the beauty of Lyons. Inspired by her mother's ambition
Pauline rejects all suitors reserving herself for some great
marriage. *ii* Exterior of a small village inn. Beauseant
devises with his friend Glavis a plan to humble proud
Pauline. Claude Melnotte, a gardener's son, is known by
his fellows as the Prince. About four years ago Old Melnotte died leaving a considerable sum of money. A great
change came over Claude. He took to reading Latin and
learned to paint. He hired a professor, a fencing-master, a
dancing master and a music tutor. He took to wearing
fine clothes. He too aspires to Pauline. Beauseant suggests
to his friends that they set Claude up as a prince and use
him to humiliate Pauline. *iii* The interior of Melnotte's
cottage. Melnotte has sent verses to Pauline. These are returned and his messenger is soundly beaten. Hard on this
rejection comes a letter from Beauseant promising to help
him obtain Pauline.
Act II,*i* The gardens of M Deschappelles' house. Beauseant's plot has been entirely successful. Claude has been
introduced and accepted by Pauline and her mother as
the Prince of Como. He has been lent a snuff box by
Beauseant and a ring by Glavis. Melnotte admires the
gardens and inquires who planned them. He is told one
Melnotte who knew his station which is more than can
be said for his son who has had the impudence to send
verses to Pauline. Melnotte behaves with princely munifi-
cence. He bestows snuff box and ring on Pauline. Damas

sees the whispering between Glavis, Beauseant and Claude provoked by these gifts and suspects some juggle. He questions Claude in Italian. Melnotte covers his inability to understand by making fun of Damas' poor pronunciation. Damas is furious that a colonel in the French army should be used as a butt for a trickster's ridicule. He challenges Claude. Pauline questions Claude about his principality. He evades the request by describing a home, which he does not say he possesses, but to which he would lead her 'could Love fulfil its prayers'. Claude begs Beauseant to release him from his oath to carry the masquerade through to the point of marrying Pauline. Beauseant insists he keep his oath. Damas returns with swords. He and Claude fight. He is easily disarmed. As far as Damas is concerned anyone who can fence as well as Claude is a gentleman and deserving of his friendship. Beauseant pretends to have received a message that the authorities suspect the 'Prince of Como' of being an enemy to the Republic. A marriage ceremony is hurriedly arranged before the 'Prince' can be arrested.

Act III,*i* The exterior of the Golden Lion inn. Claude and Pauline are married. Beauseant releases him from his oath but Claude is unable to confess the trick to Pauline. *ii* Melnotte's cottage. In his own house Claude is forced to admit the deception. Pauline, in spite of her anger, is strangely moved. Now it is Claude's pride which prevents him begging for forgiveness which comes between them. He promises to take her home the next day.

Act IV Melnotte's cottage as for the previous scene. Melnotte gives Pauline a letter consenting to their divorce. Claude intends to ask Damas to procure him a commission in the army of the Republic. He goes to redeem the noble heritage inherited from his father – a proud conscience and an honest name. Beauseant arrives to reap the reward of his plotting. He has calculated that Pauline will be so disgusted with Claude that she will be prepared to go away with him. She refuses. Impatient with her hesitation Beauseant tries to force her to his carriage at pistol point. Claude returns and hurls his rival across the stage. Still his pride prevents him from making his peace with Pauline. He surrenders her to her parents and goes off to join the army.

Act V,*i* The streets of Lyons. There are two main topics of conversation, one is the bravery of Colonel Morier, the hero of Lodi, the other is that Pauline is to marry Beauseant. We discover that Melnotte and 'Morier' are one and the same. *ii* A room in the house of M Deschappelles. Pauline's father is on the brink of bankruptcy. This very day he requires a large sum to meet demands that cannot be denied. Beauseant has agreed to advance the money if Pauline will agree to marry him. The deed is on the point of being signed when Claude snatches it and tears it up. He gives M Deschappelles twice the sum offered by Beauseant. Thus he and Pauline are at last united.

Critical commentary

Bulwer is the only established mid-century man of letters to enjoy real theatrical success. His earnings show a marked improvement over those of his predecessors. Sheridan Knowles, the leading dramatist of the 1820s and 1830s, could only total £46,000 over his whole career, earning at the height of his fame approximately £400 a play as against the £600 to £800 commanded by Bulwer. Even so there was still no financial attraction in playwriting. Playwrights tend to be already interested in the theatre, either as actors or as members of theatrical families rather than as in Lytton's case men of a purely literary turn. It may be that his initial interest was almost a reaction to the harsh treatment his early novels received from stage adaptors and his decision to turn dramatist motivated in part by a desire to expose the inefficiencies of the pirates. Whatever the reasons he appreciated the need to master dramatic form and his early work shows

that he had conned the lessons of French Romantic theatre
in general and Dumas and Hugo in particular. The result
is that species of Victorian drama which defies formal
classification but which is compounded of intrigue, sensation, idealism and domestic sentiment which promises
tragedy but always concludes with a comfortably happy
ending. It is an ideal compromise between tragedy and
melodrama.

Bulwer and Knowles share melodrama's preoccupation
with home life and the family, for however illusory the
delights of the palace by the lake described by Claude,
they are no less an ideal, while his relationship to his
mother and his dead father's memory is in essence the
same as that depicted with satisfying regularity in the
minor theatres when the sailor son returns to find his
mother turned out into the snow. Knowles had partially
concealed this lessening of the taste gap between the minor
theatres and the patent houses by the use of blank verse.
Bulwer is less self consciously literary and the result is a
marked improvement. Although still partially bogged
down in the toils of blank verse, there is nothing of the
fake Elizabethan about it and the greater part is written
in a direct and vigorous prose. The pace thus achieved is
a definite improvement on Knowles' stately measures, and
Lytton is more adept at integrating his arias into the
action of the play so that one is less conscious of the
author providing opportunities for the actor.

Lytton, perhaps with his own marital circus to inspire
him, obviously enjoys puncturing Pauline's pride but he
balances this with his skilful portrait of a young man's
climb up the class ladder. In spite of both Macready's and
Bulwer's denial of political implications the play's radical
sentiments, discreetly dressed in period costume are, at the
least, topical in the decade of the Reform Bill, and played
a large part in its success. Basically the philosophy Bulwer is advocating is that expressed slightly later in the
century in Samuel Smiles' *Self-Help* (1859) which taught

that by education, diligence, thrift, patience and abstemiousness, self-improvement was within reach of all. Self-help in one of the commonest themes of late nineteenth-century fiction, particularly that written for boys. The decision of Claude to cleanse his honour fighting for his country is closely paralleled by the decisions of the heroes of Henty and in *The Four Feathers* and by it Bulwer has anticipated a best selling formula which was to seduce the youth of the entire nation in the last two decades of the century and the first twenty years of the next. It is interesting, while on this subject, to note that Claude's father had left him well off. In spite of a sentimental American belief to the contrary, in England the rags to riches fantasy offered no reality. It took more than effort alone to ascend the class ladder. It could be done in two generations, or it could be done by the benevolence of a patron but it was necessary to acquire money and class. Lytton carefully provides Claude with both.

Even allowing for radical sentiment, good construction and a 'best-selling' plot, Bulwer could not have succeeded at this point in the theatre's history without the support (almost the collaboration) of the performers. They had their following, thus what they dignified by their art became respected. This play also marks the return of royalty to the theatre and the Royal Command Performance before the Queen and Prince Albert emphasized the growing respectability of the theatre.

London Assurance
Dion Boucicault (1820–90)

Dionysius Lardner Boucicault was born in Dublin on 26 December 1820. His mother, Anne Darley, was the sister of the poet and pseudo-Elizabethan dramatist George Darley. His father was almost certainly not her husband, Samuel Smith Boursiquot or Boucicault, but rather his guardian Dr Dionysius Lardner, the encyclopaedist and popularizer of scientific knowledge. He was educated in London, where he spent one year at London University studying civil engineering. He appeared as an actor in the provinces under the name of Lee Morton (or Moreton) before achieving his first London success as a dramatist under the name of Boucicault with *London Assurance* (1841). Several further comedies failed to establish him and in 1845 he went to France which was then the fountain head of dramatic taste. While there he married, according to doubtful and probably exaggerated anecdote, a lady of title and money, almost twice his age, who considerately fell over a cliff in the Swiss Alps during their honeymoon. Whatever the truth of this story he returned to England in 1848 having thoroughly absorbed the lessons of the French theatre. The immediate result was a series of 'cape and sword' melodramas written mainly for Charles Kean's management of the Princess Theatre. The best known of these are *The Corsican Brothers* (1852) and *Louis XI* (1855).

In 1853 Boucicault quarrelled with Kean and he left for

America taking with him as his wife the leading *ingenue* of the Princess company and Kean's ward, Agnes Robertson. As actors they were a highly acclaimed husband and wife team. In America Boucicault turned towards more contemporary subjects, first with *The Poor of New York* (1857) and its many variants, then even closer to reality, with *The Octoroon* (1859), which deals with slavery in the southern states and has as its climax the unmasking of the villain by photography. His greatest success came when he exploited his Irish background with *The Colleen Bawn* (1860). This success prompted his return to England. He took the play to Webster at the Adelphi. Instead of the normal payment Boucicault and Webster entered into an agreement to share the profits which was to eventually revolutionize playwriting by making the rewards greater and thus attracting talents who might otherwise have preferred journalism or the novel.

Although for the next ten years he lived in London, he continued to visit America to oversee the production of his work there. From 1873 onwards his plays originate more and more on the other side of the Atlantic and from 1876 he resided permanently in New York, where he continued to bring out new plays in which he played the leading comic roles. Boucicault's biography hints at a varied and tempestuous sex life and it was hardly a surprise when in 1885 he eloped to Australia with the considerably younger actress, Louise Thorndyke, whom he may or may not have bigamously married. Agnes Robertson divorced him.

The last years of Boucicault's life are a tawdry anti-climax. He had always lived well beyond his means, none of his previous wealth remained. His ability to write had deserted him. He became too old for the acrobatic comic roles which were his speciality. He turned to journalism and in 1888 accepted a teaching appointment in the newly formed school of acting at Madison Square Theatre. The one thing that remained was his optimism and we learn he was planning a new play just a few days before his death, in New York, on 18 September 1890.

He probably was connected as author, adaptor, translator and play doctor with over 250 scripts, and although authorship of many of his plays is disputed he would seem to have been the sole author of over fifty original plays, among the best known of which are: *London Assurance* (1841); *Used Up* (1844); *Don Caesar de Bazan* (1844); *The Corsican Brothers* (1852); *Faust and Marguerite* (1854); *Louis XI* (1855); *The Poor of New York* (English versions *The Poor of Liverpool*, *The Streets of London*, *The Streets of Dublin* etc); *The Octoroon* (1859); *The Colleen Bawn* (1860); *Arrah-na-Pogue* (1864); *Rip Van Winkle* (1865); *The Long Strike* (1866); *The Shaughraun* (1874); *The O'Dowd* (1880).

Confusion as to the dates of Boucicault's plays arises from our practice of dating by the first London production, thus the student will find in some reference books *The Octoroon* (1861); *Arrah-na-Pogue* (1865); *The Shaughraun* (1875).

DATE 1841

CAST

Sir Harcourt Courtly

Charles Courtly, his son

Max Harkaway

Mr Adolphus 'Dolly' Spanker

Dazzle

Mark Meddle, a lawyer

Cool, a valet

Simpson, a butler

Martin

Mr Solomon Isaacs

Lady Gay Spanker

Grace Harkaway, niece to Max

Pert, her maid

SCENE London and Gloucestershire

Plot

Act I An ante-room in Sir Harcourt Courtly's house in Belgrave Square. Charles, with the connivance of his father's valet Cool and the other servants, has deluded his father into believing that he is a sober youth unsullied by any contact with society. The truth is the reverse. Charles is on the point of arrest for debt. The play opens at half-past nine in the morning. Charles is brought home rather the worse for drink by his friend of one night's standing, Richard Dazzle, late of the unattached Volunteers, vulgarly entitled the Dirty Buffs. Dazzle and Cool smuggle Charles upstairs as his father appears. Sir Harcourt Courtly is sixty-three but admits to forty. He has retained his figure, thanks to sound corsetry, and has not a grey hair on his head, thanks to a wig ('I say, whose head grew your hair, eh?'). He is promised in marriage with the eighteen-year-old niece of his friend Max Harkaway. The match was arranged eight years ago by her father, a penurious, miserly old scoundrel who supplied Sir Harcourt's extravagances with large sums of money on mortgages upon his estates which were contiguous to old Harkaway's: it being Harkaway's great desire to unite the two properties under Sir Courtly's title. To this end he left a will decreeing that if, on attaining the age of nineteen, Grace should refuse to marry Sir Harcourt these deeds and her fortune should revert to his heir. Rather than face beggary she has agreed. Max Harkaway calls to invite Sir Harcourt to Oak Hall to prepare for the wedding. Meeting Dazzle he takes him for a relation of the Courtlys' and extends an invitation to him. Charles reappears. He is irritated to find Dazzle still on the premises. This irritation is replaced by gratitude when Dazzle invites him to 'his' country house, Oak Hall. Charles gratefully accepts in order to avoid his creditors. His absence will not be noticed as he is supposed to be returning to Oxford the next day.

Act II The lawn before Oak Hall. Grace Harkaway is an extraordinarily businesslike and balanced young lady, who, far from resenting the provisions of her father's will, considers that a young husband might expect affection and nonsense which it would be deceit in her to render:

> ... nor would he permit me to remain with my uncle.
> – Sir Harcourt takes me with the encumbrances on his estate, and I shall beg to be left among the rest of the livestock.

Meddle expects to have the drawing up of the marriage contracts. A tireless worker for the law Meddle is always hopeful of charging for his advice or suing someone for libel. To this end he is to be found in the most unexpected of places listening to conversations which he might turn to his professional advantage. Charles Courtly and Dazzle arrive. Charles is greatly taken with Grace and appalled to discover that she is about to be married. Charles is passing himself off as Mr Augustus Hamilton. He is horrified to find out that his father is also a guest but backed up by Dazzle and Cool he brazens it out. Sir Harcourt allows himself to be convinced that 'Hamilton' is not his son, firstly because he is not keen to lay claim to a son as old as Charles and secondly because that young man's haughty denials and indignation are so unlike his customary mild behaviour to his father and his clothes so much more fashionable.

Act III A morning room in Oak Hall. Sir Harcourt has sent a summons to Charles to join the house party. Charles, in his character of Augustus Hamilton, is pursuing his courtship of Grace. A contrast to her seriousness is provided by her cousin Lady Gay Spanker, 'a devilish fine woman', 'to whom nature in some frolic mood stole joy's brightest harmony to thrill her laugh, which peals out sorrow's knell'. 'Her cry rings loudest in the hunting field – the very echo loves it best, and as each hill attempts to ape her voice, earth seems to laugh it made a thing so glad.' Sir Harcourt is much taken with her. Taking advantage of the grand hiatus upon Lady Gay's arrival Cool informs Charles of his father's summons. Dazzle promises to devise a scheme to prevent the marriage between Grace and Sir Harcourt, by exploiting his father's fancy for Lady Gay. Dazzle encourages Sir Harcourt by warning him to shun Lady Gay's society as she is evidently much struck with his address. Sir Harcourt who, until this point, has exercised a healthy contempt towards Dazzle now becomes quite affable. He inquires how it was that Max Harkaway came to meet him at Belgrave Square. Dazzle, ever the opportunist, embarks on a complicated explanation as to how he discharged a debt for Charles which Charles in his turn had incurred on behalf of a poor unfortunate man with fifteen children and half a dozen wives. Sir Harcourt promises to reimburse Dazzle. Dazzle then gets young Courtly's signature on a bill corresponding to his tale: thus not only continuing the duping of Sir Harcourt but providing Charles with funds at his expense. Charles is about to disappear as 'Hamilton' prior to returning in his own person. He tries to bring his courtship of Grace to an abrupt conclusion. That she does not scream:

... is not for your sake – that – but it might
alarm the family.

Lady Gay catches them kissing. Grace exits in confusion. Charles admits that he is Sir Harcourt's son and thus is unable to carry out Lady Gay's suggestion that he remove his rival by challenging him to a duel. She promises to help end his father's engagement by encouraging his attentions.

Act IV A drawing room in Oak Hall. Augustus Hamilton has been suddenly called back to London and Charles has reappeared soberly dressed as himself. Sir Harcourt, fully occupied by Lady Gay, orders his son to amuse Grace. She has seen through Charles' identity and uses this to his discomfort and her and the audience's amusement. Lady Gay encourages Sir Harcourt to arrange to elope with her. Meddle, ever on the look out for business, informs Lady Gay's husband, a mild man totally under her domination. Act V The next night, scene the same. Sir Harcourt is about to elope. Meddle appears with witnesses. Spanker, at his wife's instigation, challenges Sir Harcourt to a duel. Sir Harcourt accepts. Lady Gay is distraught. She had thought that as Sir Harcourt was a coxcomb it would follow that he was a poltroon. She is terrified that he will kill her husband. Two shots are heard. Great is her relief when Max Harkaway enters to inform the company that he fired the shots having taken the pistols from the combatants. This affair means that Sir Harcourt has resigned his title to Grace and her father's estate to his son. A final complication occurs with the arrival of Mr Solomon Isaacs to arrest Charles for debt. This leads to a full confession from Charles and the exposure of Dazzle's opportunism.

The Colleen Bawn
Dion Boucicault

DATE 1860

CAST

Mrs Cregan

Anne Chute, the Colleen Ruaidh

Eily O'Connor, the Colleen Bawn

Sheelagh

Kathleen Creagh

Ducie Blennerhasset

Hardress Cregan, son of Mrs Cregan

Kyrle Daly, a college friend to Hardress

Hyland Creagh

Mr O'Moore

Servant

Father Tom, parish priest of Garryowen

Mr Corrigan, a pettifogging attorney

Danny Mann, the hunchbacked servant

Myles-na-Coppaleen

SCENE Ireland in the 1790s

Plot

Act I,*i* Before Torc Cregan, the residence of Mrs Cregan on the banks of Killarney. Hardress Cregan, an impoverished Irish aristocrat is secretly married to the peasant girl, Eily O'Connor, known as the Colleen Bawn. With the help of his faithful hunchbacked servant Danny Mann he has installed her in the care of Danny's mother, Sheelagh, in a cottage on Muckross Head on the other side of the lake. Most nights Danny either rows Hardress across the lake or carries a message between them. Danny is Hardress' shadow. They were foster brothers and playmates. Ten years ago Danny was maimed for life by Hardress during a boyhood fight. Hardress nursed him for months and the accident instead of alienating the foster brothers forged an even stronger bond between them. Not only is the peasant girl Eily an unsuitable match for one of Hardress' position but the situation is further complicated by the fact that the only way of redeeming the crippling mortgages on the Cregan estate is for him to marry his cousin Anne Chute to whom he is engaged. His college friend Kyrle Daly is in love with Anne. Anne favours Kyrle but Danny with a twisted loyalty to Hardress contrives to insinuate that it is Kyrle who visits the girl on Muckross Head, backing up his insinuations by letting drop an unsigned letter from Emily. The late Mr Cregan's agent, Corrigan, described as a squireen – a half sir and a whole scoundrel, visits Mrs Cregan with a demand for £8,000 to redeem the mortgage. Mrs Cregan assures him that the money will be paid within a month. He knows of Hardress's visits to Muckross Head and warns Mrs Cregan not to count on Anne's dowry. He follows this information with an offer to pay the mortgage if Mrs Cregan will marry him. Either mother or son must be sacrificed for the estate. *ii* The Gap of Dunloe. Corrigan intercepts Myles-na-Coppaleen. A year ago Myles was a thriving horse dealer but he has abandoned civilization to live as a poacher and distiller of illicit whisky near Eily, whom once he courted and now watches over as a brother. Corrigan, who is ignorant of the identity of the girl on Muckross Head, offers to set up Myles in a snug farm and stock it with pigs and cattle if he will spy on the cottage. Myles flies at the lawyer in a fit of anger, then controls himself and seems to fall in with Corrigan's plans. *iii* In-

terior of the cottage on Muckross Head. Father Tom,
Myles and Sheelagh and Eily are drinking punch. Hardress interrupts this peasant idyll. He is irritated by his
wife's peasant brogue, although he harshly remarks it is
ridiculous for him, a member of a family which will be
beggared next day, to give himself airs:

> ... And d'ye think I'd like to see you dragged down
> to my side – ye don't know me – see now – never call
> me wife again – don't let on to a mortal that we're
> married – I'll go as a servant in your mother's house
> – I'll work for the smile ye'll give me in passing and
> I'll be happy if ye'll only let me stand outside and
> hear your voice.

Hardress hints that there is one way the Cregan estates
might be preserved. The priest who married them is dead.
There was no witness to the ceremony but Danny Mann.
The only proof is his word and the certificate Eily keeps
next to her heart. Reluctantly she offers this to Hardress.
Before he can take it and destroy it Myles interrupts them.
Hardress exits. Father Tom makes Eily swear never again
to offer to give up the paper.

Act II,*i* The Gap of Dunloe. Hardress admits to Danny
that he was mad to marry a peasant girl. Danny offers to
kill Eily. Hardress reacts violently, nearly choking the life
out of his foster brother. Danny cowers away promising
never to touch a hair of Eily's blessed head – unless Hardress should change his mind and give him a glove as a
signal. *ii* A room in Torc Cregan. Anne questions Kyrle,
accusing him of loving two. He denies her accusations and
she promises that if she finds him true she will marry him.
She orders her groom to prepare her horse. She intends to
visit Muckross Head and prove Kyrle's faith one way or
another. Mrs Cregan, still unaware of the secret marriage,
asks Hardress to give Eily up for the sake of the estate. He
refuses. Corrigan enters to receive Mrs Cregan's answer to
his offer of marriage. She is about to accept when Har-

dress has the lawyer thrown out of the house. Danny hints
to Mrs Cregan that Eily might be kidnapped and packed
off to America if she could only persuade her son to send
Danny his glove as a signal. Mrs Cregan fetches one of
Hardress's gloves from the hall and gives it to Danny. *iii*
Exterior of Eily's cottage. Anne visits Eily. The name of
the man is never mentioned and the two women talk at
cross purposes, Anne presuming they speak of Kyrle, Eily
of Hardress. Anne exclaims that she can only despise
someone who has brought a girl so beautiful and simple
to shame and misery. To defend Hardress Eily admits that
she is legally married. Danny spins Eily a tale that the
Cregans are ruined. He tells her Hardress has appointed a
meeting place on the island and he will have a boat waiting for her later that night. *iv* The old weir bridge.
Anne's horse bolted when she dismounted to open a gate
and she is stranded. It begins to rain. Myles enters and
leads her to shelter in a ruined chapel. Eily is worried that
Danny is too drunk to manage the boat. Danny answers:

> The Dhrunker I am, the better I can do the work
> I've got to do.

Anne's horse had returned home on its own and Hardress
is seeking her. Myles takes the opportunity to give him a
letter from Eily imploring a meeting but hinting that if
he does not come she will commit suicide. *v* The exterior
of Myles' hut. *vi* The interior of the cave under Myles'
hut, containing his whisky still. The lake can be seen
through a large opening at the back. To the cave come
Danny and Eily. He tries to force her to give up her marriage certificate and when she refuses he throws her into
the water. Myles is out poaching. He takes a movement on
the rocks for an otter and shoots. Danny is hit and falls
into the water. Scrabbling in the water for the otter he
thinks he has killed, Myles rescues Eily.
Act III,*i* Interior of an Irish hut ten days later. Danny is
dying. Ten days previously he returned home saying he

had been shot by keepers when poaching salmon. Since then he has been delirious with fever. Much has happened. Eily's cloak was found floating in the reeds and she is presumed dead. Anne has agreed to marry Hardress. The wedding is next day. Danny confesses to his mother and Father Tom that he murdered Eily at, as he thinks, Hardress's instigation. This confession is overheard by Corrigan. *ii* A room in Castle Chute. For the last ten days Anne has been moody and bad tempered while Kyrle, unable to understand her sudden change of manner towards him, has been in a state of shock. This flares up into her taxing him with being married to Eily. Kyrle immediately realizes her mistake but holds his tongue for Hardress's sake. *iii* Exterior of Myles' hut. Father Tom questions Myles. He is astonished to learn that Eily is still alive. Eily wishes to let Hardress believe she is dead. *iv* Exterior of Castle Chute. In revenge for being rejected and thrown out of Torc Cregan, Corrigan brings the soldiers to arrest Hardress for murder. *v* The ballroom in Castle Chute. Hardress confesses his marriage to Eily to Anne. Although she loves Kyrle, and realizes how deeply she has wronged him, honour demands that she goes through with the marriage to Hardress. Mrs Cregan enters with the news that Hardress is accused of murder. The soldiers break in. Corrigan accuses Hardress of inciting Danny to murder Eily, insisting that Danny was sent Hardress's glove. Mrs Cregan realizes the real meaning of her conversation with Danny in Act Two. She confesses that it was she who gave Danny the token. Tragedy is averted when Myles enters with Eily. Mrs Cregan accepts her as a daughter-in-law and rather than waste the preparations for a wedding Anne agrees to marry Kyrle.

Critical commentary

There are certain plays, *London Assurance* is one, Bulwer's *Money* is another, that seem to defy classification.

Money at first sight, is a play written twenty years earlier than we expect it and *London Assurance* might seem to have more in common with Murphy and Sheridan. Again we are being led into pitfalls because of too superficial a knowledge of the drama which precedes it. It is easy to say that five-act main piece comedy lost popularity in the years 1800–40 and virtually disintegrated as a form. Few would quarrel with such an assessment but it should be made from a position of knowledge of what was available. This is the more important because comedy comes to mean something completely different in the twentieth century and the road to full understanding of this change in purpose lies through early nineteenth-century comedy.

The norm at the beginning of the century is Thomas Morton's *Speed The Plough* (1800). The action of the frame plot begins twenty years before Act One. Sir Philip Blandford discovered his brother making love to his fiancée. He stabbed him and fled abroad. His estates fell into the hands of the mysterious Morrington. Morrington is of course Sir Philip's brother and the play ends with their reconciliation. There is a suitably Gothic castle whose library contains a secret panel in which is concealed the blood encrusted dagger. The climax is the rescue of the heroine by Morrington's illegitimate son from a burning house. Such as the above would hardly seem to fit any previous definition of comedy, yet five characters out of the twelve are comic and in spite of the fine sentiment and melodramatic language (Sir Philip, a satisfactorily brooding baronet, speaks of 'the canker that hath withered up my trunk', and on being inquired to as to whether he has a heart replies 'Yes; of marble. Cold and obdurate to the world – ponderous and painful to myself'.) it is the comic characters that are dominant. For the first three acts our interest is mainly held by the incompetent inventions of Sir Abel Handy and the mistaken belief of his son Bob that he can do everything better than everybody else, while the play's claims to immortality rest with the unseen Mrs Grundy whose opinion on matters large and small terrorizes her Hampshire village. In this play the old and the new coexist. Sir Abel Handy and his son are eighteenth-century characterizations, first cousins to Bob Acres and Tony Lumpkin while Susan's perfect accents (in contrast to the country speech of her father and friends) express the domesticity we will come to associate with the nineteenth century. 'Oh man! ungrateful man! it is from our bosoms alone you derive your power; how cruel then to use it in fixing in those bosoms endless sorrow and despair.'

This is the format of melodramatic comedy which Boucicault was to take over lock, stock and barrel in the 1860s. It shares with *The Colleen Bawn, The Shaughraun,* and *Arrah-na-Pogue* sensation, romance and domestic subject matter. It even has, in the burning house scene, the embryo of the sensation scene which we now consider Boucicault's trade mark. If Boucicault's maturest work is rooted in the drama of the turn of the century, we can expect his apprentice pieces to show even greater signs of derivation, and from the farcical comedy which was the alternative to comic melodrama.

This was the style for *London Assurance*: farcical plotting which strains to sustain five acts, exaggerated comic characters such as the Spankers and the gulled fop of eighteenth-century drama discovering a distinctly nineteenth-century voice when in the final speech Sir Harcourt rebukes Dazzle for imposing upon them all:

Bare-faced assurance is the vulgar substitute for gentlemanly ease; and there are many who, by aping the vices of the great imagine that they elevate themselves to the rank of those whose faults alone they copy. No, sir! The title of gentleman is the only one out of any monarch's gift, yet within the reach of every peasant. It should be

> engrossed by Truth – stamped with Honour – sealed with
> good-feeling – signed Man – and enrolled in every-true
> young English heart.

London Assurance is a good play and we know that it
works on stage but it is not nearly so removed from the
main stream as some would have us believe. One must not
be sidetracked by the fact that the morality of the minor
theatres, which treated such subjects as drunkenness,
divorce and debt with thoroughly moral outrage, is con-
tradicted in this play. This is not so much a pastiche of
old values as the beginnings of an aristocratic disdain
which could remember not to be moral. It marks the beginning of the return of society to the theatre.

Boucicault knew exactly what he was doing as is evi-
denced by the letter he wrote to Squire Bancroft in 1871:

> The public pretend they want pure comedy; this is not so.
> What they want is domestic drama, treated with broad
> comedy character. A sentimental, pathetic play, comically
> rendered, such as *Ours, Caste, Colleen Bawn, Arra-na-Pogue*.
> Robertson differs from me, not fundamentally, but
> scenically; his action takes place in lodgings or
> drawing-rooms – mine has a more romantic scope.

Ironically, when one considers the massive scenes of spec-
tacular effect in his later plays: such as the attempted
drowning in *The Colleen Bawn*, the exploding steamboat
in *The Octoroon*, and the house consumed by fire in *The
Poor of New York*, it was in its settings that *London Assurance* made a seminal contribution to the development
of the theatre. It was staged at Covent Garden by the
Vestris-Mathews management in one of the first box sets,
using 'not stage properties, but *bona fide* realities'. If it
was the set which first attracted attention, much of the
credit remained to the play's eighteen-year-old author, his
success story only slightly marred by the claims. There
may well be truth in this for Boucicault is seldom an

original playwright. Given a starting point he can improve and build but he is a counter-puncher rather than an inventor. The origins of *The Colleen Bawn* are typical of this.

In 1859 Boucicault was working at Laura Keene's theatre in New York. His comedy *Vanity Fair* failed and Miss Keene required a filler for the remaining weeks of the season. He had nothing on the stocks but on the way home from the theatre he called in at a basement bookshop on Lower Broadway and bought a mass of dime novels. Among these was Gerald Griffin's *The Collegians* (1829). By the next morning he was able to send the following message to Miss Keene:

> I send you seven steel engravings of scenes around Killarney. Get your scene painter to work on them at once. I also send a book of Irish melodies with those marked I desire Baker to score for the orchestra. I shall read one act of my new play tomorrow; we rehearse that while I am writing the second, which will be ready on Monday; and we rehearse the second while I am doing the third. We can get the play out in a fortnight.

He did. His dramaturgy reveals the meretriciousness which mars all his work. The original is a strong comment on the disastrous effects of over possessive mother love. Hardress's marriage and subsequent behaviour are uncompromisingly treated. The marriage ceremony is more clearly uncanonical, being performed by an unfrocked priest, but it is between the endings that there is the greatest difference. In the book Hardress instigates the drowning and Eily is killed. Overwhelmed with remorse he savagely beats Danny who in revenge informs against him. He is arrested as he is about to marry Anne.

Boucicault's reconstructions all seem calculated to appeal to American sentimentality. By introducing a villain threatening to foreclose on a mortgage he alters weakness to self-sacrifice, thus excusing Hardress's bigamous invitations towards Anne. He then throws his hero completely in the shade by building up his own role, Myles, so that the subordinate comic, by rescuing Eily, becomes the comic hero.

Again a major interest in the work is scenic. For the sensation scene on the lake the stage was covered with gauze to represent the transparent waters over which the boat was worked to give every appearance of being actually rowed on the water. A large flat rock was raised slightly off stage centre. Danny forced Eily to land on this, and demanded the paper. She refused and was pushed into the gauze. She clung to the rock, covered to the waist by the gauze. He pushed her off and she disappeared under it. Danny was shot and followed her under the gauze. Myles entered the cave from above down a ladder, dived into the gauze and, as he returned to the surface with Eily in his arms, the curtain fell.

Caste
T. W. Robertson (1829–71)

Thomas William Robertson represents the fifth generation of a theatrical family. His great grandfather had been
a celebrated comedian with the York Theatre in the
eighteenth century and had even written several plays.
The next three generations had produced undistinguished actor managers. His grandfather James Robertson had been a playwright of sorts, a scene painter and
the author of a volume of comic songs published at Peter-
borough in 1804. The Robertson family established themselves as managers of the Lincoln circuit, and in the 1830s
from the age of five, Master T. W. Robertson appeared in
children's roles. In 1851 Robertson was the author of a
two act comic drama called *A Night's Adventure*. This
was a failure and he joined the Sadler's Wells company as
a small part actor. Robertson supplemented his income as
an actor by adapting popular French plays, he also wrote
several dramas in blank verse. In the 1850s Robertson was
a typical mid-Victorian minor dramatist, his work indis-
tinguishable from his contemporaries. In 1854 Robertson
became prompter at the Olympic, then under the management of Charles Mathews and Madame Vestris. Mathews
believed in and encouraged Robertson but even this formidable backing was not sufficient to guarantee his future.
In the middle fifties he was still acting and subsidizing
this with journalism. He first attracted notice when the
American actor E. A. Sothern began to search for a vehicle

with which to follow his performance as Lord Dundreary in *Our American Cousin*. Robertson had a version of a French play *Sullivan*, called *David Garrick*, on the stocks. This is a piece in the style of *Kean* fictionally contrasting a drunken private life with the romantic image. Any one of Robertson's contemporaries might have written it and it was hardly the break through. Indeed he was still so undervalued that Buckstone, the manager of the Haymarket, rejected his comedy *Society*. This was probably Robertson's greatest stroke of fortune. *Society* was tried out at Liverpool and taken up by Bancroft for the Prince of Wales. Marie Wilton, Bancroft's wife, had been in some of Robertson's earlier work and his association with the Prince of Wales was initially due to her influence. His early work had contained travesty, burlesque, melodrama and spectacle but his comedies, written for the Bancroft company, break the convention of mere story telling and reveal genuine insight and comment. This is indicated by the changes in his titles; his earlier plays show their narrative nature by being called *The Muleteer of Toledo*, *Jocrisse the Juggler*, *The Half-Caste* etc, his later titles reveal an attempt at wider themes. The Robertson-Bancroft collaboration is generally taken as the start of the movement which led to the social drama at the end of the century, and while the quotation from Mathews above indicates previous movement in that direction he is one of the few successful revolutionary dramatists in English theatre history. His literary reforms were not immediately taken up by the next generation of playwrights. Writers such as H. J. Byron and Sydney Grundy returned to the mechanically contrived situations of the French dramatists and it was not until the 1880s that the change promised by Robertson's work really makes itself felt. His main plays are *Society* (1865); *Ours* (1866); *Caste* (1867); *Play* (1868); *Progress* (1869); *School* (1869); *Home* (1869); *MP* (1870); *Birth* (1870); and *War* (1871).

DATE 1867

CAST

Hon George D'Alroy   Dixon
Captain Hawtree   Marquise de St Maur
Eccles   Esther Eccles
Sam Garridge   Polly Eccles
SCENE London

Plot

Act I,*i* The living room of Esther Eccles' house at Stan-
gate. It is a rather shabby room decorated with theatrical
portraits hung over dingy wallpaper. The aristocratic
George D'Alroy is in love with the actress Esther Eccles.
His friend, the slightly dandified but amiable Captain
Hawtree points out that such a marriage is forbidden by:

> Caste! – the inexorable law of Caste! The social law,
> so becoming and so good, that commands like to mate
> with like, and forbids a giraffe to fall in love with a
> squirrel.

Such a marriage as George proposes might be all very
well in a novel or in a play where the characters have
neither friends nor relatives and there is no life outside
the action of the story. In reality 'It's utter social and
personal annihilation and damnation.' We are quickly
introduced to the reality of Esther's drunken father,
Eccles, who isn't on stage over a minute before he contrives to part George from half a sovereign. Eccles exits,
very obviously to the pub. Hawtree attempts to light a
cigar. George stops him, pointing out that he wouldn't
smoke in front of a lady. Hawtree puts away his cigar case,
remarking that: 'The morals is a disease like the measles/
that attacks the young and innocent.' (Were the author
Oscar Wilde and not Tom Robertson such a line would
be held up as an epigram.) Esther and her sister Polly
enter. Esther is the spotless heroine, every inch the lady,

in spite of her humble origins. Her sister Polly is the good-hearted rough diamond type. Hawtree at first mistakes her easy behaviour as indicating easy virtue but quickly discovers his error. Robertson uses Hawtree to show how each class has a distinct set of good manners. Characters such as George and Esther can accommodate themselves to each others' rules but the socially assured Hawtree is given detailed business which makes him appear gauche and out of place in the Stangate household. As for example when he is handed a kettle, an object in his previous experience handled by servants, in an attempt to get rid of it he places it first upon a ham and then incongruously leaves it on the mantlepiece. Hawtree's tea table awkwardness is contrasted to the rough naturalness of Sam Gerridge, who is walking out with Polly. Like Hawtree, Sam is conscious of class:

> ... People should stick to their own class. Life's a railway journey, and mankind's a passenger – first class, second class, third class. Any person found riding in a superior class to that for which he has taken his ticket will be removed at the first station stopped at, according to the bye-laws of the company.

In spite of the opposition of Hawtree and Gerridge, George and Esther become engaged. The act ends with the drunken re-entrance of Eccles.

Act II The D'Alroys' lodgings in Mayfair. Six months have passed since the end of Act One. George and Esther are now married. George's mother, the formidable Marquise de St Maur, has been in Rome. The marriage has been kept secret from her. The audience learn, early in the act, that George's regiment has been ordered to India, that he has still to tell Esther of this and that this is his last night in England. Before this news can be broken his mother enters. Her reaction to Polly, Eccles and other unsuspected connections injects an element of near farce which further heightens the tension of the act, which ends with George's departure for India.

Act III As for Act One, a year later. George has been reported killed and all the money he left for Esther and their child has been drunk by Eccles. In order to survive she has moved in with Polly and returned to the theatre. The Marquise enters, prompted by a letter from Eccles, and crudely attempts to buy her grandson. Esther spurns her offers of 'help'. Sam and Polly, now formally engaged, pledge themselves to give genuine aid. The dénouement is George's unheralded return, which opens the way for a reconciliation between him and his mother.

Critical commentary

The significance of Robertson's appointment as prompter at the Olympic Theatre should not be underestimated. Mathews, in his autobiography, describes the reforms initiated there:

> The lighter phase of comedy, representing the more natural and less laboured school of modern life, and holding the mirror up to nature without regard to the conventionalities of the theatre, was the aim I had in view. The Olympic was then the only house where this could be achieved and to the Olympic I at once attached myself. There was introduced for the first time in England that reform in all theatrical matters which has since been adopted in every theatre in the kingdom. Drawing-rooms were fitted up like drawing-rooms, and furnished with care and taste. Two chairs no longer indicated that two persons were to be seated, the two chairs being removed indicating that the two persons were not to be seated. A claret coloured coat, salmon coloured trousers with a broad black stripe, a sky blue neckcloth with a large paste ribbon no longer marked the light comedy gentleman, and the public at once recognised and appreciated the change.

There is no better position for concentrated observation than that of prompter and the naturalism achieved by Robertson in plays such as *Caste* and *Society* was assimilated during this period.

Robertson's ideas are often dismissed as commonplace, although, in fact, in the penultimate speeches of *Caste*, Robertson presents startling ideas as if they were commonplace:

> *Hawtree* Yes, best to marry in your own rank of life.
> *George* If you can find *the* girl. But if ever you find the girl, marry her. As to her station?
>> 'True hearts are more than coronets
>> And simple faith than Norman blood.'
> *Hawtree* Ya-as. But a gentleman should hardly ally himself to a nobody.
> *George* My dear fella, nobody's a mistake – he don't exist. Nobody's Nobody! Everybody's Somebody!
> *Hawtree* Yes. But still – Caste.
> *George* Oh, Caste's all right. Caste is a good thing if it's not carried too far. It shuts the door on the pretentious and the vulgar; but it should open the door very wide for exceptional merit. Let brains break through its barriers, and what brains can break through love may leap over.

The Victorian and Edwardian attitudes to class are something which appear outside the range of modern criticism. The present academic convention is to affect left-wing attitudes without any attempt to appreciate the Victorian system. If we compare *Caste* with St John Hankin's *The Cassilis Engagement* (1907) where an aristocratic mother breaks her son's engagement to the bookmaker's daughter, Ethel Borridge, by inviting the girl and her ghastly mother to stay at a country house and thus politely demonstrating the gap between the classes, then Robertson's play is a superficial statement. If on the other hand we compare it with previous treatments of the same theme such as *The Colleen Bawn* and *The Lady of Lyons* it appears a penetrating study. It is surely better criticism to mark the positive advance over the previous generation than to condemn it because it fails to come to twentieth century conclusions.

Many of the realities are still not answered. What for example will be the future relationship between Sam and the Marquise or even Sam and George? Sam is the play's strongest advocate of order. He knows and is content with his place and perhaps no answer is given because the question would have been irrelevant or even impertinent in the 1860s. All Victorians were class conscious but there was a deal more upward movement than some of our contemporaries are prepared to admit. What was essential was that those who aspired to higher status had to accept the manners, standards, responsibilities and all external attributes of the class they moved into. There was no going back. The classes did not mix socially. A fourth act might have shown Sam and Polly accepting their lower social status while remaining private friends of the D'Alroys. Sam would have been as acutely embarrassed to find himself in the company of George's upper class friends on their own ground as Hawtree is shown to be on Sam's. Esther can make the transition because she is ladylike and her behaviour, as demonstrated throughout the play, no way different from that of her higher born sisters. In *Society* Robertson is critical of the socially ambitious Chodds, not because of their aspirations, but because they think they can buy themselves a dispensation from manners and social graces:

> I wish for the highest honours – I bring out my cheque-book. I want to go into the House of Commons – cheque-book. I want the best legal opinion in the House of Lords – cheque-book. The best house – cheque-book. The best turn out – cheque-book. The best friends, the best wife, the best trained children – cheque-book, cheque-book and cheque-book.

A desire to protect the standards and ideals of the upper classes should not, as it too often is today, be interpreted as evidence of superficial snobbishness.

Robertson's main evolutionary achievement was not in his widening of the focus of the drama but in the means he used to do this. At first reading we recognize all the stock characters of the previous age: spotless heroine, honest second girl, drunken father, eccentric dowager, light comedy man, honest lower class type and hero. It must be borne in mind that Robertson had a directional responsibility for this play and was thus able to impart subtlety in the representation which is not instantly apparent in the writing. The stock characters of *Caste* don't quite group as expected or Hawtree would marry Polly. The ending leaves the drunken father unreformed. Robertson is a key figure in the destruction of the stock approach to characterization.

London by Night
Dion Boucicault and others

DATE 1868

CAST

Henry Marchmont, a naval officer

Frank Marchmont, his brother

Jonathan Hawkhurst alias Bernard Jackson, a character
not unknown to the police

Shadrack Shabner, a bill discounter of the Hebrew persuasion

Mr Fairleigh, a wealthy merchant banker, living in Kent

Robert Willis, also known as the drunkard Dognose, a dram
drinker

Ankle Jack, a shoe-black

Ned Dawkins, a crossing-sweeper and member of the cadging
fraternity

Mr Nobley Cole, a popular entertainer

Chairman at the Apollo public house

Louisa Willis, deserted and betrayed

SCENE London and its suburbs

Plot

Act I, *i* Exterior of a London railway terminus. There is
the bustle of newspaper boys, shoe-blacks and passengers.
A passenger, Henry Marchmont recognizes in one of the
shoe-blacks his old schoolfellow Ankle Jack. Some years
ago Henry joined the navy intending to make his fortune
before returning to claim the hand of Louisa Willis. Since

his arrival in London he has learnt that her name is branded with infamy. A more favoured rival has taken advantage of her credulous and unsuspecting disposition and she is betrayed to ruin, shame and dishonour. She, who might have shared Henry's name and wealth, is not the wife but the mistress of another man. Henry, being too old a salt to allow himself to drift on the quicksand of a woman's perfidy, has no intention of trying to trace either the girl or her lover. He is in London to seek out his only brother Frank whom he has not seen for many years and whom he presumes will by now be a wealthy and prosperous man. He is quickly disabused of these hopes by Ankle Jack. Frank is without a penny and the associate of some of the worst characters in London. Hawkhurst enters with his associate Shadrack Shabner to whom he puts a proposition. When breaking into the house of Mr Fairleigh, a wealthy Kentish banker, Hawkhurst discovered a paper from which he learnt of a proposed marriage between Henry and Fairleigh's daughter. It is his suggestion that he and Shadrack pass Frank Marchmont off as Henry for a cut from the dowry. *ii* The banks of the Thames and Adelphi Arches by moonlight. Ankle Jack and Henry discover Frank living among the underworld community of drunks and drop-outs. Henry decides not to identify himself until he has found out why Hawkhurst and Shabner are also seeking Frank. The villains offer to set Frank up in style and he goes with them. A young girl tries to commit suicide by throwing herself from Waterloo Bridge. She is rescued by Dognose, the dram drinker. *iii* A dilapidated garret. The girl turns out to be Louisa. We learn that her ruin was caused by Frank. It is also made clear, although there is no recognition between them, that the semi-imbecile Dognose is Louisa's father, much degraded since they last met. Henry promises to reunite Louisa with Frank. Meanwhile Ankle Jack has discovered Hawkhurst's plans and prepares to counter them. *iv* The saloon of a fashionable café restaurant in the neighbourhood of Leicester Square. Hawkhurst and Shabner divulge to Frank the full extent of their plans. He is at first reluctant because Louisa is still alive but allows himself to be persuaded. He signs a bond promising forty thousand pounds to his associates. Henry enters and seizes the bond. *v* The exterior of the café. Hawkhurst and Shabner decide that it is necessary to their plans that Louisa and Henry are murdered. *vi* The back room of a low public house. The Chairman calls for Mr Nobley Cole to sing a song. At its conclusion Hawkhurst and Shabner enter. They have arranged a rendezvous with Henry. It is a trap. When he enters they demand the return of the bond. He refuses and is set upon. He shouts for help but the patrons of the pub are to a man associates of Hawkhurst. There is a desperate struggle. They gag his mouth and thrust him through a trap door. The police arrive but too late for the trap door has shut.

Act II,*i* A public tea garden in the suburbs of London. Ankle Jack is arrested for not paying his bill but by veiled references to the Apollo public house persuades Hawkhurst to believe he saw him murder Henry and Hawkhurst settles for him. Hawkhurst's behaviour confirms Ankle Jack's suspicions that Henry has been murdered. Hawkhurst recognizes, in Dognose, Robert Willis, wrongly convicted as a felon, who on his return to England discovered his wife had been murdered by an unknown woman and his daughter dishonoured. Hawkhurst uses this knowledge by persuading Dognose he can discover to him his wife's murderess. She will identify herself by the phrase 'I saw Amy Willis die'. It is Hawkhurst's plan to have Willis kill his own daughter. *ii* A room in the Cedars, at Wandworth, the residence of Mr Fairleigh the banker. Frank again expresses reluctance to be a party to Hawkhurst's scheme. Hawkhurst re-persuades him by promising to spare Henry's life (although Hawkhurst is confident that Henry died in the cellar of the Apollo). Fairleigh enters. Just in time he has been warned against Hawkhurst. He refuses to sign the marriage contract. Henry, who was miraculously rescued from the cellar after passing two days without food or drink, summons the police. Hawkhurst draws a revolver and escapes after wounding several police officers. *iii* The brick-fields at Battersea, a railroad track at the back. It is night time. Dognose waits for his wife's murderess. Louisa enters. She utters the fatal words 'I saw Amy Willis die'. Dognose hesitates; he questions her. Father and daughter are reunited. The real murderer was Bernard Jackson. Hawkhurst (alias Jackson) is returning to see if Dognose has despatched Louisa. Dognose hides her in a hut to protect her from their enemy. Dognose attacks Hawkhurst but is overpowered and left senseless across the railway line. A train is heard approaching. Louisa struggles to force the door and succeeds just in time to snatch her father from the track as the train thunders across the back of the stage. All the characters rush in except Hawkhurst. Frank is reunited with Louisa. As for Hawkhurst:

> He is now a prisoner of the law. As Bernard Jackson,
> your old enemy, let the law punish him. Your existence
> hitherto has been a long night, but there is a morning.
> Let us hope that it will bring sunlight, genial gales
> and comfort to your future days, while it banishes the
> remembrance of those scenes which have been enacted in
> London at Night.

Critical commentary

The half-amused contempt which was meted out to this genre ten years ago is in fact being replaced by an awareness of a triple importance. Most obviously it is now recognized as the mean of the mid-century theatre. Positioned as it is in this survey it serves as a sharp reminder that the progress towards the new drama, as represented by the plays of Pinero and Jones, is not nearly

as smooth as studies of this kind are sometimes in danger
of implying. As late as 1896, after the first skirmishes on
behalf of and against Ibsen, the most popular plays in
London were not problem plays or social dramas but
Edward Rose's versions of *The Prisoner of Zenda* and
Under the Red Robe. Plays of this type are also of great
significance to the new subjects of film and television.
Many of the scenic innovations of Boucicault are the starting point from which D. W. Griffith devised a funda-
mental grammar of film. Cross-cutting, panning, tracking
and mixing all have their origins in this type of theatre,
although not all these are represented in the present play.

   The final reason for reconsideration is purely literary,
for the study of scripts of this kind reveals the seamy side
of nineteenth-century playwriting and explains why many
authors were unwilling to involve themselves with the
medium. The history of *London By Night* typifies the
vast bulk of mid-century entertainment. The starting
point is a collection of low life tales collected by Eugène
Sue under the title *Les Mystères de Paris* (1842–3). No
sooner were these in print than they were seized upon to
furnish forth plots for the popular stage. Among the earliest derivations from this source was *Les Bohémians de
Paris* by Dennery and Grangé. This play opens in the
courtyard of the Messageries Royal, the stage coach terminus, with all the accompanying activity of travellers arriving and pedlars milling about. Two bohemians (the
mid-century term for petty criminals) are planning to
substitute Paul, a down and out, for his brother Charles
whom he closely resembles. Charles is engaged to be
married to an heiress to half a million francs. Paul reluctantly consents to fall in with the plan. He signs a bond
guaranteeing two hundred thousand francs to the villains.
Paul is married to Louisa. On the instigation of his men-
tors he deserts her. His brother Charles unexpectedly returns from the Orient. Louisa's father Crévecour, like
Paul, has descended to the bohemian fraternity. He lives

with a vagabond community under the Pont Neuf. He
sees Louisa try to commit suicide by throwing herself from
the bridge. He does not recognize her until after she has
been rescued by Charles. Crévecour has a long standing
grudge against Digonard, one of the bohemians, who seduced his wife years ago and started the old man on the
downward path. Louisa helps to restore her father's self
respect and he becomes the main instrument against the
bohemians. In the last act Charles is persuaded to enter a
low dive in the hope of recovering the bond signed by his
brother. He is drugged, pushed through a trap door and
the dive set on fire. Crévecour, who has followed him to
the rendezvous, makes his way to the cellar and rescues
him and the papers at the same time. The villains are un-
masked and Paul and Louisa reunited.

The next stage in the story of *London by Night* is W.
T. Moncrieff's *The Scamps of London* (1843). In this
adaptation the settings and names of the characters are
anglicized. The play now opens in a London railway
terminus. The Seine becomes the Thames. Other scenes
include a fashionable café and a low dive, while the
recognition scene between Louisa and her father takes
place in a moonlit brick-field. The similarity of settings
indicates that although Boucicault acknowledged only a
debt to Grangé and Dennery, he was aware of and pirated
Moncrieff's play. The similarity of names (Louisa John-
son/Louisa Willis; Frank and Herbert Danvers/Frank
and Henry Marchmont; Hawksworth, Shabner and
Devereux/Hawkhurst and Shadrack Shabner) is further
evidence of this.

All that is really required is the railway train scene and
this is taken over with a minimum of change from Augustin Daly's *Under the Gaslight* ironically itself plagiaristic
of Boucicault.

Apart from the simple job of morticing this sensation
scene (where a concertina-like train was slowly expanded
across the stage with wheels revolving and pistons driving,

to the sound of bells and whistles, the whole further
embellished by steam and a magnesium headlight suddenly blinding the audience to any defects in the illusion)
to the main play Boucicault's function is merely to update
the settings and slang.

Charley's Aunt
Brandon Thomas (1856–1914)

Walter Brandon Thomas was born in Liverpool. He was
educated first by a tutor and then at a private school. The
family suffered a financial reverse. He left school prematurely and was apprenticed to a Liverpool shipwright. He
then became clerk to a firm of timber merchants in Hull.
While in the second occupation he began to establish a
reputation reciting pieces he had written for himself. He
made his professional stage debut with the Kendals at the
Court Theatre in 1879. At first he found himself confined
to small parts and matinée engagements and he was glad
to accept a contract to tour America with Miss Rosina
Voke's company as a light comedian. He was very popular
in America and on his return established himself as a
dependable actor-dramatist. He was one of the first legitimate actors to appear on the Halls where he performed
comic songs written by himself. He wrote thirteen plays
in all: *Comrades* (1882); *The Colour-Sergeant* (1885);
The Lodgers (1887); *A Highland Legacy* (1888); *The Gold
Craze* (1889); *The Lancashire Sailor* (1891); *Charley's
Aunt* (1892); *Marriage* (1892); *The Swordsman's Daughter*
(1895); *22a Curzon Street* (1898); *Women Are So Serious*
(1901); *Fourchette & Co.* (1904); and *A Judge's Memory*
(1906). He appeared in leading roles of many of these but
none equalled the success of *Charley's Aunt* which, with
W. S. Penley in its title role, ran for four years on its
initial run. Since when it has remained a favourite with

repertory theatres and amateur companies and has received several London revivals. In the early ones Thomas himself recreated the title role. It was filmed, turned into the musical *Where's Charley?* (which had great success in New York in 1948 but failed in London ten years later) and has been seen on television with Danny La Rue as the 'Aunt'. It has proved to be one of the most popular plays ever written, at one time running simultaneously in forty-eight theatres in twenty-two languages, among them Afrikaans, Chinese, Esperanto, Gaelic, Russian and Zulu.

DATE 1892

CAST

Stephen Spettigue, solicitor, Oxford

Colonel Sir Francis Chesney, Bt, late Indian Service

Jack Chesney

Charley Wykeham   }   undergraduates at St Olde's

Lord Fancourt Babberley }   College, Oxford

Brassett, a college scout

Donna Lucia d'Alvadorez, from Brazil

Kitty Verdun, Spettigue's ward

Amy Spettigue, Spettigue's niece

Ela Delahay, an orphan

SCENE Oxford, during Commemoration Week, 1892

Plot

Act I Jack Chesney's rooms in college. Jack is having trouble with composing a letter to Kitty. To him comes Charley who is having similar trouble with his own letter to Amy, for although he has begun awfully well with 'My Dear Amy', he finds himself unable to proceed and thus has come to Jack, who always knows what to say and do, for advice. Charley's problems are complicated by the imminent and unexpected arrival of an aunt, whom he has never seen as she went out to Brazil before he was

born. This gives Jack the 'clinking good idea' of inviting
the girls to lunch to meet Charley's aunt, Donna Lucia
d'Alvadorez. It is now necessary to provide themselves
with an extra man to keep the old 'croc' occupied while
they pluck up courage to propose to the girls. Their choice
lights on Fanny-Babbs (Lord Fancourt Babberley). Coin-
cidentally Babbs enters, bent on stealing some of their
champagne. He is press-ganged into joining the lunch
party. Babbs, for the first time in his life, is preparing to
appear in amateur theatricals. He offers the fact that he
has to try on a woman's dress as an excuse to escape. Charley and Jack forestall him by sending out their scout Brassett for the said dress. The girls arrive but leave almost
immediately when they learn that the aunt has yet to
arrive. Jack's father unexpectedly calls. Sir Francis has
come into the family debts and difficulties along with the
family title. Jack suggests he stay to lunch to meet Charley's fabulously wealthy aunt, as a good marriage could
solve his financial problems. These plans receive a severe
jolt when the following telegram arrives for Charley:

Important business, don't expect me for a few days.
Lucia d'Alvadorez

The girls arrive. Babbs, almost dressed in his old lady's
costume, is a ready made solution. (The important things
to note when he is impersonating the aunt are that he has
never acted in his life before and never worn women's
clothes. The part must never degenerate into effeminate
female impersonation.) He tries to lighten his voice when
he is first introduced, and it cracks appallingly. After that
he speaks naturally, being careful not to use the deep
tones of his voice except to Jack, Charley and Brassett,
who know who he really is, or again when he forgets he is
supposed to be a woman. He looks a nice old lady of the
Victorian era. Apart from the obvious fun to be derived
from the girls confiding secrets and behaving with increasing familiarity with one whom they believe to be of

the same sex as themselves, there are further complications. Mr Spettigue arrives back from London unexpectedly and calls in search of his niece and ward. The girls hide. Babbs rises to the occasion and treats him with a glorious disdain. Spettigue leaves but returns when the company are about to sit down to lunch. His anger melts when he recognizes the name Donna Lucia d'Alvadorez as that of the celebrated millionairess from Brazil where the nuts come from and the act ends with his joining the luncheon party. It is necessary to note one further hare that is started. Babbs confides to his friends how a year before he met and fell in love with Ela Delahay, but lost touch with her after her father died when a rich lady from Latin America, travelling incognito, took charge of her and brought her to England.

Act II The garden outside Jack Chesney's rooms. Mr Spettigue and Sir Francis have both spent lunch making up to the supposed Donna Lucia. The masquerade is proceeding very well, so well in fact that both Sir Francis and Spettigue have decided to propose. Sir Francis does so and to his great relief is refused. The real Donna Lucia, accompanied by Ela Delahay, arrives. Donna Lucia has invested some money which Ela's father won at cards from Lord Fancourt Babberley and she is not quite the penniless orphan described by Babbs in the first scene. We also learn that in the distant past when Donna Lucia was a sentimental young lady she was called 'the angel of the watch' by a shy young officer named Francis Chesney. The first person she meets is Sir Francis. From him she learns that Charley Wykeham has borrowed his son's rooms to entertain his aunt from Brazil (where the nuts come from). Donna Lucia decides to preserve her incognito a little longer. After many interruptions Jack at last manages to propose to Kitty and is accepted. Charles is similarly successful with Amy. Before these engagements can be announced it will be necessary to obtain Mr Spettigue's written consent. Halfway through the act Babbs, thor-

oughly fed up with his skirts, takes off the dress and insists
on having a drink. It is only after a scuffle that Jack and
Charley succeed in bundling him back into it. It is necessary that the masquerade continue until Babbs has
tricked Spettigue into giving his consent to the engagements. Babbs is introduced to the real Donna Lucia. He
is panic stricken when she informs him that she knew his
late husband intimately. In an attempt to get 'Donna
Lucia' on his own Spettigue invites them all to dinner.

Act III The drawing-room at Mr Spettigue's house. Brassett has been hired to buttle for the evening for Mr Spettigue. Babbs enters. He is desperate to escape so as to
resume his own identity and make himself known to Ela.
He is stopped by the entry of the ladies who have withdrawn from the dinner table. His embarrassment in this
totally feminine situation is hysterical and when he thinks
them about to indulge in risqué stories he is close to collapse. He is not made to feel any easier when Donna Lucia
relates an anecdote of her late husband. Babbs in desperation accedes to a proposal of marriage from Mr Spettigue
in return for his written consent to the marriages. Donna
Lucia catches him indulging in a cigar; great is his relief
when she provides him with the excuse that smoking is
habitual among Brazilian ladies. His relief is short lived
when he is crucified by the embarrassment of having to
listen to Ela's confidences about the noblest man she has
ever met who deliberately lost money at cards to her
father and with whom she is in love. Babbs exits in confusion. Upon learning of Spettigue's engagement Sir Francis confides to Donna Lucia that he himself had mercen-
ary designs upon the lady but after meeting her again is
unable to carry them to their conclusion. Still unaware
that she is the real millionairess he offers her his impoverished heart and is accepted. Spettigue makes a formal
announcement of the engagements of his niece, his ward
and himself. The last causes the imperturbable Brassett
to drop a tray. Charley's sense of honour cannot allow the

deception to continue. He admits the whole trick. Babbs's voice is heard off stage. Spettigue orders that that woman be turned out of the house but before this can be done Fancourt Babberley enters in evening dress as himself. He still clutches Spettigue's letter of consent to the engagements. Before Spettigue can repossess himself of this Donna Lucia twitches it out of Babbs's hands. She calmly announces that the letter is addressed and has been delivered to Donna Lucia d'Alvadorez. Spettigue protests that Babbs is not Donna Lucia. Donna Lucia introduces herself. Babbs makes up for inadvertently being the recipient of Ela's confidences by offering her his lifelong devotion. He is accepted. No one takes much notice of Spettigue's threats to report Babbs to the college authorities.

Critical commentary

With the rise of a social drama where the distinctions between comedy and tragedy become increasingly blurred, comedy comes to acquire a different meaning. In plays like *London Assurance* there is at least a pretence of one of the characters being taught a lesson, ending a play wiser and better, and thus by transference the improvement of the audience.

Comedy suffered even more than tragedy from the change in audience composition in the first years of the nineteenth century. The new audience, mainly working-class, were not particularly interested in the doings of a society of which they had little knowledge unless these doings were presented in a farcical or burlesque fashion. Yet comedy, unlike farce and melodrama, continued to deal with the restricted social focus of the middle-class. This meant that when in 1843 it became legal to play legitimate comedy, in the minor theatres it was virtually ignored. The whole comic repertory of the eighteenth and early nineteenth centuries which fill the volumes of Bell

.and Cumberland suddenly disappeared. Laughter was provided by farce, and by the comic side of melodrama. Thus a play like *Our American Cousin*, originally conceived as a melodrama, became totally dominated by Lord Dundreary the comic relief. It is from such beginnings that the form of comic society melodrama employed by Wilde derives. Another contributory factor to the decay of comedy as a clearly defined legitimate form is the Romantic criticism, which by setting out to elevate Elizabethan tragedy had overturned the neo-classical regard for comedy. The result was that by the 1860s there was a comic vacuum. Into this poured the basically English form of burlesque. English burlesque differs from satire and comedy in its uncritical enjoyment of its subject matter. It celebrates without any commitment to improve beyond pricking any bubbles of pomposity that lie in its way. True burlesque, such as pantomime, the fairy extravaganzas of Planché and Byron, and even the early experiments of Gilbert in what we would now call Theatre of the Absurd, lie outside the scope of this work. Yet it is from these pieces that the funniest nineteenth-century plays derive. Plays which are not strictly comedy, but which their authors so term, came to be written, changing the very meaning of the word so that comedy came to be used to describe a funny play rather than a work with any formal comic purpose. The devices inherited from eighteenth-century comedy were incorporated into a drama which intermingled the tea cup realism of Robertson with the secrets, compromising or revealing letters, and women with a past, of melodrama.

Charley's Aunt is a mixed comedy of this type. The dénouement is pure melodrama in that a secret is revealed to the confusion of the 'villain', in this case metamorphosed into the unfortunate Spettigue. The piece even has its woman with a past in Donna Lucia, even if her past is no more than an innocent flirtation with Francis Chesney. The basic idea of a disguise and the use of Spettigue's written consent to the marriage both have their origins in the clichés of melodrama. From the directional innovations of Robertson come the realistic detail of the setting and use of props such as fans, cigars, champagne bottles and the like. Indeed the delightful comic *lazzi* of the first act when Babbs, wishing to tip Brassett for fetching the dress box, borrows from Jack, who borrows from Charley who borrows from Brassett, is taken from the scene in The Owls' Roost in Act Two of *Society* where the chain of borrowing is extended through seven characters. The basically drawing-room set is identical to that employed for serious plays. One possible concession to the traditional reforming purpose of comedy is the humiliation of Spettigue for making up to Donna Lucia for her money. It is very doubtful that Thomas intended any moral from his happenings. Spettigue is pompous, self-opinionated, assertive and not given to argument but he has, according to his creator, a charming smile, 'so that in spite of everything, you can't help liking him'. The bubble of his pomposity is pricked but one can not really discover a deep satirical purpose behind his fate. Any criticism of marriage 'where money is' is further undermined by the fact that all four engagements are financially advantageous to the men.

The purpose of *Charley's Aunt* is enforced laughter raised by genuinely amusing situations within a tightly constructed plot, rather than by contrived dialogue or eccentric characterization. The economy and restraint of its craftsmanship, its respect for the conventions of society (best exemplified by the refusal of the girls to remain in Jack's chambers without a chaperone), its elaborate verisimilitude of setting and elegance are typical not only of the comedy but also of the serious drama of the period. In everything, except its unique central idea of a man playing a woman (we have to go back to Jonson's *Epicoene* for a repetition of this device), *Charley's Aunt* is typical of the representative drama of the period.

An Ideal Husband
Oscar Wilde (1854–1900)

Oscar Fingal O'Flaherty Wills Wilde was the son of the well known Irish surgeon Sir William Wilde and Jane Francisca Elgee, who published prose and verse under the pen-name 'Speranza'. He was educated at Trinity College, Dublin, from whence he proceeded to Magdalen College, Oxford in 1874. In 1878 he won the Newdigate prize for English verse with his poem Ravenna. He had already acquired a reputation for idleness and affectation, becoming an apostle of J. M. Whistler's aesthetic movement. As a leading 'aesthete' he became a prominent and much quoted personality. Two of his plays were printed in the early 1880s, Vera: or the Nihilists (1880) and a blank verse tragedy The Duchess of Padua (1883). Neither of these were performed in Britain during this period, although Vera had an unsuccessful New York production during his lecture tour of America in 1882 while The Duchess of Padua was also performed in New York in 1893. During the 1880s he mainly confined himself to short stories, novels and poems, but his general attitude was already stirring up prejudice against him. The Picture of Dorian Gray (1891) in spite of its brilliance was widely criticized as decadent. The years 1892–5 were Wilde's halcyon period. He became an established dramatist and society figure. It was during this period that he wrote Lady Windermere's Fan (1892), A Woman of No Importance (1893), An Ideal Husband (1895) and The

Importance of Being Earnest (1895). A further dramatic work *Salome*, written in French and translated by Lord Alfred Douglas, was published in 1894. It was to have been seen in London at the Palace Theatre with Sarah Bernhardt in the title role but the Lord Chamberlain refused a licence. It was performed in Paris in 1894. *Salome* lies outside the scope of this work in that it is a French play and not fairly judged if considered in translation by the criteria used for native English work, when it appears florid, artificial and unrooted.

During the period of his prosperity Wilde became ever more careless of the rules of society. He flaunted his homosexuality in public, entertaining male prostitutes and other disreputable characters in public places. Society was prepared to turn a blind eye till Wilde allowed himself to be persuaded by his friend Lord Alfred Douglas to sue Lord Alfred's father, the notorious Marquis of Queensbury, for labelling him as a sodomite in 1895. The Marquis was acquitted and Wilde was arrested and charged with homosexuality. The first trial ended in disagreement among the jury, the second with Wilde's conviction, followed by a sentence of two years hard labour. Society was forced to notice what it had previously ignored. He was hounded in the press and disowned. His plays were of course withdrawn.

After his release in 1897 he took up residence in France, under the assumed name of Sebastian Melmoth. His health gradually worsened and he died from cerebral meningitis on 1 December 1900.

DATE 1895
CAST
The Earl of Caversham, KG
Viscount Goring, his son
Sir Robert Chiltern, Bt, Under-Secretary for Foreign Affairs
Vicomte de Nanjac, Attaché at French Embassy
Mr Montford

Mason, butler to Sir Robert Chiltern
Phipps, Lord Goring's servant
James and Harold, footmen
Lady Chiltern
Lady Markby
The Countess of Basildon
Mrs Marchmont
Miss Mabel Chiltern, Sir Robert Chiltern's sister
Mrs Cheveley
SCENE London

Plot

Act I The octagon room at Sir Robert Chiltern's house in Grosvenor Square. A political party is in progress. Into this society is introduced the mysterious Mrs Cheveley. Nobody seems to know very much about her except Lady Chiltern, who admits having been to the same school. Mrs Cheveley tells Sir Robert there is something she wishes him to do for her and drops into this initial conversation the name of Baron Arnheim to Sir Robert's obvious discomfort. An unlikely guest amid the attachés and politicians is Lord Goring introduced as the idlest man in London. He is clever but would not like to be thought so. A flawless dandy, he would be annoyed if he were considered romantic. He is fond of being misunderstood. It gives him a point of vantage. He admits to once having been engaged to Mrs Cheveley. Mrs Cheveley's request to Sir Robert concerns the Argentine Canal Company. Sir Robert believes it to be a swindle and intends to report to the House of Commons to this effect. Now comes the first revelation. Sir Robert Chiltern, most upright of parliamentarians who can always be relied upon to take a firm moral stand, sold the secret that Britain was going to invest in the Suez Canal to the financier Baron Arnheim. His whole career is founded on having once sold a Cabinet secret. Mrs Cheveley possesses his letter to the Baron and

intends to publish this unless he withdraws his opposition
to the Argentine Canal scheme. He agrees. Most of the
guests depart. Mabel Chiltern discovers a diamond brooch
half hidden by a cushion. Lord Goring recognizes it as
one he once gave as a present. He takes charge of it requesting Mabel to tell him if anyone enquires after it.
Lady Chiltern tells Sir Robert that Mrs Cheveley was
expelled from school for thieving. The conversation
passes on to the Argentine scheme. Lady Chiltern is horrified to learn that her husband has agreed to Mrs Cheveley's request to support the project. She forces him to
write to her to the effect that he has changed his mind.

Act II The morning-room at Sir Robert Chiltern's house.
With some vigour Sir Robert maintains to Lord Goring
that there are temptations so terrible that it requires courage and strength to yield to them. He goes on to explain
that what tempted him was not the money offered by
Baron Arnheim but the power over his fellow men that
that money would bring. Confession is out of the question.
He must fight the thing out. Lord Goring urges him to
tell his wife. Sir Robert refuses and retires on the excuse
he has some letters to write, when Lady Chiltern returns
from an afternoon at the Women's Liberal Association.
Lord Goring tries to warn her and then abruptly leaves
after melodramatically placing himself at her disposal
should she require a friend. He has not long left when
Lady Markby and Mrs Cheveley call. The latter inquires
after the diamond brooch. Lady Markby takes her leave
promising to return in a quarter of an hour. Lady Chiltern makes it very clear to Mrs Cheveley that she is not
a welcome visitor. Stung into a retort Mrs Cheveley tells
the whole story of Sir Robert's lapse. He admits the story
is true:

> Don't come near me. Don't touch me. I feel as if you
> had soiled me for ever. Oh! what a mask you have been
> wearing all these years! A horrible painted mask! You

sold yourself for money. Oh! a common thief were
better. You put yourself up for sale to the highest bidder!
You were bought in the market. You lied to the whole
world. And yet you will not lie to me.

An ideal has been shattered and Sir Robert can only
reply:

Let women make no more ideals of men! Let them not
put them on altars and bow before them or they may
ruin other lives as completely as you – you whom I have
so wildly loved – have ruined mine!

Act III The library of Lord Goring's house in Curzon
Street. Lord Goring receives the following message from
Lady Chiltern:

I want you. I trust you. I am coming to you.

He realizes that she must have discovered the secret. Lord
Caversham provides a brief interlude by calling on his
son to try and persuade him to marry. Goring hustles his
father out of the room, quietly giving Phipps instructions
that if a lady calls she is to be shown into the drawing-
room. Mrs Cheveley arrives. Phipps takes her for the
expected lady and leaves her in the library while he fetches
candles for the drawing-room. She reads and is about to
steal Lady Chiltern's note when Sir Robert is announced.
She pushes it quickly under a blotter and retires to the
drawing-room. Sir Robert starts talking very freely and
then realizing someone is in the next room tries to enter.
Lord Goring, presuming it is Lady Chiltern, tries to prevent him. Sir Robert is insistent and returns to the library
to demand an explanation for the presence of 'that
woman'. Lord Goring, still unaware of the identity of his
visitor, protests that the lady is stainless and guiltless of
all offences towards Sir Robert. After some hard words
Sir Robert sweeps out and Mrs Cheveley enters, looking
radiant and much amused. She offers to surrender the in-

criminating letter to Lord Goring if he will marry her. This offer is refused. He goes on to upbraid her with deliberately trying to degrade a husband in the eyes of his wife. Mrs Cheveley defends herself by explaining that she only called on Lady Chiltern to inquire after a brooch which she had mislaid the previous night and was stung into her revelations by her hostess' moral sneers. Lord Goring fetches the brooch from a drawer but instead of pinning it on her dress fastens it on her arm as a bracelet. Ignorant that it could be so worn, and not knowing the secret of the clasp, Mrs Cheveley is unable to take it off. Lord Goring accuses her of stealing it from his sister ten years previously. He threatens to send for the police unless she gives him the incriminating letter. Mrs Cheveley capitulates but no sooner has she handed over one letter than she manages to gain possession of Lady Chiltern's appeal which she had previously hidden under the blotting paper. She triumphantly makes her exit promising to send this to Sir Robert.

Act IV The morning-room of Sir Robert Chiltern's house. Lord Goring and his father are waiting for Sir Robert to return from the House where he has just made a brilliant speech denouncing the Argentine Canal Company. Lord Goring assures his father that he has considered his advice of the previous evening and is seriously contemplating matrimony. He proposes to and is accepted by Mabel Chiltern. He tells Lady Chiltern that Mrs Cheveley has stolen her letter, begging her to let him tell Sir Robert the truth. She refuses. Sir Robert has already received the letter but has accepted it as addressed to himself. It seems that everything has come right for him. He is repossessed of the original incriminating letter; he is repossessed of his wife's love; and to fill his cup Lord Caversham offers him, on the Prime Minister's behalf, a seat in the Cabinet. Lady Chiltern makes it obvious that she thinks he should decline. He accepts her lead and retires to write an explanation to the Prime Minister. Lord Goring takes the opportunity of his friend's absence to warn Lady Chiltern that if she forces her husband to retire from public life she will destroy him. When he returns Lady Chiltern tears up his letter refusing the PM's offer. It only remains for Lord Goring to go through the formality of asking his friend's permission to marry his sister. He is astonished when this is refused, because of Mrs Cheveley's presence in Lord Goring's rooms the previous evening. Lady Chiltern confesses the misunderstanding and the play concludes with Sir Robert's acceptance of a post in the Cabinet and the engagement of Lord Goring and Mabel Chiltern.

The Importance of Being Earnest
Oscar Wilde

DATE 1895

CAST

John Worthing JP
Algernon Moncrieff
Rev Canon Chasuble DD
Merriman, a butler
Lane, a manservant
Lady Bracknell
Hon Gwendolen Fairfax
Cecily Cardew
Miss Prism, governess to Miss Cardew

SCENE London and Hertfordshire

Plot

Act I The morning-room in Algernon Moncrieff's flat in Half Moon Street. Mr Ernest Worthing calls on his friend Algernon Moncrieff. Ernest is in love with Algernon's cousin Gwendolen Fairfax, who is, together with her Aunt Augusta (Lady Bracknell), expected for tea. Algy questions Ernest as to the meaning of an inscription in his cigarette case, which he had left in Algy's rooms. The inscription reads:

From little Cecily, with her fondest love to her dear Uncle Jack.

Ernest explains how he was adopted as a little boy by the
late Mr Thomas Cardew, who made him in his will
guardian to his grand-daughter Miss Cecily Cardew.
Cecily, who addresses him as uncle from motives of respect
which Algy could not possibly appreciate, lives at Jack's
place in the country under the charge of her admirable
governess, Miss Prism. As it is necessary to adopt a high
moral tone on all subjects when one is a guardian, a high
moral tone can hardly be said to conduce very much
either to health or happiness, so, in order to get up to
London, Jack has invented a younger brother of the name
of Ernest, who lives in the Albany and gets into the most
dreadful scrapes. Algy is delighted: as Jack has invented
a brother to be able to come up to town, so he has invented
an invaluable permanent invalid called Bunbury in order
that he can escape into the country. These explanations
are interrupted by a Wagnerian ring at the doorbell. Aunt
Augusta arrives with Gwendolen. Algy contrives to with-
draw Lady Bracknell thus giving Jack a chance to propose. Gwendolen accepts him because it has always been
her intention to marry someone of the name of Ernest. In
the middle of his proposal he is discovered by Lady Bracknell in his semi-recumbent position on one knee. She
cross-examines him with a view to discovering his eligi-
bility:

Lady Bracknell I have always been of opinion that a man
who desires to get married should know either everything
or nothing. Which do you know?
Jack [after some hesitation] I know nothing Lady
Bracknell.
Lady Bracknell I am pleased to hear it. I do not approve
of anything that tampers with natural ignorance. Ignorance
is like a delicate exotic fruit; touch it and the bloom
is gone. The whole theory in modern education is radically
unsound. Fortunately, in England at any rate, education
produces no effect whatsoever. If it did it would prove

a serious danger to the upper classes, and probably lead
to acts of violence in Grosvenor Square.

The replies continue along a similarly satisfactory course
until Jack admits that he has lost both his parents, or
rather they seem to have lost him and that he was found
by the late Mr Thomas Cardew in a handbag in the cloak-
room at Victoria Station and, as that gentleman happened
to have a first class ticket for Worthing in his pocket, he
gave him the name of Worthing. Lady Bracknell does not
regard such antecedents as an assured basis for a recognized position in good society, and she orders Jack to find
one or both parents before again applying to her for permission to marry Gwendolen.

Act II The garden at the Manor House, Woolton. Algy
arrives claiming to be Mr Ernest Worthing. Cecily, Jack's
ward, is very taken with him. He proposes only to find
that according to her diary they have been engaged on
and off for the last three months. It has always been a
girlish dream of hers to love someone whose name was
Ernest. Jack now enters in the deepest mourning claiming
that Ernest has died in Paris. He is hardly pleased to be
confronted with a flesh and blood brother. Gwendolen
arrives to become instantly bosom friends with Cecily.
This friendship lasts until they discover that they are both
engaged to Mr Ernest Worthing. There follows a confrontation over the tea table between the Alice in Wonderland
logic of Cecily's country manners and Gwendolen's society
sophistication. The quarrel ends and the interrupted
friendship is resumed after the entry of Jack and Algernon
with the resulting discovery that there is no Mr Ernest
Worthing.

Act III The drawing-room at the Manor House, Woolton. Lady Bracknell, having been apprised of her
daughter's flight by her trusty maid, whose confidence she
has purchased by means of a small coin, has followed her.
On discovering that Miss Cardew is in no way connected

with any of the larger railway stations and that she possesses about a hundred and thirty thousand pounds in funds, she is prepared to agree to her engagement with Algy. Jack, still forbidden to aspire to Gwendolen, refuses his consent. The impasse is resolved by the discovery of a guilty secret of Miss Prism, Cecily's governess. Twenty-eight years ago she left Lord Bracknell's house in Upper Grosvenor Street in charge of a perambulator that contained a baby of the male sex. She never returned. The perambulator was later discovered containing the manuscript of a three-volume novel of more than usually revolting sentimentality. The plain facts of the case are that on the morning of the day in question Miss Prism had with her a handbag in which she intended to place the manuscript. In a moment of mental abstraction she deposited the manuscript in the basinette and the baby in the handbag. She deposited the handbag in the cloak room of Victoria Station. Jack is Algy's long-lost elder brother. As he was christened Ernest John, Gwendolen's conditions are met and he realizes for the first time in his life the vital Importance of Being Earnest.

In the original draft there was a further scene between the last two acts in which Algernon was arrested for debt. A glance at this shows how right Wilde was in cutting it.

Critical commentary

The Importance of Being Earnest is by far the best work of Oscar Wilde, but the commonplace idea that better work remained unwritten is based not on informed consideration of the improvement shown in this play but rather on an over romantic sympathy for the scandal which cut short his career.

He needed to develop theatrical craft and a more mature philosophy. The first signs of the former are apparent in *Earnest* but the latter is absent. It is the undergraduate approach to life reflected in all his work which brought about his downfall. The critical problem is stripping away the cult surrounding the man in order to get at the work. In the 1920s his own estimation of himself as expressed in *De Profundis* 'I was a man who stood in symbolic relations to the art and culture of my age', was accepted. For many, adoration at his shrine became an escape from the boredom of the first quarter of the twentieth century. Even as early as 1876, when he left Oxford, he was well known and regarded by many as one of the leading lights, if not the originator of the 'Aesthetic Movement'. As an aesthete Wilde advocated the artificiality of art maintaining that all bad poetry sprung from genuine feeling:

> To be natural is to be obvious, and to be obvious is to be inartistic.

With hindsight we can recognize much of Wilde's theorizing on art as a second-hand misapplication of the ideals of the Romantics. Certainly his first two plays *Vera, or the Nihilists* and *The Duchess of Padua* are of that ilk from which derive *The Cenci* and *The Borderers*. *Vera* is turgid melodrama, a half-remembered, half-digested rag bag of dramatic cliché which any reasonably literate teenager should have been able to throw off in a week. It is incredible that its existence in manuscript form did not undermine his position as a wit. *The Duchess of Padua* is little better. It is a pastiche of *The Cenci*. The colourful obscurity of the verse cannot hide the lack of thought and observation. Most interesting, in the light of the plays which we have outlined above, is the lack of original characterization. It contains not one but three villains: Moranzone, the Duke of Padua and Papa Germont; a pair of juveniles requiring good voices and the capability of looking romantic in tights; a stock cardinal with silver hair and sterile manner; a coterie of low-comics and walking gentlemen of the Augustus Colpoys, Tom Wrench variety; and a caricature of Sarah Bernhardt able to ladle and spout rodomontade for four acts and sustain in the fifth a several-hundred-line death scene while she struggles about the stage, carefully avoiding the scenery, under the effects of a fatal poison.

It is a remarkable achievement that anybody who could write as badly as this was ever able to discipline himself to the conventions of the professional theatre. This was achieved not by Wilde learning to control or exploit his expressed theories but by a careful copying of the work of his contemporaries. His first produced play *Lady Windermere's Fan* (1892) is usually described as a comedy. It would be more correctly described as a society melodrama. The cast list is as unoriginal as that of *The Duchess of Padua*. Lady Windermere is the good woman and distressed wife; Lord Windermere the distraught husband; Lord Darlington the society cynic; and least original of all there is Mrs Erlynne – the woman with a past. Adventuresses who have broken the rules had been stage favourites ever since a succession of Lady Audleys had begun pushing people down wells, setting fire to inns, laughing wildly, pressing their hands upon their hearts and falling senseless with all the technical skill required for a prone backfall in the 1860s. The final statements on this character still remained to be made by Pinero with *The Second Mrs Tanqueray* and Henry Arthur Jones with *Mrs Dane's Defence*. Both Jones and Pinero had the talent to initiate discussion of the code in their plays. Wilde can only either accept the code, as he does in his melodramas, or burlesque it as in *The Importance of Being Earnest*. A play can show merit and originality for two reasons: it can be innovatory in form and structure, or the playwright can employ the conventional theatrical mechanism of his age to communicate some special quality. Boucicault, Robertson and Gilbert are formal innovators with, one must confess, no striking philosophical contribution. In contrast Shaw, in spite of his expressed critical contempt for 'Sardoodledum', takes over nineteenth-century theatrical conventions lock, stock and barrel. His 'woman with a past' play is *Mrs Warren's Profession. Arms and the Man* is romantic drama. *The Man of Destiny* uses all the tricks of French theatre, such as concealed identities, compromising letters and filched dispatches and *The Devil's Disciple* is pure melodrama, even down to the scaffold scene with its accompanying last minute reprieve. Shaw is however able to use these conventions to communicate his original if sometimes perverse ideologies. Any comparison between Wilde's ladies with a past and Mrs Warren must be detrimental to Wilde's creations. Instead of providing us with but another aspirant to a place in society, Shaw exposes the labour conditions which drove women to prostitution. *Arms and the Man, The Devil's Disciple* and *The Man of Destiny* have a much deeper debunking quality than anything in *The Importance of Being Earnest*. All Wilde can really offer of his own is the lighthearted society banter which passes for wit. The flashes of this in *Lady Windermere* and *An Ideal Husband* are certainly refreshing but they seem a part of the setting rather than an organic necessity:

> If you pretend to be good the world takes you very
> seriously, If you pretend to be bad it doesn't.
> I can resist everything except temptation
> [*Lady Windermere's Fan*]

> Questions are never indiscreet. Answers sometimes are.
> Only dull people are brilliant at breakfast.
> ... a woman's first duty in life is to her dress maker
> ... What the second duty is no one has yet discovered.
> [*An Ideal Husband*]

Remarks such as these may have amusing implications but they hardly demonstrate sufficient originality of insight to justify revival of these plays over so much better constructed works by unknown authors as Charles Haddon Chambers' *The Tyranny of Tears*, 1899, or St John Hankin's *The Cassilis Engagement*. This is the irritating thing about the Wilde myth. Such is the glamour and reputation of the man that, propped up by the efforts of set designers and costumiers, his work is constantly revived and his short stories turned into pastiches at the expense of a body of sound plays which are in grave danger of being forgotten. Even the early Shaw which we have compared with Wilde's work has less stage currency.

In an attempt to justify the position established for Wilde in the 1920s, Nicoll and other critics have seen in *An Ideal Husband* an improvement over *Lady Windermere's Fan* and *A Woman of No Importance*. It is dangerously tempting to credit Wilde with prefiguring Shaw's satirical treatment of social *mores* by interpreting the greater worth of the 'idle' Lord Goring in comparison to the apparent respectability of Sir Robert as a questioning of social values. Such a conclusion denies the late nineteenth century respect for the amateur. Lord Goring is cut from the same cloth as Sir Christopher in *The Liars* and Adolphus Cusins in *Major Barbara*. It is left to Shaw to make a genuine comment on the gentleman dabbler. Nor is it strictly correct to say that the use of aphorisms and paradoxes of the kind we associate with Wilde is more completely integrated into the fabric of the play, for what we might call 'Wildean' dialogue is mainly confined to the first act and the scenes between Lord Goring and his father and Lord Goring and Mrs Cheveley. In other words *An Ideal Husband* is just as surely a society melodrama as *Lady Windermere's Fan* and *A Woman of No Importance*. All three plays, to all intents and purposes, share the same cast list. In *A Woman of No Importance* Mrs Arbuthnot is the Lady with a Past, in *An Ideal Husband* it is Mrs Cheveley. The distressed wives Lady Windermere and Lady Chiltern are interchangeable as are Lord Windermere, Sir Robert Chiltern and Lord Illingworth. All three plays turn on the stage convention of a secret disclosed early to the audience but held from certain of the characters. This is obviously a good device for building suspense and holding interest, but it is a gift of craftsmanship rather than genius. There is a definite improvement in craft between *Lady Winder-mere* and *An Ideal Husband*. In the former Wilde is forced to employ a technique of direct communication with the audience reminiscent of melodrama, while by the latter he is able to expose the details of his plot through conversation without recourse to soliloquy.

The Importance of Being Earnest is a topsy-turvy, paradoxical use of the same techniques. It is almost as if Wilde was deliberately mocking the conventions of his own earlier work. The time worn devices are tricked out in such a startling form that we are taken by surprise and surprise is a major element in humour. Miss Prism, the spinster governess, is the woman with a past. Jack's origin in a handbag is the guilty secret. The sensational climax which reveals Jack as Lady Bracknell's long-lost nephew is a gorgeous burlesque of a thousand clichéd dénouements. *The Importance of Being Earnest* is deservedly acclaimed. It is a very good play. The thrust in aphorisms of Wilde's earlier plays seem utterly natural and we have no feeling that we are being served up a reheated dish but, before we lose ourselves in superlatives, it is worth considering how original the play really is. The world in which it is set had been previously charted by W. S. Gilbert. In *Engaged* Gilbert combined the realistic drama of Robertson with the ludicrously logical world of farce. The plot of *Engaged* is extraordinarily thin, three hours being taken up in trying to establish the legality or otherwise of Belinda Scot's marriage to Cheviot. *The Importance of Being Earnest* draws on Gilbert's play for incident rather than plot or theme. Bunburying, the compulsive eating of the young men when under strain and even the appearance of Jack in full mourning for his brother Ernest all echo *Engaged*. Granted that these devices are totally

assimilated into *Earnest* it is arguable that if we were
more familiar with *Engaged*, their surprise would be
lessened and with it their ability to make us laugh. *Engaged* is certainly the deeper play. It is a nearly Aristophanic criticism of Victorian social values. *Earnest* on the
other hand is a brilliantly executed trick. Wilde has
taken the conventional viewpoint and constructed epi-
grams by proclaiming the opposite. In these he is almost
predictable. Gilbert has simply exaggerated a rather unpalatable truth. Wilde is absurd to a point of unreality,
where Gilbert is shockingly over real. Attention should
be paid to Bernard Shaw's criticisms:

> It amused me of course; but unless comedy touches me as
> well as amuses me, it leaves me with a sense of having
> wasted my evening. I go to the theatre to be moved to
> laughter, not to be tickled or bustled into it; and that is
> why, though I laugh as much as anybody at a farcical
> comedy, I am out of spirits before the end of the second
> act, and out of temper before the end of the third, my
> miserable mechanical laughter intensifying these symptoms
> at every outburst. If the public ever becomes intelligent
> enough to know when it is really enjoying itself and when
> it is not, there will be an end of farcical comedy.

Wilde has been guilty of borrowing previously. *An Ideal
Husband* exploits the Rajputana Canal incidents from
Pinero's *The Cabinet Minister* and Lord Windermere's
patronage of Mrs Erlynne closely parallels Lady Twomb-
ley's social canvassing on behalf of Mrs Gaylustre.

Wilde has profited retrospectively from the tragedy of
his trials. Hands off say the supporters of oppressed
minorities, and a true assessment of his work is prevented
by a sentimental attempt to repair the judgement of his
own time. It was perhaps fair that a judgement passed on
the man but enlarged to include his work should have
been reversed by reconsideration of the man obscuring
the true quality of the work, but the truth is not always

fair and however much we may wish to show sympathy
for the persecution and humiliation meted out to the
man it is ridiculous to attempt this by reinstating his
work to a position it never fully achieved and certainly
never deserved. *Earnest* must be grateful to the players
who have served it well but if these same talents might be
persuaded to apply themselves elsewhere, we might find
Wilde's plays removed from the courses and anthologies
which they now inhabit in favour of more worthy examples of the theatre of this period. While they are
studied we must continue to assess them but let us study
them coldly and critically against other representative
plays of the period, uninfluenced by emotional consideration of Wilde's personal tragedy.

The Liars
Henry Arthur Jones (1851–1929)

The son of a farmer, Jones was born at Grandborough, Buckinghamshire. At the age of twelve he went to work at his uncle's draper's shop at Ramsgate. He then worked in another draper's shop, a London warehouse and for ten years as a commercial traveller in the London, Exeter and Bradford districts. His spare time was devoted to self-education and unsuccessful writing. He was twenty-seven before his first play *It's Only Round the Corner* was produced at the Exeter Theatre. Four years later he scored his first great success with *The Silver King* (1882) written in collaboration with Henry Herman. He has some claim to originating the new school of 'unpleasant' plays on serious social problems with *Saints and Sinners* (1884) which deals with religion and hypocrisy in a country town.

He lectured and wrote with great influence on the theatre's claim to social and artistic recognition. His lectures were reprinted under the title *The Renascence of the English Drama* (1894). In later life he involved himself in social and political controversy, particularly with Shaw and Wells, whom he addressed in *My Dear Wells: A Manual for the Haters of England* (1921). In this field he also wrote *Patriotism and Popular Education* (1919) and *What is Capital?* (1925).

His main dramatic works are: *It's Only Round the Corner* (1879); *A Clerical Error* (1879); *The Silver King* (with H. A. Herman) (1882); *Wealth* (1889); *The Middle-man* (1889); *Judah* (1890); *The Tempter* (1893); *Michael and His Lost Angel* (1896); *The Rogue's Comedy* (1896); *The Liars* (1897); *The Physician* (1897); *The Manoeuvres of Jane* (1898); *Mrs Dane's Defence* (1900); *Whitewashing of Julia* (1903); *The Heroic Stubbs* (1906); *Dolly Reforming Herself* (1908); *The Ogre* (1911); *Mary Goes First* (1913); and *The Lie* (1914).

DATE 1897

CAST

Colonel Sir Christopher Deering
Edward Falkner
Gilbert Nepean
George Nepean
Freddie Tatton
Archibald Coke
Waiter at the Star and Garter
Taplin
Gadsby
Footman
Mrs Crespin
Beatrice Ebernoe
Dolly Coke
Ferris
Lady Rosamund Tatton
Lady Jessica Nepean
SCENE London and the South of England

Plot

Act I Interior of a large tent which has been erected on the lawn of Freddie Tatton's house in the Thames Valley to cater for a Thames Regatta house party. Freddie is henpecked by his wife Lady Rosamund Tatton. She has insisted on including among the guests Edward Falkner, a national hero after his exploits in Africa. Her sister

Lady Jessica Nepean, who is rather incongruously married to the humourless Gilbert Nepean, has been encouraging Falkner's attentions and is indeed on the river with him as the play begins. The bulk of the first act is taken up with people having words with Falkner and Lady Jessica about their conduct. Gilbert is called away on business but his equally priggish brother George remains as an unwanted watch-dog. Falkner receives a message from the Foreign Office asking him to return to Africa. He asks Jessica for a last meeting. Her words are a refusal but a refusal couched in such a fashion that it must be interpreted as a promise to meet him in five days time at a small riverside hotel called the Star and Garter. Contrasted with the wild attraction between Falkner and Jessica is the respectful wooing of Beatrice Ebernoe by Falkner's friend Sir Christopher Deering. Mrs Ebernoe is a widow. Her husband was killed in Africa. She herself was rescued by Falkner. Although she has great respect for Sir Christopher she can't quite forget the past.

Act II A private sitting room in the Star and Garter five days later. Falkner has ordered a sumptuous meal. Lady Jessica arrives. Falkner, impatient with Jessica's expertise in keeping the conversation flirtatious, makes a very real declaration of love. She avoids the moment by sending him to stop a barrel organ which is playing outside. While he is out of the room George Nepean arrives. Falkner returns. There is an awkward pause. George looks very significantly at the preparations for dinner and leaves promising to tell his brother. Falkner is at first delighted at the accident. There will be a scandal and Jessica has no alternative but to leave Gilbert and go away with him. Jessica begs him to try and save her. Coincidence brings Rosamund and Freddie to the hotel *en route* to dine with Mrs Crespin. They cannot break this engagement but Rosamund does write a letter to George on the hotel's notepaper asking him to call on her the next day for an explanation of her sister's conduct. They agree that their story will be that Jessica dined with Freddie and Rosamund. Falkner is to call at Rosamund's about an hour after George to find out how they have succeeded. Lady Jessica's maid, Ferris, arrives with news that Gilbert is unexpectedly returning home that night. Although very hungry she is too frightened to eat and returns home immediately. Falkner is left alone with his sumptuous meal. The waiter is just serving this when Sir Christopher Deering turns up. He is surprised to discover how well Falkner seems to do himself when on his own. He questions him as to whether he has come to his senses over Jessica and appears satisfied with the answers. Falkner leaves the room for a moment, while he is absent Deering finds Lady Jessica's stylograph. This discovery explains the mysterious excellence of the meal and there is no doubt as Deering pockets the pen but that he has guessed a good deal of what has gone before. The waiter returns with a message that Falkner has been called away and the act ends with Sir Christopher beginning to dine.

Act III Lady Rosamund's drawing-room at Cadogan Gardens. It is the next morning. Lady Jessica enters. She tells her sister that when she returned home she found a second telegram stating that Gilbert had not after all completed his business and would not return till the next morning. George has already called on Rosamund and means to be very horrid. Freddie for once refuses to take his wife's hints that his presence is unnecessary and they are forced to involve him in the subterfuge. The circle is widened still further when Sir Christopher arrives to return Jessica's pen. He is told the whole story, Jessica explaining that she and her sister have arranged to tell things not perhaps exactly as they were but as they ought to have been. In that way 'a lie becomes a sort of idealized and essential truth'. This carefully erected edifice is shattered when Mrs Crespin tells them that she let it slip to George that Freddie and Rosamund dined with her last night. A new lie must be concocted. Dolly Coke and her husband are drawn into the tale. She agrees to swear that it was with her that Jessica dined. Unfortunately George arrives before her story is quite settled. He obviously does not believe it and refuses to listen to Sir Christopher's plea that he should leave well alone and not embitter his brother and Lady Jessica's whole future by sowing jealousy and suspicion between them. Gilbert's entry further strains the explanation which totally collapses when Falkner joins the party; unaware that the original story that Jessica dined with Lady Rosamund has been changed, he undermines any credibility in the idea that her partner was Dolly Coke. Jessica quietly asks him to tell the truth. This he does, concluding:

> If you think there was anything more on your wife's side than a passing folly and amusement at my expense, you will wrong her. If you think there is anything less on my side than the deepest, deepest, deepest love and worship, you will wrong me. Understand this. She is guiltless.

Act IV The drawing-room in Sir Christopher's flat in Victoria Street. He is preparing to leave for Africa. He proposes to Beatrice. She accepts. She will accompany him. There is no fooling, no flirtation – simply comradeship. Gilbert calls. Without excusing Jessica's folly, Sir Christopher apportions some of the blame to the husband's inability to understand his wife. He advises Gilbert to drop the matter and take her out for a good dinner to make up for the one she missed the night before. Gilbert, about to accept this advice, leaves to be replaced almost immediately by Falkner. He has received a letter from Lady Jessica which holds out every hope that she is about to leave her husband. Amid the debris of his own preparations for Africa, Sir Christopher tries to recall his friend to a sense of duty. He points out that he is the one man who can deal with the African situation. The appeal to patriotism having failed he describes the realities of ignoring the unwritten rules of society. He admits that

there is nothing to say in the abstract against running
away with another man's wife. He acknowledges that there
may be planets where it is not only the highest ideal
morality, but where it has the further advantage of being
a practical way of carrying on society:

> But it has one fatal defect in our country today – it
> won't work! You know what we English are, Ned. We're
> not a bit better than our neighbours, but, thank God!
> we do pretend we are, and we do make it hot for
> anybody who disturbs that holy pretence.

He goes on remorselessly to describe those of their
acquaintance to have flouted these dictates. Falkner and
Jessica part: Jessica to go to dinner with her husband at
the Savoy, Falkner to leave for Africa with Sir Christopher
and Beatrice.

Critical commentary

Jones is almost always coupled with Pinero as one of those
who did most to establish turn of the century society
drama, and, as judgement has been passed in favour of
the younger man, criticism of his work often tends to
come as an appendage to remarks on Pinero so that it is
perhaps just that we should restore his actual seniority for
it must be allowed that he was attempting serious subjects when Pinero was still predominantly a *farceur*. Like
Pinero, Jones served a long apprenticeship in the traditional theatrical forms and much of his early work was
produced by that High Priest of melodrama Wilson
Barrett. Yet as early as 1884 he stated in an address reprinted in his *Renascence of the English Drama:*

> Our great need is, then, for a school of plays of serious
> intention, plays that implicitly assert the value and dignity
> of human life, that it has great passions and great aims, and
> is full of meaning and importance.

Nor is this empty oratory for earlier he had shocked audiences with his treatment of the familiar, girl seduced by
the squire dying in her sweetheart's arms after to some
extent annulling her shame with good works, story. For in
Saints and Sinners he made the girl the daughter of a non-
comformist minister and reserved his strongest antagonism for the hypocritical congregation that drove them
from their home. His own dissenting upbringing gave the
play a reality and simmering energy which would have
been commonplace in 1900 but was quite extraordinary
in 1884.

A leading spokesman of conventional attitudes was
Clement Scott, best remembered today for the stand he
took against Ibsen when the battle lines were drawn in
the early 1890s. In an article 'Why Do We Go to the
Play' printed in the *Theatre* (March 1888) he wrote:

> The dramatist who trumpets forth the bad, and conceals the
> good, is unworthy of his calling. The play that belittles
> and degrades the manhood, and the womanhood, of those
> who watch it is unworthy of public recognition ... There is
> no pleasure in revelling in what is unwholesome and
> disagreeable. The playhouse is not a charnel house; the
> drama is not a dissecting knife. When I am asked 'why we
> go to the play', I should answer thus: Not to enjoy the
> contemplation of the baseness, and brutality, of life; not
> to return to our daily work more oppressed, more
> discontented, more dissatisfied, more heartless, but to
> believe in hope, in faith, in purity, in honour, in nobility of
> aim and steadfastness of purpose. We must enforce the good,
> without showing the bad.

It is at this point in the struggle that Jones is at his best.
At heart he is a preacher and, though his dialogue appears
to the reader less stiff than that of his contemporary (it is
doubtful whether there is any noticeable difference in
performance), he lacks Pinero's sophistication. He
achieved his height in the period 1897–1900, with *The*

Liars and *Mrs Dane's Defence*. After this period he seems to be looking for new battles to fight, while at the same time revisiting his past. His Victorian inability to compromise, a gift Pinero possessed, made him a comparative failure in the Edwardian theatre and perhaps is the reason he must now take second place to Pinero. There is something rather sad about the way the champion of the new drama in the 1880s became, particularly after the Great War, the leading spokesman for the establishment. His antagonism to Shaw and Wells in the latter period of his life obscured his contribution to the theatre of ideas. In the Dedication of the unperformed *The Divine Gift* (1913) to Gilbert Murray, who had called him old-fashioned, he complains that the new drama was simply: '... an eavesdropping photographic reporter, taking snapshots, and shorthand notes'.

He goes on to explain his own attitude to his successors:

> A drama without ideas is empty and sterile. That we all allow. But a drama that sets out to exploit and enforce ideas and opinions is of the nature of a political caucus and ends by grinding out wind ... The field of the modern drama is strewn with disabled riders who have hastily mounted raw colts of ideas, and never got home with them, but lie crippled and groaning while their ideas are aimlessly kicking and stampeding the country.

So might Scott have written of him in the 1880s when he was vigorously campaigning through lectures and articles for a serious theatre.

The Liars deserves an established place in our repertory if only for the brilliance of the third act and if we may carp at Deering's inability after so much speechifying on the subject to offer better marital advice to Gilbert than to take his wife out to dinner at the Savoy, can we in fact think of better? The controlled attack on the new woman is the more effective for its lack of recrimination. The advice is clear whether to those who busied themselves with flirtation or those who flirted with business – Go home. The solution of despatching Edward to the colonies may seem today a little grotesque but there is a certain reality behind the idea obtained from the drama that they were peopled with repentant ne'er-do-wells, disappointed lovers and women with a past.

Trelawny of the 'Wells'
Arthur Wing Pinero (1855–1934)

Pinero was the son of a solicitor of Portuguese-Jewish descent, the family name originally being Pinheiro. He was born in Islington, leaving school at the age of ten to become apprenticed to the law. He spent some time involving himself in amateur drama before throwing over the law to become an actor with the Edinburgh stock company. He made his first professional stage appearance at the Theatre Royal, Edinburgh on 22 June 1874. He served his theatrical apprenticeship as an actor for ten years, although before abandoning this aspect of his career he had already begun to write for the stage. His first play was *Two Hundred a Year* produced at the Globe in 1877. His early plays tend to be farce or melodrama, and like all apprentice writings are typical of the theatre of his time. It is with *The Squire* (1881) that he begins to expand the directions of his theatre. William Archer tells us:

> In the course of the very curious and interesting
> controversy which raged for some time after the production
> of 'The Squire,' Mr Pinero published the memorandum
> in his note-book which formed the germ of his drama.
> It ran as follows: 'the notion of a young couple secretly
> married, the girl about to become a mother – finding
> that a former wife is still in existence. The heroine amongst
> those who respect and love her. The fury of a rejected

lover who believes her to be a guilty woman. Two men
face to face at night-time. Qy – Kill the first wife?'

True this is still the stuff of melodrama and French theatre
but Pinero begins to relate material of this kind to the
society of his day. *The Squire* looks forward to his plays
on 'unpleasant' subjects which, while still owing more to
French and native influences than to Ibsen, take the
British theatre into the twentieth century. Such a play
was *The Profligate* written in 1889 to inaugurate Hare's
management at the Garrick. This tells the story of a libertine who believes himself contentedly married only to
meet one of the several women from his past. His wife
leaves him and, in his original version, Pinero ends with
his suicide. Hare insisted on reconciliation which weakens
the seriousness of the play's purpose but it looks forward
to the uncompromising *The Second Mrs Tanqueray*
(1893). This is now thought of as a theatrical milestone,
boldly facing facts and rejecting the artificiality and contrivance of the past. In our terms this is not true. Many
of the characters are reminiscent of other plays, as for
example Paula, the second Mrs Tanqueray, who is the
familiar lady with a past, and there is something of the
early Wilde in the coincidence of the affair between her
stepdaughter, Ellen, and one of her lovers. However,
Paula's moments of self-knowledge, such as 'I believe the
future is only the past again, entered through another
gate', and her suicide, while maintaining the code, hint
at possible alternatives and at the code's cruelty rather
than its fairness.

Although much of his later work, sensitive to the desires of an audience who wanted to feel they were being
seriously entertained, tends towards sermonizing he had,
when he wanted, a delicate lightness. His farces *The
Magistrate* (1885), *The School Mistress* (1886) and *Dandy
Dick* (1887) are among the funniest plays of the period.
He appears to have suddenly lost his ability to respond

to audience taste during the First World War and his last play *A Cold June* (1932) was a sad anticlimax to a brilliant career. He was knighted in 1909.

DATE 1898

CAST

Theatrical folk

James Telfer
Augustus Colpoys
Ferdinand Gadd
Tom Wrench
Mrs Telfer (Miss Violet Sylvester)
Avonia Bunn
Rose Trelawny

} of the Bagnigge Wells Theatre

Imogen Parrott, of the Royal Olympic Theatre
O'Dwyer, prompter at the Pantheon Theatre
Non-Theatrical folk
Vice-Chancellor Sir William Gower, Kt
Arthur Gower
Clara de Foenix } his grandchildren
Miss Trafalgar Gower, Sir William's sister
Captain de Foenix, Clara's husband
Mrs Mossop
Mr Ablett
Charles
Sarah
SCENE London in the 1860s

NOTE Bagnigge (locally pronounced Bagnidge) Wells – formerly a popular mineral spring in Islington, situated not far from the better remembered Sadler's Wells. The gardens of Bagnigge Wells were at one time much resorted to. Bagnigge Wells, unlike Sadler's Wells, has never possessed a playhouse. Sadler's Wells Theatre, always familiarly known as the 'Wells' still exists. In later editions Pinero struck out all mention of Bagnigge Wells and frankly referred to the company of the 'Wells' as 'of

Sadler's Wells Theatre', describing Rose as 'the best juvenile lady the "Wells" has known since Mr Phelps' management'.

Plot

Act I Mr and Mrs Telfer's lodgings at No 2, Brydon Crescent, Clerkenwell. May. The lodgings are littered with theatrical clutter in a manner somewhat reminiscent of the opening scene of *Caste*. A cold collation is arranged. Miss Rose Trelawny is leaving the company and the profession. She is engaged to be married to Arthur Gower. The date of the wedding is still to be arranged, for before the Gower family positively say yes to the union, Miss Trelawny is to make her home with them in Cavendish Square in order to habituate herself to the West End. Tom Wrench is the first of the theatre folk to arrive as his share in the interpretation of the immortal works of Sheridan Knowles does not necessitate his remaining after the first act. The next is Imogen Parrott, late of the Wells, but now risen to the heights of the Olympic Theatre. The two laugh at the inadequacies of Tom's theatrical wardrobe which, although it must accommodate itself to many periods, never fails to provide laughter for the gallery boys. They move on to the subject of Tom's plays. The trouble with these are they have such ordinary words and short speeches that they do not provide opportunities for leading actors. To fashion heroes out of actual, dull, everyday men – the sort of men you see smoking cheroots in the club windows in St James's Street – and heroines from simple maidens in muslin frocks is to ignore all recognized conventions of dramatic practice. The company assemble under the chairmanship of Telfer, an old-fashioned actor, ably supported by Gadd, a Byronic juvenile, and Colpoys a wizened little fellow who is unable to forget he is a low-comedian. Toasts are drunk and a sad farewell is taken.

Act II The drawing-room of Sir William Gower's house in Cavendish Square one month later. It is half an hour after dinner. Sir William and Trafalgar are asleep. The young people, Rose, Arthur and the de Foenixes converse hardly at all in muted tones. The well bred silence is obviously getting on Rose's nerves. From the street come the strains of a barrel organ playing the song Rose sang in *The Pedlar of Marseilles.* It was this song which first attracted Arthur to Rose. Rose begins to describe the scene, illustrating her description with speeches. These wake Sir William and Trafalgar. Sir William gives orders that the organ be silenced. Sir William then complains that Arthur, who is for the sake of propriety lodged round the corner with the de Foenixes, has been seen under Rose's window at night. Rose is furious and states dramatically that she is being killed as surely as Agnes in *The Spectre of St Ives.* She will, she says, be found dead of no recognized disorder. The company settle down at Sir William's command to a very serious game of whist. Rose goes into the next room and starts to accompany herself on the piano. Sir William suspends the game while the young lady performs her operas. Rose is left alone. Charles, the footman, slips her a note. Her friends from the Wells are waiting in the square on the chance of her being able to slip out for a word. A storm begins. Rose, with Charles's connivance, smuggles her friends into the house. Gadd and Avonia have just married and are celebrating by a sight-seeing trip to the West End; they are accompanied by Colpoys and Tom Wrench. They have been drinking and although not drunk are certainly a little affable. They take a little more wine. Gadd starts to sing. He and Colpoys quarrel. The card table is overturned. Bells start to ring violently all over the house. Sir William and Trafalgar appear in their night things. The actors are turned out of the house. This is Rose's breaking point. She turns to Arthur who has arrived from the square:

Oh, I'm very sorry Arthur. Indeed I am very sorry, Sir
William. But you are right – gipsies – gipsies! Yes, Arthur,
if you were a gipsy, as I am – as these friends o' mine are,
we might be happy together. But I've seen enough of your
life, my dear boy, to know that I'm no wife for you. I
should only be wretched, and would make you wretched;
and the end, when it arrived, as it very soon would,
would be much as it is to-night!

Act III Another apartment in Mrs Mossop's lodging
house for actors at No 2 Brydon Crescent, Clerkenwell.
Six months have passed. Rose is not the actress she was.
Since her return she has been reserved and subdued. She
always was a lady-like actress, she has now become a lady-
like human being. She can no longer, in Tom Wrench's
words 'spout, she can no longer ladle, the vapid trash'.
Tom confides to Avonia that Arthur Gower has become
an actor. Rose enters having received her notice. She delivers a diatribe against the contemporary theatre:

We are only dolls, partly human, with mechanical limbs
that will fall into stagey postures, and heads stuffed with
sayings out of rubbishy plays. It isn't *the* world we live in,
merely *a* world – Such a queer little one! I was less than a
month in Cavendish Square, a very few people came
there; but they were real people – real!

The jobs of most of the group, which met so confidently
a month earlier for Rose's farewell party, are endangered.
The Telfers have been dismissed, Gadd is forced to play
the Demon in pantomime and even Imogen Parrott feels
insecure at the Olympic. It is stressed that the theatre
needs to be changed. The time is ripe for Tom Wrench's
new kind of drama. Imogen is prepared to put up half
the money towards taking a theatre to produce one of his
plays. Sir William Gower calls in search of Arthur. Avonia
gives him a piece of her mind. She tells him that Rose's
stay at Cavendish Square has ruined her acting. Sir

William thaws. He becomes even more amenable when
he learns that Rose's mother acted with Kean, whom he
remembers as Richard. They apply to him for further
backing for Tom's play. The act ends with Tom beginning to read for Sir William 'Life', a comedy by Thomas
Wrench.
Act IV The stage of the Pantheon Theatre. The Telfers enter first. Pinero allows his representatives of the
old theatrical order great dignity in their retiral. Telfer
is to play 'an old, stagey, out-of-date actor' while his wife
is the wardrobe mistress but, as she says:

> . . . if we are to scrub a floor – and we may come to that
> yet – let us make up our minds to scrub it legitimately –
> with dignity.

Sir William is allowed to watch the rehearsal from a box.
He is astonished to discover that Arthur is cast for the
leading man. He accepts the situation and the curtain
falls as the rehearsal begins.

Critical commentary

Trelawny of the 'Wells' is an exact picture of the English
theatre in the 1860s, and must rank as one of the best
plays about the theatre ever written. Tom Wrench is the
young Tom Robertson wrenching the drama into new
channels. It is only just that Pinero, who owed so much
of his technique to Robertson, should pay this gentle
tribute. Thirty years had gone by since Robertson had
stirred theatrical audiences with his new methods but
those thirty years had seen the total eclipse of an established repertory and an established style of acting so that
there is sufficient contrast between the theatre of 1898 and
the theatre of 1860 for him to be able to deal with the
changes without recourse to burlesque. Robertson's battle
is long won and Pinero, the *avant garde* dramatist of
the 1880s, is the foremost playwright of the decade. He

is now the establishment already under attack from the forces which would become suddenly, during the Vedrenne-Barker season of 1904–7 at the Royal Court Theatre, the theatre of ideas. There is something sadly prophetic in the lines of the Telfers in the last act:

> *Telfer* And so this new-fangled stuff, and these dandified people are to push us, and such as us, from our stools! *Mrs Telfer* Yes, James, just as some other new fashion will, in course of time, push *them* from their stools.

The push was about to come. Symbolic of the kind of theatre produced by Pinero and Jones was the drawing-room, symbolic of the forces of change is Shaw's use of a dentist's surgery for the opening set of *You Never Can Tell* (1897). Ironically Trelawny demonstrates Pinero's ability to depict life at less than £5,000 a year and as he does it from observation and recollection he does it very well. He himself defended his preoccupation with the drawing-room in a conversation with William Archer recorded in *Real Conversations* (1904). Archer began by accusing the establishment dramatists as a body of concentrating their attentions too exclusively on the Hyde Park Corner of life. Pinero replied that Archer wished to limit him to playing chess with pawns. He pointed out that a dramatist was restricted by the realities of life:

> You must take into account the inarticulateness, the inexpressiveness of the English lower-middle and lower classes – their reluctance to analyse, to generalise, to give vivid utterance to their thoughts or emotions.

This is fair comment and Shaw's articulate dustmen and out of work students of Tom Paine have a certain air of unreality. The problem remains with us today and there is no doubt that future critics are going to be as vastly impressed by the social awareness of the shop stewards, factory hands and counter assistants of our own age as we are by the expert word play of the Elizabethan clown.

They will either recognize the unreality of our contemporary drama, or, as is quite possible (if utterly ironic), put us down as an age of exceptional literacy. It is no accident that Shaw often found himself forced back to the drawing-room he despised and the next generation merely replaced it with the sitting-room. O'Casey and Barrie were able to break this pattern only because of the superior fluency of the Scots and Irish working classes. Actors offer Pinero an articulate contrast to his society characters.

Pinero, like all the best playwrights, worked hard to acquire an individual voice. His apprenticeship was served adapting from the French. He turned these lessons to original account with his farces, which are the better for their atypical serious moments. The best Pinero is very well constructed. It was the critical pose of the 1950s and 60s to despise craftsmanship as a minor talent, but it is essential to as disciplined a medium as the theatre. Very few other writers of the period are in as complete control of the four act form. In many cases plays tend to peak in the third act and rather run down in the fourth. Jones is sometimes guilty of this, and even *The Liars*, which is one of his best constructed plays, uses the fourth act mainly for long sermons from his *raisonneur* and the matter might have been better shortened and included in Act Three. Pinero's last acts are always much more than a simple winding up process and while they may be predictable, as in *Trelawny*, they are necessary to round off our entertainment. The improvements of one age became the clichés of the next. The modern reader may find the interminable explanatory conversations between butler and parlourmaid, companion and faithful friend, two unimportant guests, or, as in *Trelawny*, between a character inside the group (Wrench) and a character who has been absent (Imogen) a tediously conventional method of exposition. It is a marked improvement on the soliloquy which Wilde is still guilty of in *Lady Windermere's*

Fan and more visually interesting than our own conventional use of the phone conversation. Pinero, unlike many of his contemporaries (and even Priestley and Coward), for the most part avoids the contrived upper and lower servant exchange, managing to introduce naturally into the play a character who knows as little as the audience and, by informing them, informs us.

His language suffers from being read rather than heard. Speeches which would pass unnoticed in performance, when delivered either by gentlemen able to act or actors able to appear gentlemen, appear as starched and unnatural when read.

It is not irrelevant to digress thus for the reader obtains little help from the theatre towards greater understanding of Pinero. When he is revived his craft is flouted in that his stage directions are often ignored. In his lifetime he was a theatrical dictator ruling every pause, every necktie and every tea cup. It should not be forgotten that he, as much as anybody, restored the dignity of the dramatist. He tells us in the preface to *The Times* (1891) how, when he started writing, a playscript was:

> ... a dissolute-looking and formless thing mercilessly
> scarred by the managerial blue pencil and illuminated
> by those interpolations with which desperate actors have
> helped to lift the poor material into temporary, unhealthy
> popularity.

In this he paved the way for Shaw's pictorial stage directions and extensive prefaces and perhaps he rather than Shaw should be acknowledged as the cleanser of the Augean stable of English drama.

Bibliography

DRYDEN

The Tempest, ed A. Morgan (The Bankside-Restoration Shakespeare series for the Shakespeare Society of New York); *Alterations and Adaptations of Shakespeare*, F. W. Kilbourne (1899); *The Life of John Dryden*, C. E. Ward (1961); *Dryden as an Adaptor of Shakespeare*, Allardyce Nicoll (1922); *The Dramatic Works of John Dryden*, ed Montague Summers (1932); *Essays of John Dryden*, ed W. P. Ker (1926); *Restoration Comedy 1660–1720*, Bonamy Dobrée (1924); *English Restoration Drama. Its Relation to Past English and Past and Contemporary French Drama*, M. Ellenhange (1933); *The Nobler Pleasure: Dryden's Comedy in Theory and Practice*, F. H. Moore (1963); *Five Heroic Plays*, ed Bonamy Dobrée (1962); *Dryden's Heroic Drama*, Arthur C. Kirs (1965); 'The Significance of Dryden's Heroic Plays' in *Proceedings of the Leeds Philosophical and Literary Society V* (1940), D. W. Jefferson (reprinted in *Restoration Drama: Modern Essays in Criticism*, ed John Loftis 1966); 'The Significance of Dryden's Aureng-Zebe' from *ELH*, vol 21 (1962), Arthur C. Kirsch (also reprinted in *Restoration Drama*); *Selected Dramas of John Dryden*, ed G. R. Noyes (1910); *Restoration Drama*, ed Eugene Waith, preface by John Gassner (1968); *The Intellectual Milieu of John Dryden*, Louis I. Bredvold (1934); *The Herculean Hero*, Eugene Waith (1962); *Dryden: A Collection of Critical Essays*, ed B. N. Schilling (1963).

BOYLE

The Dramatic Works of Roger Boyle, Earl of Orrery, ed William Smith Clark, 2 vols (1937).

VILLIERS

The Rehearsal, ed Montague Summers (1914); *Three Restoration Comedies (The Country Wife, The Way of the World, The Rehearsal)* ed G. G. Falle (1964); *The Burlesque Tradition in the English Theatre after 1660*, V. C. Clinton-Baddely (1952).

WYCHERLEY

The Complete Works of William Wycherley, ed Montague Summers (1924); *The First Modern Comedies; The Significance of Etherege, Wycherley and Congreve*, N. N. Holland (1959); *Brawny Wycherley*, W. Connely (1930); *Four Great Restoration Plays (All For Love, The Beaux Stratagem, The Way of the World, The Country Wife)*, eds Louis B. Wright and Virginia A. Lamar (1964); *Wycherley's Dramas*, Rose A. Zimbardo (1965).

ETHEREGE

The Works of Sir George Etherege, ed H. F. B. Brett-Smith (1927); *The Gay Couple in Restoration Comedy*, J. H. Smith (1948); *The Dark Comedy*, J. L. Styan (1962); *Etherege and the Seventeenth-Century Comedy of Manners*, Dale Underwood (1957); *The Letterbook of Sir George Etherege*, ed Sybil Rosenfield (1928).

TATE

The History of King Lear, Nahum Tate, eds Black and James (1975).

OTWAY

The Works of Thomas Otway, ed J. C. Ghosh (1932); *Otway and Lee*, R. G. Ham (1931); *Next to Shakespeare*, A. M. Taylor (1950).

CONGREVE

Three Restoration Comedies (The Man of Mode, The Country Wife, Love for Love), ed Gamini Salgado (1968); *The Restoration Comedy of Wit*, T. H. Fujimura (1952); *Preface to Restoration Drama*, J. H. Wilson (1965); *Crabbed Age and Youth: The Old Men and Women in the Restoration Comedy of Manners*, Elizabeth L. Mignon (1947); *The Complete Plays of William Congreve*, ed Herbert Davis (1967); *William Congreve, the Man*, John C. Hodges (1941); *Restoration Tragedy: 1660–1720*, Bonamy Dobrée; *Congreve Considered*, A. Williams (1971); *Comedies by William Congreve*, ed Bonamy Dobrée (1925); *A New View of The Way of the World*, P. and M. Mueschke (1958); *Comedy and Society from Congreve to Fielding*, John Loftis (1959); *Short View of the Immorality and Profaneness of the English Stage*, Jeremy Collier (1698); *Restoration*

Theatre, eds J. R. Brown and B. Harris (1964); *The Comedy of Manners*, J. Palmer (1913).

VANBRUGH

The Complete Works of Sir John Vanbrugh, ed Bonamy Dobrée (1927–8); *Sir John Vanbrugh, Architect and Dramatist*, Laurence Whistler (1939); *Congreve and the Century's End*, Clifford Leech, *Philological Quarterly, XLI* (1962).

STEELE

The Plays of Richard Steele, ed Shirley Strum Kenny (1971); *Richard Steele*, ed G. A. Aitken (1894); *A Life of Richard Steele*, 2 vols, G. A. Aitken (1968) (repr 1889 ed); *Sir Richard Steele*, W. Connely (1934); *Richard Steele and the Sentimental Comedy*, M. E. Hart (1970); *Steele at Drury Lane*, John C. Loftis (1973); *Tracts and Pamphlets by Richard Steele*, ed Rae Blanchard (1944); *The Correspondence of Richard Steele*, ed Rae Blanchard (1941); *The Drama of Sensibility*, Ernest Bernbaum (1915).

FARQUHAR

The Complete Works of George Farquhar, 2 vols, ed Charles Stonehill (1930); *The Recruiting Officer*, ed M. Shugrue (1965).

ADDISON

Cato (1976, repr 1713 ed); *Essays in Criticism and Literary Theory*, Joseph Addison, ed John Loftis (1975); *Miscellaneous Works of Joseph Addison*, 2 vols (1914, repr 1971).

ROWE

Jane Shore, ed H. W. Pedicord (1974); 'The Nature of Tragedy in Rowe's *The Fair Penitent*', *Papers on Language and Literature*, vol 2 (1966), Frank J. Kearful; 'Pathos and Personality in the Tragedies of Nicholas Rowe', *English Writers of the Eighteenth Century*, ed John H. Middendorf (1971); *An Introduction to Eighteenth-Century Drama*, F. S. Boas (1952).

GAY

Gay's Beggar's Opera: Its Content, History and Influence, W. E. Schultz (1923); *The Beggar's Opera*, ed E. V. Roberts (1969); *Ballad Opera*, E. M. Gagey (1937); *John Gay, Favourite of the Wits*, W. E. Irving (1940); *John Gay, His Place in the Eighteenth Century*, P. F. Gaye (1938); *The Beggar's Opera and Companion Pieces*, ed C. F. Burgess (1966); *John Gay, Social Critic*, Sven M. Armens (1954); *Polly*, ed Oswald Doughty (1922).

FIELDING

*The Tragedy of Tragedies or The Life and Death of Tom Thumb
the Great*, ed J. T. Hillhouse (1918); *Henry Fielding, Playwright,
Journalist and Master of the Art of Fiction*, H. K. Banerji (1930);
The History of Henry Fielding, 3 vols, Wilbur L. Cross (1918);
Henry Fielding, His Life, Work and Times, 2 vols, F. Homes Dudden
(1952); *Henry Fielding: Complete Works*, ed W. E. Henley, 16 vols,
(1903); *A Century of English Farce*, Leo Hughes (1956).

LILLO

The Works of the Late Mr George Lillo (1740); *The Works of
Mr George Lillo with some account of his life*, T. Davies, 2 vols
(1775, 1810); *The London Merchant and Fatal Curiosity*, ed ·
A. W. Ward (1906); *The London Merchant, or the History of
George Barnwell*, ed M. R. Booth (1965).

MOORE

*Edward Moore: Dramatic Works; to which is prefixed a short
account of the author's life* (1788); *The Life and Works of Moore*,
J. H. Caskey (1927); *Edward Moore: Poems, Fables and Plays*
(1969, repr 1756 ed).

HOME

Douglas, ed G. D. Parker (1972); *Home: a study of his life and
works, with special reference to the tragedy of Douglas and the
controversies which followed its first representations*, A. E. Gipson
(1917); *John Home: Works now first collected, to which is prefixed
an account of his life by Henry Mackenzie*, 3 vols (1822).

MURPHY

Eighteenth-Century Afterpieces, ed R. W. Bevis (1970); *'The Way
to Keep Him' and Five Other Plays by Arthur Murphy*, ed
John P. Emery (1956); *The Works of Arthur Murphy*, 7 vols (1786);
The Life of Arthur Murphy, J. Foot (1811); *The Dramatic Career
of Murphy*, H. H. Dunbar (1946).

GARRICK

David Garrick, Dramatist, Elizabeth P. Stein (1938); *The
Theatrical Public in the Time of Garrick*, William Pedicord (1954);
The Dramatic Works of David Garrick, 3 vols (1798); *Memoirs of
the Life of David Garrick Esq*, Thomas Davies, 2 vols (1780, repr
1969); *The Life of Garrick*, Arthur Murphy, 2 vols (1801, repr 1969);
Life of David Garrick, Percy Fitzgerald, 2 vols (rev edn 1899);
Garrick's Letters, ed D. M. Little and G. M. Kahrl, 3 vols (1964).

COLMAN

Dramatic Works, 4 vols (1777); *Memoirs of the Colman Family*,
R. B. Peake (1842); *George Colman the elder, essayist, dramatist,
and theatrical manager 1732–94*, E. R. Page (1935); *The Amiable
Humorist: A Study in the Comic Theory and Criticism of the
Eighteenth and Early Nineteenth Centuries*, (1960).

CUMBERLAND

Richard Cumberland: His Life and Dramatic Works, Stanley
T. Williams (1917); *Memoirs of Richard Cumberland, Written by
Himself* (1806 repr 1969); *Quick springs of Sense: Studies in the
Eighteenth Century*, ed L. S. Champion (1974); *English
Sentimental Drama*, Arthur Sherbo (1957); *The Beggar's Opera and
other Eighteenth-Century Plays*, selected John Hampden,
introduction David Lindsay.

GOLDSMITH

Collected Works of Oliver Goldsmith, 5 vols, ed Arthur Friedman
(1966); *Oliver Goldsmith: A Georgian Study*, Ricardo Quintana
(1967).

SHERIDAN

The Dramatic Works of Richard Brinsley Sheridan, ed Cecil Price
(1973); *The Letters of Richard Brinsley Sheridan*, ed Cecil Price
(1966); *Sheridan's Plays now printed as he wrote them and his
Mother's unpublished Comedy*, ed W. Fraser Rae (1902);
The Linleys of Bath, Clementine Black (1926); *The Plays and Poems
of Richard Brinsley Sheridan*, ed R. Crompton Rhodes (1928);
English Theatre Music in the Eighteenth Century, R. Fiske (1973);
Sheridan, 'Edited by a Constitutional Friend' (1816); *Speeches of
the Managers and Counsel in the Trial of Warren Hastings*, ed
A. E. Bond (1859–61); *The Political Career of Richard Brinsley
Sheridan*, Michael T. H. Sadlier (1912); *Dramatic Character in the
English Romantic Age*, Joseph W. Donohue Jr (1970).

LEWIS

The Castle Spectre, M. G. Lewis (1798); *The Life and
Correspondence of Lewis*, 2 vols (1839); *Monk Lewis and the Tales
of Terror*, O. F. Emerson (1923); *They Called Him Monk*,
W. Thomas (1966); *German Influence in the English Romantic
Period 1788–1818*, Frank Woodyer Stokoe (1963).

SCOTT

Doom of Devorgoil, Sir Walter Scott (1830); *The Waverley Dramas*

(1870); *Memoirs of the Life of Scott*, J. G. Lockart (1837–8); *The Rise and Fall of the French Romantic Drama with special reference to Scott*, F. W. M. Draper (1925); *Scott and the Medieval Revival*, A. Chandler (1965); *Essays of Chivalry, Romance and the Drama*, Sir Walter Scott (1887).

SHELLEY

The Complete Works of Shelley, Julian edition, eds R. Ingpen and W. E. Peck, 10 vols (1926–9); *The Life of Percy Bysshe Shelley*, J. T. Hogg, 2 vols (1933); *A Study of Shelley's Drama The Cenci*, E. S. Bates (1908); *Shelley, Godwin and their Circle* (1913); *Shelley and Calderon*, S. De Madariaga (1920); *Prometheus Unbound: An Interpretation*, C. Grabo (1935); *William Godwin and his World*, R. Glynn Grylls (1953); *Shelley: His Thought and His Work*, Desmond King-Hele (1960).

KNOWLES

English Plays of the Nineteenth Century, vol I Drama 1800–1850, ed M. R. Booth (1969); *The Dramatic Works*, J. S. Knowles, 3 vols (1841); *Knowles and the Theatre of his time*, L. H. Meeks (1933); *The Life of James Sheridan Knowles*, R. B. Knowles (1872); *Macready's Reminiscences*, ed Sir Frederick Pollock (1875).

BULWER

Dramatic Works, Bulwer (1841); *Works*, 38 vols (1874); *Bulwer-Lytton's Plays*, P. J. Cooke (1894); *An Introduction to the Prose Romances, Plays and Comedies of Bulwer*, E. G. Bell (1914).

BOUCICAULT

London Assurance, ed Ronald Eyre (1971); *Nineteenth-Century Plays* (The World's Classics), ed George Rowell (1953); *The Career of Dion Boucicault*, Townsend Walsh (1915); *The Art of Acting*, Dion Boucicault (1926); *The Stage Irishman*, G. C. Duggan (1937); *Stage to Screen: Theatrical Method from Garrick to Griffith*, A. Nicholas Vardac (1949); *John Brougham: An Autobiography*, ed William Winters (1881); *Victorian Melodramas*, ed James L. Smith (1976); *Blood and Thunder*, M. W. Disher (1949); *Melodrama*, James L. Smith (1973); *English Melodrama*, M. R. Booth (1965); *The World of Melodrama*, Frank Rahill (1967); *Enter Foot and Horse*, A. H. Saxon (1968); *Melodrama: Plots that Thrilled*, M. W. Disher (1954); *Penny Plain, Two Pence Coloured*, A. E. Wilson (1952).

ROBERTSON

The Principal Dramatic Works of Thomas William Robertson,
2 vols (1889); *Life and Writings of T. W. Robertson*, T. Edgar
Pemberton (1893); *T. W. Robertson: His Plays and Stagecraft*,
Maynard Savin (1950).

THOMAS

Charley's Aunt, French's Acting edition.

WILDE

The Collected Works of Oscar Wilde, 15 vols, ed Robert Ross
(1922); *Complete Plays*, Oscar Wilde, introduction Tyrone Guthrie
(1954); *Oscar Wilde: The Critical Heritage*, ed Karl Beckson (1970);
Bibliography of Oscar Wilde, Stuart Mason (1914); *Oscar Wilde, a
Study*, André Gide (1905); *Oscar Wilde, His Life and Confessions*,
Frank Harris (1916).

JONES

Late Victorian Plays 1890–1914, ed George Powell (1968); *The Old
Drama and the New*, William Archer (1923); *Life and Letters of
Henry Arthur Jones*, Doris Arthur Jones (1930); *The Renascence of
the English Drama*, Henry Arthur Jones (1894); *Henry Arthur Jones*,
P. Shorey (1925); *Henry Arthur Jones and Modern Drama*,
R. A. Cordell (1932).

PINERO

Trelawny of the 'Wells', A. W. Pinero (1899); *Trelawny of the
'Wells'* (1936); *Pinero: a critical biography with letters*,
W. D. Dunkel (1943); *Arthur Wing Pinero*, H. Hamilton Fyfe (1902);
Sir Arthur Wing Pinero's Plays and Players, H. Hamilton Fyfe
(1930); *The Rise and Fall of the Well-Made Play*, John Russell
Taylor (1967); *The Social Plays of Pinero*, ed C. Hamilton, 4 vols
(1917–22); *Modern English Playwrights*, J. W. Cunliffe (1927).

Index

Abbott, The 314
Absalom and Achitophel 61, 96
Achilles 175
Adelphi Theatre 357
Addison, Joseph 26, 35, 100, 139, 158–64
Adonais 316
Aeschylus 323, 337
Aesop 119
Agis 208, 209
Alcibiades 102
Alfred 209
All For Love, or The World Well Lost 34, 72, 90–95, 129, 191, 207
All In the Wrong 214
Alonzo 209
Altemira 44
Alzuma 214
Ambitious Stepmother, The 165
Ambrosio, or The Monk 283, 289
Ancient British Drama 313
Andria 140
Animated Nature 249
Antony and Cleopatra 34, 93–5
Arbuthnot, John 174
Archer, William 423, 430
Arden of Faversham 195, 198, 199, 288
Arms and the Man 409
Arrah-na-Pogue 358, 369, 370
Atheist, The 103
Auchindrane, or The Ayrshire Tragedy 302
Aureng-Zebe 65, 68–74, 207
Author's Farce, The 189

Barrett, Wilson 419
Barrie, J. M. 431
Battle of Sedgemoor, The 61
Beaumont, Francis 34, 58, 65, 119, 230
Beaux Stratagem, The 149
Beggar's Opera, The 174–9, 181, 183–8, 273–4
Bell, E. G. 13, 332, 393
Bentley, Richard 239

Bevis, R. W. 218
Birth 374
Biter, The 165
Black Prince, The 44
Bondman, The 240
Bonduca 230
Bon Ton, or High Life Above Stairs 220
Booth, Michael R. 12
Borderers, The 407
Boswell, James 187
Boucicault, Dion 314, 356–72, 381–7, 408
Bourgeoises à la Mode 119
Boyle, Roger, 1st Earl of Orrery 43–52, 65, 66, 72, 110
Brady, Nicholas 96
Bravo of Venice, The 283
Brecht, Bertholt 288, 334
Britannia and Batavia 196
British Drama, The (Bell) 13
British Drama, The (Dicks) 13
British Plays (Bell) 13
British Theatre 13
Brutus of Alba 96
Buckhurst, Charles, Lord 23, 33
Bulwer, Edward 346, 348–55, 367
Byron, Lord George 291, 316, 334
Byron, H. J. 374, 394

Cabinet Minister, The 412
Caius Marius 103
Caius Gracchus 340
Captain O'Blunder 258
Captives, The 174
Carmelite, The 240
Cassilis Engagement, The 378, 410
Caste 370, 373–80
Castle Spectre, The 17, 101, 130, 212, 221, 283–91, 297
Cato 100, 158–64, 186, 198, 345
Cenci, The 316–22, 334–7, 339, 347, 407
Centlivre, Mrs Susanna 221, 275–6
Chambers, Charles Haddon 409–10

Champion, The 195
Chances 61
Chapman, George 72
Charles I 316, 339
Charley's Aunt 388–95
Cheats of Scopin, The 102–3
Chekov, Anton 10, 137
Chevely, or The Man of Honour 349
Choleric Man, The 234
Christian Hero, The 139, 196
Cibber, Colley 120, 124–5, 137
Cibber, Theophilus 103, 119, 199, 281
City Madam, The 24
Clandestine Marriage, The 229–38, 245
Clarissa 267
Cleone 205–6, 213
Clerical Error, A 414
Cockpit Theatre 32
Cold June, A 425
Coleridge, Samuel Taylor 334, 340
Colleen Bawn, The 357, 358, 363–7, 369–72, 378
Collegians, The 371
Collier, Jeremy 112, 119, 120, 140
Colman, George (elder) 10, 28, 225, 229–38, 239, 254, 269
Colour-Sergeant, The 388
Comical Revenge, or Love in a Tub, The 83
Comrades 388
Comus 230
Confederacy 119
'Congreve and the Century's End' 137
Congreve, William 10, 11, 25, 26, 34, 35, 57, 58, 72, 111–18, 127–31, 132–8, 139–40, 144, 145, 154, 155, 225, 265
Conquest of Granada, The 34, 62, 64
Conscious Lovers, The 140
Constant Couple, The 148, 245
Corneille, Pierre 48–9, 191, 206, 314
Corsican Brothers, The 356, 358
Country Girl, The 220–28

see also The Country Wife
Country House, A 119
Country Wake, The 185
Country Wife, The 75, 88, 118, 136, 225–7, *passim*
see also The Country Girl
Court Theatre 388
see also Royal Court Theatre
Covent Garden 13, 26–7, 175, 209, 229–30, 249, 259–60, 314, 334, 370
Cox and Box 66
Critical Review 247
Critic, The 63, 225, 258–9
Cuckold's Haven 96
Cumberland's British Theatre 13
Cumberland's Minor Theatre 13
Cumberland, Richard 225, 234–5, 239–47, 394
Cunningham, Allan 313
Curzon Street 388

Daly, Augustin 386
Danby, John F. 338
Dandy Dick 424
Darley, George 356
D'Avenant, Sir William 31–3, 34–42, 62, 66
Davies, Robertson 12, 266
Davy Crockett 315
Darwin, Charles 337
David Garrick 374
Dennery 385–6
Dennis 140
Dépit Amoureux 119
Dibdin, T. J. 13, 212, 312
Dickens, Charles 30, 246, 340
Dicks Standard Plays 13
Dicks 13
'Discourse upon Comedy' 156
Distressed Wife, The 175
Divine Gift, The 421
De Profundis 407
Devil's Disciple, The 409
Dobrée, Bonamy 11, 21, 93, 129
Dodsley, Robert 205, 213
Doggett, Thomas 185
Dolby's British Theatre 13
Dolly Reforming Herself 415
Don Caesar de Bazan 358

Don Carlos 103
Don Quixote in England 189
Doom of Devorgoil, The 307–15
Double Dealer, The 112
Douglas 198, 205, 206, 208–13, 240
Drama and Society in the Age of Jonson 18
Drummer, The 158
Drury Lane 13, 26–7, 28, 148, 158, 220–21, 237, 258, 259, 260, 265, 299–300, 314, 334, 341
Dryden, John 11, 23, 31, 33–42, 48, 50, 53–60, 61, 62, 65, 66, 68–74, 87, 90–95, 96, 102, 110, 129, 131, 140, 148, 154, 163, 169–70, 193, 274, 276, 313, 332
Duchess of Padua, The 396, 407–8
Duenna, The 265, 270–76
Duke and No Duke, A 96
Duke of Milan, The 240
Dumas, Alexandre 315, 354
Dunciad, The 194
D'Urfey 145, 185

Ecclesiastical Policy (Hooker) 22
École des Femmes, L' 227
Edinburgh Review 28
Edward III 345
Elgee, Jane Francisca ('Speranza') 396
Elmerick 196
Engaged 411–12
English Plays of the Nineteenth Century (Booth) 12
Epicoene 230, 395
Essay of Dramatick Poesy 33
Etherege, Sir George 10, 23, 25, 58, 72, 83–9, 111, 118, 125, 136, 137, 145, 154, 155
Eunuch, The 227
Evelyn, John 58
Evening's Love, or The Mock Astrologer, An 34, 53–60, 274–5

Fables for the Female Sex 202
Factory Lad, The 288

Fair Penitent, The 165, 166, 170
Falkland 348
Fall of Coriolanus, The 96
False Delicacy 249
False Friend, The 119
Farquhar, George 11, 26, 145, 148–57, 245
Fashionable Lover, The 235, 246–7
Fatal Curiosity 196, 288
Fatal Discovery, The 209, 213
Faust 337
Faust and Marguerite 358
Fielding, Henry 63, 65, 189–94, 195, 339
Fifty-One Fables in Verse 175
First Modern Comedies, The 81
Fletcher, John 34, 48, 51, 58, 61, 119, 230
Florizel and Perdita 229
Foote, Samuel 214, 230, 258, 339
Forced Marriage 102
Fortunes of Nigel, The 301
Foundling, The 202
Fourchette & Co 388
Four Feathers, The 355
Frankenstein 316
French, Samuel 13
Friendship in Fashion 103
Funeral, or Grief à la Mode, The 139–47, 155, 236

Galsworthy, John 350
Gamester, The 202–7, 288
Garrick, David 19, 202, 209, 218, 220–28, 229, 237, 254, 258, 259, 265, 268
Gay, John 174–88, 202, 273
Gentleman Dancing Master, The 75
Gentleman, The 140
George Barnwell 173, 231
   see *The London Merchant*
Gilbert, W. S. 339, 394, 408, 411–12
Gil Blas 202
Godwin, Mary 316
Godwin, William 338
Goethe, Johann Wolfgang von 337
Gold Craze, The 388

Golden Farmer, The 315
Goldsmith, Oliver 10, 140, 213, 216, 218, 225, 234–5, 237, 238, 247, 248–57
Good Natured Man, The 249, 256
Gorboduc 49, 51, 345
Grangé 385–6
Gray's Inn Journal, The 214
Grecian Daughter, The 214
Griffin, Gerald 371
Griffith, D. W. 385
Grub Street Opera 189
Grumbler, The 249
Grundy, Sydney 375
Guzman 44

Half-Caste, The 374
Hamlet 103, 220
Hankin, St John 378, 410
Haymarket Theatre 29, 175, 189, 350, 374
Hazlitt, William 100, 138, 273, 340, 345
Hellas 316
Henri III et sa Cour 315
Henry V (Boyle) 43–52, 65, 110
Henty, G. A. 355
Herman, Henry A. 414, 415
Herod the Great 44
Heroic Stubbs, The 415
Highland Legacy, A 388
High Life Below Stairs 236–7
Historical Register, The 189
History of Early Nineteenth Century Drama 1800–50, A 12
History of England 249
History of English Drama 1660–1900 16, 21, 216, 234
History of Greece 249
History of Late Eighteenth Century Drama 1750–1800, A 12
History of Late Nineteenth-Century Drama 1850–1900, A 12
History of Restoration Drama 10–11
History of the Rebellion of 1745 209
History of Rome 249

History of the Spanish Conspiracy against the State of Venice 107
Hit or Miss 302
Hoadley, John 195
Hoadly, Benjamin 235
Hobbes, Thomas 22
Hogarth, William 236
Holland, Norman 11, 81
Home 374
Home, John 198, 205, 208–13, 240
Horace 206
Horne, R. H. 345
Howard, Sir Robert 33, 34
Hume, David 208
Hugo, Victor 354
Hunchback, The 340
Hurlothrumbo, or The Supernatural 189

Ibsen, Henrik 10, 200, 201, 288, 291, 334, 385, 420, 424
Ideal Husband, An 396–402, 409–12
Importance of Being Earnest, The 396–7, 403–9, 411–13
Imposters, The 240
Indian Emperor, The 34, 62, 71, 148
Indian Queen, The 34, 62
Injured Love 96
Innocent Usurper, The 194
Iron Chest, The 101
Ishmael and other poems 348
Island Princess, The 96
It's Only Round the Corner 414
Ivanhoe 301, 314

James, Henry 81
Jane Shore 165–73
Jealous Wife, The 229, 235
Jew, The 240
Jocrisse the Juggler 374
Johnson, Dr Samuel 73, 100, 184, 273, 332
Johnson, Samuel 189
Jones, Henry Arthur 10, 200, 345, 384, 408, 414–22, 430–31
Jones, Inigo 39
Jonson, Ben 10, 25, 31, 34, 50, 87, 88, 89, 100, 117, 137, 145,

Jonson, Ben *continued*
  250, 265, 332, 395
Joseph Andrews 189
*Journal of a West Indian
  Proprietor* 283–4
Journey to London 119–20
Judah 315
Judge's Memory, A 388
Julius Caesar 108, 192
Jupiter 258

Kabale u Liebe 283
Katherine and Petruchio 220
Kean, Charles 29, 356–7
Kean, Edmund 340
Kean 374
Keats, John 311
Keene, Laura 371
Kelly, Hugh 249
Kemble, John Philip 27–9, 259
Kenilworth 301
Killigrew, Thomas 31–3
*Kind Keeper, or Mr Limber-
  ham, The* 34
King Lear (Tate) 96–101, 162
King Lear (Shakespeare) 96,
  97–8, 99, 335, 338, 339, 346
Knight of the Burning Pestle
  65, 194
Knights, L. C. 11, 18, 81
Knowles, James Sheridan 312,
  340–47, 353–4
Know Your Own Mind 214
Kotzebue, August Friedrich
  Ferdinand von 260, 283,
  289, 299, 300

Lady Jane Grey 166
Lady of Lyons, The 346,
  348–55, 378
Lady Windermere's Fan 396,
  408, 409–12, 431–2
Lamb, Charles 80–81, 100,
  156, 332–3, 334, 340
Lancashire Sailor, The 388
Lee, Nathan 72, 129, 131, 194
Leech, Clifford 11, 124–5, 137
Le Sage 119, 202
Les Bohémians de Paris 385
Les Mystères de Paris 385
Letters on the English Nation
  75
L'Évasion de Marie Stuart 314

Leviathan 22
Lewis, M. G. 283–91, 316, 333,
  335
Liars, The 410, 414–22, 431
Lie, The 415
Lillo, George 195–201, 205
Little Theatre 189, 230
Lives of the English Poets 73
Lives of the Poets 103
*Lives of the Poets of Great
  Britain and Ireland* 199
Lodgers, The 388
Loftis, John 11
London Assurance 356–62,
  369–70, 393
London by Night 381–7
*London Merchant, or George
  Barnwell, The* 173, 195–201,
  205, 207, 288
London Stage 13, 211
London Theatre 13
Long Strike, The 358
Louis XI 356, 358
Loutherbourg, Philip Jaques
  de 221
Love for Love 111–18
Love In a Bottle 148
Love in a Wood 75
Love in Several Masques 189
Love's Labour's Lost 89
Love's Last Shift 119, 124–5, 281
Loyal General, The 96
Luke the Labourer 288
Lying Lover, The 140

Macarthy, Mary 256
Macaulay, Thomas Babington
  137
Macbeth 335
Macklin, Charles 220
Macready, William Charles
  28–9, 297, 302, 340, 347, 350,
  354
Magistrate, The 424
Magpie or the Maid?, The 302
Maid's Tragedy, The 51, 108
Maison de Campagne 119
Major Barbara 410
Manoeuvres of Jane, The 415
Man of Destiny, The 409
*Man of Mode, The, or Sir
  Fopling Flutter* 22, 71, 83–9,
  118

Marina 196
Marker, Frederick and Lisa-
  Lorne 12
Marlowe, Christopher 18, 49,
  72
Marriage 388
Marriage-à-la-Mode 57, 64,
  236
Mary Goes First 415
Massinger, Philip 24, 48, 240
Mathews, Charles 370, 373,
  374, 377
Maugham, Somerset 350
Measure for Measure 321
Memoirs (Cumberland) 240,
  247
Memorials (Whitelock) 31
Merchant's Daughter, The 315
Michael and His Lost Angel
  415
Middleman, The 415
Middleton, Thomas 58
Midsummer Night's Dream, A
  217
Miller and his Men, The 302,
  313
Minister, The 283
*Minstrelsy of the Scottish
  Border* 301
Misfortunes of Arthur, The 51
Miss in her Teens 220, 268
Mistake, The 119
Modern Prophets, The 185
Molière 25, 102, 119, 227
Moncrieff, W. T. 312, 386
Money 350, 367–8
Monsieur de Pourceaugnac 119
Monthly Chronicle 349
Moore, Edward 202–7
Morning Chronicle 274
Morton, J. H. 66
Morton, Thomas 368
Mourning Bride, The 112,
  127–31, 186
MP 374
Mr Anthony 44
Much Ado About Nothing 57
Mrs Dane's Defence 408, 415,
  421
Mrs Warren's Profession 409
Muleteer of Toledo, The 374
Murdock, F. H. 315
Murphy, Arthur 205, 214–19,

  225, 368
Murray, Gilbert 421
Mustapha 44
Mysterious Mother, The 333–4

Nabbes 256
Natural Son, The 240
Necessity of Atheism, The 316
New Monthly 349
New Spirit of the Age, A 345
New Way to Pay Old Debts, A
  22
*Nice Valour, or the Passionate
  Madman, The* 58
Nicoll, Allardyce 10–11, 12,
  16, 20, 57, 216, 234, 282, 410
Night's Adventure, A 373
Nineteenth-Century Plays 12

O'Casey, Sean 431
Octoroon, The 357–8, 370
Ode to the West Wind 316
O'Dowd, The 358
Oedipus 194, 300
Ogre, The 415
Old Bachelor, The 111–12
Old Drury Lane 341
Old Wives' Tale, The 65
Olympic Theatre 373, 377
'On the Artificial Comedy of
  the Last Century' 81
'On the Theatre' 234
'On the Tragedies of Shake-
  speare, Considered with
  Reference to their Fitness
  for Stage Presentation' 332
Orphan of China, The 102,
  103, 205, 214
Ossian 209
Otway, Thomas 72, 102–10,
  129, 130, 154, 163, 169, 187
Our American Cousin 374,
  394
Ours 370, 374
Oxberry's Edition 13
Oxberry, W. 298

Parthenissa 44
Pasquin 189
*Patriotism and Popular
  Education* 414
Paul Clifford 13
Peele, George 49, 65

Peep Behind The Curtain, A
  225
Pelham 349
Penley, W. S. 388
Pepys, Samuel 22–3, 58
Phelps, Samuel 29
Physician, The 415
Picture of Dorian Gray, The
  396
Pilgrim 119
Pills to Purge Melancholy 185
Pinero, Arthur Wing 10, 200,
  237, 345, 384, 408, 412,
  419–21, 423–32
Pizarro 260, 292–300
Plain Dealer, The 75
Planché, J. R. 130, 312, 394
Play 374
Plutarch 94
Pocock, Isaac 301–6, 312, 313
Political Justice 338
Polly 175, 180–88
Polly Honeycombe 229, 268–9,
  274
Poor of Liverpool, The 358
Poor of New York, The 357,
  358, 370
Pope, Alexander 35, 163, 174,
  175, 332
Powell, George 12
Pride and Prejudice 267
Priestley, J. B. 350, 432
Prisoner of Zenda, The 385
Profligate, The 424
Progress 374
Prometheus Bound 323, 337
Prometheus Unbound 316,
  323–7, 337–8
Provok'd Husband, The 120
Provok'd Wife, The 119
Pygmalion 257

Quentin Durward 301
Quin, James 220

Racine, Jean 102
Rape of the Lock, The 194
Ravenna 396
Real Conversations 430
Recruiting Officer, The 148–57
Redgauntlet 301
Rehearsal at Goatham, The
  175

Rehearsal, The 34, 61–7, 194
*Relapse, or Virtue in Danger,
  The* 118, 119–26, 137, 157,
  225, 227, 280–82 *passim*
Reminiscences 212
*Renascence of the English
  Drama* 414, 419
Rent Day 288
Restoration Comedy (Dobrée)
  11, 21
'Restoration Comedy: the
  Reality and the Myth' 81
Restoration Tragedy 1660–1720
  93–4, 129 (Dobrée)
*Revels History of Drama in
  English, The* 12, 268
Richardson, Samuel 165
Richelieu 349
Rich, John 175, 188
*Richard II, or The Sicilian
  Usurper* (Tate) 96, 345
Richard II (Shakespeare) 339,
  345
Richard III 103, 168, 172, 322
*Rightful Heir, The (The Sea
  Captain,* revised) *see* The
  Sea Captain
Rip Van Winkle 358
Rival Ladies, The 50
Rivals, The 226, 254, 258–9,
  273, 274–5, 300
Robber's Bride, The 302
Robertson, T. W. 347, 350,
  370, 373–80, 394–5, 408, 411,
  429
Robinson Crusoe 302
Rob Roy Macgregor 301–6,
  313, 314
Rogue's Comedy, The 415
Rollo 283
Roman Father, The 205–6
Rosamund 158
Rose, Edward 385
Rowe, Nicholas 26, 103, 129–31
  passim, 154, 163, 165–73, 194,
  198, 332
Rowell, George 12
Royal Convent, The 165
Royal Court Theatre 430
Rural Sports 174

Sadler's Wells 29, 373, 425–6
Saints and Sinners 414, 420

Salome (Wilde) 397
Sara Sampson 200
Scamps of London, The 386
Scanderberg 196
Schiller, Johann Christoph
   Friedrich von 283, 289
School 374
School for Action 140, 256
School for Guardians, The 214
School for Scandal, The 226,
   245–6, 254, 259, 260, 266
School Mistress, The 424
Scott, Clement 420
Scott, Sir Walter 28–9, 39, 213,
   301–16, 421
Sea Captain, The (revised as
   The Rightful Heir) 349–50
Second Mrs Tanqueray, The
   408, 424
Sedley, Sir Charles 33, 87
Self-Help 354–5
Shadwell, Thomas 96, 145
Shakespeare (Bell) 332
Shakespeare, William 9, 10,
   18, 24, 32, 34, 38–9, 49, 42,
   49–51, 57, 59, 72, 88, 93–5,
   96, 97, 99, 100, 101, 108, 129,
   145, 166, 168, 172, 191, 194,
   213, 220, 237, 282, 332, 333,
   335, 339, 349
Shaughraun, The 358, 369
Shaw, G. B. 10, 146, 163, 237,
   257, 266, 408–9, 410, 414, 421,
   430
Shelley, Percy Bysshe 311,
   316–39
Sheridan, Richard Brinsley
   10, 63, 216, 218, 225, 227,
   234, 237, 238, 245–6, 247,
   254, 256, 257, 258–69, 270–82,
   288, 292–300, 341, 368
She Stoops to Conquer 140,
   248–57
She Would if She Could 83
Shirley, James 24, 25, 57
*Short View of the Profaneness
   and Immorality of the English
   Stage* 140
Siege of Aquileia, The 209
Silver King, The 414
Sir Marmaduke Maxwell 313
Smiles, Samuel 354
Smith, Adam 208

Society 374, 378, 379, 395
Soldier's Fortune, The 103
Sothern, E. A. 373–4
Southern, Richard 12
Southey, Robert 334
Spanish Armada, The 63
Spectator 139, 140, 146, 158,
   162
Speed the Plough 368
Squire, The 423–4
Squire Treloolsy 119
Steele, Richard 10, 26, 125,
   131, 139–47, 154, 155, 158,
   169, 170, 236, 245, 256, 268
Stirling, Edward 340–41
St Irvyne 316
Stranger, The 299
Streets of Dublin, The 358
Streets of London, The 358
Strindberg, J. A. 10
Suckling, Sir John 32
Sue, Eugene 385
Sullivan 374
Swellfoot the Tyrant 328–30,
   339
Swift, Jonathan 111, 171–2,
   174, 175, 184, 258
Swordsman's Daughter, The
   388
Sylvia 196

Tale of Mystery, A 130
Talisman, The 301
Tamerlane 165
Taming of the Shrew, The 220
Tate, Nahum 96–101, 162, 166
Tatler 139, 158, 170
*Tempest, or The Enchanted
   Island, The* 31–42
Tempest, The (Shakespeare)
   39
Tempter, The 415
Temple Beau, The 189
Tender Husband, The 140,
   256, 268
Terence, Publius 140, 227, 229
Theatre, The 140, 420
The Times 29, 432
Thoughts on Various Subjects
   171–2
Three Hours After Marriage
   174
Timon of Athens 240

Timour the Tartar 283
Thomas, Brandon 388
Thompson, Benjamin 299
Titus and Berenice 102, 103
To a Skylark 316
Tom Jones 189, 229, 245
Tottenham Court 256
Townley, James 236
Tragedy of Tragedies, or The Life and Death of Tom Thumb the Great, The 189–94
Traître Puni 119
Trappolin 96
Trelawny of the Wells 345, 423–32
Trewin, J. C. 297
Trip to Scarborough, A 225, 227, 277–82
True Briton, The 299
Tryphon 44
Two Hundred a Year 420
Tyrannic Love 34
Tyranny of Tears, The 410

Ulysses 165
Uncommercial Traveller, The 30
Under Milk Wood 337
Under the Gaslight 386
Under the Red Robe 385
Used Up 358

Vampire, The 130
Vanbrugh, Sir John 35, 118, 119–26, 137, 139, 154, 280–82 passim
Vanity Fair 371
Venice Preserved, or A Plot Discovered 102–10, 129, 172, 174, 187
Vera: or the Nihilists 396, 407
Vicar of Wakefield, The 249
Victorian Theatre, The 12
Villiers, George, 2nd Duke of Buckingham 34, 61–7
Virginius 340–47
Volpone 88
Voltaire, François Marie Arouet de 75, 205, 214, 299

Walpole, Horace 333

Walpole, Sir Robert 175, 187, 189
War 374
Waverley 301
Way of the World, The 25, 112, 117, 118, 132–8, 140, 155
Way to Keep Him, The 214–19, 279
Wealth 415
Webster, Ben 42, 130, 315, 357
Wells, H. G. 414, 421
Welsh Opera, or The Grey Mare the Better Horse, The (later *Grub Street Opera*) 189
West Indian, The 226, 235, 239–41
What D'ye Call it? 174
What is Capital? 414
Where's Charley? 388
Whistler, J. M. 396
White Devil 335
Whitewashing of Julia, The 415
Wife of Bath, The 174
Wilde, Oscar 394, 396–413, 424, 431
Wild Gallant, The 57, 63
Wilks, Robert 148–9
William Tell 340
Will's coffee house 35, 148
Winter's Tale, The 220
Wit Without Money 58
Woman of No Importance, A 396, 410
Women Are So Serious 388
Wonder, a Woman Keeps a Secret, The 221, 275–6
Wordsworth, William 334
World Drama 57
Wycherley, William 10, 23, 34, 75–82, 87–8, 111–12, 118, 125, 137, 145, 154, 155, 223, 226, 227–8

Yorkshire Tragedy, A 198, 199, 288
You Never Can Tell 430

Zastrozzi 316